Teacher's Annotated Edition

Spanish
today 1

Nancy A. Humbach
Mercedes Uribe Wall
Geraldine Antoine
Sue Carol McKnight

ANNOTATIONS BY
Dorothy Gonsalves

HOUGHTON MIFFLIN COMPANY   **Boston**

Atlanta   Dallas   Geneva, Illinois
Hopewell, New Jersey   Palo Alto   Toronto

Acknowledgments

The authors and publisher wish to thank the following persons who reviewed various stages of manuscript: Professor Pablo Valencia (College of Wooster, Wooster, Ohio), Professor Mario Iglesias (Ohio State University, Columbus, Ohio), Fabiola Betancourt Perry, F. Isabel Campoy, Dorothy Gonsalves, Lourdes Sandoval de Collins, Professor William H. Heflin, Jr. (University of Tennessee, Knoxville, Tennessee), Anthony J. Bent, Dr. Maria E. Arcocha (Ottawa Hills High School, Toledo, Ohio), Joy Renjilian-Burgy (Wellesley College, Wellesley, Massachusetts), and Rosario Centeno Caso.

The publisher also wishes to thank Rosa María C. Pérez del Río for her help in preparing the section *Accommodating Native Speakers* and the following teachers in Texas who piloted one chapter with their students: Idella Wilson and Tomacita Olivares (Stephen F. Austin High School, Austin), Susan Pardue (John F. Kennedy High School, San Antonio), Mel Turner (Robert E. Lee High School, San Antonio), Don Hall (Spring Branch Senior High School, Houston), Mildred Davis (Forest Oak Middle School, Fort Worth), and Rebecca Stevenson (Western Hills High School, Fort Worth).

Printed in U.S.A.
Student's Edition ISBN: 0-395-29295-6
Teacher's Edition ISBN: 0-395-29510-6

Contents

Scope-and-sequence chart

1 ¿Quiénes somos?
Photo essay   1

		NOTAS CULTURALES	ESTUDIO DE PALABRAS
CAPÍTULO 1 *Los Ángeles, California*	**¿Quién soy?** 8 ¿Quién eres? ¿Qué idioma hablas? ¿Quién es ese chico?	Hispanic influence in Los Angeles Shaking hands Greetings First names	Descriptive adjectives Greetings and leave-takings
CAPÍTULO 2 *Miami, Florida*	**¡Al colegio!** 25 En la clase de biología El horario de Luis Lleras	**La pequeña Habana** Dominoes School day **El bachillerato**	Numbers 0–12 Classroom objects Days of the week
CAPÍTULO 3 *San Antonio, Texas*	**Con los amigos** 43 Un regalo de cumpleaños ¿Cuántos años tienes? ¿Me prestas tu calculadora?	Mexican Americans in Texas **Quinceañera** **Santo** vs. **cumpleaños** Regional variations Independence Day	Numbers 13–31 Months of the year
CAPÍTULO 4 *Nueva York, Nueva York*	**En casa** 62 Llaman por teléfono Fotos de familia ¡Cállate!	Puerto Ricans in New York Extended family Spanish surnames	Family Health expressions (with **tener, estar**)
CAPÍTULO 5 *Chicago, Illinois*	**Trabajo y pasatiempos** 82 ¿Qué quieres ser? Solicitud de empleo	Spanish speakers in Chicago Women and job titles ID's Columbus Day	Occupations Numbers 32–99 Height and weight
	Algo más 102		

PRONUNCIACIÓN Y ORTOGRAFÍA	GRAMÁTICA
Vowels [a] [e] [i] [o] [u]	Present tense of **ser**: singular forms Expressing origin with **ser** Gender of nouns Agreement of adjectives ending in -o or -a Agreement of adjectives ending in -e Making sentences negative Tag questions (¿no? ¿verdad?) *En resumen* *Repaso*
[l]: l [y]: ll, y	Gender and definite articles **el** and **la** Plural of nouns and definite articles Verb form **hay** Subject pronouns **yo, tú, él,** and **ella** Present tense of **tener**: singular forms Definite article with days of the week Formation of **sí-no** questions *En resumen* *Repaso*
[s]: s, c (i,e), z	Indefinite articles **un** and **una** Definite articles with dates Possession with **de** (+ name) Descriptive **de** phrases Possessive adjectives **mi, tu, su** (singular and plural) Questions with question words Exclamations with **qué** *En resumen* *Repaso*
[k]: c, k, qu Stress	**Tú** and **usted** Subject pronouns Present tense of **estar** Agreement of adjectives (singular, plural, and mixed gender) Position of adjectives Plural indefinite articles *En resumen* *Repaso*
[ch]: ch Silent *h* Linking	Present tense of **ser** Possessive adjectives **nuestro** and **su** **Querer** + infinitive (singular) Present tense of regular -ar verbs *En resumen* *Repaso*

A nuestro alrededor
Photo essay 241

PRONUNCIATIÓN Y ORTOGRAFÍA	GRAMÁTICA	LECTURA
Strong vowels (a, e, o)	Preterit tense of regular -ar verbs Definite articles with nouns in a general sense Preterit tense of verbs in -car, -gar, -zar Preterit tense of -ar stem-changing verbs Preterit tense of ir and ser Preterit of ver and dar Al + infinitive *En resumen* *Repaso*	Los huicholes
Diphthongs: weak + strong	Preterit tense of decir Preterit tense of hacer Preterit tense of -er and -ir verbs Nada, nadie and nunca Alguno and ninguno Double-object pronouns with me, te, nos Double-object pronouns with le and les *En resumen* *Repaso*	La leyenda del coquí
Diphthongs: strong + weak	Reflexive constructions Definite articles with clothing Preterit tense of poner Preterit of stem-changing -ir verbs *En resumen* *Repaso*	La Tuna (with song, La Aurora)
Diphthongs: weak + weak Vowel combinations with accent marks	Present progressive tense Definite articles with parts of the body Object pronouns with present participles Preterit tense of tener, poder, poner *En resumen* *Repaso*	Simón Bolívar, el Libertador
Syllabication	Preterit with spelling changes Infinitive after prepositions Si-clauses in the present tense Preterit tense of estar *En resumen* *Repaso*	El horóscopo de la semana

Teacher's guide

Introduction

Spanish Today speaks for itself. As soon as you open the texts you see how efficiently each chapter is organized, how naturally cultural material is integrated with language content, and how many ways students are engaged in active and personal participation. These features, in combination with vivid art and photography, create a dynamic two-year program that stresses language as a tool of people's lives and an instrument of their cultural expression. With such an emphasis, *Spanish Today* provides students with a sound basis for learning Spanish as it is spoken and written today.

Communication and culture

The program's most important purpose is to enable students to *use* Spanish. This focus on communicative competence is woven into every aspect of *Spanish Today,* so that students completing the course will be able to use each of the four language skills to do a number of things.

Speaking. From the start, *Spanish Today* helps students develop practical speaking skills: asking for information; reporting what others say; stating individual opinions and concerns about home, school, shopping, eating, travel, entertainment. Whatever the topic, students are encouraged to express their own moods and feelings; they learn to do more than give pat "yes or no" answers.

Listening. Listening skills have a practical emphasis, too. Students learn to understand the same things they learn to say. In addition, they learn to understand the gist of more complicated exchanges and other communications.

Reading. Students develop the skills to read everything they can say, without the help of a dictionary. *With* the aid of a dictionary, they will be able to read short newspaper and magazine articles, simple stories, and many other kinds of straightforward prose.

Writing. With guidance, students will be able to write complete sentences on many factual topics, express simple opinions, and write reports, descriptions, anecdotes, and personal letters.

A second aim of the program is to foster in students a sensitive appreciation of the Spanish-speaking world. The kinds and quality of cultural information in *Spanish Today* help students become keenly aware of the diversity of the peoples and customs throughout the world. As students gain insight into the lives and feelings of Spanish speakers, they should realize that cultural appreciation can help bring people together and avoid misunderstandings.

Key strengths

Organization. There are several facets to the organization of *Spanish Today:* the organizational clarity of the chapters, the manner in which topics were chosen and sequenced, and the program's unique superstructure. *Spanish Today* is a two-level continuous course divided into six Stages. As students move from Stage to Stage, they progress from personal and local concerns to ever widening circles of cultural scope and focus. Stage 3 overlaps the two levels of the program to provide smooth articulation from one school year to the next. The Stages add a level of organization to the program that gives both teacher and student an opportunity to assess the work accomplished and consider the goals ahead.

Cultural integration. Cultural content is integrated with most elements of *Spanish Today*. Each of the six Stages opens with an eight-page, full-color photo essay that illustrates some of the themes of the Stage in settings around the Spanish-speaking world. The names used for the characters in the text and the settings for the dialogues, readings, and other core material are all authentic, taken from various countries where Spanish is spoken. A section entitled "Spanish Around You" opens the first-year book and shows students some of the many connections that exist between English and Spanish. Suddenly it should seem to students that the language they are about to learn is not so foreign after all.

Student involvement. The "Spanish Around You" section is just one way that Spanish is brought close to home for students. Throughout the program there is an emphasis on the student's personal and active participation in the learning process. The majority of the activities that follow core material are on a personal level; students may choose to respond in a variety of ways that parallel everyday conversation, as they express points of view, state their preferences or ideas, or ask questions. Even in the word study and grammar sections, open-ended activities urge students to use words and phrases imaginatively rather than merely to manipulate structures. This focus on self-expression builds students' confidence and skill in the use of the language.

Completeness of the program

Spanish Today is a complete program. Although the Student Text can stand entirely on its own and constitutes a total course, you may wish to take advantage of the full complement of materials available with *Spanish Today, One* to increase students' chances of reaching a high level of competency in Spanish. The program consists of the following components:

Student Text. Much of what follows in this Teacher's Guide is a detailed description of the Student Text, after the brief summaries below of the ancillaries.

Teacher's Annotated Edition. Both a teaching aid and a resource, the Teacher's Annotated Edition includes this Teacher's Guide and an Annotated Student Text. The Teacher's Guide suggests procedures and activities for *Spanish Today* and ways to adapt the program to different teaching styles and learners' needs. To acquaint the teacher with possible strategies for a typical lesson, sample lesson plans are given for Chapter 3 (Stage 1) and Chapter 8 (Stage 2). You will also find resource materials for teachers, including games and

classroom expressions in Spanish. Annotations overprinted in the Student Text provide specific suggestions for introducing and practicing core material, varying exercises and activities, further personalizing activities, and expanding cultural information. These annotations appear on the relevant pages, right where they are most useful.

Workbook. The 112-page Workbook reinforces and strengthens a student's ability to write Spanish correctly. Pages are perforated so that assignments can be handed in for correcting. Each chapter of the Student Text has a corresponding chapter in the Workbook. In addition, the Workbook has two pages of culminating activities for students to do at the end of each Stage. Line art and realia illustrate the Workbook and heighten the exercise material's appeal to students.

Tests. A set of sixteen Chapter Tests is offered, one for each chapter in the Student Text. Each test is three pages long, and is supplemented by a pre-test worksheet with questions intended to check test readiness, as well as an extra worksheet consisting of optional sections, which teachers may choose to treat as extra-credit work, include as part of the basic test, or simply omit.

Cassettes. Cassette recordings aid development in aural/oral skills. A set of 20 cassettes includes core material, pronunciation and vocabulary drills, grammar exercises, and readings from the Student Text. Special listening comprehension exercises, which do not appear in the Student Text, are also included for each chapter. Listening comprehension sections of the Tests are also provided on tape.

Posters. The Posters are valuable visual aids. They are especially useful for introducing core material and vocabulary, drilling structures, and stimulating conversation. They can be adapted for individual or small group assignments as well as for use with the full class. The set contains 64 posters, 17 x 22 inches.

Flashcards. Handy in size, the Flashcards can be used for classroom activities such as vocabulary presentation and drill, and some grammar drills. The Flashcards can also be used in conjunction with the Posters to stimulate more complex and varied activities. The set includes 200 cards: 199 with a picture on one side and a word or phrase on the other, and an index card for quick reference.

Organization of the program

Spanish Today, One contains sixteen chapters, and *Spanish Today, Two* contains fifteen chapters (plus a number of special sections, which are discussed below). As mentioned earlier, the program also has an organizational superstructure that divides the thirty-one chapters of the two-year sequence into six Stages.

Each Stage has a theme that effectively broadens the scope of the student's communicative abilities. The six Stages might be graphically depicted as a set of concentric circles, with Stage 1 at the center and Stage 6 outermost, representing the progression from the individual's immediate environment and everyday concerns to cultural issues of more lasting and widespread impact. Each Stage is introduced by an eight-page full-color photo essay. Culminating activities, called *Algo más,* are provided at the end of each Stage (and at the end of the first year) for a change of pace.

The organization of the program into Stages offers several benefits. First, considered from the standpoint of language acquisition, the Stage structure roughly reflects the sequence in which human beings expand their powers of communication and spheres of interest. The second benefit, though less linguistically based, is equally important. The Stages offer variety in both content and format, with the intent of maintaining a fresh level of interest for both students and teachers throughout the course of study. A third benefit is the ease of articulation between the first and second years that is made possible by having Stage 3 bridge the two levels.

The following is a brief summary of the Stages of *Spanish Today.* See the Scope-and-sequence chart on pages TAE 4–9 for a detailed listing of the content of *Spanish Today, One.*

Stage 1: ¿Quiénes somos? Students learn basic forms of greeting, leave-taking, and thanking. They learn to identify and describe themselves, their families, and their friends with respect to age and certain traits of personality and appearance; and

they learn to solicit such information from others. Students also learn to ask and answer questions about where they live, their health and personal moods, their school routine, occupations, and activities. They also learn to express surprise, pleasure and displeasure, disbelief; to state some simple opinions; to ask for help; and to express and ask for agreement and disagreement. Stage 1 covers Chapters 1–5 of *Spanish Today, One.*

Stage 2: De día en día. The focus of this stage is on the practicalities of everyday life: finding one's way in the city and country, discussing the weather, using public transportation, shopping, eating out, making short trips, and engaging in sports and hobbies. Students learn to extend and accept invitations or to decline them for appropriate reasons. They increase their range of communication skills to include expressing likes and dislikes, opinions and desires, indifference, certainty, as well as fear and anger. They learn to make comparisons and simple evaluations, and to ask for and offer advice or assistance. Stage 2 covers Chapters 6–11 of *Spanish Today, One.*

Stage 3: A nuestro alrededor. In this stage, students learn to increase their linguistic flexibility to deal with unpredictable or out-of-the-ordinary events: natural phenomena, entertainment, vacation travel, accidents, and family quarrels. Students practice summarizing past events, arguing, blaming, and forgiving; expressing disappointment and regret; complimenting; persuading; and apologizing. They also learn to express personal reactions to events with calm, fear, impatience, or decisiveness. Stage 3 covers Chapters 12-16 of *Spanish Today, One* and Chapters 1 and 2 of *Spanish Today, Two.*

Stage 4: En contacto. Within the context of a filmmaking session, television program, student newspaper, and a farewell party, students learn to use language to instruct, persuade, promise, advise, offer or refuse to do something, and correct others. Students talk about future plans, food and its preparation, mass media, and party customs. In this stage students increase their ability to read for meaning. Stage 4 covers Chapters 3-6 of *Spanish Today, Two.*

Stage 5: Nuevos horizontes. Students consider arguments related to various issues, such as ecology and the environment, use of the automobile, education, elections, employment, and money. They learn to evaluate arguments, to justify and defend a point of view, to suggest and instruct, to predict, and to express their personal feelings more completely. They are encouraged to consider others' points of view, rather than merely reporting or supporting their own. Stage 5 covers Chapters 7-10 of *Spanish Today, Two.*

Stage 6: El alma hispánica. In this stage, students deal more extensively with culture and the Hispanic heritage: the celebrations of Carnival, the role of sports in daily life, poetry and music, crafts and fine arts, and a contemporary short story. Students learn to read, analyze, and discuss prose and poetry. Stage 6 covers Chapters 11-15 of *Spanish Today, Two.*

Features of the Student Text

The following special sections supplement the sixteen chapters of *Spanish Today, One.* Suggestions for their use are contained in the section of the Teacher's Guide entitled ''Suggested procedures and activities,'' which begins on page TAE 14.

Spanish Around You. This four-page section highlights some of the ways in which Spanish speakers have influenced the English language and American culture. This light and appealing introduction to the course points out to students that they already know more Spanish than they think they do by virtue of borrowed words, cognates, and the increasing use of Spanish in the United States.

Maps. Four maps are found on pages xii-xv: Spain, Mexico, Central America and the Caribbean, and South America.

Photo essays. Each Stage is introduced by eight pages of full-color photographs, which have been selected for their relevance to the themes and topics of the Stage. The photo essays are designed to stimulate interest in the Spanish-speaking world and may be used as the basis for numerous activities.

Culminating activities. At the end of Stages 1 and 2, and following Chapter 16 are Culminating Activities, entitled *Algo más.* These culminating activities offer a variety of enjoyable ways for students to combine and apply the skills they have learned in the preceding Stages.

Reference section The following elements are found in the reference section at the end of *Spanish Today, One:* (1) a list of common Spanish first names; (2) a group of supplementary word sets, categorized according to topic and chapter; (3) English equivalents for the core material of Chapters 1–11; and (4) grammar charts, which include pronouns, articles and adjectives, and verb forms; (5) Spanish-English End vocabulary; (6) English-Spanish End Vocabulary; and (7) an Index of the principal grammar and pronunciation topics and word sets introduced in the text.

Chapter format

A typical chapter of *Spanish Today, One* contains the following elements:

Chapter opening text. A brief passage in English opens each chapter. It gives some information about the geographical setting of the chapter and sets the scene for the core material and cultural notes.

Core material and activities. Monologues, dialogues, and simulated realia (schedules, notes, want-ads, etc.) introduce the cultural themes, new vocabulary, and grammatical structures. Two or more core material selections are presented in each chapter. Every selection is followed by activities, called *Extensión,* that check and reinforce comprehension of the core material, present small amounts of new vocabulary, and provide opportunities for students to personalize the core material. Beginning in Stage 2, comprehension checks are introduced in the *Comprensión* sections following the core material.

Cultural notes. In each chapter there are three or more cultural notes in English. These notes, located in various places in the chapter, provide specific information on the customs, social conventions, or geography of a region; on special uses of language that occur in the core material; or on other matters of interest related to the theme or setting of the chapter.

Estudio de palabras. The word study section presents word sets or groups of related words to help students expand their vocabulary. Each presentation is followed by related exercises and activities.

Pronunciación y ortografía. The sound-spelling sections provide practice with specific sounds, patterns of stress, and intonation.

Gramática. The grammar sections consist of examples and brief explanations of the grammar points. Each presentation is followed by related exercises. The grammar sections also contain open-ended activities called *¡Vamos a hablar!*

Lectura. A reading selection that recombines familiar vocabulary and structures is found in every other chapter in Stage 2 and in every chapter of Stage 3. New words that are not cognates are glossed in the margin as a reading aid. One or more *actividades* follow the reading selection.

En resumen. The grammar summary is a reference section. It provides a concise overview of the grammar topics of the chapter. Where appropriate, material from previous chapters is summarized along with related new material.

Repaso. The review exercises focus on vocabulary and grammar of a given chapter and re-enter material from previous chapters.

Vocabulario. The end-of-the-chapter vocabulary lists the active new vocabulary with English equivalents.

Suggested Procedures and Activities

Every group of students has different interests, needs, and abilities; every teacher has different ideas and techniques. No book or teacher's guide can replace the imagination, ingenuity, and sensitivity of the teacher. The guidelines in this section, therefore, are merely *suggestions* for effective use of the various elements of *Spanish Today, One.* Each teacher should adapt and alter the procedures described to suit her or his style and situation.

Learning objectives

The formation of learning objectives is a good way to ensure that teachers and students alike are aware of the goals of the course. Such goals are necessarily an individual matter, and what is reasonable — or even possible — in one school or class may be out of the question elsewhere. There is no single correct set of objectives. A wide range of views exists, not only as to what level of expectation is proper, but also as to what form learning objectives should take and how detailed they should be. The following suggestions, therefore, are intended to help the teacher form learning objectives within the context of *Spanish Today* that fit her or his own situation.

Several aspects of the instructional process need to be considered in forming learning objectives. First and foremost is the content: *what* is to be learned. Since few students will truly master all of what is taught, it is further necessary to determine what percentage of the content and what degree of accuracy constitute a minimally satisfactory level of attainment. Next to be considered is the amount of time within which students are to learn the material. Finally, one must decide how students are to demonstrate that they have learned the material. Again, there is no one answer to the question of what is adequate, reasonable, or fair. Teachers simply have to exercise their own judgment in light of what they know about their school, their students, and the amount of time available.

A useful tool for the process of forming learning objectives is the Scope-and-sequence chart on pages TAE 4 to TAE 9. This chart categorizes the course content according to the various kinds of information students should learn: cultural information, word sets (and vocabulary in general), pronunciation, grammar. The individual teacher can decide and then inform students exactly what will be expected, and to what level of proficiency or accuracy, within each of the categories. This procedure begins, but does not complete, the formation of meaningful learning objectives.

What will require a little more effort on the part of the teacher, but what is ultimately perhaps even more important, is a listing of the kinds of things students ought to be able to do with language by the time they finish a given chapter. This will involve analyzing the vocabulary, the topics and content of the various core material selections, and the kinds of expressions presented in the activities. The teacher should keep in mind what students are learning *to do* with language rather than just think about the grammatical structures or individual words students are supposed to learn. For each chapter, it should be possible to identify three to five "communication skills." Since these really form the heart of each chapter, around which the grammar, vocabulary, and the cultural information have been organized, it is important for students to know what the skills are and to be encouraged to master them.

A few examples will perhaps help. In Chapter 1, for instance, students learn (among other things) to exchange greetings and take leave of each other, to identify themselves and others, to describe themselves and others, and to ask and answer some simple questions. At the end of the chapter, each student ought to be able to do each of those things, even if only on a fairly elementary basis. Similarly, in Chapter 3 they learn to discuss ages and birthdays, to offer gifts or thanks for gifts, to extend birthday greetings, and to express incredulity and surprise. In later chapters the communication skills become more complex. In Chapter 6, students give and respond to directions; in Chapter 8, to express anxiety and reassurance; in Chapter 13, to blame, deny, and apologize.

Expressed in the form of communication skills, the goals of the course are more likely to make sense to students than goals that include only lists of vocabulary words or grammatical structures. Those are also important, of course, but their importance is frequently not as obvious or convincing to students as to teachers. By including among the objectives the kinds of communication skills the students should be trying to develop, teachers can help students see the point of what they are learning, and help them see language as a tool for a variety of tasks. Once again, since these *uses* of the language and the active participation that they require of the student are really the basis of the whole *Spanish Today* program, their inclusion in the learning objectives is extremely important.

Special sections of the program

Spanish Around You. This section is an especially important feature because it comes at the very beginning of the first-year book. How students get started is likely to be a crucial factor in determining their attitude toward language study. Hence, the emphasis here is on the ways in which at least some bits and pieces of Spanish and Hispanic culture — in the form of cognates and borrowed words, place names, signs, and labels — are not really so foreign after all. The point is to stress for students, at the outset, the familiar or common aspects of Spanish rather than to overwhelm them with what is different or unusual about Spanish. For many students learning a foreign language is a new experience, which can be filled with frustration. One of the aims of this section is to make students feel more comfortable with the experience of learning Spanish by drawing attention to linguistic and cultural features they already know.

The degree to which the material presented in this section is, in fact, familiar will vary from class to class (even from student to student) and from one part of the country to another. But even if a student does claim total ignorance of everything on these pages, enthusiastic and vigorous presentation on the part of the teacher at this point can do much to overcome the beginner's feeling that everything having to do with Spanish is completely foreign. Stress to students that in a real sense Spanish is becoming the second language of the United States. Over 14 million inhabitants of the United States speak Spanish. Most students will have had some contact with the language or the culture.

A number of different kinds of activities can be devised to make these pages both an effective teaching device and a source of fun. One of the easiest ways to get students started is to look for things to add to each of the categories represented here. Newspapers and magazines, phone books, street maps and atlases, should all help produce additional examples of the influence of Spanish. Students should be encouraged to contribute personal anecdotes about their experiences with Spanish-speaking people. Students may want to learn the meanings, if they do not already know them, of the items that are presented on pages viii-xi of the Student Text. One word of caution should perhaps be expressed, however. Since the main purpose of this section is to get students interested and involved, and to help them overcome their shyness, diffidence, or indifference toward Spanish, it is important to treat these pages in a relaxed manner, to emphasize similarity and familiarity, and the usefulness of exposure to Spanish as a way of enriching one's sense of English. Above all, it should be borne in mind that these pages are most likely to fulfill a useful purpose if they are treated as a lively means of introducing new material rather than as something to be presented and then tested. "Spanish Around You" is important as much for its capacity to help set a positive tone as for its actual content.

Finally, one should keep in mind that this section is an introduction both to the language and to the culture. "Spanish Around You" is just the first step in the *Spanish Today* program, where language and culture are never really separated. In the material on these pages, partly because "grammar" is not at issue, teachers have an opportunity to help students see language as one part of a vast cultural complex. How students look at "Spanish Around You" will have much to do with their success and their attitudes throughout their study of Spanish.

You may wish to introduce (or try to elicit from students) some of the following words and phrases that are not included in the "Spanish Around You" section. (These words and expressions are introduced in *Spanish Today, One* unless indicated otherwise.)

Cognates

Music

el clarinete	la orquesta
el concierto	el piano
la guitarra	la trompeta
el instrumento	el violín
la música	

Occupations (all have feminine forms)

el dentista	el piloto
el intérprete	el pintor
el mecánico	el policía
el médico	el profesor

Class/school

el álgebra	el examen
la biología	la historia
la clase	la música
el/la estudiante	

Locatives

el banco	el museo
la estación	el parque
el garaje	el restaurante
el hospital	el teatro
el hotel	

Miscellaneous

el accidente	la familia
el agente	fantástico
el aire	favorito
la ambulancia	la foto(grafía)
el café	la idea
el centro	la información
el cine	inteligente
el color	interesante
contento	la inundación
la costa	el león
delicioso	la línea
la dirección	la memoria
económico	la montaña
elegante	la patata
la emoción	la persona
enorme	el problema
la ensalada	el/la radio
especial	la raqueta
estupendo	el silencio
excelente	la televisión
la excursión	la temperatura
la experiencia	las vacaciones
fabuloso	la victoria
la fama	el volumen

Cognates not in text

el tigre	la elección
la botella	el ministro
el arte	el voto
la universidad	la libertad
el apartamento	la democracia

Borrowed words

adios	loco
aficionado	olé!
arroyo	patio
arroz con pollo	plaza
cacao (tree)	pronto
chile (con carne)	pueblo
conquistador	rodeo
corral	sierra
coyote	siesta
fiesta	sombrero
guacamole	taco
guerrilla	tapioca
jaguar	tortilla
junta	

For additional Spanish place names in the United States, consult a map or atlas. You may wish to use an overhead projector and point out Spanish names state by state, or you may wish to have students work in small groups (or pairs) to uncover Spanish names in various regions or groups of states. In the latter instance you may need to assist students in their search. Supply English equivalents for students.

The following place names are a sampler and may be used as a basis for further discussion and research. Literal translations are given in parentheses.

Names of states

Florida (*flowering, in bloom*)
Colorado (*colored, red*)
Nevada (*covered with snow*)
Montana (*mountain*)

Cities with religious names

San Diego	Santa Cruz
San Francisco	San Antonio
Los Angeles	Santa Fe

Alabama

Andalusia (*province in Spain*)	Gordo (*fat*)
	Lavaca (*the cow*)
Corona (*crown*)	Perdido (*lost*)

Arizona

Casa Grande (*large house*)
Sierra Vista (*view of the sierra*)
Dos Cabezas (*2 heads*)
Ganado (*cattle*)
Nogales (*walnut trees*)

California

Chico (*boy*)
El Cajon (*large box*)
El Centro (*the center*)
El Toro (*the bull*)
Carpinteria (*carpentry*)
Tiburon (*shark*)
La Puente (*bridge*)
Mariposa (*butterfly*)
Pajaro (*bird*)

Colorado

La Junta (*gathering, junction*)
Cuchara (*spoon*)
Salida (*exit*)
Mosca (*fly*)
Pueblo (*town*)

Florida

Alturas (*heights*)
El Portal (*the portal*)
Naranja (*orange*)
Molino (*mill*)
Punta Gorda (*fat point, promontory*)
Largo (*long*)

Georgia

Alamo (*poplar tree*)
Buena Vista (*good view*)

Illinois

Alhambra (*Moorish palace in Spain*)
Cerro Gordo (*fat hill*)
Cisne (*swan*)
Eldorado (*the golden one*)
El Paso (*the pass*)

Maine

Mexico (*country*)
Peru (*country*)

Nevada

Alamo *(poplar tree)*
Caliente *(warm, hot)*
Cobre *(copper)*
Las Vegas *(the plains, meadows)*
Mina *(mine)*

New Jersey

Buena *(good)*
Malaga *(city in Spain)*
Bogota *(city in Colombia)*

New Mexico

Alcalde *(mayor)*
Arroyo Seco *(dry stream)*
Bosque *(woods)*
Capitan *(captain)*
Casa Blanca *(white house)*
Cebolla *(onion)*
Cuervo *(crow)*
El Porvenir *(the future)*
Las Cruces *(the crosses)*
Gallina *(hen)*
Lajoya *(the jewel)*
La Luz *(the light)*
La Plata *(the silver)*
Ojo Caliente *(hot eye)*
Pinos Altos *(tall pines)*
Portales *(portals)*
Raton *(mouse)*
Ruidoso *(noisy)*
Truchas *(trout)*

New York

Cuba *(country)*
Lima *(city in Peru)*
Leon *(city in Spain)*

Ohio

Toledo *(city in Spain)*
Lima *(city in Peru)*

West Virginia

Cinco *(five)*
Leon *(lion)*

Photo essays. The full-color photographs at the beginning of each Stage are valuable for several reasons. The pure visual appeal of colorful pic-tures, which simply make the book more fun to use, is an obvious benefit. Likewise, the photographs are of self-evident value as a means of illustrating the places and topics described in the text and of giving the student a sense of reality and substance. The usefulness of the photo essays as the basis for activities, however, is more easily overlooked. A photograph can give rise to a practically unlimited number of comments and descriptions, especially with the help of a few timely suggestions from the teacher.

If a picture is worth a thousand words, in a foreign language course there is much to be said for elicit-ing as many of those words as possible from the students. Techniques for doing so range from ask-ing students to make simple statements about a picture to asking them to "step into" a scene and create an appropriate narrative or conversation. Students can make up or answer factual questions about what is depicted; they can state their personal feelings about what they see; they can invent names for people, explanations for situations, or results of occurrences; they can say of what, where, or whom a picture reminds them.

You may wish to review the photographs from time to time as you prepare lesson plans, looking for ways to use them to elicit particular words and structures. Many pictures can serve repeatedly as cues for different kinds of utterances.

Most teachers prefer to keep to a minimum the amount of English spoken in the classroom. Cer-tainly it is desirable to promote as much use of Spanish as possible in talking about illustrations as in other activities. However, you may find that per-mitting occasional discussion of the photographs in English is worthwhile if it enables students to in-crease their awareness and understanding of the cultures that are represented.

Culminating Activities. Review and reinforce-ment are basic to a successful foreign language program. The ongoing re-entry that is included throughout the chapters of *Spanish Today* is com-plemented by the Culminating Activities *(Algo más)* at the end of each Stage and at the end of the first-year book. This special section serves as the basis for a kind of "time-out," a break in the regular work pattern that acknowledges or reflects the nat-ural plateaus students typically reach in the process of learning a language. Skills and topics from several chapters are used in these activities, helping tie together individual bits of information and concepts so that students can see the total picture and fully appreciate the communicative powers that they have acquired. Moreover, the section offers new and enjoyable ways for students to work with familiar material, as well as ways to expand their cultural awareness. While the section does provide review, the activities are meant to be fun rather than to be used as tests of any sort.

It is not expected that any one student will do all of the activities; rather, it is hoped that at least one or two activities will appeal to each student. The printed directions plus your imagination and help should suffice as guidelines. Some of the activities are intended for individual work (writing a letter), others for pairs or small groups (skits and displays), and still others for the entire class (games and large projects). The activities provide both oral and written practice; many involve use of visuals. At least one Culminating Activity in each Stage is keyed to the color essay that introduces that Stage. Students are asked to develop a conversation, skit, or simple narrative based on one or more of the photos. One activity — creating an album or scrapbook — is an ongoing project continued through the first year. Students are asked to contribute to their album during the course of each Stage, adding realia and other visuals, items related to the content of the Stage, handwritten and printed materials that reflect their own personalities and activities.

You may want to spend parts of several days working on this section, possibly alternating individual projects with group projects. (Some of these activities may be started before the end of the Stage.) Additional enjoyable activities such as slide shows, songs, and talks by visitors can be included during this period as part of the consolidation process that helps to give students the desired sense of accomplishment and understanding.

Chapter material

Chapter opening text. Students should begin the study of each chapter by reading the brief introductory text in English. You may wish to expand on this material with information based on your own knowledge of the area. Depending on the ability of the class, you may wish to paraphrase this information in Spanish beginning in Stage 2 or 3, in order to give the students extra practice in listening comprehension. Be sure that students can locate the places discussed on a map. The maps in *Spanish Today* will be useful, as well as a globe or various wall maps. Increasing geographic awareness is a worthwhile objective in the study of a foreign language.

Besides providing a few details about the locale of the chapter and establishing a context for the core material, the opener may be used to stimulate discussion of current events and personal experiences and attitudes. Use newspaper articles, slides, or films of the area, if they are available. Ask students about their knowledge or impressions of the places mentioned in the text. At the end of the chapter you may wish to ask them how their earlier impressions have changed or broadened.

In Stages 2 and 3, this text may be used as the basis for brief warm-ups and re-entry. Try asking short comprehension questions in Spanish about the information, eliciting previously learned structures and vocabulary.

Core material and activities. The dialogues, narratives, and simulated realia (bulletin board notes, posters, want ads, etc.), which constitute core material, have several important functions. First, the core material establishes a theme for the chapter, which is reflected in most of the other sections of the chapter as well. Second, core material introduces vocabulary and grammatical structures, many of which are treated in depth later in the *Estudio de palabras* and *Gramática* sections. Third, cultural features are an integral part of the core material; many of these features are treated in cultural notes. Finally, one of the most important functions of the core material is to present examples of various categories of communication, which are then practiced and expanded upon in the *Extensión* sections that follow core material.

The suggested strategies for teaching core material and activities can be summarized briefly and emphatically as follows: (1) present the material in several short sessions rather than fewer, longer ones; (2) return to material frequently for re-entry, variation, and reinforcement; (3) exploit to the greatest possible degree the interests, imagination, and creativity of both the students and the teacher.

None of the core material selections is intended to be memorized. A more useful objective is for students to be able, at the end of a chapter, to understand and use the material in new contexts. This ability to comprehend and to produce language outside the familiar context in which it was presented marks true communicative competence.

With respect to comprehension, therefore, students should reach a point at the end of each chapter where they can answer questions based on the core material, paraphrase the material, and use the language correctly, within the parameters of familiar vocabulary and structures. They should be able to do so both orally and in writing, in response to either spoken or written cues.

There are many ways of presenting core material, in order to facilitate comprehension- but a few general guidelines are appropriate. Students should hear, rather than simply read, the selection the first time it is presented in class. In many cases, it is advisable to do the initial presentation with books closed, in order to maintain the necessary emphasis on listening comprehension. Make it clear to students that they are not expected to understand fully on the first exposure to the material, but encourage them to try to get a general idea of the meaning. There will be frequent opportunities to return to the selection and fill in the gaps in comprehension. Remind students frequently of basic techniques for understanding new material: logical guessing based on context; attention to morphological clues such as cognates and words related to other known words; attention to intonation, tone, and non-verbal clues such as gestures and facial expressions.

Begin each core material session with an uninterrupted reading or playing of the recording. During this initial presentation, the material should be modeled at normal, conversational speed, without exaggeration or distortion. Then you may wish to reread the material with pauses to check on comprehension. Basic comprehension questions as you work through a section can help point out key elements and ensure that nobody gets lost. Visuals such as drawings, magazine cut-outs, and props are useful devices in checking comprehension. The same is true of gestures, pantomime, and dramatization. As students progress, you may wish to clarify vocabulary by means of Spanish definitions, synonyms or antonyms, or by pointing out root words. It is important to elicit these types of confirmation of understanding from students wherever

possible, prompting as necessary, rather than merely to provide the information.

After the initial reading of the core material and checking comprehension, model the phrases and sentences for student repetition. Aim for correct pronunciation and intonation based on teacher (or tape) model. It is here that the basis for proper pronunciation is laid. Students should be able to produce utterances at normal conversational speed, without unnatural emphasis or exaggeration. While it is important not to set unreasonably high standards, one should keep in mind that it is easier to correct pronunciation errors at the outset than to change bad habits once they have been established. Corrections should be made in a positive way. Having the entire class repeat a corrected response before asking an individual to do so is often a good idea. Another technique is to have several individuals repeat a word or phrase, rather than just the student who makes an error in pronunciation.

Many of these same techniques for presenting and checking comprehension of dialogues and narratives can be used for simulated realia, with one notable exception. Since items such as want-ads or posters in real life are designed to be read, not heard, and since they are often illustrated, students should be able to see the text as they hear it. You may wish to display the material on an overhead projector or suggest that students follow in their books. You should read the material with intonation that might be used in actually reading such an item; one reads abbreviated material differently from full prose. Then have students practice reading it in the same way. Make sure they understand what they are saying by occasionally asking them to paraphrase the information. In Stages 2 and 3 students should try to paraphrase in Spanish.

After the initial presentation, students can be encouraged to make slight variations. For example, in the bulletin board ad on page 45, the telephone number and the age requirement could be changed, within the limits of the students' vocabulary.

It is very important not to spend too much time on a given section of core material without breaking to a different activity. In most circumstances, fifteen minutes is probably the maximum time that should be spent on any one activity. One may easily fall into the trap of trying to analyze the material exhaustively during one session, with the result that students' concentration and level of interest are diminished. A more effective strategy is to limit the scope of each session, in terms of both the time spent and the material covered, and return to the selection the next day or even later in the same class period. Once the initial presentation of a section of core material has been completed, it is usually desirable to return to it two or three times during the study of that chapter. Most students will not master the material before several such presentations have taken place. The teacher's judgment will determine the time spent on new material. While students should not be allowed to become bored, they should not become frustrated by having to move ahead before they reach a reasonable level of understanding.

The activities in the *Extensión* sections that follow every selection of core material are among the most important features of *Spanish Today*. The way in which they are used can greatly affect the students' success in learning to communicate in Spanish. All of the activities exist for the purpose of encouraging students to use Spanish, often to talk about their own feelings and experiences. The teacher and students will frequently think of ways to expand or adapt the activities; such creativity is to be encouraged.

A limited amount of new vocabulary and structures is used in the activities. New material is indicated with a raised degree mark (°); English equivalents are provided in the end-of-chapter vocabularies. Much of this new material is analyzed later in the chapter. Many useful expressions may be treated as lexical items with little or no discussion of the grammar. In any case, it is usually best to do the activities first with minimal analysis, since the idea is to get the class started *using* the material as quickly as possible. After having worked on the appropriate parts of the *Estudio de palabras* and *Gramática* sections, you may choose to go back to the activities to reinforce the students' understanding of how the words and concepts are put into practice.

Many activities are in the form of a question (or statement) followed by a series of varied responses. Often these responses represent a variety of attitudes or moods, so that students can come close to presenting their own point of view in a given situation. Make clear to students that the printed variations do not represent all possible responses. Rather, they are a selection of useful conversational tools covering a range of meanings. The activities will be most effective if students are allowed to choose the forms that actually express their own feelings — or their whims — and to invent or recall other expressions from previous chapters, and are not obliged to respond in set ways just so that everybody practices saying everything. Generally, in fact, all of the printed variations will eventually be used by somebody (if need be, the teacher can take a role and produce those that students do not use), and ideally the class will come up with a number of utterances to add to the ones provided. By returning to the activities several times during the course of a chapter (they can be used effectively as warm-ups), the teacher can make sure that all of the material is learned and practiced in an enjoyable way.

Activities can be taught in much the same way as core material: presentation, practice, then reinforcement through variation. Initial presentation can be done with books open or closed, but subsequent practice should be done with books closed in order to maintain spontaneity. Most of the activities are suitable for work involving pairs of individuals, and it is recommended that this technique be used whenever possible. Where questions are given, students can ask the questions of one another. Often a chain drill can be set up simply by having each student end her or his utterance by saying ''y tú?'' to somebody else. Many activities are explicitly presented for a cue-response approach involving two people. Sometimes the teacher may wish to take one of the roles at the beginning, then have students take both parts once the pattern is established. Whatever specific devices are used, the more often students are led to interact with one another as well as with the teacher, the more readily they will perceive Spanish as a form of communication instead of an academic exercise.

A new type of printed activity is introduced in Stage 2: *Comprensión*. These checks are not only valuable in assessing student comprehension of core material; they also help students interpret the simulated realia.

Teachers may wish to adjust the level of difficulty of a question to the ability of each student. The question can be slightly modified but still reinforce the structure being practiced, or sentence fragments may be accepted as responses. Often the same question can be asked of two or three students in succession, so that the weaker student may have the opportunity to hear the correct answer before being asked to respond.

As students progress in their mastery of the language, they should be given frequent opportunity to make up their own questions. Too often the teacher does all the asking and the students do all the responding. Students should be encouraged to work in pairs and in small groups as they ask and answer questions. Also, students should be given the opportunity to ask the teacher questions for practice with the formal form of address. The teacher's responses will provide extra listening comprehension practice.

Cultural notes. Promoting awareness of diverse cultures is an integral part of *Spanish Today*. The cultural notes are numerous and varied; their aim is to offer insights into the life of Spanish-speaking people. It is not possible (or desirable) to include lengthy commentary and exhaustive details in the notes; they should serve instead as the basis for further discussion and in some cases, research. Annotations in the TAE provide additional information that you may wish to share with the students. Encourage students to be alert for news items and other references to the topics and locales of the book, and to bring them to the attention of the class. Many of the things they study in their other courses, especially social studies, literature, and art courses, are relevant to the subject matter of *Spanish Today;* helping students to perceive such relationships among their different courses greatly benefits them and the entire school community.

All of the cultural notes of *Spanish Today, One* are in English so that the information will be easily accessible and students will not consider them an added burden. As in the case of the other English sections of the text, you will want to use your own judgment as to how much time to allow for discussion in English. You may want to have students read the notes outside of class, then set aside a few minutes for class discussion afterwards. Perhaps you will wish to make up simple comprehension questions, to be asked and answered in Spanish, based on the notes or the photos, drawings, or rea-

lia that complement them. Whatever method of handling them you prefer, it is hoped that the cultural notes and related activities or projects will prove enjoyable and informative.

Estudio de palabras. The word study sections provide the basis for classroom activities designed to increase the students' basic vocabulary. New words are presented in related groups, since it is easier for students to learn vocabulary in logical groups than as isolated words or expressions. Two or three such word groups are included in most chapters.

The majority of the groups are lexical word sets, such as sports terms, weather expressions, or food. Most word sets are presented through the use of illustrations to minimize interference from English and to place the vocabulary in context. Beginning in Stage 2, some sections are included that focus on linguistic features such as cognates, diminutives, the superlative suffix-*ísimo,* and adverbs in -*mente.* Such topics help students increase not only their vocabulary but also their word-building skills.

Several topics are presented in each *Estudio de palabras* section. Each topic generally relates to one of the core material selections; the topic can be presented after the core material selection has been introduced. Sometimes one or another of the topics lends itself to use as an introduction to the core material selection and could therefore be presented first. This technique will facilitate variation of the core material.

The exercises and activities that follow each presentation can be done with the entire class, small groups, or pairs of students. Exercises should be done orally first and can be followed by written work, if desired. Stress to students the need for mastering these words, which are intended to become part of their active vocabulary. It is suggested that you not spend too much time on a particular section during a single class period; once again, varying the kinds of things done in class will generally produce better results.

Pronunciación y ortografía. Each sound-spelling section contains brief, simple explanations of one or two features of the Spanish sound system, drills for practicing these features, and a few sentences to provide pronunciation and reading practice in context. The illustrated proverb within each section offers students additional pronunciation practice, as well as a way to have fun learning set phrases that are an integral part of Hispanic culture. The proverbs are generally related to the sound being practiced, though sometimes more to one of the themes of the chapter.

Phonetic symbols are used in the sound-spelling sections, primarily for convenience of reference and to remind students that sounds and letters do not always correspond. Students are not expected to learn these symbols. Most of them are identical to symbols in the International Phonetic Alphabet. *Palabras claves* are given for each sound, so that students can learn to associate that sound with specific spellings. The *palabras claves* are generally high-frequency words, and most of them are recently introduced vocabulary.

The speech patterns covered in these sections of *Spanish Today, One* are representative of the generally accepted, standard Spanish pronunciation of Latin America. The goal of *Spanish Today* is to help students acquire the fundamentals of standard Spanish pronunciation; no attempt has been made to include all the sounds of the language or discuss the fine points of regional variations. However, a few cultural notes in the Student Text and annotations in the TAE do point out major regional variants.

Students will attain widely varying degrees of proficiency in regard to pronunciation. One criterion for determining what constitutes acceptable pronunciation is whether or not a given utterance would be comprehensible to a native speaker not familiar with the text. Many factors, including innate aptitude, self-confidence, and motivation, will influence the extent to which an individual student's pronunciation may surpass the minimum acceptable level.

A student who clearly has difficulty distinguishing and reproducing the sounds of Spanish should not be expected to achieve near-native pronunciation. On the other hand, a student who gives evidence of having a "good ear" and an ability to imitate sounds and speech patterns should be encouraged to improve her or his pronunciation as much as possible. Your perception of a student's relative potential, therefore, will determine to a considerable extent the kinds of corrections you make of that student's speech.

All of the pronunciation drills are included in the *Spanish Today, One* recordings. Whether or not you use the recordings, you will probably want to model and then have students repeat the examples. Walk around the room as you model the words, so that students can see how the mouth and various muscles are involved in producing the sounds. Alternate choral repetition with individual practice, encouraging students to speak clearly and in full voice. It is important also to speak at a natural tempo, with normal stress patterns.

On occasion, you may find it necessary to isolate a difficult phoneme for special attention, but this isolated practice should always be followed immediately by repetition of the utterance spoken at normal tempo.

When presenting the proverbs, try first to elicit from students some possible interpretations or English equivalents, prompting as necessary. (English equivalents are provided in the annotations.) In many cases cognates, familiar words, and the illustration itself provide enough clues to point students in the right direction. Students should not be concerned about unfamiliar vocabulary and structures; the proverbs are not intended for active mastery, and linguistic analysis of them, especially early in the course, is unlikely to be profitable. As an optional activity, you might encourage students to come up with different artistic renderings of the proverbs and post the drawings on a bulletin board.

It is advisable to do portions of a pronunciation section over a period of several days, rather than attempt to cover it in one class period. Quick, lively drills on one or two sounds, repeated at appropriate points in later class periods, will produce better results than a concentrated one-time session.

Gramática. The grammar section of each chapter presents several grammar points, and each of these presentations is followed by two or more exercises for immediate practice and reinforcement of the topic. Two or three open-ended activities (*¡Vamos a hablar!*) are interspersed throughout the grammar section.

Each presentation begins with an example of the grammar point at issue, either in a chart form or as a Spanish phrase or sentence. This example is followed by a succinct explanation in English. Grammar presentations may be done inductively or deductively, at your discretion. For example, you may wish to present some topics by having students do one of the exercises and then try to derive a grammar statement about the pattern practiced. In other instances, for a change of pace, you may wish to present examples and the explanation first, and then have students practice the concept in the related exercises. Alternating the use of inductive and deductive approaches, depending on the complexity of the particular grammar point, is one effective way of varying class procedures. In addition, this kind of variety can be a real help to the students; since not all students learn equally well with both approaches, the variety gives more of them a better chance of comprehending the material.

Most grammar exercises are given in context so that students can practice communicating with a purpose. Initially, drills should be done orally and with books closed, in order to focus students' attention on what they are saying. An extension of this oral practice is for the teacher to model the cues and responses for the students, who then write the responses after oral repetition. As a change of pace, students should cue the exercises instead of the teacher. As a general rule, intensive oral work should precede any written assignments. When dealing with a particularly difficult structure, many teachers find it helpful to repeat a drill, or a slightly modified version of it, two or three times within the same week. It may be helpful to assign troublesome exercises as written homework after oral drill in class. Annotations often suggest variations for the drills. Students should be encouraged to offer their own variations; such variations are an important step toward competence in the language. *¡Vamos a hablar!* activities are provided at strategic intervals to offer students greater freedom in the manipulation of new structures, in a new and personalized context. Students can do these activities in pairs or small groups. For a change of pace, they can be done with the full class.

Lectura. The reading selections recombine familiar vocabulary and structures. *Lecturas* are introduced in Stage 2, where they occur in every other chapter; in Stage 3 they occur in every chapter. Unfamiliar words that are not obvious cognates are glossed in the margin as a reading aid; they should be treated as passive vocabulary. The *Lecturas* are designed to give students an added cultural slant on the geographical setting of the chapter. They offer students the opportunity to read extended blocks of material and provide training in understanding unfamiliar passages.

In most cases the reading selections can be presented in much the same way as the core material and activities are. It is best to begin the presentation by reading the entire selection through once (or by playing the recording). After this introduction to the material, you may wish to analyze it carefully for students, paragraph by paragraph, clarifying the meaning of unfamiliar vocabulary, pointing out cognates, and using other techniques for ensuring comprehension. (See pages TAE 19–22.) As you work through the readings, encourage students to make intelligent guesses; they should try to use contextual clues to comprehend a word or phrase.

The amount of time spent on a given reading selection will depend on the mood of the class as well as the nature of the reading selection. It is a good idea to vary the purpose for which a selection is read. At first, students should be asked to read for the gist of the story; later they should read for specific details or with an eye to retelling the story (orally or in writing). *Actividades* after the *Lectura* have several aims: they help ensure that students understand the material and can manipulate it; they may expand on the theme of the reading by personalizing the material and relating it to the students' own experience; and they may suggest research to further the students' cultural awareness.

En resumen. This handy reference section summarizes the grammar points from the *Gramática* and sometimes presents additional information, for example, *vosotros*-forms. Intended for recognition only, they are not practiced actively. The grammar summary brings together the topics presented piecemeal in the *Gramática* section. In some cases material from previous chapters is reentered and summarized, along with related new material.

Grammar points are frequently presented in charts and tables for the purpose of quick review. Capital letters in parentheses following the grammar headings refer back to corresponding exercises in the *Gramática*. If students are having difficulty with any of the grammar topics, they should be encouraged to repeat the appropriate drills in that section before taking the chapter test. Since this section is intended for reference, most teachers will not want to take class time to cover it.

Repaso. Systematic review and re-entry are key features of *Spanish Today*. The review exercises in the *Repaso* focus on the vocabulary and grammar of the chapter where the material is taught and they re-enter such material from previous chapters. These exercises are intended for either oral or written work; some can be done both ways. In the earlier units especially, it is advisable for teachers to go over exercises orally before assigning them as written homework. You may wish to assign selected exercises after the corresponding section of the grammar is completed or wait until the entire chapter is finished. The *Repaso* is extremely useful as a pre-test review.

Vocabulario. The chapter vocabulary is a reference list of active new vocabulary with English equivalents. Students should master the words and expressions before going on to the next chapter. Vocabulary items are alphabetized within each of several categories as a learning aid: *sustantivos, verbos, otras palabras, expresiones,* and other categories as appropriate to the chapter. The *expresiones* include idiomatic expressions as well as isolated words and set phrases introduced in core material or activities that students should learn as lexical items.

The vocabularies are intended to be used for reference, not assigned for homework. While some students may want to memorize the lists of words, teachers should encourage them to learn new vocabulary in context — something reference lists do not provide. Most vocabulary items should be mastered during class sessions, so the vocabularies may be useful as review or check-up aids. Teachers can help make vocabulary learning more enjoyable for students by using class time for word games such as *Hola,* Categories, Add-an-element, Hangman, Scrambled Letters, Acrostics, and Crossword Puzzles. Directions for various games are given in the annotations and on TAE pages 31–33.

Reference section

Appendix A. The first Appendix is a list of common boys' and girls' names in Spanish. You may wish to assign names to students or allow them to choose their own. Name cards, made from 5″ x 8″ cards, can be folded in half lengthwise to stand up on student desks. Letters should be large enough so that the name can be read from across the room. These name cards will be useful in the first few days of the course for doing many of the activities in Chapter 1. Some teachers may wish to use them as an initial introduction to reading and to make students aware of sound-spelling correspondences.

Appendix B. English equivalents of core material for Stages 1 and 2 (chapters 1–11) are given in the second Appendix. They are intended mainly as a reference for home study, or for students who were absent when core material was introduced. Some teachers may wish to use the English equivalents in paraphrasing the Spanish core material during its presentation. Occasionally, you may wish to give students the English equivalents and ask them to express the same ideas in Spanish.

Appendix C. The list of supplementary word sets is a useful tool in helping students increase the number of things they can say and write during the course of a chapter. In some of the activities such as conversations, letters, or skits, students may wish to use words not in their active vocabulary. Since it is unrealistic and pedagogically unsound to present long lists of words in a given group or set that all students must learn, these supplementary (and optional) word sets are made available to students with special interest in a topic. Some of the words presented are introduced as active vocabulary in later chapters.

Appendix D. The grammar summaries include charts and tables on the agreement of adjectives, possessive and demonstrative adjectives, and pronouns. The verb charts show regular *-ar, -er,* and *-ir* verbs, stem-changing verbs, verbs with spelling changes, reflexive verbs, and selected irregular verbs in the present and preterit tenses, as well as affirmative *tú*-commands and present participles.

Spanish-English Vocabulary. The end vocabulary gives the basic words and expressions introduced in the core material, activities, and *Estudio de palabras* sections plus the chapter number where they are introduced. Teachers will find the chapter references useful in preparing additional exercises or quizzes. Words from headings, photo captions, scene setters, and *lecturas* are included also (except obvious cognates), but these are listed without chapter references.

English-Spanish Vocabulary. This vocabulary is a selected list of common words that students will find helpful for some of the *Repaso* exercises and *Lectura* activities, as well as for skits and other open-ended activities.

Index. The Index at the end of the Student Text indicates the page(s) on which a grammar topic is introduced or summarized. The Index also contains page references to topics in the *Estudio de palabras* and the *Pronunciación y ortografía* sections.

Sample Lesson Plans

Non-Linear teaching

Sample lesson plans for Chapter 3 (Stage 1) and Chapter 8 (Stage 2) are outlined below to demonstrate how a non-linear treatment of this text could be implemented. The exact amount of time needed to complete a chapter will depend on many factors, including the age and maturity of the students, the teacher's pacing, the length of the class period, and the amount of supplementary material used. These two plans show how to spread the teaching activities for each chapter over 10 days. Such an organization will make it possible to cover the 16 chapters of *Spanish Today, One* in 160 days, a pace that should still give teachers ample flexibility to adapt the plans to specific situations in their schools. Extra days can be used profitably doing the Culminating Activities for each Stage, showing slides or films, or special language attractions.

No one plan will work equally well for every class, but these suggestions may serve as models for teachers in preparing to teach the two chapters under discussion here as well as the remaining chapters. Perhaps the single most important general reminder is that variety and change of pace are crucial to a lively class. And keeping things lively is an important component in maintaining student interest, which in turn is the only really effective way to ensure student involvement. Active student participation is an essential aspect of making the best use of the variety of exercises and activities to be found throughout *Spanish Today, One*. One way to

achieve variety is to begin each chapter a little differently. Although the first piece of core material may be the most obvious and perhaps the easiest way to begin a chapter, there are other possibilities. A cultural note or a photo essay can serve as the basis for discussion that will help set the tone for a chapter, especially valuable when the chapter is set in a place that the students have not yet become familiar with. A topic from the *Estudio de palabras* section may on occasion provide a good launching pad. The same is true of a topic in the *Gramática* section. And in some instances, one or more of the activities in an *Extensión* section may be a way of getting into a chapter, where you first help students master the variety of ways of responding to a comment or question before exposing them to the particular situation in the core material that calls such use into play.

A second consideration is the need to break up the longer sections of a chapter, especially grammar presentation and practice. Typically, these are the parts of the chapter students find the least stimulating, which doesn't mean the grammar can be omitted, but does make it important to keep the doses small. You may want to intersperse some of the grammar exercises with core material selections without waiting for the latter to be fully mastered. If the core material has not been mastered, some of the vocabulary in the exercises may need presentation and practice first, but the value gained in change of pace is probably worth the extra effort at that point.

Variety in technique is another way to build a successful language program. Probably nothing bores students faster than knowing that they can expect nothing other than teacher presentation followed by student response, in every class. Getting students to work in small groups or pairs occasionally, having student take over the role of "teacher" at least to the extent of asking the questions, and working in chain drills rather than always having the teacher pose the next question or problem all help. One technique that can work well to give students a sense of being in some control of what goes on is to set aside three to five minutes at the beginning of the class during which students ask the teacher as many questions as they can think of. This activity is a good warm-up drill; the object of the game is to see how fast students can ask questions — with the teacher required to answer only when the questions have been posed accurately. This helps develop fluency (because it is a race against the clock), boosts self-confidence, and generally gets the class off to a lively start.

Learning a foreign language within the rigid confines of a school class period does, of course, require practice and a certain amount of "dry" drill. But varying the sequence of activities and the instructional techniques and trying to keep things spontaneous will help make the language seem more like a real tool for communication rather than just a puzzle to be figured out. These sample lesson plans may help give you some ideas about how to proceed.

Planning a lesson

The detailed lesson plan for Chapter 3 and the somewhat abbreviated plan for Chapter 8 assume a fifty-minute period. The numbers in parentheses represent a suggested number of minutes for each activity. If your class periods are shorter than fifty minutes, you can eliminate certain activities or spend less time on them. If your class periods are longer, you can stretch the time by increasing the number of activities or spending more time on some of them. Annotations frequently provide suggestions for games and supplementary activities. You may wish to use workbook exercises as extra practice in class or as homework assignments. Some teachers include a few minutes at the end of the period for students to begin their homework. Five or ten minutes is usually enough to make sure students understand what is required, and give a welcome change of pace.

A teacher's time is at a premium; certain shortcuts can lead to more efficient and effective use of that time. It is useful to plan the lesson for an entire Stage at a time, leaving activities flexible enough to allow for changes in schedule. Prepare the visuals, hand-outs, and props for that Stage and file them in folders or manila envelopes. Make a list of these items or write them in your TAE so that you (or a student assistant) can pull out the appropriate materials for each chapter. Make a note in the margin of the TAE beside activities for which you have prepared special materials, or place a checkmark beside an annotation that suggests the use of visuals. Another technique that saves time is checking homework on overhead transparencies prepared ahead of time. This procedure frees the teacher to answer students' questions, and it completes the correction in less time than writing the answers on the board. Finally, it is important to leave the lesson plans flexible enough to allow for days during which students can catch up on work missed or review materials they did not master.

Chapter 3 (Stage 1)

Day 1

Materials: Map of Texas and Mexico, flashcards for numbers 1–31.

(3) 1. Warm-up: Greet students in Spanish and elicit proper responses. Ask personal questions at random, about students' classes and teachers (to review content of previous chapters).

(10) 2. Discuss tests from Chapter 2.

(3) 3. Present learning objectives for Chapter 3. (See Scope-and-sequence chart on pages TAE 4–5 and guidelines for forming learning objectives on pages TAE 14–15.)

(5) 4. Present cultural opener (p. 43). Ask students about their own observations and impressions of Mexican influence in Texas. Locate San Antonio on map and point out other major cities, especially those with Hispanic names. Discuss history of the region. Expand by having students discuss photo essay on pp. 54–55.

(10) 5. Introduce *Un regalo de cumpleaños* (p. 44). (See suggestions for teaching core material, beginning on page TAE 19.) Personalize dialogue with students' names.

(7) 6. Introduce activities A and B (p. 44). Review days of the week; cue Act. A with different days of the week. Have students vary cue by replacing *la fiesta* with other events, e.g., *la clase, el examen.* Have students practice in pairs.

(3) 7. Present cultural note on *quinceañera.*

(9) 8. Review numbers 0–12. Present numbers 13–31 in *Estudio de palabras,* using flashcards (if available). Do Ex. A (p. 47).

Assignment: Give students 8 statements or questions. Have them write one rejoinder for each one, to help them prepare for warm-up on Day 2. e.g.,

La fiesta es hoy; no hay examen mañana. (This activity will be used for warm-up on Day 2.)

Day 2

Materials: Flashcards for numbers, telephones (or Telephone Company Teletrainer Kit), timer or stopwatch.

(3) 1. Warm-up: "Beat the clock." Give students 5 Spanish statements or questions to which they must respond orally with as many rejoinders as they can within a specified time limit. Keep score of the number of correct rejoinders. (Repeat this activity two more times during the chapter to see if students can beat this day's record.)

(7) 2. Review *regalo* dialogue (p. 44). Have students vary dialogue by changing ages and substituting names of students.

(10) 3. Review Act. A and B (p. 44). Introduce Act. C and D. Have students practice in small groups or pairs. Use telephones for Act. D, if available.

(8) 4. Present *un* and *una* (p. 50). Have students find examples in first dialogue and in the activities. Do Ex. A and B.

(12) 5. Review Act. C (p. 44), and re-enter gift item vocabulary from Chapter 2, e.g., *libro, lápiz.* Write nouns on the board. Have students suggest gift items for each other. Cue with *¿qué le compro a [José]?* Be sure students use correct indefinite articles.

(7) 6. Present [s] sound (p. 49). Do drill A. Dictate ten words with the [s] sound, e.g., *cinco, quizás, buscar.* Correct on board or with overhead projector.

(3) 7. Do Ex. B (p. 47) for additional practice of numbers.

Assignment: Prepare an invitation, based on Act. D (p. 44), for oral presentation.

Day 3

Materials: Telephones, saint's day calendar.

(3) 1. Warm-up: Have students create a biography of an imaginary student, Carlos, by having them respond to questions, such as *¿Dónde vive? ¿Es simpático? ¿Es bi-*

lingüe? ¿Qué idioma(s) habla? ¿De dónde es? ¿Cuál es su clase favorita? etc.

(15) 2. Students work in pairs. Have them practice party invitations with a partner, then present them, using (toy) telephones.

(8) 3. Present months of the year (p. 48). Do Ex. C and D. Do Ex. D as chain drill. Have students listen carefully to birthday months and say which month has the most birthdays.

(5) 4. Discuss cultural note on first names. Use calendar of saints' days. Ask students, *¿Cuándo es tu santo?*

(12) 5. Introduce dialogue *¿Cuántos años tienes?* (p. 45). Vary dialogue by substituting students' names and their actual birthdays. Review numbers and months if necessary.

(7) 6. Introduce Act. A and B. Have students practice in small groups. One student in each group should lie about her/his age and try to convince the others in the group that the age is genuine.

Assignment: Write out Exercise A of *Repaso* (p. 58). First do orally in class.

Day 4

Materials: Mock job ads.

(4) 1. Warm-up: Ask students personalized questions about their birthdays and ages.

(8) 2. Review *años* dialogue and Act. A and B (p. 45). Ask short comprehension questions as you go. Have students act out core material.

(11) 3. Introduce Act. C and D. For practice with C, announce good news and bad news and have students respond accordingly. For practice with D, distribute mock job ads and have students pair off to interview each other.

(8) 4. Present grammar topic on definite article with dates (p. 51). Do Ex. C orally, then have students write answers. Correct in class. Do *¡vamos a hablar!* as chain drill.

(7) 5. Review spelling of [s] sound. Model *palabras claves* again and have students repeat. Check pronunciation carefully. Do drill B.

(5) 6. Do Ex. B in *Repaso* (p. 58) orally.

(7) 7. Game: *¡Ojo!* for numbers practice. (See annotation on p. 47.)

Assignment: Students write out their own birthdays and those of five friends.

Day 5

Materials: Timer or stopwatch.

(3) 1. Warm-up: "Beat the clock." Repeat warm-up activity for Day 2, changing cues; see whether students can improve their previous record by giving more responses. Remind them they will have one more chance to beat their record during this chapter.

(12) 2. Introduce and practice dialogue *¿Me prestas tu calculadora?* (p. 46).

(11) 3. Introduce Act. A–C of *Extensión.* Encourage variations. Have students practice in small groups.

(3) 4. Collect or correct homework.

(5) 5. Repeat pronunciation drill B (p. 49). Ask students for other words containing [s] sound. Do drill C orally, then have students dictate words to each other in pairs.

(5) 6. Present proverb. Ask students what they think it means. Remind them not to be concerned about unfamiliar words or structures. Point out differences between Spanish and English equivalent: *diente* vs. *mouth.*

(5) 7. Discuss cultural note on *ceceo.* Point out that [ø] is typical of Castile; locate on map. (Optional: Have students practice *ceceo* by repeating drills B or C with [ø] instead of [s].)

(6) 8. Present question words (p. 56). Remind students of other ways to form questions: tag questions and *sí-no* questions (with rising intonation or inverted word order). Do Ex. I orally. Then have students work in pairs and prepare four questions for their partners to answer.

Assignment: Write out Ex. I (p. 56).

Day 6

Materials: Objects (or flashcards of objects).

(3) 1. Warm-up: Continue biography of Carlos (see warm-up for Day 3). Expand to include his age and birthday, names of his friends, and their ages and birthdays.

(3) 2. Collect or correct homework.

(10) 3. Present possession with *de* (p. 51). Do Ex. D and E orally. Students then write Ex. E. Correct in class.

(7) 4. Review *calculadora* dialogue and Act. A–C. Display various objects (or flashcards) and cue activities with other nouns. Do Act. A and B as chain drills, with students asking new questions each time: *¿Me prestas tu grabadora? ¿Tienes mi bicicleta?*

(5) 5. Game to practice possession with *de: ¿De quién es?* (See annotation on p. 52.)

(4) 6. Present descriptive *de*-phrases. Elicit additional examples. Do Ex. F (p. 52).

(3) 7. Cultural note on *día de la Independencia* (p. 52).

(15) 8. Photo essay (pp. 54–55). Read caption aloud and discuss meaning. Break class into small groups. Each group must select one photo and describe the people in a short narrative for presentation.

Assignment: Write out *Repaso* Ex. D (p. 59) to hand in for correction.

Day 7

Materials: Timer or stopwatch, objects (e.g., toy bike, glasses, watch) or flashcards with pictures of such objects.

(5) 1. Warm-up: Have students ask you as many questions as they can think of during a specified time period. You should answer only those questions that are posed accurately. Keep score of the number of correct questions. (Students will be given several opportunities throughout the course to beat their record.)

(10) 2. Dictation. Select 4–5 lines from the dialogues in the chapter.

(10) 3. Present possessives *mi, tu, su* (p. 53). Demonstrate with objects (or flashcards). Do Ex. G and H and *¡vamos a hablar!* orally.

(8) 4. Personalize Ex. H. Have students display objects on their desks. Ask *sí-no* questions about the objects: *¿Es de Pilar el*

reloj? —Sí, es su reloj. (—No, no es su reloj. Es de Paco.)

(10) 5. Repeat Act. A–C (p. 46). Cue with objects; mix singular and plural nouns to practice forms of possessives.

(7) 6. Review names of months and numbers. Have students give their telephone numbers (or make up numbers), to personalize numbers drill.

Assignment: Write out Ex. E and F of *Repaso* after oral presentation.

Day 8

Materials: Timer or stopwatch.

(3) 1. Warm-up: "Beat the clock." (See warm-up for Day 2.)

(8) 2. Present exclamations with *qué* (p. 56). Demonstrate with an announcement, such as *¡Mañana hay examen!*, and have students react. Do Ex. J and K orally.

(10) 3. Students write five statements to shock or surprise; other students will react with appropriate exclamations.

(7) 4. Review possessives. Collect objects from everyone. Ask erroneous questions (or have a student do so) about ownership of objects.

(6) 5. Do *Repaso* Ex. C (p. 59) orally, books open. Repeat, books closed; vary cues somewhat and encourage students to re-enter responses from chapters 1 and 2.

(6) 6. Pronunciation practice. Model *palabras claves* again and repeat drill A (p. 49).

(10) 7. Team dictation to reinforce sound-spelling correspondences. Divide class into two teams. Send two members of opposing teams to the board and dictate 2–3 words containing [s] sound. Team with more correctly spelled words wins.

Assignment: Write out *Repaso* Ex. G (p. 60). (Optional: Precede with oral work on Ex. G in class.)

Day 9

Materials: Objects.

(3) 1. Warm-up: Give students cue lines from chapter core material selections and activities and have them respond appropriately.

(3) 2. Correct homework.

(8) 3. Give listening comprehension exercise to practice numbers. Dictate to students ages and phone numbers. Students write down arabic numbers to demonstrate understanding.

(10) 4. Review core material selections and *Extensión* activities.

(5) 5. To review *tener* and indefinite articles, place several objects on a table or desk. Have individual students remove (and replace later) one or more items and identify what they have.

(6) 6. To practice and review chapter vocabulary, play *Anagrams*. Ask for English equivalents of words when deciphered. (See instructions on TAE p. 33)

(15) 7. Review as needed for the Chapter Test.

Assignment: Prepare for test on Chapter 3.

Day 10

Give test for Chapter 3.

Chapter 8 (Stage 2)

Day 1

1. Discuss tests from Chapter 7.
2. Learning objectives for Chapter 8.
3. Cultural opener (p. 156).
4. Core material: first half of *Monserrate* dialogue (p. 157).
5. Word study: weather expressions (p. 161); do Ex. A orally.
6. Write out grammar Ex. A (p. 161) and Ex. H of *Repaso* (p. 174).

Day 2

1. Core material: second half of *Monserrate* dialogue.
2. *Comprensión* and *Extensión* (pp. 157–158). Pronunciation: flap [r] and trilled [rr]; do drills A and B (pp. 162–163).
3. Write out *Comprensión* (p. 157).
4. Grammar: *me gusta(n)*; do Ex. M (p. 169). Chain drill. Repeat Act. C (p. 158) with variations.

Day 3

1. Pronunciation: review flap [r] and present trilled [rr]; do drill C (p. 163).
2. Grammar: stem-changing verbs *e > ie;* do Ex. A, B, and *¡Vamos a hablar!* (pp. 164–165).
3. Review *Monserrate* dialogue.
4. Write out grammar Ex. A and B (p. 164).

Day 4

1. Cultural note on Bogotá (p. 158).
2. Core material: *La tierra caliente* (p. 159) and *Comprensión.*
3. Word study: expressions with *tener* (p. 162); do Ex. C.
4. Grammar: stem-changing verbs *o > ue* (p. 165); do Ex. C, D, E.
5. *Repaso* Ex. B and C (pp. 172–173).

Day 5

1. Pronunciation: review trilled [rr] and drill C; do drill D and present proverb (p. 163).
2. Review core material on *la tierra caliente* (pp. 159–160); do *Extensión.*
3. Grammar: review stem-changing verbs; write Ex. C and D (p. 165).

Day 6

1. Word study: review weather expressions (p. 161); do Ex. B.
2. Cultural note (p. 161).
3. Grammar: personal *a;* do Ex. F and G (p. 166); direct-object pronouns; do Ex. H and I (p. 167).
4. Review core material selections.

Day 7

1. Review sound-spelling of flap [r] and trilled [rr].
2. Grammar: direct-object pronouns with infinitives (p. 168); do Ex. J.
3. *Lectura* and *actividades* (p. 170).

Day 8

1. Review Act. C (p. 158) and *tierra caliente* dialogue (p. 159).
2. Dictation: flap [r] and [rr].
3. Grammar: direct-object pronouns *me, te, nos;* do Ex. K and L (p. 168).
4. *Repaso* Ex. A, D, and E (p. 173).

Day 9

1. Review *Lectura* and *Actividades.*
2. *Repaso* Ex. F and G (pp. 173–174).
3. Vocabulary game.
4. Review for test.

Day 10

Give test for Chapter 8.

Resource Materials

Games

This section contains detailed instructions for games referred to in the annotations, plus additional suggestions for games. There are also instructions for games in the annotations themselves. You may adapt the games to your own classes and teaching style, create your own games, or have students contribute games for class use.

Acrostic. Team competition for vocabulary practice with word sets. Write in large letters on the board (vertically or horizontally) two key words of equal length for each team to build from. For example: To practice classroom vocabulary, use *LA CLASE* and *COLEGIO.* The word *papel* can be linked to A, E, or L of *la clase,* or to E or L of *colegio.* The first team to build a word from each letter in their key word wins. The game may also be played with one key word or a phrase, and in groups or individually.

Ta Te Ti (Tic Tac Toe). Can be used for practice of verb forms (using subject pronouns or nouns as cues) and for vocabulary (using picture cues). Play, using the chalkboard, a pegboard with hooks for hanging cards, or a board with pockets for holding cards. If the chalkboard is used, draw nine equal squares, 3 down and 3 across. For verb practice, write subject pronouns in the squares. Label horizontal squares 1, 2, and 3; label vertical squares A, B, and C. Divide the class into two teams, one with X as a symbol, and the other with O. The player must say, *"Quiero A2"* and give the correct form of the verb cued. The first team to complete three squares across, down, or diagonally wins.

Buscapalabras. For recognition of written words. Use word sets and play on the chalkboard or on a large sheet of paper on the wall. Make a grid of squares (for example, 10 × 10) and choose the words to be hidden. Write the words in the squares (one letter per square), horizontally, vertically, diagonally, backward, forward, or upside-down. Fill in the empty squares with other letters and list the hidden words below the grid. For competition, form two teams. With each team using a different color, team members circle the hidden words. The team that circles more words wins. At the end of the game, check the words with choral repetition, asking *"¿Está bien?"* The game may also be dittoed for individual use, or students can prepare their own *buscapalabras* and exchange papers with classmates.

Béisbol (fútbol, básquetbol). Use for practice of verb conjugations, cueing with a subject and infinitive; for information questions on dialogues or readings; or for vocabulary practice, cueing with English words or with visuals. Form two teams and assign a pitcher and scorekeeper for each team. The pitcher gives a cue or asks a question; the batter responds. A correct answer gains a base; a mistake is an out. After three outs, the second team goes to bat. The team with the higher score after a determined number of innings wins. For soccer and basketball, a correct answer is a goal or basket. Play goes to the opposing team after an incorrect answer.

College Bowl. To check comprehension of dialogues or readings. Prepare questions to ask students. Questions may all be worth the same amount or graded according to difficulty. Announce point values of questions. Ask a question, first of one team and then the other, being sure that each student has an opportunity to answer. A correct answer wins points for a team. If a student gives an incorrect answer, the opposing team receives a "free" question that any member of the team may answer. The higher scoring team wins.

Concentración. For practice of verb forms and corresponding subject pronouns, opposites (prepositions, adjectives), and categories (beverage/ milk, meat/ham). This game is for small groups of students (5 or 6). Prepare 20 cards: write numbers from 1 to 20, one on each card; choose matching pairs and write them on the other side of the cards. For example: with opposite prepositions, write *cerca de* on one card and *lejos de* on another. To play, place the cards number side up in a square formation. Students then choose two cards by number, saying *"Quiero el 5 y el 10."* If the two cards chosen are a match, the student keeps the cards and chooses again. If the cards are not a match, the cards are replaced number side up and a second student chooses, etc. The student with the highest number of matches wins.

Hola (Bingo). For practice of numbers, word sets, or verb forms. Prepare dittoed grids of 4 rows of 4 squares, or have students make their own. With the class, list on the board the items that will be used for calling, such as numbers from 1 to 31, foods, parts of the body, present or preterit verb forms. Have a student write each word on a slip of paper to use for calling. Students fill in their grids, choosing words from the list on the board. Assign a caller who draws from the slips of paper. A win may be vertical, horizontal, four corners, diagonal, or four center squares.

Password. To review vocabulary. Choose teams of two students each, plus a leader, a timekeeper, and a scorekeeper. One member of each team receives a vocabulary word from the leader. This member must give a one-word clue within ten seconds to her/his partner. Clues may not be another form of the word given: if the word is *amigo,* the clue may not be *amiga.* The partner has ten seconds to give a response. If the answer is incorrect, the second team has a turn to give a clue. The word value drops one point per clue, beginning with 10 points. The first team to reach 20 points wins the game. Select a new team to replace the losers and play another round. The audience sees the word each time to increase student interest and appreciation of the clues.

Simón dice. Can be used with commands, classroom objects and instructions, clothing vocabulary, and parts of the body. Tell the class to do what you say, or to point to the item you name, only when you start with *"Simón dice."* Students who do what Simón does not instruct are eliminated from the game.

Spelling bee. Two teams take turns giving words for their opponents to spell orally. Award a point for each correct spelling. Or, as you dictate a word, have a member of each team write it on the chalkboard.

Anagrams. For vocabulary practice during the last few minutes of class. Write a jumbled word on the board and have students guess the word. For example: *ilobgoaí = biología.*

Voy a [México]. In succession, students name an object or person they are taking to [Mexico]. Each person must name all preceding items in correct order to remain in the game.

Veinte preguntas. Choose an object, either animal, vegetable, or mineral. Students have twenty *sí-no* questions to guess the word. The student who guesses correctly chooses the next word.

La Horca (Hangman). Think of a word and write on the board a blank space for each letter. Have the class guess each letter in Spanish. If the guess is correct, write the letter in the space it occupies. If the guess is incorrect, draw a part of the hanged man, until he is complete, or until students guess the word.

Question, please. For speaking practice with questions. Give a statement and have students form a question, using a question word. For example: *Juan vive en Montana. ¿Dónde vive?* or *¿Quién vive en Montana?*

Synonym-Antonym. One team gives a word. The opposing team must give either a synonym or antonym, as required, of the word given.

Word Factory. Write a long word on the board and have students write as many words as they can, using only the letters contained in the word. Set a time limit. Afterwards, have students read their words aloud (a different word each time). List them on the board. Award a prize to the student with the highest number of words.

Finish the story. Begin a story and have each student add one sentence to complete the tale.

Record the story and play it back to students to hear the results.

Crucigrama (Crossword puzzle). On a blank sheet of paper, have students create short, original crossword puzzles. Use a crossword from a newspaper as a guide. Have students prepare their puzzles in small groups. Groups may then exchange puzzles and fill them in.

Classroom expressions

Terms of praise and disapproval

Bien.	Fine.
Muy bien.	Very good.
Excelente.	Excellent.
¡Magnífico!	Wonderful!
¡Perfecto!	Perfect!
Bien hecho.	Well done.
Eso es.	That's it; that's right.
Tienes razón.	You're right.
Buena idea.	Good idea.
Mucho mejor.	Much better.
¿Estás seguro/a?	Are you sure?
¿Quién sabe la respuesta?	Who knows the answer?
No está bien.	That's not correct.
¡Ay, no!	No.

Instructions

Abran (Abre) los libros.	Open your books.
Al fondo de la página.	At the bottom of the page.
Aprendan (Aprende) de memoria.	Memorize.
Cierren (Cierra) los libros.	Close your books.
Contesten (Contesta).	Answer.
Corrijan (Corrige).	Correct.
Digan (Di).	Say.
En coro; todos juntos.	All together.
En español.	In Spanish.
En inglés.	In English.
Al principio de la página.	At the top of the page.
En voz alta.	Out loud.
En voz baja.	Quietly.

¿Es difícil?	Is it hard?	No tengo [lápiz].	I don't have a [pencil].
¿Es fácil?	Is it easy?	¿Para cuándo es la tarea?	When is the homework due?
Escriban (Escribe).	Write.		
Escuchen (Escucha).	Listen.	Presente.	Present.
¿Están listos?	Are you ready?	¿Qué quiere decir?	What does this mean?
Haga (Haz) el papel de [Raúl].	Take the role of [Raúl].	Repita Ud., por favor.	Please repeat.
Hagan [Haz] una pregunta.	Ask a question.		

¿Hay preguntas? — Are there any questions?

Levanta la mano.	Raise your hand.
Miren (Mira).	Look.
Otra vez.	Once again.
Pasen (Pasa) a la página [diez].	Turn to page [ten].
Pasen (Pasa) a la pizarra.	Go to the board.
Pásenme (Pásame) la tarea, por favor.	Hand in your assignment, please.
Pregunta a [tu compañero/a].	Ask [your classmate].
Presten (Presta) atención.	Pay attention.
Repitan (Repite).	Repeat.
Saquen (Saca) los libros.	Get out your books.
Siéntense (Siéntate).	Sit down.
Sigan (Sigue) el modelo.	Follow the model.
Silencio, por favor.	Quiet, please.
Todo el mundo; todos.	Everyone.
Voy a pasar lista.	I'm going to take attendance.

Courtesy Expressions

Adiós.	Good-by.
Buenos días.	Good day.
Buenas tardes.	Good afternoon.
(Con) permiso.	Excuse me.
De nada.	You're welcome.
Gracias.	Thank you.
Hasta mañana.	Until tomorrow.
Lo siento.	I'm sorry.
Pasa (Pase Ud.).	Go ahead.
Perdón.	Excuse me.
Por favor.	Please.
Salud.	Gesundheit.

Student responses

¿A qué hora?	At what time?
Ausente.	Absent.
¿Cómo se deletrea?	How do you spell?
¿Cómo se dice?	How do you say?
¿Cuándo hay examen?	When is there an exam?
Me hace falta [papel].	I need [paper].
No entiendo; no comprendo.	I don't understand.
No estoy preparado/a.	I'm not prepared.
No sé.	I don't know.

Useful addresses

The following organizations may be helpful in obtaining cultural information and materials for classroom use. In addition, foreign language journals may contain useful addresses as well as information regarding study programs abroad.

ERIC Clearing House for Language and Linguistics
Center for Applied Linguistics
1611 N. Kent Street
Arlington, Virginia 22209

Mexican National Tourist Council
405 Park Avenue
New York, New York 10021

ONCE *(for pen pals)*
M. Frances Taylor
Rhode Island College
Providence, Rhode Island 02908

Organization of American States
17th and Constitution
Washington, D.C. 20006

Sociedad Honoraria Hispánica
Dr. Frank Figueroa
Collegium of Comparative Cultures
Eckerd College
St. Petersburg, Florida 33733

Spanish Heritage Association, Inc.
115-10 Queens Blvd.
Forest Hills, New York 11375

Spanish National Tourist Office
665 Fifth Avenue
New York, New York 10022

Accommodating Native Speakers

The backgrounds, abilities, and interests of native speakers in a beginning Spanish class may differ markedly from those of non-native speakers. For non-native speakers the beginning course focuses primarily on the acquisition of the language skills of listening and speaking, and secondarily on the skills of reading and writing. Many native speakers may be proficient in listening and speaking but may wish to improve their reading and writing skills, as well as enrich their vocabulary, and be exposed to the culture (e.g., literature and fine arts) of their native language. This section of the Teacher's Guide suggests possible ways to adapt *Spanish Today* to accommodate native speakers.

Course content

Personalize culture. The cultural aspects of the program can be emphasized and explored fully with native speakers. Let them bring their life experiences into the classroom. Students can be asked to expand on the cultural notes, especially those in Stage 1, which deal with the experiences and observations of Hispanics in the United States. Students can be asked whether they have had experiences similar to those described in the core material, observe similar customs at home, or how their situation is different. They should be encouraged to relate anecdotes, stories, or personal experiences.

Stress vocabulary development. Some native speakers can understand Spanish very well but may have a very limited active vocabulary, even orally. The *Extensión* sections can be fully utilized to aid in vocabulary development. Native speakers could be encouraged to master all the varied responses to a given statement or question. They should be given frequent opportunities to supply additional responses, either previously learned material or new responses. In addition, they can be encouraged to create new dialogues based on the conversational exchanges in the *Extensión* sections. While for non-native speakers most class work with these sections will be oral, for native speakers this work could be largely written. With both groups of students, stress that the material in the *Extensión* sections helps them to function in the language.

The other key section in each chapter of *Spanish Today* for the development of vocabulary, the *Estudio de palabras,* could also be fully utilized with native speakers. Where appropriate, native speakers could be assigned extra words for oral and written mastery, in order to expand their active vocabulary. (See the Supplementary Word Sets in the Appendix of the Student Text, pages 364–367).

Emphasize reading and writing. Spanish-speaking students have generally heard the language for a number of years but, because their schooling since the early grades may have been in English, they may have had little exposure to written Spanish. Such students should be given ample opportunities for written assignments, in contrast to their English-speaking classmates, who will profit more from oral assignments. Many exercises in *Spanish Today,* though intended primarily for oral work, can easily be adapted for written work. In addition, the focus of the *Pronunciación y ortografía* sections should be more on sound-spelling correlation rather than on pronunciation practice. You may wish to assign native speakers additional words that reinforce certain sound-spelling patterns.

The *Lecturas* can also be useful points of departure to develop reading and writing skills. Native speakers can be asked first to re-tell and then to re-write (i.e., prepare a resume or capsule version of) a *Lectura.* This kind of assignment gives them credit for being able to read already (where the non-native speaker of Spanish may well have to struggle a bit), but requires them to read carefully, because they then have to put the story into their own, presumably simpler, Spanish version.

One technique for improving writing skills is for the students to write short, descriptive poems and sketches about themselves or other topics of interest. Asking students to keep a journal or notebook with at least three entries per week may also help improve their writing skills and self-confidence. Another writing assignment that could be of benefit to everyone in the class would be to have native speakers put the English cultural notes into Spanish. You should stress that strict translation is not what they are being asked to do (translation is really a separate and very complex skill), but rather that they simply are to give some of the same, or related additional information, in their own words in Spanish. You may wish to have them compare versions with other native speakers, and as a group present the agreed-upon best Spanish cultural note to the class. Finally, if there is a school newspaper, it might be possible to have a special Spanish-language section of it in each issue, written by the native speakers in your class. Short of that, a "class reporter" kind of paper — a single page each week might be a way to start — could be written by the native speakers for the rest of the class. Or the native speakers could head up a class-reporter project, where non-natives help them produce a mini-newspaper to be distributed to other Spanish classes.

Focus on grammar as a tool. Grammar is the backbone of the language and must be taught, but — particularly with native speakers — it should be taught as a means to an end and not as an end in itself. It can be approached as a tool for helping make oneself understood by as many people as possible. Native speakers should be encouraged to see that a knowledge of grammar can assist them in expressing themselves even better, with greater variety of effect, especially in instances where their speech contains many colloquial expressions or features that may be considered non-standard Spanish. Too heavy an emphasis on grammar can lead to a rejection of or apathy towards the study of Spanish among native speakers if they feel their native fluency is being questioned. However, native

speakers can be shown that, while the use of colloquialisms may be acceptable, there are other, perhaps more widely understood, ways of saying the same things. They should be encouraged to master both.

Teaching techniques

Spanish-speaking students can be of real assistance in a Spanish class, but a word of caution is in order. Native speakers should not be assumed to be experts in the language just because they speak it; such an assumption could lead to considerable frustration for students who do not have a good command of the grammar and who feel they are being "tested." Furthermore, some native speakers are bound to feel they already know the language, and may well refuse to work at improving their skills. Hence, Spanish teachers have to be particularly sensitive to the different levels of experience and ability among the native speakers in the class and to the needs of those students. With the proper kind of encouragement, they can do a lot to spark a class. For example, native speakers can be paired (reciprocal teaching style) with non-native speakers for both formal and informal practice of Spanish. Also, native speakers can be group leaders once in a while for conversation practice and pronunciation drills. Teaching techniques and classroom activities need to be planned according to the number of native speakers in the class, and the extent of their knowledge of both Spanish and English.

Another common teaching technique is individualized study, or special projects for native speakers. It is more beneficial to keep such students working on special projects in class, rather than isolating them, since students learn so much from each other. Projects on special topics, or ways Spanish affects their home life may be especially appropriate. After a reasonable length of time (a week or a month, depending on the project assigned) students can have a "show-and-tell" for their classmates. You may want to avoid charges of favoritism by seeing to it that all class members are assigned special projects at some point, suited to their individual abilities and interests.

Special projects

Some special class and outside projects for Spanish speakers, as well as projects for the entire class, that are designed to increase cultural awareness are suggested below:

1. Collect stories from different regions, such as tales, legends, and superstitions, and encourage students to discuss them.
2. Invite Spanish-speaking visitors to class, such as people who can recall important events in the history of the area, professors from neighboring universities, or professionals from the community who use Spanish in their daily lives. Where appropriate, encourage students to be aware of the variety in pronunciation among speakers from different countries.
3. Encourage the students to speak in class and to participate in class discussions. Students can relate stories, personal experiences, jokes, etc. Do not correct students every time they use regional variations. However, you should encourage them to speak only in Spanish.
4. Encourage student organizations that recognize outstanding students of Spanish and that promote its cultural development, such as the Spanish Honor Society, a Spanish drama club, and others.
5. Encourage school activities that recognize the importance of the learners' culture, such as *Posadas* during the Christmas season; celebration of national holidays; literary contests, Spanish language assemblies, and Spanish publications in the local paper.
6. Develop culture packets with the students on a specific Spanish-speaking region, depending on the ethnic make-up of the class. Topics that might be covered include the following: history (especially the various strands of cultural influence), famous men and women, music, family dynamics, games and riddles, plays and playwrights, short stories and poetry, foods, and contemporary problems. Such culture packets are an important tool in helping students discover the history of their forebears and their contributions to society.

Spanish
today **1**

Spanish
today 1

Nancy A. Humbach
Mercedes Uribe Wall
Geraldine Antoine
Sue Carol McKnight

HOUGHTON MIFFLIN COMPANY **Boston**

Atlanta   Dallas   Geneva, Illinois
Hopewell, New Jersey   Palo Alto   Toronto

About the Authors

Nancy A. Humbach teaches Spanish at Finney-town High School in Cincinnati, Ohio, and is the editor of the quarterly newsletter *¡Albricias!* She has been president of the Ohio Modern Language Teacher's Association (OMLTA) and has served on the executive councils of OMLTA, the American Association of Teachers of Spanish and Portuguese (AATSP), and the *Sociedad Honoraria Hispánica.*

Mercedes Uribe Wall, a native of Colombia, has taught Spanish to elementary and high-school students in this country, and to adults in Mexico, Puerto Rico, and the United States. She has given workshops on foreign language methodology, and co-authored a workbook to accompany *En contacto* (Houghton Mifflin Company).

Geraldine Antoine teaches Spanish at Lincoln High School in Gahanna, Ohio. She has taught methodology courses at Otterbein College and presented workshops on foreign language teaching and testing. She has also been president of OMLTA and served on the executive councils of OMLTA and AATSP.

Sue Carol McKnight has taught Spanish at various levels in high school and college. Most recently she was Spanish teacher at Finneytown High School in Cincinnati, Ohio. She has also taught Spanish to adults and participated in summer institutes at Rice University and at the *Universidad Autónoma de México.*

ANNOTATIONS

Dorothy Gonsalves is former chairperson of Foreign Languages at Sehome High School, Bellingham, Washington.

LISTENING COMPREHENSION EXERCISES

Dorothy Gonsalves

WORKBOOK

Evelyn Smith teaches Spanish at Beverly High School, Beverly, Massachusetts.

CHAPTER TESTS

Carol E. Klein is coordinator of Foreign Languages for the Worcester Public Schools, Massachusetts.

Copyright © 1982 by Houghton Mifflin Company

Printed in U.S.A.
Student's Edition ISBN: 0–395–29295–6
Teacher's Edition ISBN: 0–395–29510–6

Contents

2

De día en día

3

A nuestro alrededor

Spanish
around you

As you begin to learn Spanish, you will discover that you know more Spanish than you think you do.

el mapa

You can probably guess what the Spanish words illustrated on this page mean, because they resemble English words. Words that are related in spelling and meaning and are derived from the same source language are called *cognates*. There are thousands of Spanish-English cognates derived from a common ancestor, often Latin.

la policía　　**la fruta**　　**el teléfono**　　**el elefante**

hacienda

armada

Over the years, speakers of English have borrowed many Spanish words that are now a part of the English language. Much of the borrowing has occurred in the southwestern part of the United States through contact with the Spanish-speaking population there. How many words on this page do you know?

poncho

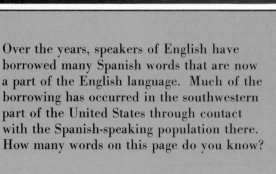

adobe   chihuahua   frijoles

**Boca Raton
(Florida)**

**Mesa
(Arizona)**

**Conejos
(Colorado)**

The Spanish language and culture have been present in the United States since the first explorers and settlers came to this country from Spain. Many place names in the United States are Spanish. Some towns and cities are named for saints, while others are named for a geographical feature or a characteristic of their location.

Today many Spanish speakers live in the United States, and as a result, Spanish is increasingly evident in the media, on buildings and signs, and in business and government forms. Look around you and you'll find that cognates, borrowed words, and Spanish place names and signs have given you a head start in learning Spanish.

Buena Vista
(Georgia)

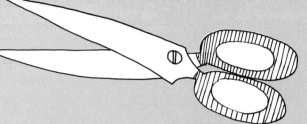

Tijeras
(New Mexico)

Los Gatos
(California)

MAR CANTÁBRICO

FRANCIA

Santander

Bilbao
San
Sebastián

ANDORRA

• La Coruña
• Santiago
de Compostela

• León

Pamplona

PIRINEOS

ATLÁNTICO

• Burgos

Río   Duero

Río   Ebro

• Barcelona

PORTUGAL

• Salamanca

Segovia
• Ávila

SIERRA DE GUADARRAMA

Madrid
☆

ISLAS
BALEARES

Menorca

Mallorca

SIERRA DE GREDOS

Río   Tajo

• Toledo

Río   Guadiana

Valencia •

Ibiza

OCÉANO

Guadalquivir

Río

• Córdoba

Alicante •

MAR MEDITERRÁNEO

• Sevilla

Granada •
• Málaga

SIERRA NEVADA

• Cádiz

Estrecho de Gibraltar

ÁFRICA

| 0 | 100 | 200 km |
| 0 | 50 | 100 | 150 mi |

MARRUECOS

ISLAS CANARIAS

Lanzarote

La Palma

Tenerife

Fuerte-
ventura

Gomera

Gran Canaria

Hierro

OCÉANO
ATLÁNTICO

ESPAÑA

ISLAS
CANARIAS

ÁFRICA

ÁFRICA

ESPAÑA

xii

Barranquilla
Cartagena
Maracaibo
Isla de
Margarita
Caracas
Río Orinoco
GUYANA
Medellín
Bogotá
COLOMBIA
VENEZUELA
GUAYANA
FRANCESA
Cali
SURINAM
Quito
ECUADOR
Río Negro
ECUADOR
Guayaquil
Río Amazonas
PERÚ
CORDILLERA
BRASIL
Callao
Lima
Machu
Picchu
Cuzco
Brasilia
DE
La Paz
BOLIVIA
Lago Titicaca
Sucre
Potosí
LOS
Río Paraná
São Paulo
PARAGUAY
TROPICO DE
CAPRICORNIO
Asunción
Río de Janeiro
CHILE
San Miguel
de Tucumán
OCÉANO
PACÍFICO
ARGENTINA
ANDES
Córdoba
Santa Fe
Aconcagua
Valparaíso
Santiago
URUGUAY
OCÉANO
Buenos Aires
La Plata
Montevideo
Río de la Plata
ATLÁNTICO
Concepción
Río Colorado
PAMPAS
San Carlos
de Bariloche
PATAGONIA
0   400   800 km

0   200   400   600 mi
Punta Arenas
TIERRA DEL FUEGO
Estrecho de Magallanes
CABO DE HORNOS

AMÉRICA DEL SUR

Tijuana

Mexicali

ESTADOS   UNIDOS

GOLFO

DE

CALIFORNIA

BAJA CALIFORNIA

Ciudad
Juárez

Hermosillo

Chihuahua

Río

Bravo

Nuevo Laredo

SIERRA MADRE OCCIDENTAL

Torreón

Monterrey

SIERRA MADRE ORIENTAL

GOLFO DE MÉXICO

Mazatlán

San Luis Potosí

Tampico

*BAHÍA DE
CAMPECHE*

Mérida

Guanajuato

Guadalajara

YUCATÁN

México, D.F.

Toluca

Puebla

Veracruz

Cuernavaca

Taxco

SIERRA MADRE DEL SUR

Oaxaca

BELICE

OCÉANO PACÍFICO

Acapulco

*Lago
Izabal*

*GOLFO DE
TEHUANTEPEC*

Guatemala

*Lago
Ilopang*

*Lago
Atitlán* Antigua

GUATEMALA

San Salvador

EL SALVADOR

0   200   400 km

0   100   200   300 mi

MÉXICO, AMÉRICA CENTRAL Y LAS ANTILLAS

xiv

OCÉANO ATLÁNTICO

LAS BAHAMAS

La Habana
CUBA
Guantánamo
Santiago de Cuba

HAITÍ

REPÚBLICA
DOMINICANA

Santo Domingo

San Juan
Mayagüez • Río Piedras
• Ponce
PUERTO RICO

JAMAICA

MAR CARIBE

HONDURAS
Tegucigalpa

NICARAGUA

Managua
Lago de Nicaragua

San José • Limón

COSTA RICA

Canal de Panamá
Colón
Panamá
PANAMÁ

COLOMBIA

VENEZUELA

1

¿Quiénes somos?

1

¿Quiénes somos? The people shown here depict some of the many faces of the Spanish-speaking world. Left: Two Guatemalan students, a soccer game in Spain, men selling clothing in Mexico. Right: Colombian girls in school uniform, Spanish woman knitting, Guatemalan woman at a market, Mexican students playing basketball, and flamenco dancers in Spain.

Life in the cities and towns of Spanish-speaking countries presents varied scenes: a park corner in Veracruz, Mexico; a balloon vendor in Mexico city; replacing a street lamp in Seville, Spain (left); a stroll along the colorful **Ramblas** in Barcelona, Spain; the **Plaza Mayor** of Salamanca, Spain; and an enthusiastic soccer fan in Barcelona (right).

The whitewashed homes of a town in southern
Spain and a village in the Pyrenees present a
peaceful view of rural life. Women with jugs, a
Mexican girl carrying firewood, and men repair-
ing fishing nets in Venezuela reflect the common
tasks associated with small-town life.

capítulo 1

¿Quién soy?

■ Los Angeles County is home to many Mexican Americans who have lived in the United States for several generations. It also attracts thousands of Mexican citizens who have immigrated to the United States in hopes of finding employment in southern California. Students whose families have just arrived from Mexico are able to take advantage of bilingual programs in the schools to help them learn English and adjust to life in the United States.

¿Quién eres?

See Appendix for English equivalents of core material (dialogues and readings).

It's the first day of school in Los Angeles. Ana García greets a new classmate who has recently arrived from Mexico.

ANA	¡Hola! Soy Ana García. ¿Y tú?
PEDRO	Soy Pedro López. Mucho gusto, Ana.
ANA	¿Eres de aquí?
PEDRO	No. Soy de México.

extensión

A. A classmate tells you her/his name, and then asks you what your name is. Identify yourself in one of the following ways.

■III Soy [Inés/Paco]. Y tú, ¿cómo te llamas?°

Me llamo° [Ana/José].
Soy [Lola/Pablo].
[María Smith].

B. Check your memory and try to identify several classmates. Your classmates should let you know whether you're right or wrong.

■III ¿Eres [Pedro]?

No, soy [Diego].
Sí°. Me llamo [Pedro].
¿Quién? ¿Yo°?

C. An exchange student in your class wants to know where you're from. Choose a suitable answer.

■III ¿Eres de aquí?

Sí, soy de [los Estados Unidos°].
No, no soy de aquí.
No, soy de [San Diego].

D. Introduce yourself to a classmate seated next to you, and shake hands as your classmate acknowledges the introduction. Notice that a girl says *encantada* and a boy says *encantado*.

■III Soy [Susana Díaz], ¿y tú?

[Pepe Torres]. Mucho gusto.
[María Chávez]. Encantada°.
[Marcos Paz]. Encantado°.

¿Qué idioma hablas?

Optional: Take role in Spanish: *Voy a pasar lista.* Have students respond with *presente.*

Warm-up: Ask class questions from activities on p. 9.

Teresa and Felipe are on their way to class. Teresa has just moved to Los Angeles and speaks very little English.

TERESA	Hablas inglés, ¿verdad?
FELIPE	Sí, soy bilingüe. Y tú también, ¿no?
TERESA	Pues, no. Sólo hablo un poco de inglés.

extensión

Variation: Expand activities by re-entering suitable responses from previous activities. Vary question slightly to elicit other responses: *¿Hablas francés? ¿Hablas inglés?*

A. Find out whether your classmates are bilingual. Start with the classmate on your left.

■⫶⫶ ¿Eres bilingüe? No, no soy bilingüe.
Sí. Hablo inglés y también [francés°].
Yo no°. Sólo hablo un poco de español°.

B. A classmate asks you whether you speak Spanish. Not much? A little perhaps? Select a suitable answer.

■⫶⫶ ¿Hablas español? No mucho°.
Sí, un poco.
Sí, hablo español.

Optional: After activities have been mastered, have students act out dialogue. Encourage variation of lines.

¿Quién es ese chico?

Isabel asks her friend Carlos about another boy.

ISABEL   Ese chico es Juan Tovar, ¿no?
CARLOS   No. Es mi amigo Paco González. Es muy simpático.
ISABEL   ¿Vive aquí en Los Ángeles?
CARLOS   No. Vive en Santa Bárbara.

extensión

Ese and *esa* are treated as vocabulary in early lessons. Point out to students that *ese* is used with a m.s. noun and *esa* with a f.s. noun.

You may wish to introduce adjectives from word study and have students repeat Act. B.

Illustrate Act. D on board. Ask class to contribute answers, then have students work in pairs.

Younger people will always shake hands in introductions to adults. Close friends or relatives usually kiss each other on the cheek. *Hola* is also used to attract attention.

A. Ask a classmate to identify a boy and then a girl in your class.

■Ⅲ   ¿Quién es ese chico?   Es mi amigo [Carlos].
                                      Lo siento°. No sé°.

■Ⅲ   ¿Quién es esa° chica°?   Es mi amiga° [Susana].
                                      Lo siento. No sé.

B. Describe a friend briefly to a classmate.

■Ⅲ   ¿Cómo es° tu° amigo   Es muy simpático.
       [Pedro]?   Es inteligente°.

■Ⅲ   ¿Cómo es tu amiga [Elena]?   Es simpática°.
                                      Es alegre°.

C. A classmate wants to know if you live in the same town. How would you respond?

■Ⅲ   Tú vives aquí, ¿verdad?   Sí, vivo aquí.
                                      No, vivo en [Palo Alto].
                                      No, no vivo aquí.

D. Interview a classmate, using the following guidelines.

Tú: ¡Hola! ¿Quién . . . ?   Compañero/a: Soy . . .
      ¿Vives . . . ?   No, vivo . . .
                                 (Sí, vivo . . .)
      Hablas . . . , ¿no?   Sí, y también . . .
                                 (No. Sólo hablo . . .)

Spanish speakers tend to shake hands more often than Americans. They frequently shake hands when they are introduced to someone, when they greet friends, and also when they say good-by to an individual. Students who see each other every day or during school activities may simply say **¡Hola!** or wave a hand.

Estudio de palabras

¿Cómo es?

Introduce using visuals, mime, photos. Point out *-o* endings for males, *-a* endings for females, but emphasize meaning. Formal presentation of adjectives is in *Gramática.*

Paco es **alto.**

María es **alta.**

Manuel es **bajo.**

Emilia es **baja.**

Tomás es **moreno.**

Dolores es **morena.**

Antonio es **rubio.**

Ana es **rubia.**

Alberto es **perezoso.**

Rosa es **perezosa.**

Carlos es **estudioso.**

Teresa es **estudiosa.**

Juan es **simpático.**

Isabel es **simpática.**

José es **antipático.**

Lucía es **antipática.**

A Ask a classmate about the persons pictured above.

Personalize: *¿Cómo es [name of student]? [. . .] es simpático.*

■॥ ¿Cómo es Tomás?   *¿Tomás? Es moreno.*

■॥ ¿Cómo es Emilia?   *¿Emilia? Es baja.*

B Describe two classmates. Make two statements about each person, one in the affirmative and one in the negative.

■॥ *Carmen es simpática . . .*

■॥ *Felipe no es moreno . . .*

¡Hola y adiós!

¡hola! hi!
buenos días hello, good morning
buenas tardes good afternoon

adiós good-by
hasta mañana until tomorrow
hasta luego see you later

C You're on your way to class and meet a friend. Greet her/him hurriedly and then say good-by.

■III *Hola, [Eduardo]. Hasta . . .*

D Your teacher greets you as you enter the classroom. Return the greeting.

■III Buenos días, [Susana].   *Buenos días, [señor°/señora°/señorita°].*

Greet students daily in Spanish and have them reply using proper title.
T: *Buenos días, clase.*
S: *Buenos días, Sra./Srta./Sr.* + name.

Speakers of Spanish and English use different greetings, depending on the situation and the person or persons spoken to. **¡Hola!** is generally used to greet a friend, but **buenos días** and **buenas tardes** are more appropriate when greeting a teacher or stranger. **¡Adiós!** may be said as a hello and good-by all at once. For example, if you pass a friend on the street and you're in a hurry, you might just wave and say **¡Adiós!**

Pronunciación y ortografía

In Spanish, as in English, sounds and letters do not always correspond. Spanish has more consistent pronunciation and spelling patterns than English, however. In the pronunciation sections of this book, symbols within brackets are used to represent specific sounds. For example, the symbol [a] represents the sound of the letter **a** in **casa**. **Palabras claves,** or key words, are given for each sound to help you associate that sound with specific letters.

vowel sounds

Spanish has five basic vowel sounds: [a], [e], [i], [o], and [u]. All basic Spanish vowel sounds are pronounced sharply and clearly.

palabras claves

[a] casa
[e] mes
[i] sí
[o] poco
[u] mucho

Have students observe your mouth movements as you pronounce vowels. Model key words and have students repeat. Be sure students pronounce vowels without a glide. Contrast to English vowels.

A Pronounce the following words after your teacher. Be sure that each vowel sound is sharp and distinct.

Display words on board, overhead projector, or use book. After full class practice, have half of class close eyes. Student pronounces a word for group with eyes closed to repeat. Stress listening practice and importance of correct pronunciation.

[a]	
alta	baja
cama	dama
casa	mapa

[e]	
me	de
mes	nena
eres	cena

[i]	
sí	mi
fila	vive
amiga	chica

[o]	
sólo	como
poco	oso
noto	foto

[u]	
tu	tus
luna	cubo
mucho	nube

B Read aloud the following sentences to practice your pronunciation of Spanish vowels.

Optional: For quick practice of vowels teach: *Ba be bi bo bu, el burro sabe más que tú.* Or practice with student names.

1. Mucho gusto, Paco.
2. Tomás es alegre.
3. Isabel es simpática.
4. Esa chica vive en Santa Bárbara.

El ejercicio hace maestro.

Proverb: Practice makes perfect.

Gramática

Present tense of **ser**: singular forms

As you begin to teach formal Spanish grammar, you may find it helpful to review some English grammar. Ask class: What is a subject? subject pronoun? verb? adjective?

Soy Ana García.   *I am* Ana García.
¿Quién **eres?**   Who *are you?*
Es Pedro López.   *He is* Pedro López.

The verb **ser,** like its English equivalent *to be,* has special forms in the present tense.

A   Felipe wants to be sure he knows everyone in his class. Take his role and ask each student her/his name.

Optional: Use chain drill technique with students' real names. S¹: *¿Eres [Ana Phillips]?* S²: *Sí, soy [Ana Phillips]. ¿Y tú? ¿Eres [Tomás Green]?* Start chain to demonstrate.

■ⅲ   Luis Portillo   Felipe: *¿Eres Luis Portillo?*
Luis: *Sí, soy Luis Portillo.*

1. Carlos Dávila
2. Alicia Molina
3. Pedro Martínez
4. Ana García
5. José Luis Centeno
6. Marcos Pacheco
7. Marta Díaz

B   Rosa is pointing out who some of her friends are. Take her role and identify the following persons.

Variation: S¹ points to another and asks, *¿Quién es?* S² replies, *Es mi amiga, Ana.*

■ⅲ   Ana   *Es mi amiga Ana.*

■ⅲ   Felipe   *Es mi amigo Felipe.*

1. Clara
2. Alfredo
3. Ángela
4. Ricardo
5. Isabel
6. Manuel

¡vamos a hablar!

¡vamos a hablar! activities are intended for personalized practice and re-entry and recombination of previously learned material.

A friend is introducing you to a cousin who is visiting your town. Shake hands and greet her/him. Then find out some facts about your friend's cousin. Here are some phrases to get you started.

Hola. Mucho . . .
¿Eres de . . . ?
¿Hablas . . . ?
¿Vives . . . ?

Encourage students to expand: *¿Vives aquí? ¿Hablas francés? ¿Eres estudioso?*

Expressing origin with ser

Pilar **es de** Los Ángeles.	Pilar *is from* Los Angeles.
Soy de aquí.	*I'm from* here.

A form of the verb **ser** + **de** is used to express the place of origin of a person or thing.

C Pedro wants to verify where some of your friends are from. Tell him whether he is right or wrong.

■Ⅲ Elena es de aquí.   *Sí, es de aquí.*
   (No, no es de aquí.)

1. Alicia es de Barcelona.
2. Carlos es de México.
3. Felipe es de Lima.
4. Elena es de San Juan.
5. Luisa es de Buenos Aires.
6. Susana es de Panamá.
7. Miguel es de Quito.

Gender of nouns

Es mi **amigo** Tomás.	He's my *friend* Tomás.
Es mi **amiga** María.	She's my *friend* María.

All Spanish nouns have gender, that is, they are either masculine or feminine. A noun that refers to a male is masculine and usually ends in **-o.** A noun that refers to a female is feminine and usually ends in **-a.**

D Identify each of your friends to a new classmate.

■Ⅲ José Luis   *Es mi amigo José Luis.*

1. Rosa	3. Fernando	5. Diego
2. Elena	4. Isabel	6. Manuel

José María Pardo Merino
Asunción Martínez de Pardo

Amelia Pineda Neumann
Vda. de
Juan Arzadón Ibarrarán

Participan a Ud. el próximo enlace de sus hijos

José Manuel y Rosa Amelia

que se celebrará (D. m.) el día 25 de Mayo, a las siete y media de la tarde, en la Iglesia de los Jesuitas de Areneros (I.C.A.I.), Santa Cruz de Marcenado s/n.

The use of two first names is common in Spanish. Girls' names are often a compound of **María,** such as **María Teresa, María del Carmen,** or **Ana María.** Common compound boys' names are **José Luis, Juan Manuel,** or **Miguel Ángel.**

Agreement of adjectives ending in **-o** or **-a**

Fernando es **alto.**   Fernando is *tall.*
María Teresa es **alta.**   María Teresa is *tall.*

In Spanish, an adjective changes form according to whether it describes a male or a female. An adjective ending in **-o** describes a male. An adjective ending in **-a** describes a female.

E Say that Ana has the same characteristics as each of the following boys.

▪III   Juan es rubio.   *Ana es rubia también.*

1. Tomás es bajo.
2. José Luis es antipático.
3. Diego es perezoso.
4. Juan Manuel es estudioso.

F Your brother is mistaken about what your classmates are like. Correct him, telling who has the characteristic in question.

▪III   María es estudiosa, ¿verdad?   *No, Alfonso es estudioso.*
(Alfonso)

1. Tomás es bajo, ¿verdad? (Teresa)
2. ¿Elena es simpática? (José)
3. ¿Julio es perezoso? (Carmen)
4. Alberto es alto, ¿verdad? (Mateo)
5. Sara es morena, ¿verdad? (Manuel)
6. ¿Alicia es rubia? (Marta)

Agreement of adjectives ending in **-e**

Roberto es **inteligente.**   Roberto is *intelligent.*
Mariana es **inteligente.**   Mariana is *intelligent.*

An adjective ending in **-e** can be used to describe either a male or a female.

G Tell a friend what the following people are like.

▪III   Manuel / alegre   — *¿Cómo es Manuel?*
— *Es alegre.*

▪III   Dolores / estudiosa   — *¿Cómo es Dolores?*
— *Es estudiosa.*

Variation: Books closed. S¹ supplies name, S² gives adjective, S³ makes statement: *Teresa es rubia.*

1. Miguel Ángel / bajo
2. Elena / antipática
3. Carmen / inteligente
4. Diego / perezoso

5. Pilar / alegre
6. Juan / bilingüe
7. Carlos / rubio
8. Susana / alta

Making sentences negative

María **no** es bilingüe.   María is *not* bilingual.
Ese chico **no** vive aquí.   That boy does *not* live here.

In Spanish, the word **no** is used before a verb to make a statement negative.

H   Luisa is in a bad mood today and contradicts everything your friends say. Take her role.

◾⫿   Elena es alta.   *Elena no es alta.*

1. Paco vive en México.
2. Pedro es muy simpático.
3. Marta es de Los Ángeles.
4. Felipe es bilingüe.
5. Rosa es muy estudiosa.
6. Lucía vive en San Diego.
7. José Luis es de aquí.
8. Esteban vive aquí.

Game: Have students write self descriptions in *¡vamos a hablar!* Collect papers and read, playing *¿Quién soy yo?* Student who guesses correctly reads next description.

¡vamos a hablar!   Tell about yourself in three sentences. Make at least one of your statements negative.

Me llamo Susana. Soy de México
y no hablo mucho inglés . . .

Tag questions

Variation: Have students write 5 true or false statements about classmates. S¹ makes tag question of a statement, S² must reply.

Marcos es inteligente, **¿verdad?**   Marcos is intelligent, *right?*

Esa chica es Teresa, **¿no?**   That girl is Teresa, *isn't she?*

A tag question is a short phrase that is "tagged on" to the end of a statement to make it into a question. Common tag questions are **¿no?** and **¿verdad?**

I   Verify some information about various people. Ask a question, using *¿verdad?* or *¿no?*

Have students answer questions in Ex. I: *No es perezoso. Es estudioso.*

◾⫿   Ese chico es perezoso.   *Ese chico es perezoso, ¿no?*

1. Tu amiga es de aquí.
2. Felipe es muy antipático.
3. Hablas un poco de inglés.
4. Esa chica es Alicia.
5. Rosa es de México.
6. Juan vive aquí.
7. Tomás es bilingüe.

The *En resumen* is for reference and review. Refer students to section to help prepare for tests. Or review orally, providing or eliciting examples.

En resumen

The letters in parentheses that follow headings indicate related exercises in the **Gramática** section of the chapter.

Infinitive and verb forms

INFINITIVES	VERB FORMS	ENGLISH EQUIVALENTS
hablar	(Yo) **hablo** inglés.	*I speak* English.
comprender	(Tú) **comprendes** el español.	*You understand* Spanish.
vivir	Juan **vive** en México.	Juan *lives* in Mexico.

1. The basic form of the verb (the form listed in vocabularies and dictionaries) is the infinitive. English infinitives usually consist of *to* + a verb, such as *to speak*. Spanish infinitives consist of a single word ending in **-ar, -er,** or **-ir.**

2. Subject pronouns, such as **yo** and **tú,** are often omitted in Spanish since the verb form and the context of the sentence usually help identify the subject of a sentence.

3. Most Spanish verbs, like **hablar, comprender,** and **vivir,** are regular. Their forms change according to set patterns. Other verbs, like **ser,** are irregular and have special forms.

Present tense of **ser**: singular forms (A–C)

SER	TO BE
soy	I am
eres	you are
es	he/she is

A form of the verb **ser** + **de** is used to indicate the place of origin of a person or thing: **Soy de los Estados Unidos.**

Gender of nouns (D)

Ese **chico** es Juan.	That *boy* is Juan.
Esa **chica** es María.	That *girl* is María.

Spanish nouns referring to people often change form according to whether the person referred to is male or female. A noun referring to a male is masculine in gender and often ends in **-o.** A noun referring to a female is feminine in gender and often ends in **-a.**

Noun-adjective agreement (E–G)

MASCULINE	FEMININE
Raúl es rubi**o**.	Ana es rubi**a**.
Felipe es bilingü**e**.	María es bilingü**e**.

In Spanish, an adjective must agree with the noun to which it refers. An adjective ending in **-o** is used to describe a male. An adjective ending in **-a** is used to describe a female. An adjective ending in **-e** can be used to describe either a male or a female.

Making statements negative (H)

Pedro **no** es muy alto.	Pedro is *not* very tall.
Elena **no** vive aquí.	Elena does *not* live here.

The word **no** before a verb is used to make a statement negative. There is no Spanish equivalent for the auxiliary verb *do* or *does* in negative statements.

Tag questions   (I)

Hablas inglés, **¿verdad?**	You speak English, *right?*
Vives en Los Ángeles, **¿no?**	You live in Los Angeles, *don't you?*

A statement can be made into a question by adding a tag question like **¿no?** or **¿verdad?** to the end of the statement.

Written Spanish

1. Spanish questions begin with an inverted question mark and end with a question mark: **¿Quién eres?**
2. Spanish exclamations begin with an inverted exclamation mark and end with an exclamation mark: **¡Hola!**
3. In Spanish, accent marks and certain other symbols are an important part of the spelling of the language: **tú, bilingüe, español.**

La calle Olvera en Los Ángeles.

21

Repaso

In early lessons, go over exercises orally before assigning as written homework.

The **Repaso** section at the end of each chapter will help you practice the Spanish you have learned in the chapter. Some of the exercises also review material from previous chapters.

A Agree or disagree with the following descriptive statements, according to the pictures.

Luis es inteligente, ¿verdad?

Sí, es inteligente.

Ana es alta, ¿no?

No. No es alta.

María Teresa es simpática, ¿no?

Juan Manuel es bilingüe, ¿verdad?

Paulina es alegre, ¿verdad?

Enrique es perezoso, ¿no?

B Make two statements about each of the following people, choosing from the adjectives below.

Game: Place in hat slips of paper with adjectives: *alta, rubio, perezosa, simpático.* Student draws a word and gives a truthful statement about a classmate: *Carmen es alta. Marcos no es estudioso. Yo soy simpático.*

bilingüe	**alta**
alto	**simpático**
simpática	**estudioso**
alegre	**perezoso**

Clara   *Clara es simpática. No es estudiosa.*

1. Marta
2. Luis
3. mi amiga
4. Pedro
5. Alfredo
6. mi amigo

C Complete the following paragraph with the correct forms of *ser.*

Yo ＿＿ Ana García. Y esa chica ＿＿ mi amiga Susana Gómez. Susana ＿＿ de México y ＿＿ bilingüe. Y tú, ¿quién ＿＿?

D Give a logical response to the questions, choosing from the responses on the right.

Variation: Repeat Ex. D with books closed. Student asks a question, another gives any logical answer.

1. ¿Cómo te llamas?	Sí, un poco.
2. ¿Hablas español?	Es mi amigo Luis.
3. Ana García vive aquí, ¿verdad?	Me llamo Inés González.
4. ¿Quién es ese chico?	Sí, hablo inglés y español.
5. Eres Carmen González, ¿verdad?	Adiós.
6. Tú eres bilingüe, ¿no?	No, soy Paula Ortiz.
7. Hasta luego.	No vive aquí. Vive en San Diego.

E Restate the following sentences in the negative.

■‖ Soy María Alba. *No soy María Alba.*

1. Vivo en San Diego.
2. Hablo francés.
3. Marcos es mi amigo.
4. Es bilingüe.
5. Esa chica es mi amiga Elena.
6. Elena es de Los Ángeles.
7. Es muy simpática.
8. Eres muy alto.

F You meet a Mexican student, Alicia Molina, at a dance. Tell or ask her the following things.

1. Introduce yourself to Alicia. Tell her where you live and what languages you speak.
2. Ask Alicia who her (male) friend is.
3. Ask Alicia if her friend lives in your town, and what he's like.

G Prepare a brief autobiographical sketch. Include your name, where you live, what languages you speak, and what you are like.

■‖ *Me llamo . . .*

23

Vocabulario

SUSTANTIVOS

el amigo, la amiga   friend
**el compañero, la
compañera**   classmate
la chica   girl
el chico   boy
el español   Spanish
(language)
los Estados Unidos   the
United States
el francés   French
(language)
el idioma   language
el inglés   English
(language)
México   Mexico
el señor (*abbrev.* **Sr.**)   Mr.
la señora (*abbrev.* **Sra.**)
Mrs.
la señorita (*abbrev.* **Srta.**)
Miss

VERBOS

hablar   to speak; **hablo**   I
speak; **hablas**   you speak
ser   to be; **soy**   I am;
eres   you are; **es**   he/she
is
vivir   to live; **vivo**   I live;
vives   you live; **vive**   he/
she lives

OTRAS PALABRAS

alegre   cheerful, happy
alto, -a   tall, high
antipático, -a   unpleasant
aquí   here
bajo, -a   short, low
bilingüe   bilingual
¿cómo?   how? what?
de   from
en   in
ese, esa   that
estudioso, -a   studious
inteligente   intelligent
mi   my
moreno, -a   dark-haired,
brunet(te)
mucho, -a   much, a lot
muy   very
no   no, not
perezoso, -a   lazy
¿qué?   what?
¿quién?   who?
rubio, -a   blond(e)
sí   yes
simpático, -a   nice, pleasant
sólo   only
también   also
tu   your
tú   you
y   and
yo   I

EXPRESIONES

adiós   good-by
buenas tardes   good afternoon
buenos días   good morning
¿cómo es ...?   what is ...
like?
¿cómo te llamas?   what's
your name?
encantado, -a   I'm pleased
to meet you
hasta luego   see you later
hasta mañana   see you tomorrow
hola   hello, hi
lo siento   I'm sorry
me llamo ...   my name
is ...
mucho gusto   how do you
do
¿no?   isn't that right?
no mucho   not much
no sé   I don't know
pues   well
un poco (de)   a little
¿verdad?   isn't it?
yo no   not me

The *Expresiones* contain idiomatic expressions as well as
other words and phrases presented as set phrases, especially
where unfamiliar structures are
involved.

Photo: School in Miami.

capítulo 2

¡Al colegio!

In the past few decades, many Cubans and other Hispanics have settled in Florida, especially in and around Miami. A section of Miami is known as **la pequeña Habana** or Little Havana because of the Cuban influence there. Many Cubans have been able to continue working at their former professions and have established themselves in banking, law, medicine, and government. Others are owners of shops, factories, and radio and television stations.

En la clase de biología

Rosa and Lucía are passing notes in biology class. Rosa was absent yesterday, and she asks Lucía about the test she has to make up tomorrow.

Introduce core. Act out with teacher-class, small groups, and finally in pairs.

Introduce meanings of new words (marked with °) before doing each activity below.

See list of classroom expressions in Teacher's Guide and gradually introduce instructions in Spanish.

Lucía, ¿ es fácil el examen?

No. Es muy difícil. Hay diez preguntas muy largas.

¡Qué horror! No sé nada.

No te preocupes. Te ayudo a estudiar esta tarde.

extensión

Variation: Extend using new questions such as *¿Cómo es tu clase de álgebra? ¿música?*, or ask *¿Es [fácil] tu clase de [historia]?*

Variation: Extend with new questions such as *¿Hay examen de inglés mañana? ¿biología?*, or *¿Hay clase de álgebra? ¿música?*

A. Ask a classmate what her/his biology class is like.

■‖ ¿Cómo es tu clase de biología?   Es muy difícil.
Es fácil.
Es interesante°.
Muy aburrida°.

B. Ask a friend whether there's a Spanish test tomorrow.

■‖ [Diego], ¿hay examen de   No, no hay.
español mañana°?   Lo siento. No sé.
Sí, mañana hay examen.
Sí. ¿Te ayudo a estudiar?

C. You're caught off guard when your English teacher announces a test. Show your surprise or displeasure.

■‖ Hoy° hay examen.   ¡Qué problema!° No sé nada.
No tengo° bolígrafo°.
¡Qué sorpresa!°
¿Hoy? No, [señor]. Es mañana.

Point out to students that *hay* is used with singular and plural nouns. See *Gramática* for further practice with *hay*.

D. You have to research some questions for history class. Ask a classmate how many questions there are.

■‖ ¿Cuántas° preguntas hay?   Hay diez preguntas largas.
Sólo cinco°.
Muchas°. ¿Por qué?°

El horario de Luis Lleras

Drill orally times and subjects shown in *horario*. Elicit comments regarding capitalization. Subjects are not capitalized. Only proper names, cities, countries, and title abbreviations are capitalized.

```
                    LUNES

    8:00    álgebra     Sr. Rodríguez
    9:00    español     Srta. Ibáñez
   10:00    biología    Sra. Adams
   11:00    ALMUERZO
   12:00    historia    Sr. Hills
    1:00    inglés      Srta. Smith
    2:00    música      Sra. de Guzmán
```

Check comprehension with questions such as: *¿Dónde es Luis estudiante? ¿Cuántas materias estudia? ¿Qué tiene por la mañana? ¿Qué tiene a las once? ¿Por qué es historia su clase favorita?*

Luis es estudiante en un colegio de Miami. Estudia seis materias. El lunes por la mañana tiene álgebra con el señor Rodríguez, español con la señorita Ibáñez y biología con la señora Adams. A las once toma el almuerzo. Por la tarde tiene historia a las doce, inglés a la una y música a las dos. Su clase favorita es historia porque el profesor es muy bueno.

extensión

Assignment: Ask students to prepare a copy of their own or an imaginary *horario* for use in activities A–D. List other subjects on board or refer students to supplementary word list in Appendix.

A. Give the names of the teachers of three classes you have this year.

   ▪ꟷ   Tengo [inglés] con [la señorita Smith].

B. Tell a classmate when you have some of your classes.

   ▪ꟷ   ¿Cuándo° tienes° clase de [historia]?   Por la tarde.
                                                   Por la mañana.
                                                   A [las dos].
                                                   No tengo clase de
                                                   [historia].

C. Ask a classmate what her/his favorite class is.

   ▪ꟷ   ¿Cuál° es tu clase favorita?   La clase de [español].

   Now ask why.

   ▪ꟷ   ¿Por qué?   Porque es [fácil].
                      Es muy [interesante].
                      La profesora° es [muy buena°].
                      El profesor es [simpático].

D. Find out from a classmate which classes he/she has on Monday.

   ▪ꟷ   ¿Qué clases tienes el lunes?   Tengo español, . . .

Estudio de palabras

Los números de 0 a 12

Optional: After choral practice with numbers, have class "count off" in order, or write numbers on board and have students count down 12 to 0.

0 = cero	3 = tres	6 = seis	9 = nueve
1 = uno	4 = cuatro	7 = siete	10 = diez
2 = dos	5 = cinco	8 = ocho	11 = once
			12 = doce

A Help your little sister learn to play dominoes. Tell her the number of each domino.

For additional practice with numbers, teach equations: *dos y dos son cuatro.* Chain drill: S[1]: *dos y tres,* S[2]: *Dos y tres son cinco.*

Game: Form two teams and give equation: *cinco y dos.* Students write equation on board. First correct answer wins point for team.

  *once*

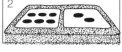 

 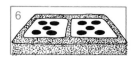

B Check a young cousin's addition homework. Read her/his answers aloud.

12 2 7 3 9 5 11 8 10 4 1 6

Dominoes is one of several favorite games of older Spanish-speaking men in many countries. The game provides relaxation as well as an occasion to get together with friends for a chat. A table at a coffee shop, cafeteria, or outdoors are common sites for late afternoon or evening games.

Optional: Have students bring domino games to class. Use for live practice of Act. A or play a game after discussion of cultural note.

En la clase

Use objects to introduce new vocabulary. Add new items gradually, continuing to drill previous words.

1. el libro
2. el lápiz
3. el cuaderno
4. el bolígrafo
5. el papel
6. la mesa
7. la silla
8. la cesta
9. la pizarra
10. la grabadora

C Point to or hold up an object for a classmate to name.

■▥ (pointing to a chair) *la silla*

Los días de la semana

Point out that some Spanish calendars begin with Monday. Obtain samples.

lunes   martes   miércoles   jueves   viernes   sábado   domingo

Game: Write scrambled days of week on board and have competition to see who can unscramble first: *usveej nmoogid eorimecls reeisvn sunle odabas smetra.*

Clara: ¿Qué día es hoy?   *What day is today?*
Pedro: Hoy es lunes.   *Today is Monday.*
Clara: ¿Y mañana?   *And tomorrow?*
Pedro: Mañana es martes.   *Tomorrow is Tuesday.*

Notice that the days of the week are not usually capitalized in Spanish.

D Identify the days of the week, starting with Monday.

■▥ ¿Qué día es?   *Es lunes.*

E The week is moving faster than your friends believe. Say that it's one day later than they think.

■▥ Es jueves, ¿verdad?   *No. Es viernes.*

Optional: Practice days in three-part chain drill. S¹: *¿Qué día es mañana?* S²: *Mañana es miércoles.* S³: *¡Qué bueno!*

1. Es lunes, ¿no?
2. Hoy es sábado, ¿no?
3. Mañana es martes, ¿verdad?
4. Es domingo, ¿verdad?
5. ¿Es miércoles mañana?
6. Hoy es viernes, ¿verdad?

Pronunciación y ortografía

palabras claves | [l] papel
[y] yo, silla

Explain that Spanish vowel sounds are pronounced the same, but some consonant sounds vary from one country to another and often within a country. See *y* and *ll* below.

The Spanish [l] sound is similar to the [l] sound in English *least,* with the tongue held high and the tip touching the back of the upper gum ridge. The tongue is never curled as in English *fall.*

A Pronounce the following words after your teacher. Pay special attention to the [l] sound.

lápiz	colegio	papel
libro	alegre	fácil
lunes	bilingüe	español

B Read the following sentences aloud to practice the [l] sound.

1. Miguel estudia español con Isabel.
2. El lunes hay colegio.
3. El inglés es difícil.

Y and *ll* are sometimes pronounced like *s* in *pleasure* or *j* in *juice.* Have students imitate your pronunciation.

In many Spanish-speaking areas, the [y] sound is similar to English [y] in *yes.* The *ll* in words like **silla** and **llamo** is also pronounced with the [y] sound in Mexico, in some parts of Spain, and in many parts of South America.

The [ll] sound is similar to the sound of *lli* in English *million,* and is used in Spain and in some areas of Latin America. The letter **ll** is a separate letter of the alphabet. In dictionaries and vocabularies, words beginning with **ll** are listed after the group of words beginning with **l.**

En boca cerrada no entran moscas.

C   Pronounce the following words after your teacher. Imitate the pronunciation of your teacher for words containing **y** or **ll.**

<blockquote>
yo   ayudo   llama   silla
ya   mayo   llega   calle
</blockquote>

D   Read the following sentences aloud.

1. Me llamo Guillermo Padilla.
2. Yo vivo en Sevilla.
3. La silla es de Yolanda.
4. ¿Te ayudo el lunes?

Gramática

Gender and definite articles **el** and **la**

MASCULINE	FEMININE
el libro	la mesa
el cuaderno	la silla
el examen	la clase

When discussing gender, use students' Spanish names as examples. Ask who has masculine name which ends in -o. Who has feminine name ending in -a? Do the same for names not ending in -o or -a.

In Spanish, nouns that refer to objects as well as nouns that refer to persons are either masculine or feminine in gender. A masculine singular noun often ends in **-o,** and a feminine singular noun often ends in **-a.** The gender of nouns that end in a letter other than **-o** or **-a** should be memorized, since the ending does not help indicate the gender.

<blockquote>
El libro es difícil.   *The* book is difficult.
La clase es interesante.   *The* class is interesting.
</blockquote>

The definite article **el** is used with masculine singular noun; **la** is used with a feminine singular noun.

A   A classmate wants to know where the following objects are. Say that you don't know. Be sure to use the appropriate definite article with each item.

Game: Place items listed in Act. A on table. Give class one minute to study items. Cover, removing one. Lift cover and ask missing item. Re-cover and remove second item. Uncover and ask which two items are missing, etc.

▪▥   lápiz   *¿El lápiz? No sé.*

1. bolígrafo	5. mesa
2. grabadora	6. silla
3. papel	7. cesta
4. libro	8. cuaderno

B Describe each person or object, using the adjectives provided. Start each statement with the appropriate definite article.

■III libro / interesante *El libro es interesante.*

1. grabadora / buena
2. señor / alto
3. mesa / larga
4. profesora / simpática
5. señorita / bilingüe
6. examen / difícil
7. clase / aburrida
8. biología / fácil

Plural of nouns and definite articles

Optional: Show classroom object to class and have students give singular form. Show duplicate items and elicit plural form. Let students show items.

SINGULAR	PLURAL
el cuaderno	los cuadernos
la clase	las clases
el papel	los papeles

Most Spanish nouns ending in a vowel add **-s** in the plural. Most nouns ending in a consonant add **-es** in the plural. Some nouns also have a spelling change in the plural: **lápiz, lápices; examen, exámenes.**

The definite article must agree in number with the noun it modifies. **Los** is used with a masculine plural noun, and **las** is used with a feminine plural noun.

C Give the plural form of each noun and its definite article.

Acrostic: Divide class into 2 teams. Write on board *la clase* and *colegio.* Students link class objects and other words to base. First team to complete, wins.

■III el chico *los chicos*

1. el papel
2. la pizarra
3. la silla
4. el bolígrafo
5. el libro
6. la profesora
7. el señor
8. la cesta

D Assure the school principal that you have all the necessary materials for your classroom.

■III mesas *Tengo las mesas.*

1. bolígrafos
2. libros
3. sillas
4. cuadernos
5. cestas
6. lápices
7. papeles
8. grabadoras

Verb form **hay**

Hay examen mañana.
Hay dos grabadoras en la mesa.

There is a test tomorrow.
There are two tape recorders on the table.

The verb form **hay** means *there is* or *there are*. **Hay** can be used with a singular or a plural noun.

E Say how many of each item there are, based on the drawings.

Variation: Expand with questions about classroom items. ¿[*Cuántas mesas*] hay en la clase? ¿sillas? ¿libros? ¿cuadernos?

Hay cuatro bolígrafos.

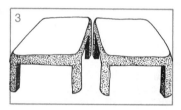

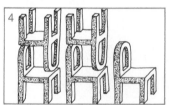

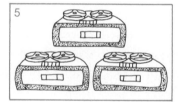

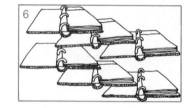

Subject pronouns **yo, tú, él,** and **ella**

yo	I	(**Yo**) soy María.
tú	you	¿(**Tú**) eres Juan?
él	he	(**Él**) es mi amigo.
ella	she	(**Ella**) es de Miami.

You have already learned that Spanish verbs are often used without a subject pronoun. The verb form and the context of a sentence usually help identify the intended subject of a sentence. Subject pronouns are generally used for emphasis, clarification, or to contrast two subjects.

F Restate each sentence, beginning with the subject pronoun that corresponds to the verb form.

■‖ Hablas inglés, ¿verdad?   *Tú hablas inglés, ¿verdad?*

1. Soy de Miami.
2. Hablo un poco de español.
3. Es muy simpática.

4. Eres bilingüe, ¿no?
5. Es un chico simpático.
6. Tiene cinco clases hoy.

Present tense of **tener**: singular forms

Tengo cinco lápices.   *I have* five pencils.
No **tienes** bolígrafo.   *You* don't *have* a pen.
Lucía **tiene** mi libro.   Lucía *has* my book.

The verb **tener** *(to have)* has irregular forms in the present tense. An article, such as *a/an,* can be omitted before a noun that follows **tener** when the noun is used in a general sense.

G You've forgotten your class supplies today. Tell what you're missing and express your concern.

Chain drill: Hide object. Student must find out who has it. S¹: *¿Tienes mi cuaderno?* S²: *No, no tengo tu cuaderno.* S?: *Sí, tengo . . .*

■‖ papel   *No tengo papel. ¡Qué problema!*

1. lápiz
2. libro

3. cuaderno
4. bolígrafo

H Marta asks if you have various items. Tell her no and that you're sorry.

■‖ mi grabadora   Marta: *¿Tienes mi grabadora?*
                           Tú: *Yo no. Lo siento.*

1. el libro de español
2. dos bolígrafos
3. mi cuaderno

4. mi horario
5. papel
6. lápiz

I Your friends are mistaken about your class schedule. Tell them that Miguel has the class in question.

Assignment: Have students write 10 original questions using tags, to ask and answer in class.

■‖ Tienes clase de música hoy, ¿verdad?   *No. Miguel tiene clase de música hoy.*

1. ¿Tienes álgebra a las doce?
2. Tienes historia a las once, ¿no?
3. Tienes biología el martes, ¿no?
4. ¿Tienes clase de inglés el martes?
5. ¿Tienes español con la Srta. Alonso?
6. ¿Tienes música con el Sr. Peterson?
7. Tienes clase de francés mañana, ¿verdad?

A friend wants to know about one of your classes. Tell her/him who your teacher is, what time of day you have the class, and what it's like.

Personalize: Have students answer questions on their own *horarios*. Use question words.

Tienes clase de [álgebra], ¿verdad?	Sí. Tengo [álgebra] con ... La clase es [por la mañana]. Es muy [difícil].

The definite article with days of the week

Tuesday (and sometimes Tuesday the 13th) is considered an unlucky day in many Spanish-speaking countries. Cite *El martes ni te cases ni te embarques.*

Tengo clase de música **el jueves.**	I have music class *on Thursday.*
Hay examen **los viernes.**	There's an exam *on Fridays.*
Los sábados no tengo clases.	I don't have classes *on Saturdays.*

The definite article **el** or **los** is used with days of the week to express *on.* **Sábado** and **domingo** add **-s** in the plural; the other days have the same form in the singular and plural.

J   Confirm that you or the people mentioned have certain subjects on the day after the one indicated.

■Ⅲ   Tienes inglés el lunes, ¿no?   *Sí, y también el martes.*

1. Luis tiene biología los jueves, ¿verdad?
2. Marta tiene música el martes, ¿verdad?
3. Sara tiene álgebra los lunes, ¿no?
4. ¿Tienes español el miércoles?
5. ¿Tienes historia el martes?

K   A classmate asks you when you'll have certain exams. Answer her/him, using any day of the week.

■Ⅲ   biología   — *¿Cuándo hay examen de biología?*
              — *Hay examen [el lunes].*

1. música	3. historia	5. inglés
2. español	4. álgebra	6. francés

The school day for high school students in many Spanish-speaking countries begins early and often ends between 4:00 and 5:30. Lunch break may be as long as two hours, and many students return home to have the midday meal with their families. In some countries, extra-curricular activities such as sports are held on Saturdays. In Mexico, Spain, and Colombia, scouting may be scheduled on Saturdays. In Cuba, Saturdays are reserved for political activities.

Formation of **sí-no** questions

Pilar es bilingüe.

Felipe tiene clase hoy.

¿Pilar es bilingüe?

¿Felipe tiene clase hoy?

In Spanish, a statement can be changed into a **sí-no** question by using rising intonation at the end of the statement.

L   Verify certain information by asking your classmates *sí-no* questions. Use rising intonation.

■||| Luz tiene clase de inglés.
— *¿Luz tiene clase de inglés?*
— *Sí, tiene clase de inglés.*
  (No. No tiene clase de inglés.)

1. Hay diez preguntas largas en el examen.
2. El profesor de álgebra es bueno.
3. Tienes biología el jueves.
4. Ese chico vive en México.

Luis tiene dos clases hoy.
La clase es fácil.
La Sra. Romero es de Miami.

¿Tiene **Luis** dos clases hoy?
¿Es fácil **la clase?**
¿Es de Miami **la Sra. Romero?**

A statement can be made into a **sí-no** question by using inverted word order and rising intonation. When the word order is changed, the verb precedes the subject. An adjective or other words, such as a **de**-phrase, often comes between the verb and its subject.

M   Change the following sentences into questions by using inverted word order. The subject should follow immediately after the verb.

Have students respond to questions positively or negatively, in three part drill. S¹: *Pilar estudia cinco materias.* S²: *Estudia Pilar cinco materias?* S³: *No, estudia seis.*

■||| Pilar estudia cinco materias.   *¿Estudia Pilar cinco materias?*

1. María tiene tres bolígrafos.
2. Diego tiene historia a las nueve.
3. Miguel estudia álgebra.
4. Rosa vive en México.

N   Change the following sentences into questions, putting the subject at the end of the question.

■||| La clase es interesante.   *¿Es interesante la clase?*

1. La Sra. White vive aquí.
2. El profesor es de Cuba.
3. Manuel estudia mucho.
4. José es moreno.
5. Carmen tiene clase de español.

Students who plan to attend a university in a Spanish-speaking country must complete the **bachillerato,** or secondary school education. Requirements for the **bachillerato** vary from one country to another, but foreign languages, science, and mathematics are generally required subjects. Other subjects may include religion, philosophy, geography, and history. There are few elective subjects. In some countries, such as Mexico and Colombia, students may have eight or more subjects a year. Class periods are short, but students often have many hours of homework weekly. A diploma is awarded at the end of the **bachillerato,** after successful completion of rigorous final exams.

Add any personal insight you might have about education in other countries.

En resumen

Gender of nouns

All Spanish nouns are either masculine or feminine in gender. A masculine singular noun often ends in **-o,** and a feminine singular noun often ends in **-a.** Some nouns, like **estudiante,** are the same in the masculine and feminine form.

Plural of nouns (C, D)

SINGULAR	PLURAL
libro	libro**s**
cesta	cesta**s**
papel	papel**es**
viernes	viernes

The plural of a noun is usually formed by adding **-s** after a vowel, and **-es** after a consonant. Days of the week that end in **-s** do not change in the plural.

Definite articles (A–D, J, K)

	MASCULINE	FEMININE
Singular	el	la
Plural	los	las

1. A definite article must agree in number and gender with the noun it modifies: **el libro, los libros; la cesta, las cestas.**
2. The definite article is used with days of the week to express *on:* **No hay clases los sábados; Tengo inglés el lunes.**
3. The definite article is used with courtesy titles such as **señor** or **señora,** unless they are used in direct address: **Tengo música con el señor Fernández,** but **Buenos días, señora.**

Verb form **hay** (E)

¿**Hay** clase de inglés hoy?   *Is there* English (class) today?
Hay tres libros aquí.   *There are* three books here.

Hay can be used with a singular or plural noun.

Singular subject pronouns (F)

yo	*I*
tú	*you*
él	*he*
ella	*she*

The pronoun **yo,** unlike its English equivalent *I,* is not capitalized unless it begins a sentence.

Present tense of **tener**: singular forms (G–I)

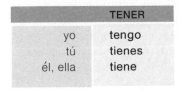

	TENER
yo	tengo
tú	tienes
él, ella	tiene

The verb **tener** *(to have)* is irregular in the present tense.

Sí-no questions (L–N)

<table>
<tr><td>STATEMENT</td><td>QUESTION</td></tr>
<tr><td>Luis tiene mi bolígrafo.</td><td>¿Luis tiene mi bolígrafo?
¿Tiene Luis mi bolígrafo?
¿Tiene mi bolígrafo Luis?</td></tr>
</table>

A statement can be made into a **sí-no** question by using rising intonation at the end of the statement, or by using inverted word order and rising intonation. When the word order is changed to form a question, the verb precedes the subject. Sometimes other sentence elements, such as a noun object or adjective, may come between the verb and its subject.

Repaso

A   Tell how many of the following items each person has. Use any number between *dos* and *doce*.

> ▪▥   Marcos / cuadernos   *Marcos tiene tres cuadernos.*

1. Marta / grabadoras
2. yo / libros
3. Carmen / cuadernos
4. Elena / lápices
5. tú / cestas
6. Alicia / bolígrafos
7. Daniel / mesas
8. María / sillas

B   Give an appropriate reaction to each of the following sentences. Choose from the list on the right.

1. El examen es muy difícil.
2. No tengo mi libro.
3. ¡Hola! Soy Pedro Hernández.
4. No hay pizarra en la clase.
5. ¿Hablas mucho español?
6. ¿Cuándo tienes clase de álgebra?
7. ¿Hay clase de música mañana?

No sé.
¡Qué sorpresa!
¡Qué problema!
¡Qué horror!
Mucho gusto.
No te preocupes.
Muy aburrido.
Por la tarde.
No mucho.

C   Tell what classes there are on different days of the week, based on the drawings below. Use any day of the week in your statements.

■||| *El lunes hay clase de inglés.*

D   Lola is talking on the phone with Pedro. He can't hear very well because of a bad connection and questions everything Lola says. Take Pedro's role and change Lola's statements to questions by using inverted word order.

■||| Marcos estudia historia.   *¿Estudia Marcos historia?*

1. Tomás es bilingüe.
2. Marta estudia francés.
3. Luis tiene seis materias.
4. La profesora tiene dos grabadoras.
5. Adela vive en Los Ángeles.
6. El examen es largo.

E   You are a teacher and it's the first day of school. What supplies do you need? What equipment is already in your classroom?

■||| *Tengo . . . No tengo . . .*

F   Prepare a brief biography of someone you know. Include such information as the person's name, where he/she lives, and what he/she is like. Tell three subjects the person studies, and what her/his favorite class is.

G   Interpret for a new student from Cuba who speaks very little English.

1. — What day is today?   — Today is Friday.
2. — Do you have a pen?   — No. I have two pencils.
3. — How many students are   — There are twelve.
   there in Spanish class?

Vocabulario

Stress importance of vocabulary study. To encourage learning, hold occasional vocabulary bees. Give English word, students supply Spanish.

SUSTANTIVOS

el álgebra   algebra
el almuerzo   lunch
la biología   biology
el bolígrafo   ball-point pen
la cesta   wastebasket, basket
la clase   class
el colegio   school
el cuaderno   notebook
el día   day
el estudiante, la estudiante   student
el examen   exam
la grabadora   tape recorder
la historia   history
el horario   schedule
el lápiz   pencil
el libro   book
la materia   subject; material
la mesa   table
la música   music
el número   number
el papel   paper
la pizarra   chalkboard
la pregunta   question
el profesor, la profesora   teacher
la semana   week
la silla   chair
la tarde   afternoon

VERBOS

estudiar   to study; **estudia** he/she studies
tener   to have; **tengo**   I have; **tienes**   you have; **tiene**   he/she has

OTRAS PALABRAS

aburrido, -a   boring
bueno, -a   good
con   with
¿cuál?   what? which?
¿cuándo?   when?
¿cuántos? -as?   how many?
difícil   difficult
él   he
ella   she
este, esta   this
fácil   easy
favorito, -a   favorite
hoy   today
interesante   interesting
largo, -a   long
mañana   tomorrow
muchos, -as   many
porque   because
¿por qué?   why?
su   his, her

EXPRESIONES

a la una   at one o'clock; **a las (dos)**   at (two) o'clock
hay   there is, there are
no sé nada   I don't know anything
no te preocupes   don't worry
por la mañana   in the morning
por la tarde   in the afternoon
¡qué horror!   how terrible!
¡qué problema!   what a problem!
¡qué sorpresa!   what a surprise!
te ayudo a (+ *infinitive*)   I'll help you to
toma el almuerzo   he/she has lunch

LOS DÍAS DE LA SEMANA

el lunes   Monday
el martes   Tuesday
el miércoles   Wednesday
el jueves   Thursday
el viernes   Friday
el sábado   Saturday
el domingo   Sunday

LOS NÚMEROS DE 0 A 12

cero   0
uno   1
dos   2
tres   3
cuatro   4
cinco   5
seis   6
siete   7
ocho   8
nueve   9
diez   10
once   11
doce   12

capítulo 3
Con los amigos

Texas, which was a part of Mexico until 1836, has a large Mexican-American population whose ancestors often date back to Spanish colonial days. San Antonio, with its historic buildings, is especially reminiscent of the Spanish heritage in Texas. The city's Mexican Americans have kept alive the Spanish language and the traditions and celebrations of Mexico.

Un regalo de cumpleaños

Felipe is caught unprepared for Rosa's birthday.

FELIPE	¿Qué tienes ahí, Pilar?
PILAR	Un regalo para Rosa.
FELIPE	¿Un regalo? ¿Por qué?
PILAR	¡Porque cumple quince años mañana!
FELIPE	¡No me digas! ¿Qué le compro?
PILAR	Una novela o quizás un disco . . . Son fáciles de buscar.
FELIPE	Oye, buena idea. Hasta pronto.

extensión

A. You've forgotten about a party. When reminded by a friend, how are you likely to respond?

■‖ La fiesta° es el viernes.

¡No me digas!
Sí, ahora recuerdo°.
¿Una fiesta?
¡Qué bueno!°
¿A qué hora?

B. A friend gives you a gift as he/she wishes you a happy birthday. What do you say?

■‖ ¡Feliz cumpleaños°, [Tomás]!

¿Un regalo? Gracias.
¡Muchas gracias!°
¡Qué sorpresa!
¿Qué es?

C. A friend wants some advice about a birthday gift for Rosa. Can you help?

■‖ ¿Qué le compro a Rosa?

Un [cassette°] quizás.
[Una novela o un disco.]
Pues, no sé.

D. Pretend that you're calling Miguel to invite him to Sara's birthday party. Be sure to tell him the day and the time of the party. Also give Miguel an idea for a gift.

Tú:	Hola, ¿Miguel? Soy . . .	Miguel:	Hola, . . .
	El lunes Sara cumple . . .		¡No me . . . !
	Hay una fiesta el . . .		¡Qué . . . ! ¿A qué . . . ?
	Es a las . . .		¿Qué le . . . ?
	Quizás . . .		Buena . . .
	Hasta . . .		Adiós, . . . Muchas . . .

Fifteen is generally a special age for Hispanic girls in Mexico and Puerto Rico, as well as for many Hispanic American girls. At age fifteen, a girl is entitled to be called **señorita,** signifying that she is no longer a child. Traditionally, a girl was then eligible for marriage. Today, a girl may be permitted to date at fifteen. **A quinceañera** or fifteen-year-old girl often celebrates her birthday with an elaborate party, dinner, and dance for family and friends. In Mexico, the celebration often begins with a Mass.

Establish parallels or differences between *quinceañera* and "sweet 16".

¿Cuántos años tienes?

Carmen and Isabel discuss a want ad on the school bulletin board. Isabel wants to apply for the job, but Carmen thinks she's too young.

> Busco joven entre 16 y 18 años para trabajar en oficina.
> Llamar por favor al teléfono 515-2627

CARMEN	Isabel, sólo tienes quince años, ¿no?
ISABEL	Sí, pero casi tengo dieciséis.
CARMEN	¡No te creo! ¿Cuándo es tu cumpleaños?
ISABEL	El veinte de noviembre.
CARMEN	¡Qué suerte! Entonces, puedes llamar para el empleo.

extensión

Point out difference between *tener . . . años* and *cumplir . . . años.* Ask students *¿Cuántos años tienes? ¿Cuántos años cumples?*

A. Ask a classmate how old he/she is.

■॥ ¿Cuántos años tienes?　　　　Tengo [catorce°] años.
　　　　　　　　　　　　　　　　Casi [dieciséis].

B. A classmate brags about being sixteen years old, but you don't believe it. What's your reaction?

■॥ Tengo dieciséis años.　　　　¿Verdad? No te creo.
　　　　　　　　　　　　　　　　¡Me tomas el pelo!°
　　　　　　　　　　　　　　　　Tú no tienes dieciséis años.
　　　　　　　　　　　　　　　　¡No me digas!

Personalize: To encourage mini-dialogues, have students ask each other if they have a job:
S¹: *¿Tienes empleo?*
S²: *Sí, . . . (No)* S¹: *¿Verdad? No te creo.*

C. A friend announces to you that he/she has a job. Share in the excitement.

■ﺍ   ¡Tengo empleo!   ¡No me digas!
                                       ¡Qué suerte!
                                       ¡Qué bueno!
                                       ¡Fantástico!°

D. You want to hire a part-time employee. Interview several students for the job, using the following guidelines.

Tú: ¿Cómo te . . . ?   Estudiante: Me llamo . . .
    ¿Dónde . . . ?   Vivo . . .
    ¿Cuántos años . . . ?   Tengo . . .
    ¿Hablas . . . ?   Sí, . . .

¿Me prestas tu calculadora?

Carlos needs to borrow a calculator, so he asks Jaime to lend him one.

CARLOS   ¡Oye, Jaime! ¿Me prestas tu calculadora?
JAIME   No puedo porque es del profesor.
CARLOS   ¡Por favor! Tengo examen mañana.
JAIME   ¡Caramba! Yo también.
CARLOS   Entonces, ¿puedo estudiar contigo?
JAIME   Buena idea.

Point out that *prestar* is used for the English verbs *to borrow* and *to lend.*

extensión

V: Chain drill with students asking original questions. *¿Me prestas tu bolígrafo? ¿lápiz? ¿grabadora? ¿cuaderno?*

A. A friend asks to borrow your bicycle.

■ﺍ   ¿Me prestas tu bicicleta°?   Sí, claro°.
                                       No puedo. Es de [Jaime].
                                       No. Lo siento.

B. Ask a friend for your watch, which you loaned her/him a week ago.

■ﺍ   ¿Tienes mi reloj°?   Sí, aquí tienes el reloj.
                                         Gracias.
                                       ¡Caramba! No recuerdo°.
                                       Yo no. Lo siento.

C. Try to locate the owner of a pair of glasses you've found in your classroom.

Mention regional vocabulary differences. *Gafas, anteojos,* and *lentes* may be used for glasses.

■ﺍ   ¿De quién° son estos°   No sé.
        lentes°?   Son de [Julio].
                                      ¡Son mis° lentes! Muchas
                                        gracias.

Los números de 13 a 31

Quickly review numbers from 0 to 12.

13 = trece	18 = dieciocho	23 = veintitrés	28 = veintiocho
14 = catorce	19 = diecinueve	24 = veinticuatro	29 = veintinueve
15 = quince	20 = veinte	25 = veinticinco	30 = treinta
16 = dieciséis	21 = veintiuno	26 = veintiséis	31 = treinta y uno
17 = diecisiete	22 = veintidós	27 = veintisiete	

veintiún chicos   veintiuna chicas
treinta y un chicos   treinta y una chicas

Veintiún and **treinta y un** are used with masculine plural nouns. **Veintiuna** and **treinta y una** are used with feminine plural nouns.

A   You're at an auction. Outbid the last offer by one dollar.

■ꓲ   ¡Veinticinco!   *¡Veintiséis!*

1. ¡Trece!   5. ¡Veintinueve!
2. ¡Diecisiete!   6. ¡Veintiséis!
3. ¡Quince!   7. ¡Catorce!
4. ¡Veintidós!   8. ¡Veinte!

B   Read the following telephone numbers in Irene's address book. Say the first number by itself, and the remaining numbers in pairs.

■ꓲ   oficina: 513-2719   *oficina: cinco, trece, veintisiete, diecinueve*
■ꓲ   María: 231-2628   *María: dos, treinta y uno, veintiséis, veintiocho*

When giving telephone numbers, pairs beginning with zero are said as two separate numbers: 231-2608 would be *dos, treinta y uno, veintiséis, cero ocho.*

Game: *Ojo,* for number practice. Class counts off in order. If a student's number contains a 3 or is divisible by 3, student says *ojo* and places index finger beneath eye in "watch out" gesture. If student says number instead of *ojo* when required, student is eliminated.

~ Teléfonos ~

oficina	513-2719
María	231-2628
José Luis	315-3029
Rosa	430-2021
David	518-1915
Sr. Fuentes	814-2426
Srta. Gómez	516-1217
Teresa	722-2531

Los meses del año

Optional: Mention that September has two acceptable Spanish spellings: *septiembre* and *setiembre*.

diciembre
enero
febrero

junio
julio
agosto

marzo
abril
mayo

septiembre
octubre
noviembre

In Spanish, the months of the year are generally not capitalized, unless they begin a sentence.

C Name the months that precede and follow the ones given.

Optional: Obtain tape or record and teach song *Uno de enero* to practice months. Explain that song refers to the running of the bulls in Pamplona in northern Spain during the July fiesta of San Fermín.

■ⅲ agosto   *julio, septiembre*

1. enero
2. septiembre
3. marzo
4. mayo
5. noviembre
6. julio

D Take a poll of the birthday months in your class.

■ⅲ ¿En qué mes es tu cumpleaños?   [*En junio*].

🔳 Spanish first names often correspond to the name of a saint in the Roman Catholic Church, and Spanish speakers may celebrate their **santo** or saint's day instead of their birthday. For example, a girl named **Carmen** may celebrate the day of **Nuestra Señora del Carmen** on July 16, and a boy named **Carlos** may celebrate the day of **San Carlos** on November 4. Although today more and more Hispanic families choose to celebrate birthdays instead of saints' days, it is customary to congratulate a friend or family member on her or his saint's day.

Pronunciación y ortografía

palabras claves ▌ [s] mesa, diez, cinco

The Spanish [s] sound is similar to the [s] sound in English *sun*. The [s] sound is spelled **s, z,** and **c** (before the vowels **e** or **i**).

A Pronounce the following words after your teacher.

Optional: *Trabalenguas:*
¿Qué precio tienen
estos seis racimos de
cerezas? Sesenta y
seis pesetas. Tell students that *peseta* is currency in Spain.

sí	marzo	cesta
silla	pizarra	cinco
son	almuerzo	doce
mesa	lápiz	once
dos	diez	fácil

B Read the following sentences aloud to practice the [s] sound.

1. Los libros son de Cecilia Silva.
2. Susana García tiene cinco lápices.
3. Cero y diez son diez.

C Dictate the following words to a classmate, and then have your classmate dictate them to you.

1. perezoso
2. fácil
3. dieciséis
4. gracias
5. pizarra
6. estudioso

A caballo regalado
no se le mira el diente.

Proverb: Don't look a gift horse in the mouth.

capítulo 3 **49**

Regional variations in pronunciation are common in Spanish. For example, the Spanish spoken in some parts of Spain differs from the Spanish of the Americas in much the same way that the English spoken in the United States differs from that spoken in Australia, Canada, and Great Britain. In some areas of Spain, the sound of **c** (before **e** or **i**) and **z** is similar to the sound of *th* in *think*.

Gramática

Indefinite articles **un** and **una**

¿Es **un** regalo?   Is it *a* gift?
Tengo **una** novela.   I have *a* novel.

The indefinite article *a/an* has two singular forms in Spanish: **un** and **una.** The form **un** is used with a masculine noun, and **una** is used with a feminine noun.

A   You're unwrapping birthday presents. Identify each gift and express your thanks. Be sure to give the correct form of the indefinite article.

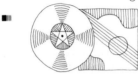   *¡Un disco! Muchas gracias.*

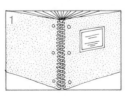

B   Tell what objects there are in the classroom, using the cues provided.

▪▥   mesa   *Hay una mesa en la clase.*

1. pizarra	3. cesta	5. libro	7. grabadora
2. calculadora	4. silla	6. bolígrafo	8. horario

Definite articles with dates

¿Es **el primero** de noviembre?   Is it *the first* of November?
No, es **el dos** de noviembre.   No, it's *the second* of November.
                                      No, it's November *second*.

In Spanish, the definite article **el** is used with dates. The first day of the month is expressed with the ordinal number **primero**. All other dates are expressed with cardinal numbers, such as **dos, tres,** and **cuatro**. In spoken Spanish, the day usually precedes the month.

C   Express the following dates in Spanish.

Optional: Ask dates of holidays. *¿Cuándo celebramos el cumpleaños de Jorge Washington? ¿el día de dar gracias?*

■Ⅲ   July 4   *Es el cuatro de julio.*

1. October 12   5. September 1
2. May 5   6. February 17
3. December 31   7. July 14
4. March 9   8. November 20

¡vamos a hablar!   Ask three classmates to tell you their birthday.

¿Cuándo es tu cumpleaños?   Es el [ocho de octubre].

Possession with de

¿**De quién** es el cuaderno?   *Whose* notebook is it?
— **Es de Felipe.**   — *It's Felipe's.*

¿**De quién** son los libros?   *Whose* books are they?
— **Son de la profesora.**   — *They are the teacher's.*

In Spanish, possession can be expressed with **de**, followed by a proper name or noun referring to a person. No apostrophe is used with a noun, as in English.

Notice that the verb form **es** is used in the singular, and **son** *(they are)* is used in the plural.

D   Report that you have the following items belonging to various friends.

■Ⅲ   los libros / Raquel   *Tengo los libros de Raquel.*

1. el disco / Fernando
2. la bicicleta / Ana
3. los lentes / Paco
4. los bolígrafos / Carlos
5. la novela / Jaime
6. el reloj / Cristina

E You're trying to locate the owner of some items that have been left on your desk. A classmate tells you who the owner of each item is.

Game: Collect items from students. Play *¿De quién es?* Leader holds item and asks, *¿De quién es?* Students respond, *Es de Marta.* Correct guesser leads next round.

 lápices / Julia — *¿De quién son los lápices?*
— *Son de Julia.*

calculadora / Tomás — *¿De quién es la calculadora?*
— *Es de Tomás.*

1. cuadernos / Marisa
2. bolígrafo / Álvaro
3. horario / Luis

4. papeles / Javier
5. bicicleta / mi amiga Elena
6. grabadoras / la profesora

Descriptive de-phrases

Elicit examples of descriptive *de*-phrases: *cuaderno de francés, libro de español, papel de álgebra, horario de clases, mes de julio.*

Es un **regalo de cumpleaños.**   It's a *birthday gift.*
Tengo **clase de música** hoy.   I have *music class* today.

The preposition **de** + a noun may be used to modify or describe another noun. The **de**-phrase follows the noun it describes.

F Inform a new student what time the following classes meet.

inglés / a las dos   *Hay clase de inglés a las dos.*

1. álgebra / a las ocho
2. biología / a la una
3. español / a las diez
4. historia / a las once
5. francés / a las nueve

El día de la Independencia is an important holiday in Hispanic countries and is often celebrated with big parades, music, and dancing. Independence Day is observed on many different dates to commemorate each nation's independence from Spain. For example, it's July 5 in Venezuela, July 9 in Argentina, and September 16 in Mexico.

In Texas, Independence Day is referred to as *el dieciséis.*

Photo: Independence Day parade in Mexico City.

Possessive adjectives **mi, tu, su**

SINGULAR			PLURAL	
mi disco	*my* record		**mis** discos	*my* records
tu bicicleta	*your* bicycle		**tus** bicicletas	*your* bicycles
su profesora	*her/his* teacher		**sus** profesoras	*her/his* teachers

Mention that it is incorrect to place sentence stress on possessive adjectives. *Su* (your, their) is presented in *capítulo 5*.

A possessive adjective precedes the noun it modifies. **Mi, tu,** and **su** can be used with a singular masculine or feminine noun. **Mis, tus,** and **sus** are used with a plural masculine or feminine noun.

The possessive adjectives **su** and **sus** can mean either *her* or *his.* Context will help tell which meaning is intended.

G   Ask several classmates if they have the following items with them.

■||| reloj   — *¿Tienes tu reloj?*
                      — *Sí, tengo mi reloj.*
                        (No, no tengo mi reloj.)

1. bolígrafos
2. papeles
3. lentes
4. grabadora
5. horario
6. lápices
7. cuaderno
8. bicicleta

H   Pilar is cleaning out her locker. Confirm who the owner is of the items she discovers in it.

Personalize: Use objects from students to ask *sí-no* questions. T: *¿Es de [Miguel] el reloj?* S: *Sí, es su reloj.* (No)

■||| La novela es de Juan, ¿verdad?   *Sí, es su novela.*

1. ¿Son de Alicia los discos?
2. ¿Son de Miguel los papeles?
3. La grabadora es de la profesora, ¿no?
4. El reloj es de Susana, ¿verdad?
5. ¿Son de Carlos los lentes?
6. ¿El horario es de José?
7. ¿La calculadora es de Elena?
8. Los libros son de Teresa, ¿verdad?

¡vamos a hablar!   A friend is looking for some missing belongings. Offer to help her/him look for them.

Busco [mis lentes].   ¿Te ayudo a buscar [tus lentes]?

54

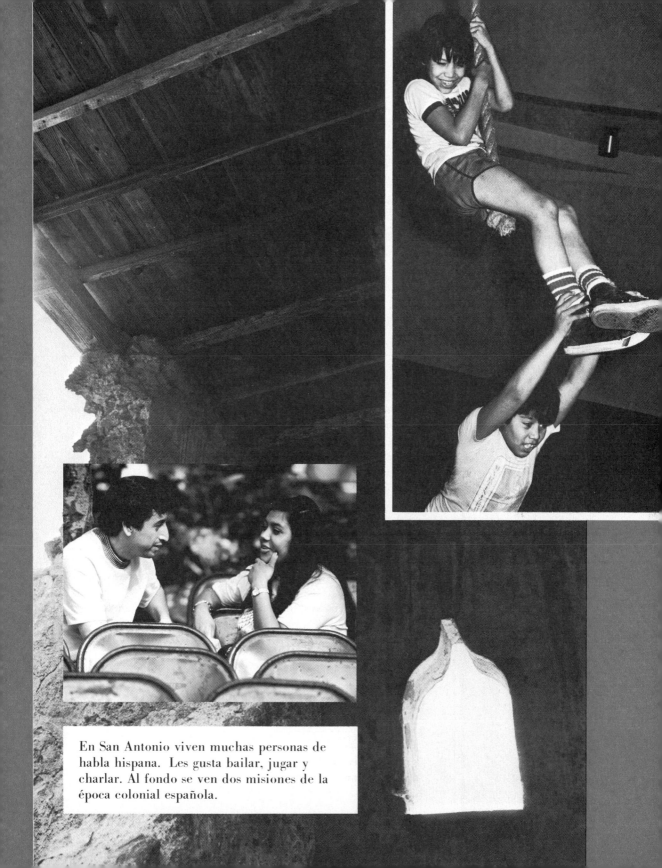

En San Antonio viven muchas personas de habla hispana. Les gusta bailar, jugar y charlar. Al fondo se ven dos misiones de la época colonial española.

Questions with question words

¿Qué es?	*What* is it?
¿Quién es esa chica?	*Who's* that girl?
¿Dónde vives?	*Where* do you live?
¿Qué idioma hablas?	*What* language do you speak?

Question words, such as **¿qué?, ¿quién?,** and **¿dónde?,** are used to ask for specific types of information. The verb usually follows the question word. A question word always has an accent.

Other question words and phrases that you have used are **¿cómo?, ¿cuándo?, ¿por qué?, ¿de quién?,** and **¿cuál?**

I You're at a noisy party and can't hear what a friend says. Ask for clarification of her/his statements, using the question words indicated.

▪◁ Juan es muy simpático. (cómo) *¿Cómo es Juan?*

1. Diego vive en Los Ángeles. (dónde)
2. Hoy es martes. (qué día)
3. Su cumpleaños es el lunes. (cuándo)
4. La novela es interesante. (cómo)
5. Miguel tiene música a las tres. (quién)
6. Estudio historia porque es fácil. (por qué)
7. María estudia inglés y español. (quién)
8. La clase es a las diez. (cuándo)

Exclamations with **qué**

¡Qué sorpresa!	*What a surprise!*
¡Qué bueno!	*How nice! Great!*

¡Qué! is used with a noun or an adjective to form an exclamation.

J React to the following sentences with an appropriate exclamation from the list below. Use each exclamation at least once.

¡Qué horror!	**¡Qué sorpresa!**	**¡Qué suerte!**
¡Qué bueno!	**¡Qué problema!**	

▪◁ Ese chico no estudia. *¡Qué problema!*

1. No sé nada.
2. ¿Un regalo? ¡No me digas!
3. ¡Tengo empleo!
4. No tengo mis lentes.
5. Hoy es viernes.
6. El examen es muy difícil.

K Express each of the following statements as an exclamation. Use the indicated word in your exclamation.

■Ⅲ Ella es *simpática.*   *¡Qué simpática!*

1. La biología es *fácil.*
2. El examen es muy *difícil.*
3. Es un chico *alegre.*
4. Ese libro es muy *interesante.*
5. Es un disco *fantástico.*
6. La fiesta es una *sorpresa.*

En resumen

Indefinite articles **un** and **una** (A, B)

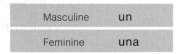

Masculine	un
Feminine	una

The indefinite article **un** is used with a masculine singular noun, and **una** is used with a feminine singular noun: **un disco, una fiesta.**

Definite article with dates (C)

1. In Spanish, the definite article **el** generally precedes the date: **Es el primero de julio, Es el diez de abril.**
2. The definite article is omitted from dates in a letter: **20 de noviembre.**

Possession with **de** (D, E)

De + a proper name or a noun referring to a person is used to express possession: **Es el libro de Luis.**

Descriptive **de**-phrases (F)

A phrase consisting of **de** + a noun is used to describe or modify another noun: **Es una fiesta de cumpleaños.**

Possessive adjectives **mi, tu, su** (G, H)

SINGULAR	PLURAL	
mi	mis	*my*
tu	tus	*your*
su	sus	*her / his*

A possessive adjective agrees in number with the noun it modifies.

Questions with question words (I)

1. Question words or phrases, such as **¿qué?, ¿dónde?,** and **¿por qué?** are used to ask for specific kinds of information.
2. The verb usually follows the question word: **¿Dónde vives?, ¿Por qué estudia español Luis?**

Exclamations with **qué** (J, K)

qué + adjective	¡Qué bueno!	*How nice! Great!*
qué + noun	¡Qué sorpresa!	*What a surprise!*

Repaso

A Tell what item each person has. Use the correct form of *tener* and the appropriate indefinite article.

∎ɪɪɪ Pilar / reloj *Pilar tiene un reloj.*

1. Sara / regalo
2. yo / calculadora
3. Rafael / novela

4. mi amigo / disco
5. tú / grabadora
6. Beatriz / bicicleta

B Announce each runner's number as he/she crosses the finish line of a two-mile race. Read each group across.

2	18	7	29	11	24	5	27	8	23
14	6	30	12	9	13	3	20	31	15 ·

C Answer or react to the sentences on the left, choosing an appropriate response from the list on the right.

1. Aquí tienes un disco.
2. ¿Me prestas tu grabadora?
3. ¡Caramba! ¿Quién tiene mi bolígrafo?
4. ¿De quién es el reloj?
5. Hay una fiesta el sábado.
6. ¿Cuántos años tienes?
7. ¡Rafael tiene empleo!

¡Me tomas el pelo!
No sé, pero aquí tienes un lápiz.
Casi quince.
Muchas gracias.
Claro.
¡Qué suerte!
¡Qué bueno!
Es de Manuel.

D Tell to whom each object belongs, basing your reponses on the drawing below. Use a *de*-phrase and *es* or *son,* as appropriate.

■ⅼⅼ   *Los papeles son de Tomás.*

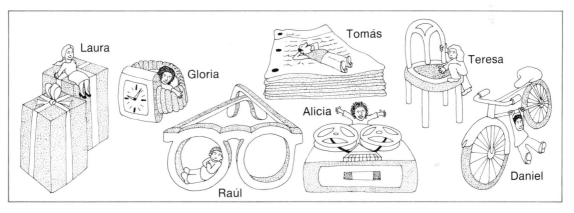

E Restate the following sentences, making the italicized elements plural. Make any other necessary changes.

■ⅼⅼ   Es mi *lápiz.*   *Son mis lápices.*

1. Es mi *silla.*
2. Es tu *calculadora,* ¿verdad?
3. El *disco* es de Mario.
4. Es su *reloj.*
5. La *novela* es de Sara.
6. Es tu *cuaderno.*

F Tell the birthday of each of the following persons.

1. Mi cumpleaños es el . . .
2. El cumpleaños de mi amigo [David] es el . . .
3. El cumpleaños de mi amiga [Carmen] es el . . .
4. El cumpleaños de mi profesor/profesora es el . . .

G   Supply the missing question words to complete the following conversational exchanges. Use *¿qué?* *¿quién?* *¿cómo?* *¿dónde?* *¿cuándo?* or *¿por qué?*

1. ¿____ es el profesor?
   — Es muy inteligente.

2. ¿____ es tu clase favorita?
   — Porque el profesor es bueno.

3. ¿____ es?
   — Un regalo para Juan.

4. ¿____ es tu cumpleaños?
   — El primero de diciembre.

5. ¿____ es esa chica?
   — María Sánchez.

6. ¿____ vive Rosa?
   — En San Antonio.

Vocabulario

SUSTANTIVOS

el año   year
la bicicleta   bicycle
la calculadora   calculator
el cassette   cassette
el cumpleaños   birthday
el disco   record
el empleo   job
la fiesta   party, festivity
el joven, la joven   young person
los lentes   eyeglasses
el mes   month
la novela   novel
la oficina   office
el regalo   gift
el reloj   wristwatch
el teléfono   telephone

VERBOS

buscar   to look for; **busco** I'm looking for
llamar   to call
ser: son   they are
trabajar   to work

OTRAS PALABRAS

ahí   there
ahora   now
casi   almost
contigo   with you
¿de quién?   whose?
del   of the
entonces   then
entre   between, among
estos, estas   these
fantástico, -a   fantastic
mis   my
o   or
para   for, in order to

pero   but
primero, -a   first
quizás   perhaps
sus   her, his
tus   your
un, una   a (an)

LOS MESES DEL AÑO

enero   julio
febrero   agosto
marzo   septiembre
abril   octubre
mayo   noviembre
junio   diciembre

EXPRESIONES

buena idea   good idea
¡caramba!   gosh! good grief!
claro   of course
¿cuántos años tienes?   how old are you?
cumplir … años   to be … years old; **cumple … años** he/she'll be … years old
feliz cumpleaños   happy birthday
gracias   thanks, thank you; **muchas gracias**   thank you very much
hasta pronto   see you soon
¿me prestas …?   can you lend me …?
¡me tomas el pelo!   you're pulling my leg!
¡no me digas!   you don't say! don't tell me!
no puedo   I can't
¡no te creo!   I don't believe you!
¡oye!   hey! listen!
por favor   please
puedes (+ *inf.*)   you can
¡qué bueno!   how nice! great!
¿qué le compro?   what shall I buy her/him?
¡qué suerte!   what luck!
recuerdo   I remember
tener … años   to be … years old
yo también   me too

LOS NÚMEROS DE 13 A 31

trece   13
catorce   14
quince   15
dieciséis   16
diecisiete   17
dieciocho   18
diecinueve   19
veinte   20
veintiuno   21
veintidós   22
treinta   30
treinta y uno   31

capítulo 4

En casa

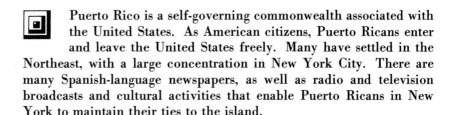

Puerto Rico is a self-governing commonwealth associated with the United States. As American citizens, Puerto Ricans enter and leave the United States freely. Many have settled in the Northeast, with a large concentration in New York City. There are many Spanish-language newspapers, as well as radio and television broadcasts and cultural activities that enable Puerto Ricans in New York to maintain their ties to the island.

¡Aló! and ¡bueno! are commonly used in Latin America to answer the phone. ¡Diga! or ¡dígame! is used principally in Spain.

Llaman por teléfono

Enrique Fuentes lives in New York City with his family. He answers the telephone. A neighbor, Mr. Pérez, wants to speak to Enrique's father.

ENRIQUE	¡Aló!
SR. PÉREZ	Soy el señor Pérez. ¿Quién habla? ¿Enrique?
ENRIQUE	Sí. Buenas tardes, señor Pérez. ¿Cómo está usted?
SR. PÉREZ	Bien, gracias. ¿Está tu padre en casa?
ENRIQUE	No. Está en Puerto Rico. Vuelve el domingo.
SR. PÉREZ	Muy bien. Llamo el domingo entonces.
ENRIQUE	Hasta luego, Sr. Pérez.

Comprehension check: ¿Quién habla? ¿Cómo está el Sr. Pérez? ¿Quién es el Sr. Fuentes? ¿Dónde está?

extensión

Have students repeat Act. A, using *tú*. See *Gramática* for contrast of *tú* and *usted*.

A. As you enter the school cafeteria, one of your teachers greets you and asks how you are. Are you fine, or just so-so?

▪▥ Hola, [Carmen], ¿cómo estás°?

Bien, gracias. ¿Y usted?
No muy bien.
Regular°, ¿y usted, [señor]?
Estoy cansado/cansada°.

B. You're working part-time in a law firm. A client comes in and asks for Mr. González. Give the information requested.

▪▥ ¿Está el Sr. González?

Sí, un momento°, por favor.
No, no está aquí.
Está en casa.
Vuelve [el martes].

C. The doorbell rings. It's a boy asking for your younger brother, who is not at home. Find out his name, tell him when your brother will be in, and say good-by.

Tú: Buenas . . .
No, . . . ¿Cómo te . . . ?
A las . . .
Hasta . . .

Un chico: Hola, ¿está . . . ?
Me . . . ¿Cuándo . . . ?
Muy . . . Gracias.
. . .

Fotos de familia

Daniel shows his photo album to his friend Fernando.

Aquí está mi familia. En esta foto están papá, mamá y el tío Ignacio.

¡Mira esta foto!
Es mi perro Sultán.

Aquí están mis hermanos con unos amigos. Manuel es mi hermano mayor y Cristina es mi hermana menor.

Estoy muy contento aquí, ¿verdad? Es mi bicicleta nueva.

extensión

A. Tell a classmate how many people there are in your family and how many brothers and sisters you have.

◼▮▮ ¿Cuántas personas hay en tu familia?

Hay [seis]. Tengo [dos hermanos y una hermana].

B. You're looking at a friend's photo album. He/she shows you a favorite picture that you think is terrible. Do you tell your friend what you really think, or do you try to be polite?

◼▮▮ Mira esta foto. Es bonita°, ¿verdad?

Sí. Es bonita.
¡Qué interesante!
No está mal°.
Pues, no. Es fea°.

¡Cállate!

It's breakfast time at the Romero's. Roberto isn't feeling well today.

MADRE Buenos días, chicos. ¿Qué tal?
ROBERTO Yo muy mal, mamá. Estoy resfriado. ¡A . . . chú!
ELENA ¡Ay, pobrecito! ¡Lo siento! ¿Y tu examen de álgebra?
ROBERTO *(In a whisper to Elena)* ¡Cállate, tonta!
MADRE ¿Tienes examen, Roberto? ¡Pues, al colegio!

extensión

Act out dialogue, once activities have been mastered. Encourage variation of lines.

A. Ask a classmate who has been absent recently how he/she is feeling today.

   ▪▥ ¿Cómo estás hoy?

   Bien, ¿y tú?
   Mejor°, gracias.
   Un poco resfriado/resfriada.
   Estoy muy mal.

B. A friend isn't feeling well. Sympathize with her/him.

   ▪▥ ¡Ay! Estoy muy mal.

   ¡Pobrecito!/¡Pobrecita!
   ¡Qué lástima!°
   ¿Verdad? ¿Qué tienes?°
   Lo siento.

C. Your brother has just discovered that you received a zero on an exam. You're afraid his loud exclamation will be heard by your parents. How do you react?

   ▪▥ ¿Cero en el examen?

   ¡Cállate, tonto!
   ¡Caramba! Siempre° hablas
      demasiado.
   No importa.°

Spanish-speaking families generally have strong family ties. The term **familia** usually refers to the "extended family" and includes mother, father, and children, plus grandparents, aunts, uncles, and cousins. Social gatherings and family celebrations frequently include numerous relatives, as well as members of the immediate family. Grandparents often live in the home of one of their children and share in the rearing of their grandchildren. An aunt or uncle may also live in the household. Young adults traditionally remain in their parents' home until marriage.

La familia de Marta Centeno

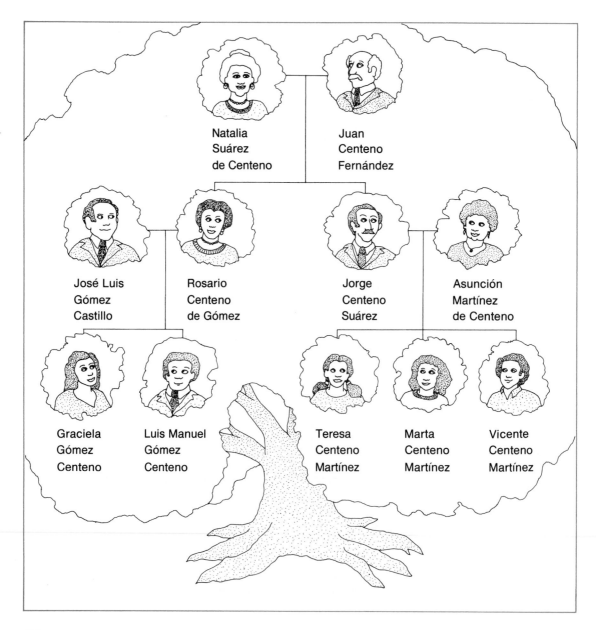

Optional: Use transparency to point out each family member as you read text.

Comprehension check: ¿Quién soy? ¿Cuántos hermanos tengo? ¿Cómo se llama mi hermana? ¿Quiénes son mis padres? ¿Quiénes son mis tíos?

Assignment: Have students prepare their own imaginary or real family tree, using two last names for each family member. Have students give an oral description of each person.

Marta Centeno introduces her family.

Yo soy Marta Centeno Martínez. Tengo dos **hermanos,** Vicente y Teresa. Mis **padres** son Jorge y Asunción Centeno. Mis **tíos** son Rosario y José Luis Gómez. Sus **hijos** son mis **primos.** Mi **prima** se llama Graciela y mi **primo** Luis Manuel. Nuestros **abuelos** son Natalia y Juan Centeno.

la abuela	grandmother	**la hermana**	sister
el abuelo	grandfather	**el hermano**	brother
los abuelos	grandparents		
		la hija	daughter
la madre	mother	**el hijo**	son
el padre	father	**los hijos**	children
los padres	parents		
		la prima	cousin *(female)*
la tía	aunt	**el primo**	cousin *(male)*
el tío	uncle		

A masculine plural noun is used to refer to two or more persons of different gender. For example, **los hermanos** may mean *brothers and sisters* as well as *brothers.*

A   Look at the family tree on page 66. Pretend that you are Luis Manuel, and identify five members of your family.

▬│| *Graciela es mi hermana. Mi padre se llama . . .*

B   Describe a member of your own family. Give information such as the person's name, age, relationship to you, and tell what he/she is like.

▬│| *Mi hermano menor se llama Miguel. Tiene once años y es muy alto.*

C   Find out from a classmate how her/his family is doing. Your classmate should reply with information about one or two family members.

▬│| ¿Cómo está tu familia?   *Bien. Mis padres . . .*

Spanish family names are usually composed of two last **names.** For example, in the name **Luisa Martínez Caso, Martínez** is the father's surname and **Caso** is the mother's surname. Sometimes the word **y** or a hyphen is used between the two last names. In conversation, the father's surname is often said alone, but both names are frequently used in written documents.

When a woman marries, she generally keeps her father's name only and adds her husband's surname, using **de** to join the two names. For example, Luisa's mother would probably use the compound surname **Caso de Martínez.**

capítulo 4   **67**

¿Qué tal?

Game: Have volunteers pantomime *Estudio de palabras* items. Class must guess each item.

Tengo dolor de cabeza.

Tengo fiebre.

Tengo dolor de estómago.

Estoy enferma.

Estoy resfriada.

Estoy mal.

D You're in the nurse's office. Describe how you feel to the nurse, using some of the expressions above.

■▥   ¿Estás enfermo/enferma?   *Sí, [tengo fiebre].*

E A friend doesn't feel well. Find out what's wrong and then sympathize with her/him. You can start by asking *¿Cómo estás?, ¿Qué tal?,* or *¿Qué tienes?*

———— Pronunciación y ortografía ————

palabras claves ‖ [k]   casa, **qu**ince, **k**ilo

Trabalenguas for practice of [k] sound: *Claudio clavó un clavo, un clavo clavó Claudio.*

The Spanish [k] sound is unaspirated. It is produced without the puff of air that often accompanies English [k]. Spanish [k] is spelled **c** (before **a, o, u,** or a consonant) and **qu** (before **e** or **i**). It is also spelled **k** in a few words of foreign origin, such as **kilo** and **kilómetro.**

A Listen and then repeat the following words after your teacher. Be sure that you produce the [k] sound without a puff of air.

casa	clase	**qué**
con	claro	**quién**
cuatro	cabeza	**aquí**
como	colegio	**quince**

B Read the following sentences aloud. Pay special attention to the [k] sound.

1. Carmen habla con cuatro chicas.
2. Carlos tiene cinco clases el miércoles.
3. ¿De quién es el cuaderno? ¿de Raquel, quizás?

stress

Spanish words of more than one syllable have a definite stress, or emphasis, on one of the syllables. The following three guidelines will help you know what part of a word to stress in Spanish.

1. Most words that end in a vowel or in **-n** or **-s** are stressed on the next-to-last syllable: do · **min** · go, **bue** · nas, e · **xa** · men.

2. Words that end in a consonant other than **-n** or **-s** are stressed on the last syllable: fa · **vor,** ver · **dad,** a · **bril.**

3. Words that are pronounced contrary to these guidelines have a written accent mark (´) over the vowel of the stressed syllable: pa · **pá, lá** · piz, sim · **pá** · ti · co.

C Pronounce the following words carefully. The stressed syllables are indicated in boldface letters.

a · **le** · gre	se · **ñor**	**fá** · cil
can · **sa** · do	es · pa · **ñol**	sim · **pá** · ti · ca
en · **fer** · mo	pa · **pel**	di · **fí** · cil
her · **ma** · na	ver · **dad**	te · **lé** · fo · no
mar · tes	tra · ba · **jar**	**lá** · piz
e · **xa** · men	us · **ted**	qui · **zás**

De tal palo, tal astilla.

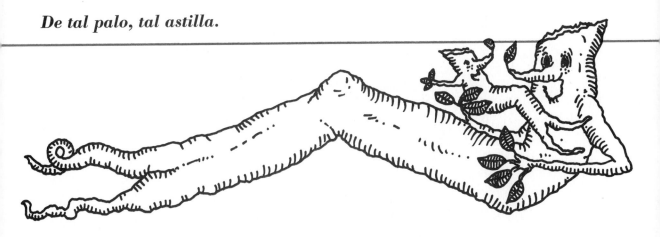

Proverb: Like father, like son; A chip off the old block.

Gramática

Tú and usted

Optional: Use photos or visuals. Have students choose between *tú* and *usted* as appropriate form of address for each person shown.

A Spanish speaker must make a choice between **tú** and **usted** when addressing an individual. In general, the use of **usted** implies a more formal relationship than **tú**. **Tú** is normally used between close friends or relatives, between students, or by an adult when speaking to a child. **Usted** is normally used by a young person when speaking to an adult, unless the adult is a close relative.

If you are not sure whether to use **usted** or **tú, usted** is safer until the person addressed indicates that you should use **tú.**

A Would you use *tú* or *usted* to address the following people?

▪⦀ tu profesora de español   *usted*

1. tu perro
2. tu mamá
3. tu abuela
4. un amigo de tu padre

5. la Sra. Molina
6. el Sr. García
7. un hermano
8. un amigo

B Ask how each of the following persons is feeling. Use *¿Cómo está usted?* or *¿Cómo estás?*, as appropriate.

Expand Ex. B by having students respond to questions.

▪⦀ Teresa   *¿Cómo estás?*

1. Sr. García
2. Srta. Jiménez
3. Enrique

4. tío Carlos
5. Cristina
6. tu papá

Subject pronouns

Cue with visuals for practice of subject pronouns. Ask which subject pronoun would be used to address or to talk about each person or group.

SINGULAR	
yo	I
tú	you *(familiar)*
usted	you *(formal)*
él	he
ella	she

PLURAL	
nosotros	we
nosotras	we
ustedes	you *(familiar and formal)*
ellos	they
ellas	they

¡David y Carmen! ¿Cómo están **ustedes?**

Vosotros forms are explained on p. 76.

In Latin America the plural form **ustedes** is used to address more than one person, whether the relationship is formal or familiar.

MASCULINE
Nosotros (David y Ana) estamos bien.
Ellos son David y Ana.

FEMININE
Nosotras (Ana y Carmen) estamos bien.
Ellas son Ana y Carmen.

The plural forms **nosotros** and **ellos** may refer to an all-male group or to a group that includes at least one male. **Nosotras** and **ellas** refer exclusively to all-female groups.

C Tell whether you would use *tú, usted,* or *ustedes* to address the following persons.

▪▥ tus tíos   *ustedes*

1. tu profesor de música
2. la Sra. Blanco
3. Ana y Eduardo
4. tus amigos Roberto y Esteban
5. tus padres
6. tu primo Andrés

D A friend tells you some news about yourself and various friends. Express disbelief, using an appropriate subject pronoun in your responses.

Vary the exclamations: *¡me tomas el pelo! ¿verdad? ¡caramba! ¡lo siento!* Have the students supply original sentences.

▪▥ Ángela está en Nueva York.   *¿Ella? ¡No me digas!*

1. Julio tiene cinco perros.
2. Tú y yo estamos cansados.
3. Mis padres son bilingües.
4. Ernesto tiene fiebre y dolor de cabeza.
5. Ana habla tres idiomas.
6. Cristina y Marisa son primas.
7. Rafael y Antonio son de San Diego.

Present tense of **estar**

Game: Play *Ta Te Ti* (tic-tac-toe) with forms of *estar*. See Teacher's Guide for games.

Remind students that *ser* is used for physical and personality traits, origin, and possession. Contrast of *ser* and *estar* is presented in *capítulo 6*.

	ESTAR
yo	estoy
tú	estás
él, ella, usted	está
nosotros, nosotras	estamos
ellos, ellas, ustedes	están

Mi papá **está** en Puerto Rico.　　My father *is* in Puerto Rico.
Ana **está** enferma hoy.　　Ana *is* sick today.
¿**Estás** contento?　　*Are you* happy?

Estar *(to be)* is used to express location, health, or moods and feelings.

E　You're tracing your family tree. Ask your mother the present location of various family members.

■III　la tía Isabel / México　　Tú: *¿Dónde está la tía Isabel?*
　　　　　　　　　　　　　　　Mamá: *Está en México.*

1. los primos Muñoz / Los Ángeles
2. el abuelo / San Juan
3. las tías de papá / Chicago
4. el primo Federico / Miami
5. los hermanos del abuelo / San Antonio
6. el tío Andrés / San Diego

F Tell how everyone is feeling today. Use the appropriate form of *estar* and *muy bien, bien, regular,* or *mal.*

Expand: S¹ ¿Cómo está Gabriel? S² Está enfermo, contento, mal, resfriado.

■||| Gabriel   *Gabriel está [bien] hoy.*

1. Ana y Carlos
2. ustedes
3. tú

4. Manuel y yo
5. yo
6. Lucía

Agreement of adjectives

SINGULAR	PLURAL
Jaime está contento.	Jaime y Pedro están contentos.
Elisa está contenta.	Elisa y Pilar están contentas.
Mi padre es moreno.	Mis padres son morenos.

Most Spanish adjectives have four forms: two singular forms (**-o, -a**) and two plural forms (**-os, -as**). A four-form adjective agrees with the noun it modifies in both gender and number.

The plural of adjectives is formed by adding **-s** after a vowel, and **-es** after a consonant. The masculine plural form of the adjective is used to modify two or more nouns of different gender.

G Say that the following people are feeling tired today.

Have students use an appropriate response: lo siento, ¡qué lástima!, ¡caramba!

■||| Julio   *Julio está cansado hoy.*

1. yo
2. Juan y David

3. la profesora
4. Teresa y Carmen

5. Nicolás
6. mis primas

Assignment: Have students write 8 original sentences, using 4 adjectives ending in -o and 4 not ending in -o.

SINGULAR	PLURAL
El disco es interesante.	Los discos son interesantes.
La clase es interesante.	Las clases son interesantes.

A singular adjective that ends in a letter other than **-o** or **-a** has two forms: one singular and one plural. A two-form adjective agrees with the noun it modifies in number only.

H Say that two of the following persons or objects fit the description given.

Personalize: Have students describe classmates, friends, school subjects, or possessions.

■||| Mi hermana es alegre.   *Mis dos hermanas son alegres.*

1. Mi amiga es bilingüe.
2. El profesor es bueno.
3. La clase es difícil.
4. El libro es interesante.

5. El chico es estudioso.
6. El estudiante es inteligente.
7. El examen es fácil.
8. La bicicleta es nueva.

I   Your father asks how your friends are doing. Tell him, choosing from the adjectives *enfermo, cansado, contento,* and *resfriado.*

■III   Miguel y Diana   Papá: *¿Cómo están Miguel y Diana?*
    Tú: *Están [resfriados].*

1. Pablo y Anita
2. Alicia y Susana
3. Rosario y su amiga
4. Rafael y Alberto

5. Roberto y Carlos
6. Marcos y su hermana
7. Carmen y José
8. Marta y Luis

¡vamos a hablar!   You're talking on the telephone with your grandmother. Tell her how everyone in the family is doing.

¿Cómo están ustedes?   *Mamá está bien, pero papá . . .*

Position of adjectives

María es una chica **bonita.**   María is a *pretty* girl.
Tengo dos discos **nuevos.**   I have two *new* records.
¿Es Fernando el chico **alto?**   Is Fernando the *tall* boy?

In noun phrases, descriptive adjectives usually follow the noun they modify.

J   You have a part-time job as a sales clerk in a department store. Assure some customers about the quality of the following items.

V: Have students describe objects, using other adjectives.
S¹: *¿Cómo es [la mesa]?* S²: *Es [bonita].*

■III   la mesa   Cliente: *¿Es buena la mesa?*
    Tú: *Sí. Es una mesa muy buena.*

1. el reloj
2. el disco
3. la calculadora

4. la bicicleta
5. la cesta
6. el bolígrafo

7. la grabadora
8. el cuaderno
9. la silla

Plural indefinite articles

Hay **unos** perros aquí.   There are *some* dogs here.
Busco **unas** sillas.   I'm looking for *some* chairs.

The plural forms of the indefinite articles **un** and **una** are **unos** and **unas** respectively. **Unos** is used with a masculine plural noun and **unas** is used with a feminine plural noun to express an indefinite quantity or number.

K   Point out to a classmate where to find some of the following items.

◼▮▮   libros / mesa   *Hay unos libros en la mesa.*

1. sillas / clase
2. papeles / silla
3. lápices / mesa
4. cuadernos / mesa
5. mesas / clase
6. fotos / mesa

En resumen

Subject pronouns (A–D)

SINGULAR		PLURAL	
yo	I	nosotros	we *(m. or m. + f.)*
		nosotras	we *(f. only)*
tú	you *(familiar)*	vosotros	you *(familiar)*
		vosotras	you *(familiar)*
usted	you *(formal)*	ustedes	you *(familiar and formal)*
él	he	ellos	they *(m. or m. + f.)*
ella	she	ellas	they *(f. only)*

1. **Tú** and **usted** both express *you* in the singular. **Tú** is the familiar form of address, and **usted** is the formal form. **Usted** is often abbreviated as **Ud.** or **Vd.**

2. **Ustedes** is used in most parts of Latin America to address more than one person, whether the relationship is formal or familiar. **Ustedes** is often abbreviated as **Uds.** or **Vds.**

    Vosotros and **vosotras** are used primarily in Spain for familiar *you* plural. In Latin America, the **vosotros**-form is sometimes used in literary works.

    In this book, the **ustedes**-form is used for *you* plural. The **vosotros**-forms corresponding to pronouns, possessive adjectives, and verbs are presented in the *en resumen* sections and *appendixes.*

3. **Nosotras** and **ellas** refer to all-female groups. **Nosotros** and **ellos** may refer to an all-male group or to a group that includes at least one male.

Present tense of estar (E, F)

	ESTAR
yo	estoy
tú	estás
él, ella, usted	está
nosotros, nosotras	estamos
vosotros, vosotras	estáis
ellos, ellas, ustedes	están

The verb **estar** *(to be)* is used to express location, health, moods, and feelings. The present-tense forms of **estar** are irregular.

Agreement and position of adjectives (G–J)

	FOUR-FORM ADJECTIVES		TWO-FORM ADJECTIVES	
	Masculine	Feminine	Masculine	Feminine
Singular	contento	contenta	fácil	fácil
Plural	contentos	contentas	fáciles	fáciles

1. Four-form adjectives have two singular forms **(-o, -a)** and two plural forms **(-os, -as).** They agree with the noun they modify in number and gender: **Las casas son bonitas.**
2. Two-form adjectives have one singular and one plural form. They agree with the noun they modify in number: **Mis padres son bilingües.**
3. Groups that include at least one male are described with masculine plural adjectives: **Marta, Alicia y Pablo están contentos.**
4. In a noun phrase, a descriptive adjective usually follows the noun: **Tengo unos discos fantásticos.**

Indefinite articles (K)

	SINGULAR	PLURAL
Masculine	un perro	unos perros
Feminine	una bicicleta	unas bicicletas

The plural form of **un** is **unos,** and the plural form of **una** is **unas.** **Unos** and **unas** usually mean *some.*

Repaso

A   Teresa and Alfredo meet each other in the park. Complete their conversation. Then create a second, similar conversation between Teresa and Mr. Fuentes.

Teresa: ..., Alfredo. ¿Cómo ...?
Alfredo: ... ¿Y tú?
Teresa: ...
Alfredo: Pues, ...
Teresa: Hasta ...

B   Describe six objects that you own, using the adjectives below.

bueno	**bonito**	**interesante**
nuevo	**feo**	**fantástico**

■ꟷ   *Tengo unos discos nuevos.*

■ꟷ   *Tengo una bicicleta buena.*

C   Tell how the following people feel or what they are like, using the words provided.

■ꟷ   mi hermana / tener / fiebre   *Mi hermana tiene fiebre.*

1. Rafael / tener / dolor de estómago
2. Alejandro y Marta / estar / cansados
3. tus primos / ser / inteligentes
4. mi amiga Raquel / ser / bonita
5. Cristina / tener / dolor de cabeza
6. Alberto y su amigo / estar / enfermos
7. Pilar / ser / alta y rubia

D   Pluralize the italicized noun phrases in the following sentences. Be sure to make all necessary changes in verb and noun agreement.

■ꟷ   *Mi hermano* está aburrido.   *Mis hermanos están aburridos.*

1. *El libro* es de Miguel, ¿no?
2. Hay *una silla* en mi clase.
3. *Mi primo* es de San Diego.
4. *Tu hermana* está en casa, ¿verdad?
5. *El perro* es feo.
6. Hay *un cuaderno* en la oficina, ¿no?
7. *El amigo* de Martín está cansado.
8. *El estudiante* está contento.

E   Identify each family member's relationship to you, based on the following descriptions.

Assignment: Have students prepare short talks about real or imaginary family: *Tengo dos hermanos. Mi hermana Marta cumple . . . Es baja y morena. Mi hermano se llama . . . Tiene . . . Es . . .*

▪▐   Es la madre de tu papá.   *Es mi abuela.*   After each talk, ask class questions: *¿Quién habla? ¿Cuántos hermanos tiene? ¿Cómo se llaman? ¿Cuántos años . . . ? ¿Cómo es?*

1.   Es el hijo de tus padres.
2.   Es el hermano de tu madre.
3.   Son los hijos de tus tíos.
4.   Es el padre de un hermano de tu padre.
5.   Es la hija de la hermana de tu madre.

F   Tell how the following persons are feeling, using the correct form of *estar*. Be sure that each adjective agrees with the subject of the sentence.

▪▐   Sara y Marta / resfriado   *Sara y Marta están resfriadas.*

1.   Roberto / contento
2.   Adela y su hermana / cansado
3.   Tomás y Carlos / enfermo
4.   Ricardo y Maribel / resfriado
5.   su prima / contento
6.   Luisa y Miguel / enfermo

G React to the following sentences, choosing the most logical response from the list on the right.

1. ¡Aló!
2. ¿Qué tal?
3. ¡Eres muy feo, Jorge!
4. ¿Me prestas tu bicicleta?
5. Tienes mi calculadora, ¿verdad?
6. Estoy muy mal.
7. Tengo dolor de estómago.
8. Diego y Raquel son hermanos.

¡Cállate, tonto!
No puedo.
¿Ellos? No te creo.
No recuerdo.
Regular. ¿Y tú?
Pobrecito.
¿Está Antonio?
¡Qué lástima!
No importa.

Vocabulario

SUSTANTIVOS

la cabeza   head
la casa   house, home
el estómago   stomach
la familia   family
la fiebre   fever
la foto   photo
el perro   dog
la persona   person

VERBOS

estar   to be
hablar: habla   he/she
   speaks, is speaking
llamar: llamo   I('ll) call

OTRAS PALABRAS

bien   well
bonito, -a   pretty
cansado, -a   tired
contento, -a   happy, content
demasiado   too much
ellos, -as   they
enfermo, -a   sick
feo, -a   ugly
hasta   until
mal   badly
mayor   older
mejor   better
menor   younger
nosotros, -as   we
nuestro, -a   our
nuevo, -a   new
regular   so-so
siempre   always
unos, -as   some
usted   you
ustedes   you (*pl.*)

EXPRESIONES

¡aló!   hello (*telephone*)
¡ay!   *expresses pain, alarm, surprise*
¡cállate!   be quiet!
en casa   at home
estar resfriado, -a   to have a cold
¡mira!   look!
no está mal   it's not bad
no importa   it doesn't matter
¡pobrecito, -a!   poor thing!
¡qué lástima!   what a shame!
¿qué tal?   how are you?
¿qué tienes?   what's the matter?
tener dolor de cabeza   to have a headache
tener dolor de estómago   to have a stomachache
tener fiebre   to have a fever
¡tonto, -a!   silly! foolish (person)!
un momento   just a minute
vuelve   he/she returns

LA FAMILIA

la abuela   grandmother
el abuelo   grandfather
los abuelos   grandparents
la hermana   sister
el hermano   brother
la hija   daughter
el hijo   son
los hijos   children
la madre (mamá)   mother
el padre (papá)   father
los padres (papás)   parents
el primo, la prima   cousin
la tía   aunt
el tío   uncle

capítulo 5
Trabajo y pasatiempos

■ Chicago has attracted an increasing number of Spanish-speaking people in recent decades. The majority are Mexican Americans from the Southwest. There are also many Puerto Ricans, Cubans, and Central and South Americans. The presence of the Spanish community is evident not only in industry and business, but in the Hispanic traditions and holidays observed in Chicago. Mexican Independence Day on September 16 and Pan American Day on April 14 are occasions for large and festive celebrations in the city.

Warm-up: Ask personalized questions, re-entering material from previous chapters.

Comprehension check: For pilot: *¿Dónde vive? ¿Por qué viaja?* Mechanic: *¿Qué quiere ser? ¿Cuándo trabaja?* Pintor: *¿Cómo es?* Intérprete: *¿Por qué es intérprete?*, etc.

¿Qué quieres ser?

A reporter from a radio station in Chicago is interviewing people on the street about their careers. Here's what four persons say about themselves.

Vivo en Chicago pero viajo mucho porque soy piloto. Cuando viajo me gusta visitar ciudades nuevas. En mi tiempo libre miro televisión o escucho música.

Quiero ser mecánico y reparar carros. Para aprender, trabajo en el garaje de mi tío los fines de semana.

Quiero ser pintor. Soy una persona independiente y creadora. Me gusta pintar paisajes y trabajar al aire libre.

Soy intérprete porque hablo tres idiomas muy bien. Mi padre es de Alemania y mi madre es de España. Me gusta ayudar a personas de otros países.

extensión

A. Ask a classmate if he/she wants to be a pilot, a painter, a mechanic, or an interpreter.

■▥ ¿Quieres ser [piloto]?

Sí, quiero ser [piloto].
¿Yo? Todavía° no sé.
No. Quizás [intérprete].

B. Find out why your classmate wants to be a pilot, a painter, a mechanic, or an interpreter.

Game: Student panto-
mimes profession and
asks: S¹: ¿Qué quiero
ser? S²: Quieres ser
[pintor]. S¹: ¿Por qué
quiero . . .

■ⅠⅠ   ¿Por qué quieres ser   Porque me gusta [viajar].
          [piloto]?   Porque soy [independiente].
                                       Me gusta [visitar ciudades
                                          nuevas].

C. Tell a classmate what you do in your free time.

■ⅠⅠ   ¿Qué haces° en tu tiempo libre?   [Escribir° cartas°.]
                                            No mucho.
                                            Me gusta [leer°].

Comprehension check:
¿Cómo se llama?
¿Dónde vive? ¿Cuál
es su teléfono?, etc.

Personalize: Have stu-
dents fill out dittoed solicitud de empleo for
class discussion.

Solicitud de empleo

Jorge Castillo has filled out the following application for a part-time job in a grocery store.

SOLICITUD DE EMPLEO

Nombre: *Jorge Castillo Santos*

Dirección: *Avenida Michigan 618, Chicago*

Teléfono: *965-7428*   Fecha de nacimiento: *20/5/68*

Nombre del padre: *Andrés Castillo*   Ocupación: *policía*

Nombre de la madre: *Elena Santos de Castillo* Ocupación: *enfermera*

Escuela: *Benito Juárez*   Grado: *10*

Trabajo que solicita: *ayudante*

Experiencia: *No tengo experiencia*

Pasatiempos: *coleccionar monedas, correr, sacar fotos*

Recomendaciones:

Nombre: *Sr. Rubén Chávez*   Teléfono: *363-1542*

Nombre: *Sra. Irene García*   Teléfono: *684-2322*

extensión

A. Tell a classmate whether or not you're looking for a job.

■ⅠⅠ   ¿Buscas trabajo?   Sí, porque quiero ganar° dinero°.
                                Todavía no. Quizás en [enero].
                                Sí, pero no tengo experiencia.

Ask students whether they have jobs. Find out why they work: to provide spending money, to help with their education, purchase a car, etc. Point out that middle- and upper-class teens in Spanish-speaking countries generally do not work, partly because it could be taken as a sign that the parents are unable to provide for them.

B. A friend invites you to listen to records. Accept or decline.

◼⫼   ¿Quieres escuchar° discos?   Sí. Buena idea.
                                   De acuerdo°. ¿Cuándo?
                                   No puedo. Trabajo hoy.
                                   No. Prefiero° [correr].

C. Ask a classmate if he/she has a favorite pastime.

◼⫼   ¿Tienes un pasatiempo favorito?   Sí, [coleccionar monedas].
                                        Me gusta [sacar fotos].
                                        No, no tengo.

D. Your school newspaper is preparing a special series on student job preferences. Tell a reporter your name and address, what you want to do for a living, and why.

Reportero/a: ¿Cómo te llamas?   Tú: Me llamo . . .
             ¿Cuál es tu . . . ?   Mi dirección . . .
             ¿Qué . . . ?   Quiero ser . . .
             ¿Por qué?   Porque . . .

Ocupaciones

el mecánico
la mecánico

la enfermera
el enfermero

el ingeniero
la ingeniera

la abogada
el abogado

el obrero
la obrera

la pintora
el pintor

el dentista
la dentista

la intérprete
el intérprete

el piloto
la piloto

la policía
el policía

Explain that distinction
between male and fe-
male is sometimes made
by saying *la mujer
mecánico/policía.*

Nouns of occupation ending in **-e** or **-ista** are usually the same in the masculine and feminine forms. Notice that **mecánico, piloto,** and **policía** are also the same in the masculine and feminine forms.

A Ask a friend the occupation of some of the members of her/his family. Choose from the jobs listed on page 86.

Refer students to supplemental list of occupations in Appendix.

■⫶ ¿Qué es tu papá?   *Es intérprete.*

■⫶ ¿Qué es tu mamá?   *Es abogada.*

B Take a poll to find out what your classmates want to be. Use the jobs given on page 86.

Expand: Have students ask *¿por qué?* or use for next class warm-up.

■⫶ ¿Qué quieres ser?   *Quiero ser . . .*

Los números de 32 a 99

Quickly review numbers 0 to 31 before introducing new items.

Game: Play *Ojo* with numbers 1 to 99. (See p. 47 for instructions.) Or have contest with equations.

32 = treinta y dos	37 = treinta y siete	60 = sesenta
33 = treinta y tres	38 = treinta y ocho	70 = setenta
34 = treinta y cuatro	39 = treinta y nueve	80 = ochenta
35 = treinta y cinco	40 = cuarenta	90 = noventa
36 = treinta y seis	50 = cincuenta	

In Spanish numbers above 30, tens are connected to units with **y: cuarenta y uno, cincuenta y dos, noventa y nueve.**

C Find out from a friend the ages of various members of her/his family. Use real or fictitious ages.

■⫶ ¿Cuántos años tiene tu [abuelo]?   *Tiene [sesenta] años.*

The image of women as mothers and housewives has long been a tradition in Hispanic countries. Today, the social scene is changing and more and more Hispanic women are choosing professions and careers once held chiefly by men. Many Hispanic women are doctors, lawyers, architects, and executives. The increased presence of women in the work force is creating changes in the Spanish language. For example, forms such as **la abogada, la presidenta,** or **la presidente** are recent adaptations of the language.

Esta señora es abogada.

La estatura y el peso

ft/in	m/cm
4'7"	1,39½
4'8"	1,42
4'9"	1,44½
4'10"	1,47
4'11"	1,49½
5'	1,52
5'1"	1,54½
5'2"	1,57
5'3"	1,59½
5'4"	1,62
5'5"	1,64½
5'6"	1,68
5'7"	1,70½
5'8"	1,73
5'9"	1,75½
5'10"	1,78
5'11"	1,80½
6'	1,83
6'1"	1,85½
6'2"	1,88

Mido 1 (metro), 57 (centímetros).   Peso 60 kilos.

D It's weigh-in time for a sports competition. Tell your coach how much you weigh. Divide your weight in half to get your approximate weight in kilos.

■‖   *Peso [cincuenta y seis kilos].*

E Find your height in meters and centimeters on the chart, then tell it to a classmate.

Equivalents: 1 in. = 2.5 cm., 1 kilo = 2.2 lbs. To give height, students may say: *Mido uno (con) cincuenta y siete.*

■‖   *Mido [uno, cincuenta y siete].*

Pronunciación y ortografía

palabra clave

‖ [ch] **chico**

In Spanish, the [ch] sound is similar to [ch] in English *church.* Spanish **ch** is a compound letter and comes after **c** in the Spanish alphabet. In a dictionary, words beginning with **ch,** like **chico,** are found after the group of words beginning with **c.**

A Read the following sentences aloud to practice the **[ch]** sound.

1. Conchita escucha música.
2. Ese chico cumple dieciocho años.
3. Esa chica estudia mucho.
4. Luisa Ochoa tiene muchos amigos.

silent h

The letter **h** does not represent a sound in Spanish. It is silent, as in English *honest*. The letter **h** must be written for correct spelling, however.

B   Listen and repeat the following words after your teacher.

hoy	hola	hijo	hermana
hay	hermano	hija	historia

C   Read the following sentences. Remember that *h* is silent.

1. Mi hermana habla con tu hermano.
2. ¡Hola! Hablas inglés, ¿verdad?
3. Mi hijo tiene clase de historia.

Use Exercise B or C as a *dictado*, having several students write on board for quick correction.

linking

In Spanish speech, words are generally pronounced in breath groups. Words spoken within a breath group tend to be linked together.

Papá_está_en casa.   **¿No_hablas_inglés?**

The final consonant or vowel of a word tends to be linked to the initial vowel sound of the word that follows. Two identical vowels or two identical consonants tend to be pronounced as one. Because **h** is silent, linking occurs with the vowel that follows it.

D   Read the following sentences aloud. Link the words as indicated.

1. Elena habla_inglés y español.
2. Tengo_una clase de_inglés_a las_siete.
3. Quiero_ayudar_a mi hermano.
4. Los hermanos de_Eduardo trabajan_en_un hospital.
5. El_estudiante_español se llama Luis_Antonio.
6. Está_en la_oficina con_una_amiga.

Optional: Have students read chapter dialogues and indicate where linking occurs.

No es tan fiero el león como lo pintan.

Present tense of **ser**

SER	
yo	soy
tú	eres
él, ella, usted	es
nosotros, nosotras	somos
ellos, ellas, ustedes	son

Remind students of uses of *ser:* physical and personality traits, possession, origin, occupation.

You have already used all the present-tense forms of **ser** except **somos.** The forms of **ser** are irregular.

El señor López es dentista.   Mr. López is *a* dentist.
Mi tía es **una** dentista buena.   My aunt is *a* good dentist.

Notice that in Spanish, the indefinite article is omitted before an unmodified noun of occupation that follows **ser.**

A   Agree or disagree with Lucía's questions and statements about you and your twin brother.

■ꟼ   Son estudiantes, ¿verdad?   *Sí, somos estudiantes.*
     (No, no somos estudiantes.)

V: Have students give different reply for each twin: *Yo soy alto, pero él es bajo. Yo soy simpático, pero él es antipático.*

1. Ustedes son de aquí, ¿no?   4. Son simpáticos.
2. Son muy altos.   5. ¿Son abogados?
3. Son bilingües.   6. Son de Santa Bárbara.

B   Imagine that you're an exchange student in Mexico. Answer some questions from students at the school you're attending.

■ꟼ   ¿Eres de los Estados   *Sí, soy de los Estados Unidos.*
     Unidos? (sí)

1. ¿Qué es tu papá? (ingeniero)
2. ¿Qué es tu mamá? (policía)
3. ¿Cuántos son ustedes? (cuatro)
4. ¿Tus hermanos son estudiantes? (sí)
5. ¿Cuáles son tus clases favoritas? (español y biología)
6. ¿Eres bilingüe? (sí)
7. ¿Cómo son tus amigos? (simpáticos)
8. ¿Cómo es el colegio en tu país? (difícil)

Citizens and residents of many Hispanic countries are required to carry identification cards. The **cédula** or **tarjeta de identidad** is a national I.D. issued at the age of eighteen or twenty-one, depending on the country. The **cédula** or **tarjeta de identidad** bears a person's name, place of residence and other personal data, thumb print, and photo. Students are often given school identification cards that entitle them to reduced fares or free rides on public transportation, and discounts or free admission to museums, concerts, or the theater.

Possessive adjectives **nuestro** and **su**

SINGULAR	PLURAL
nuestro carro	**nuestros** carros
nuestra casa	**nuestras** casas

The possessive adjective **nuestro** *(our)* has four forms. It agrees in number and gender with the noun it modifies.

SINGULAR	PLURAL
su carro	**sus** carros
su casa	**sus** casas

Practice all possessive adjectives with objects or visuals. Show item, student tells possessor: (cuaderno), tú.
S: Es mi cuaderno.

The possessive adjective **su** has two forms and agrees with the noun it modifies in number only. **Su** and **sus** may mean *his, her, its, your,* and *their,* depending on the context.

C   Ricardo asks you if the following items belong to you and your brother. Respond in the affirmative or negative.

■III   ¿Es su perro?   *Sí, es nuestro perro.*
(No, no es nuestro perro.)

1. ¿Es su carro?
2. ¿Son sus bicicletas?
3. ¿Es su casa?

4. ¿Son sus papeles?
5. ¿Son sus tíos?
6. ¿Es su hermana?

D   Verify the owners of the following items. Use the correct form of *su* in your responses.

■||| ¿Los libros son de Julio?   *Sí, son sus libros.*

1. ¿El carro es de Miguel y Andrés?
2. ¿La foto es de Ana?
3. ¿Los discos son de tus primos?
4. ¿La oficina es de la profesora?
5. ¿Los libros son de esa chica?
6. ¿Los lentes son de Jaime?
7. ¿El garaje es de sus padres?
8. ¿El reloj es de Marta?

E   Correct each of the following statements, using the cues indicated.

■||| Los tíos de Elena son de Cuba.   *No. Sus tíos son de Puerto Rico.*
        (Puerto Rico)

Assignment: Have students write ten personal statements using forms of *nuestro*. In class student reads statement aloud and other students respond: S¹: *Es nuestro perro.* S²: *Ah, es su perro, ¿verdad?*

1. El amigo de Juan tiene fiebre. (dolor de cabeza)
2. Los primos de Raúl están en Nueva York. (Los Ángeles)
3. El hermano de Santiago es policía. (obrero)
4. La abuela de Beatriz está bien. (enferma)
5. Los amigos de Manuel están bien. (resfriados)
6. Los padres de Ana son dentistas. (abogados)

Querer + infinitive

¿Qué **quieres ser?**   What do *you want to be?*
Quiero ser abogado.   *I want to be* a lawyer.
Carmen **quiere viajar.**   Carmen *wants to travel.*

A form of the verb **querer** followed by a dependent infinitive can be used to express what you want to do or be.

F   Tell what each person wants to do.

Optional: Have students bring cutouts to show what various people want to do, then give appropriate sentences: boy reading Spanish dictionary: *Carlos quiere aprender español.*

■||| Pilar / leer   *Pilar quiere leer.*

1. yo / comprar un regalo
2. Marta / mirar televisión
3. mi padre / reparar el carro
4. tú / visitar México
5. tú / escuchar música
6. yo / aprender inglés
7. Julio / estudiar
8. Teresa / buscar empleo

G   You're serving as a hospital volunteer. You ask a patient if he/she wants to do something, but get a negative reply to everything.

■Ⅲ   leer un libro   — *¿Quiere usted leer un libro?*
   — *No, no quiero leer un libro.*

1. mirar televisión
2. escuchar música
3. mirar fotos

4. hablar con el enfermero
5. pintar un paisaje
6. hablar con una amiga

¡vamos a hablar!   Invite a friend to join you in an activity after school. If he/she isn't free, invite someone else.

¿Quieres [escuchar discos]?   — Sí. De acuerdo.
   (No. Prefiero [correr].)

Present tense of regular **-ar** verbs

	HABLAR
yo	hablo
tú	hablas
él, ella, usted	habla
nosotros, nosotras	hablamos
ellos, ellas, ustedes	hablan

After presentation of *-ar* verbs, have class list known *-ar* verbs. Have one student write on board. Elicit original sentences.

The present tense of regular **-ar** verbs is formed by adding a set of endings to the verb stem (the infinitive minus **-ar**). A verb ending must agree with the subject of the sentence whether or not the subject is expressed.

Hablamos español.	*We speak* Spanish.
	We are speaking Spanish.
	We do speak Spanish.
¿Hablas español?	*Do you speak* Spanish?
	Are you speaking Spanish?
Luego **hablo** contigo.	*I'll speak* to you later.

In Spanish, the present tense tells what is happening or what generally happens. It can also be used with future meaning. A single present-tense form has several English equivalents.

H Say what you and some of your friends usually do after school.

Chain drill: S¹: *Estudio español. ¿Y tú?* S²: *También estudio español.* Supply other statements.

■ⅢⅠ yo / estudiar español   *Estudio español.*

1. Pedro / mirar televisión
2. Inés / escuchar discos
3. tú / llamar por teléfono

4. mi hermana / ayudar a mi mamá
5. yo / hablar con mis amigos
6. tú / trabajar en una oficina

I Your father asks you what you're doing. Explain that it's not you, and that your sister María is doing what he asks about.

■ⅢⅠ mirar televisión   Papá: *¿Miras televisión?*
                           Tú: *Yo no. María mira televisión.*

1. sacar unas fotos
2. estudiar biología
3. escuchar discos
4. hablar con el abuelo

5. buscar el perro
6. reparar el reloj
7. pintar la mesa
8. ayudar a mamá

J Say that you and a friend are not doing any of the following activities.

■ⅢⅠ ¿Llaman a Guillermo?   *No, no llamamos a Guillermo.*

1. ¿Miran televisión?
2. ¿Escuchan música?
3. ¿Buscan unos papeles?
4. ¿Reparan la bicicleta?
5. ¿Trabajan en el garaje?
6. ¿Sacan fotos?
7. ¿Coleccionan monedas?
8. ¿Compran un regalo?

K Tell whether or not the following people are doing the activities indicated.

V: Have students ask questions, then answer *sí* or *no*: S¹: *¿Estudian ellas en casa?* S²: *Sí . . . (No).*

■ⅢⅠ ellas / estudiar en casa   *Estudian en casa.*
                                  (No estudian en casa.)

1. nosotros / hablar con un amigo
2. ustedes / comprar un carro nuevo
3. nosotros / reparar el reloj
4. ellas / viajar a Cuba
5. ustedes / pintar paisajes
6. ellas / buscar empleo
7. ellos / ganar mucho dinero
8. ustedes / mirar unas fotos

¡vamos a hablar! Find out what a friend usually does on Saturday mornings.

¿Qué haces los sábados por la mañana?   [Ayudo a mis padres.]

Students may also respond with infinitive construction: *Ayudar a mis padres.*

Photo: New York City.

Columbus's discovery of America on October 12 is an important holiday to Spanish speakers. In Spain, the holiday is called **Día de la Hispanidad** and commemorates Spain's cultural influence in the Americas. In Latin America, it's called **Día de la Raza** and celebrates Latin America's Spanish and Indian heritage. Celebrations by Spanish speakers in the United States often include parades with music, banners, and colorful costumes.

En resumen

Present tense of ser (A, B)

	SER
yo	soy
tú	eres
él, ella, usted	es
nosotros, nosotras	somos
vosotros, vosotras	sois
ellos, ellas, ustedes	son

Possessive adjectives (C–E)

SINGULAR	PLURAL	
mi	mis	my
tu	tus	your
nuestro, nuestra	nuestros, nuestras	our
vuestro, vuestra	vuestros, vuestras	your *(plural familiar)*
su	sus	his, her, its, your, their

1. Possessive adjectives precede the noun they modify. They agree in number with the object possessed: **Es su bicicleta, ¿verdad?**
2. **Nuestro** has four forms: two singular and two plural. It agrees in number and gender with the object or objects possessed: **Es nuestra casa, Son nuestros padres.**
3. Like **nuestro,** the possessive adjective **vuestro** has four forms and agrees in number and in gender with the object or objects possessed.

Querer + infinitive (F, G)

> **Quiero** sacar unas fotos.
> ¿**Quieres** ser intérprete?
> **Quiere** viajar a California.

A form of **querer** + a dependent infinitive can be used to express what you want to do or be. Only **querer** is conjugated to match the subject.

Present tense of -ar verbs (H–K)

	MIRAR
yo	miro
tú	miras
él, ella, usted	mira
nosotros, nosotras	miramos
vosotros, vosotras	miráis
ellos, ellas, ustedes	miran

1. The present tense of **-ar** verbs is formed by adding a set of endings to the infinitive stem. The verb ending must agree with its subject.
2. A single present-tense Spanish verb form has several English equivalents. For example, **escucho** can mean *I listen, I do listen, I am listening,* or *I'll listen.*

Repaso

A Tell something about each of the following persons by completing each sentence with the correct form of the verb *ser*.

> ▪‖ Yo _____ bilingüe.   *Yo soy bilingüe.*

1. Mi mamá _____ creadora.
2. Mis hermanos _____ morenos.
3. Mi papá _____ de Cuba.
4. Tú y yo _____ estudiantes.

5. Ella _____ muy inteligente.
6. Mi hermano _____ pintor.
7. Tú _____ de México, ¿verdad?
8. Nosotros _____ primos.

B Juan is daydreaming about his weekend plans. Tell five things that he wants to do, based on the scene below.

> ▪‖ *Juan quiere mirar televisión.*

C Make clear who owns each item, using an appropriate possessive adjective.

> ▪‖ Pepe y yo miramos las fotos.   *Pepe y yo miramos nuestras fotos.*

1. Marta busca la bicicleta.
2. Buscamos el perro.
3. Sara y Manuel pintan la casa.
4. Yo escucho los discos.
5. Ustedes estudian los libros de español.
6. Tomás y tú reparan la grabadora.

D You and your friends are all doing different things on Saturday. Tell what each person is doing.

Game: Prepare and distribute cards with either an infinitive or a phrase written on each.
T: (give subject) *ellos.*
S¹: (gives appropriate verb form) *reparan.*
S²: (completes with appropriate phrase) *su bicicleta.*

■⫶ Rafael / trabajar / con su padre   *Rafael trabaja con su padre.*

1. Ana y Alejandro / estudiar / biología
2. Laura / ayudar / a una amiga
3. yo / reparar / mi bicicleta
4. tú / comprar / un regalo
5. Carlos y yo / coleccionar / monedas
6. ustedes / mirar / sus fotos
7. Fernando / pintar / al aire libre

E Help the government do a labor study in two Mexican cities by giving the totals for the following occupations.

Game: *Buscapalabras* for practice with occupations. See Teacher's Guide for instructions.

■⫶ *Hay ochenta y nueve policías.*

En Toluca hay	**En Puebla hay**
1. sesenta policías	veintinueve policías
2. dieciséis ingenieros	dieciocho ingenieros
3. cuarenta y siete abogados	treinta abogados
4. cincuenta y dos mecánicos	cuarenta y dos mecánicos
5. quince dentistas	quince dentistas
6. diez pilotos	cuatro pilotos
7. cincuenta enfermeras	cuarenta y nueve enfermeras
8. seis intérpretes	veinticinco intérpretes

F   Complete the following conversation in a logical manner.

Marta: Buenos días, Alicia.
Alicia: ...
Marta: ¿Quieres ... ?
Alicia: No, prefiero ... ¿Quieres ... mañana?
Marta: Sí, buena ... Me gusta ...

G   Interview a classmate and then report your findings to the class.

1. ¿Cómo te llamas?
2. ¿Cómo estás?
3. ¿Quieres mirar televisión?
4. ¿Estudias por la tarde?
5. ¿Qué haces mañana?
6. ¿Qué quieres ser?

▩⫴   *Ese chico se llama ...*

Vocabulario

SUSTANTIVOS

Alemania   Germany
el ayudante, la ayudante
    assistant
el carro   car
la carta   letter
la ciudad   city
el dinero   money
la dirección   address
la escuela   school
España   Spain
la experiencia   experience
la fecha   date
el fin de semana   weekend
el garaje   garage
el grado   grade
la moneda   coin
el nombre   name
la ocupación   occupation
el país   country
el paisaje   landscape
el pasatiempo   pastime
la televisión   television
el trabajo   work

VERBOS

aprender   to learn
ayudar (a)   to help
coleccionar   to collect
comprar   to buy
correr   to run
escribir   to write
escuchar   to listen to
ganar   to earn
leer   to read
mirar   to look at, to watch
pintar   to paint
querer (+ *inf.*)   to want
reparar   to repair, to fix
viajar   to travel
visitar (a)   to visit

OTRAS PALABRAS

creador, -a   creative
independiente   independent
otro, -a   other
todavía   still, yet

OCUPACIONES

el abogado, la abogada   lawyer
el dentista, la dentista   dentist
el enfermero, la enfermera   nurse
el ingeniero, la ingeniera   engineer
el intérprete, la intéprete   interpreter
el mecánico, la mecánico   mechanic
el obrero, la obrera   worker
el piloto, la piloto   pilot
el pintor, la pintora   painter
el policía, la policía   police officer

EXPRESIONES

al aire libre   outdoors
de acuerdo   okay, all right
el tiempo libre   spare (free) time
me gusta   I like
mido   I am . . . tall
peso   I weigh
prefiero   I prefer
¿qué haces?   what do you do?
sacar fotos   to take pictures

NÚMEROS DE 32 A 99

treinta y dos   32
cuarenta   40
cincuenta   50
sesenta   60
setenta   70
ochenta   80
noventa   90

algo más

A **¿Quién es?** Form two teams. Each team writes a short description of one classmate, including her/his age, birthday, appearance, number of brothers and sisters, and future occupation. Each member of one team, and then the other, asks a **sí-no** question in Spanish until the mystery person is discovered. The winning team is the one needing fewer questions to discover the opposing team's mystery person.

B **Juego.** Form two teams. Each group prepares a list of ten to fifteen original questions, or questions about the dialogues or cultural notes in Chapters 1 through 5. Each member of one team asks a person on the opposing team a question from the list. Choose a judge to keep score. The team with more correct answers wins.

C **Pequeño teatro.** Prepare a skit, working in a group of three to six people. Base your skit on a class or family scene, a birthday party or **santo,** an interview, or a theme suggested by a dialogue in Chapters 1 through 5. Create a setting and use props, costumes, or music to provide a background. Present your skit to the class.

D **Documento de identidad.** Design an ID card in Spanish. Include facts such as your name, age, address, phone number, and the name of your school and of your teacher. Add a photo or drawing of yourself. Use your ID for entrance to Spanish-related activities.

E **Collage.** Choose a location that interests you and that has a Hispanic name or background. It may be a historic site, a business run by a Spanish-speaking person, or a community where many Spanish speakers live. Work alone or in a group and prepare a collage with photos, drawings, news clippings, brochures, and anything else that you feel is appropriate. Present your collage to the class and tell about the place you have chosen.

F **El calendario.** Prepare a large calendar of events and special dates to hang in your classroom. Different groups may prepare various months. Mark Hispanic holidays, special school activities, or visits to places or events related to Hispanic culture in your area. You might plan a party to celebrate one of the Hispanic holidays on your calendar. Refer to the calendar to announce upcoming events.

G **El mundo hispano.** Collect magazine and newspaper photos and articles that pertain to Spanish-speaking people who live in or who have visited the United States. You may include sports figures, actors or actresses, musicians, politicians, artists, or other famous or newsworthy personalities. Tell the class about two of the people you have chosen.

H **Álbum.** Start an album or scrapbook in Spanish that will reflect your personality, moods, hobbies, likes and dislikes, ideas, and activities. Your album will be a long-term project that you can work on throughout the school year, so you should select an album or scrapbook that you can easily add pages to during the year. Begin with a description of yourself, your family, and your friends, using photos, drawings, or a family tree to illustrate your description. Include your class schedule, a calendar of your activities, and a favorite proverb. You may paste in tickets, fliers, comics, letters, poems, and photos. It might be interesting to illustrate school or Spanish-class activities. Provide captions or descriptions in Spanish for the items you include. Share your album with your class or friends at the end of each stage.

I **¿Quién soy?** Look at the color photographs on pages 1 through 8 and select someone you would like to talk about. Pretend you are that person and describe yourself, where you're from or live, and tell about your school, family, friends, and interests.

De día en día

La comida o un refresco proveen momentos de descanso y de charla agradable en un café de México o de cualquier parte del mundo hispano. Abajo: Pimientos y sacos con alubias en España; pescado y rábanos en México.

capítulo 6
¿Adónde vas?

Locate Mexico City on map.

A metropolis of more than fifteen million people, Mexico City requires an extensive public transportation system. Streetcars and many kinds of buses serve most of the city. Large buses called **ballenas** (whales) travel the wider streets. Express buses called **delfines** (dolphins) are able to enter secondary and narrow streets as well as the main streets. The city's fastest and newest transportation system is the **metro** or subway, which currently has a network of three lines. Future routes are planned to connect outlying areas to the Federal District.

Warm-up review: ¿Qué quieres ser? ¿Te gusta visitar ciudades nuevas? ¿viajar? ¿escuchar música? ¿Qué haces los fines de semana?

¡Qué confusión!

Model dialogue, then have students repeat. Check for proper intonation and pronunciation.

Alfredo es mensajero y quiere tomar el metro para llevar un paquete al correo.

POLICÍA	Oiga, señor, ¿adónde va?
ALFREDO	Voy al metro.
POLICÍA	Esta entrada está cerrada.
ALFREDO	¡Ay, no! Voy a llegar tarde. ¿Qué hago?
POLICÍA	No se preocupe. Usted tiene que ir hasta la esquina y luego doblar a la derecha. Allí hay otra entrada. Eso es todo.
ALFREDO	Gracias. Adiós.
POLICÍA	De nada. Para servirle.

comprensión

Have a student record questions. Ask students to answer questions with books closed.

Optional: Expand B by having students supply more detailed information.

A. Answer the following questions, based on the dialogue.

■|| ¿Qué es Alfredo? Es mensajero.

1. ¿Adónde va? ¿por qué?
2. ¿Qué está cerrada?
3. ¿Quién ayuda a Alfredo?
4. ¿Cómo va Alfredo a la otra entrada?

B. Imagine that you're going through an experience similar to Alfredo's. Reconstruct the scene, telling what happens when you try to take the subway.

■|| Quiero . . . Quiero tomar el metro.

1. Voy a llevar . . .
2. Una entrada . . .
3. Un policía pregunta ¿ . . . ?
4. Para entrar al metro, tengo que . . .
5. ¡Qué. . . !

The Spanish equivalent for bus is *un autobús (bus)* in many areas, but it is also called *un camión* (Mexico), *una guagua* (Puerto Rico), and *un colectivo* (Argentina).

Optional: Introduce place names (p. 116) and have students expand Act. B. S¹: *Voy [al hotel]*. S²: *Está en la esquina.* Explain that *a + el = al.*

A. Ask a classmate where he/she lives in relation to school. Near by? Far away?

■▮ ¿Dónde vives?   A [tres] cuadras° de aquí.
        Lejos°. Tomo el bus°.
        Cerca° de aquí.

B. You're lost in a large city. Express your confusion and need for help to a passerby.

■▮ ¡Qué confusión! ¿Dónde estoy?   ¿Adónde vas?
        No te preocupes.
        ¿Puedo ayudarte?

C. Your mother tells you that it's 9:30. You have a dentist appointment at 10:00 and can't possibly make the appointment on time. How do you react?

■▮ Son las nueve y media°.   ¡Caramba! Voy a llegar tarde.
        ¿Las 9:30 ya°? ¡No me digas!
        ¿Qué hago? No puedo ir.

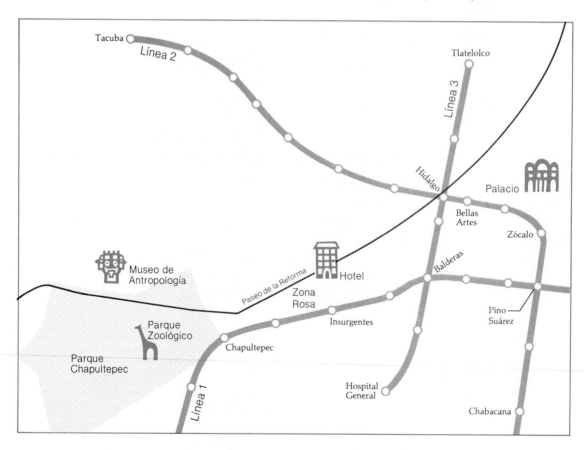

El metro de México

See cultural note, p. 122. Suggest further research by interested students.

Optional: Use transparency of metro map to show locations mentioned during reading of dialogue.

Verónica Chávez y su prima Beatriz visitan la ciudad de México por primera vez. Quieren tomar el metro, pero no saben dónde está. Verónica pregunta en la información del hotel.

VERÓNICA	Por favor, señor. ¿Dónde puedo tomar el metro?
EMPLEADO	¿Adónde va, señorita? Hay tres líneas.
VERÓNICA	Voy al Zócalo.
EMPLEADO	Estamos en el Paseo de la Reforma. Para ir al Zócalo tiene que tomar la línea número 1. Hay que bajar en la estación Pino Suárez y tomar la línea número 2.
VERÓNICA	¡Ay, dios mío! ¿Es difícil?
EMPLEADO	No, señorita. Con este mapa no hay problema.
VERÓNICA	Muchas gracias. Hasta luego.

comprensión

Check comprehension by asking questions on dialogue.

Have students show locations on map during retelling of story.

Retell the story from the point of view of the hotel employee.

■‖   Dos chicas visitan . . .   Dos chicas visitan la ciudad de México.

1. Quieren tomar . . .
2. Una chica pregunta . . .
3. Ellas quieren ir . . .
4. Para ir al Zócalo hay que . . .
5. Luego tienen que . . .

extensión

Have students work in pairs, asking and giving directions. Have them incorporate as many expressions from dialogue as possible.

Game: Students locate themselves on map (p. 114) and then give directions. Class has to guess where they are going. Winner gives next directions.

La Plaza de las Tres Culturas is located near Tlatelolco. See photo, p. 121.

A.   Use the subway map on page 114 and direct Verónica from her hotel in the Zona Rosa to the *Palacio de Bellas Artes.*

■‖   Por favor, ¿cómo voy al   Tiene que tomar . . .
       Palacio de Bellas Artes?

B.   A helpful stranger has just given you directions to your hotel, but you still don't understand. Express how frustrated you feel.

■‖   Eso es todo. ¿Comprende°?   Lo siento. No comprendo. Perdón°, ¿quiere repetir°? Más despacio°, por favor. ¡Qué confusión!

C.   You're at the Zócalo. Ask directions to Chapultepec Park or to Tlatelolco. Ask the person giving directions to slow down or repeat if you don't understand. Be sure to thank her/him.

■‖   Perdón, ¿cómo voy [al   Tiene que tomar . . .
       parque Chapultepec]?

Estudio de palabras

En el pueblo

Optional: Use place-name visuals to introduce *Estudio de palabras.* See Appendix C for additional place names.

Calle Alvarado
Avenida Cinco de Mayo
Avenida Juárez
Calle de Hidalgo
CINE
ESTRELLA

1	el banco	6	el colegio
2	el correo	7	el parque
3	el cine	8	la estación
4	el hotel	9	la plaza
5	el museo	10	la iglesia

A Help a stranger who is visiting the town illustrated above. Tell her/him the street where each place or building is located.

▪▥ ¿Dónde está el banco? *El banco está en la avenida Juárez.*

B Identify the place associated with each of the following words.

▪▥ estudiar *el colegio*

1. una carta   4. domingo
2. viajar   5. el pintor
3. el dinero   6. correr

Preposiciones compuestas

Optional: Use classroom objects to introduce prepositions. Place chair beside, in front, behind, near, far from desk. Elicit: *La silla está al lado de la mesa.*

lejos de	far from
cerca de	near
enfrente de	facing, opposite
detrás de	behind
al lado de	next to
a la izquierda de	to the left of
a la derecha de	to the right of

Remind students that the preposition *de* is required when a specific place is mentioned after the preposition.

C Imagine that you're a resident of the town pictured on page 116. Explain where each place or building shown is located in relation to the church.

■ıı *El cine está a la derecha de la iglesia.*

D Tell where you sit in the classroom in relation to your teacher and two of your classmates.

Vary by using local landmarks, school facilities, and classroom objects.

■ıı *Estoy al lado de Cristina.*

■ıı *Estoy cerca de Manuel.*

Optional: Obtain map of Mexico City to show other street names: *Avenida Juárez* for president Benito Juárez; *16 de Septiembre* for date of independence from Spain.

Photo: Monument to Columbus on Paseo de la Reforma.

Streets in Hispanic cities are often named for famous political and military figures and for important dates and events in the nation's history. Many streets and squares throughout Latin America are named for the Venezuelan leader Simón Bolívar and the Argentine general José de San Martín, both national heroes in South America's struggle for independence. In Mexico City, the key artery named **Paseo de la Reforma** recalls major agricultural and social reforms of the 19th century.

117

Pronunciación y ortografía ———

palabras claves | **stop** [b]   bajo, vez
                | **fricative** [β]   rubio, favorito

The Spanish stop [b] sound is similar to the English [b] sound in the word *bee*. The stop [b] sound occurs after a pause and after **m** and **n**.

The fricative [β] sound is similar to stop [b], but is pronounced with the lips almost touching as air is forced out. The fricative [β] sound occurs most often after a vowel and after any consonant other than **m** or **n**.

Both the [b] and [β] sounds are spelled **b** or **v,** so you must memorize the spelling of these sounds.

A   Listen and repeat the following words after your teacher. Pay special attention to the fricative [β] sound.

stop [b]		fricative [β]	
bajo	visitar	ru**b**io	favor
bien	caram**b**a	a**b**uelo	nueve
banco	nom**b**re	sá**b**ado	favorito
vez	tam**b**ién	tra**b**ajo	jueves
veinte	in**v**ierno	ha**b**lo	novela

B   Now practice the following phrases, each of which contains a fricative [β] sound.

una vez   un chico bueno
la verdad   María va
está bien   la biología

C

Have students compose sentences, using words with *b* and *v*. Or challenge students to compose *trabalenguas* for competition.

Read aloud the following sentences. Each fricative [ƀ] sound is printed with a boldface letter.

1. Voy al banco el jueves.
2. ¡Caramba! El abuelo tiene fiebre.
3. Busco veinte libros de biología.
4. Vivo a nueve cuadras de mi trabajo.

cognates

Warn students that there are false cognates: *asistir* (to attend a function), *la fábrica* (factory).

You have already learned that cognates are words that come from the same root and have similar meanings. For example, the Spanish word **estudiante** and the English word *student* are cognates.

Recognizing cognates can help to make vocabulary study and reading easier, but remember that cognates are often spelled differently in Spanish and English and they are always pronounced differently.

D   Dictate the following Spanish words to a classmate. Be sure to use correct Spanish pronunciation.

inteligente	problema	oficina
historia	agosto	mecánico
profesor	teléfono	octubre

E   Working with a partner, write fifteen cognates from this chapter and previous ones.   Optional: Refer to *Spanish Around You* to expand Ex. E.

Quien busca, halla.

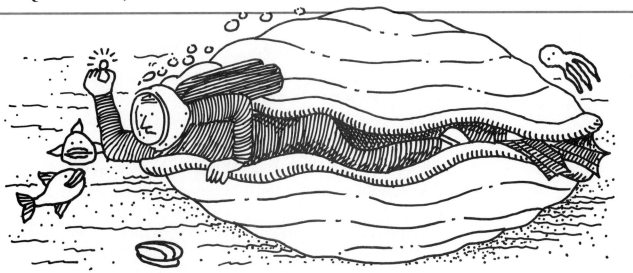

Proverb: Seek and ye shall find.

Gramática

Telling time

Optional: Use large clock with movable hands to cue time expressions. Practice hours and half hours before doing exercises.

Es la una.

Son las tres.

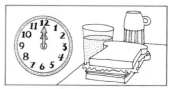

Es (el) mediodía.
Son las doce.

Es la una y media.

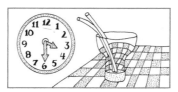

Son las tres y media.

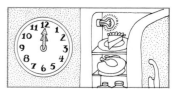

Es (la) medianoche.
Son las doce de la noche.

In telling time, **es** is used with **una, mediodía,** and **medianoche; son** is used with plural numbers. **¿Qué hora es?** is used to ask *What time is it?*

A According to your watch, you and a friend are late for your next class. Express your concern and tell her/him the time.

Game: ¿Qué hora es? Have a clock holder conceal face of clock from class, set a time, and ask: ¿Qué hora es? S: Son las tres. Clock holder: No, no son las tres. ¿Qué hora es? Student guessing correctly leads next game.

◼▥ 3:00   *¡Llegamos tarde! ¡Ya son las tres!*

1. 10:00
2. 8:30
3. 1:00
4. 12:00
5. 2:30
6. 11:30
7. 1:30
8. 9:00

¿A qué hora estudias?   *At what time* do you study?
A las siete.   *At* seven o'clock.

The expression **¿a qué hora?** is used to ask at what time an activity or an event occurs. **A la (las)** + number is used in the response.

B Tell a classmate what time you usually do the following activities.

◼▥ llegar al colegio (7:30)   — *¿A qué hora llegas al colegio?*
                                — *A las siete y media.*

1. tomar el almuerzo (11:00)
2. estudiar (7:00)
3. mirar televisión (8:00)
4. escuchar discos (9:30)
5. hablar con tus amigos (3:30)
6. ir a casa (5:30)

Contractions al and del

Cue varied place names to elicit use of al and del: el metro/al; la estación/a la.

Voy **al** museo.   I'm going *to the* museum.
Está a la derecha **del** hotel.   It's to the right *of the* hotel.
¿Está lejos **del** parque?   Is it far *from the* park?

The preposition **a** and the definite article **el** combine to form the contraction **al. De** and **el** combine to form **del.** The definite articles **la, los,** and **las** do not contract with **a** and **de.**

C   You're planning activities for the coming week. Tell where you have to go and on which day. Use the name of any day of the week.

Assignment: Have students redo Ex. C using metro, Zócalo, esquina, Palacio de Bellas Artes.

    ▪◖◗   el banco   *Tengo que ir al banco el martes.*

1. la iglesia
2. el parque
3. el correo
4. la estación
5. el cine
6. el colegio
7. la plaza
8. la oficina de papá

D   Answer the questions, identifying the owner of the following objects.

    ▪◖◗   ¿Es tu libro?   (el profesor)   *No, es del profesor.*

1. ¿Es tu disco?   (las hermanas de Pilar)
2. El mapa es de Ana, ¿verdad?   (el Sr. Rueda)
3. La calculadora es de Enrique, ¿no?   (la Srta. Gómez)
4. ¿Es el carro de Juan?   (el tío de Juan)
5. El paquete es de Pedro, ¿no?   (el amigo de María)
6. ¿Es tu grabadora?   (los padres de Antonio)

La Plaza de las Tres Culturas.

The **metro** in Mexico City is one of the most modern and beautiful in the world. The design of the system presented a special challenge to the Mexican engineers who had to overcome the problems of earthquakes and shifting subsoil. Built between 1967 and 1970, the **metro** is controlled by a sophisticated computerized electronic system and accommodates an average of more than 3,500,000 passengers daily. Marble platforms and picturesque murals decorate many stations. **Pino Suárez** station in downtown Mexico City is built around an Aztec pyramid, one of the thousands of pre-Colombian and Spanish colonial relics unearthed during the excavation work that preceded the building of the **metro.** The **Zócalo** station contains a model of the **Zócalo** as it appeared at the time of the Aztecs.

Present tense of **ir**

	IR
yo	voy
tú	vas
él, ella, usted	va
nosotros, nosotras	vamos
ellos, ellas, ustedes	van

The verb **ir** *(to go)* is irregular in all forms of the present tense.

E   Jorge is having a party on Saturday. Find out from your friends if the following persons are going.

> ■III   Beatriz   Tú: *¿Va Beatriz a la fiesta?*
> Amigo/a: *Sí, va. (No, no va.)*

1. tú
2. Pilar
3. tus primos
4. tú y tu hermana

5. Vicente
6. ustedes
7. Rosa y David
8. Ignacio

F   Tell where each of the following persons is going.

S¹ gives a subject (no-sotros). S² cues place with visual (parque). Class combines: (Nosotros) vamos al parque.

> ■III   Sara / banco   *Sara va al banco.*

1. yo / museo
2. Susana y Amelia / correo
3. Jorge / dentista
4. tú / estación

5. usted y su primo / plaza
6. nosotras / oficina de mamá
7. tú y yo / parque
8. ustedes / cine

¡vamos a hablar!

You and a friend are making plans for the weekend. Decide what time you'll go to different places.

Have students cue with visuals and clock.

> ¿A qué hora vamos [al parque]?

> A [las tres]. ¿Está bien?

Ser versus estar

Review present tense of *ser* and *estar* before explaining usage.

The verbs **ser** and **estar** are both equivalent to English *to be*, but they cannot be used interchangeably.

USES OF SER	
Physical traits	Esa chica **es** alta.
Personality traits	Tú **eres** creador.
Occupation	Alfredo **es** mensajero.
Telling time	**Son** las tres.
Origin	**Soy** de Miami.
Possession	El mapa **es** de Luis.

G   Complete the following sentences, using an appropriate form of the verb *ser.*

> ■III   Mamá / de California   *Mamá es de California.*

V: Have students ask questions. S¹: *¿Es de California mamá?* S²: *Sí, (No) . . .*

1. Uds. / hermanos
2. yo / de aquí
3. Carmen / morena
4. el perro / de mis abuelos

5. las fotos / bonitas
6. nosotros / estudiantes
7. el metro / nuevo
8. la clase de historia / interesante

USES OF ESTAR	
Moods or feelings	**Estoy** muy contento hoy.
Health	Mamá **está** enferma.
Location	Gloria **está** en México.

H Specify the location of the people, places, or objects mentioned. Use the cues in parentheses and an appropriate form of *estar*.

■III ¿Dónde está David? (en Puerto Rico) *¿David? Está en Puerto Rico.*

1. Marta busca el banco. (en la calle Colón)
2. Buscamos el metro. (en esa esquina)
3. Julio busca su grabadora. (en el colegio)
4. Ramón busca su reloj. (en casa)
5. ¿Dónde están sus padres? (en el hotel)
6. Tú buscas el libro de español. (en la mesa)
7. ¿Dónde está Elena? (en el museo)
8. ¿Dónde están tus fotos? (en la clase)

I Make a statement about each of the following people. Use a form of the verb *ser* or *estar,* as appropriate.

Explain that *de* cues origin and *en* cues location.

Optional: Have students explain why they chose *ser* or *estar,* and give cue, if any.

■III Papá / en Nueva York *Papá está en Nueva York.*

1. Marcos / en la clase
2. la profesora / en la oficina
3. yo / de California
4. mi tío / ingeniero
5. mamá / alta
6. mi amiga y yo / bien
7. tú / contento
8. mis papás / enfermos

Present tense of regular -er verbs

	APRENDER
yo	aprend**o**
tú	aprend**es**
él, ella, usted	aprend**e**
nosotros, nosotras	aprend**emos**
ellos, ellas, ustedes	aprend**en**

Review present tense of -*ar* verbs before introducing -*er* verbs.

The present tense of regular **-er** verbs is formed by adding the endings for **-er** verbs to the infinitive stem. Other regular **-er** verbs that you have seen are **comprender** *(to understand),* **leer** *(to read),* and **correr** *(to run).*

J Say that the following people are learning Spanish.

■III Marta *Marta aprende español.*

1. yo
2. el Sr. López
3. nosotros
4. tú

5. Juan y usted
6. María y Elena
7. Ana y yo
8. Uds.

K A police officer gives your school group directions to the museum. They're so complicated that no one understands them.

V: Practice *leer* or *correr. Marta lee el periódico. Paco corre en el parque.* Cue varied subjects.

■III Paco *Paco no comprende.*

1. Teresa y yo
2. ustedes
3. yo

4. Tomás
5. tú
6. los profesores

Photo: Zócalo and cathedral.

A **plaza** or main square is a common feature in Hispanic towns and cities and a favorite gathering place for town or city residents. The principal church or cathedral, government buildings, shops, and cafés often border the **plaza.** The **Zócalo,** Mexico City's main square, has been the site of government and religious buildings from the time of the Aztecs whose temples and structures faced the area. Today, the city's Cathedral, National Palace, Supreme Court, shops, and hotels are located around the **Zócalo.**

Arte y artesanía en México. Izquierda: Museo de Antropología y dos artesanos que trabajan el cobre y la cerámica. Derecha: Mural de Tenochtitlán de Diego Rivera.

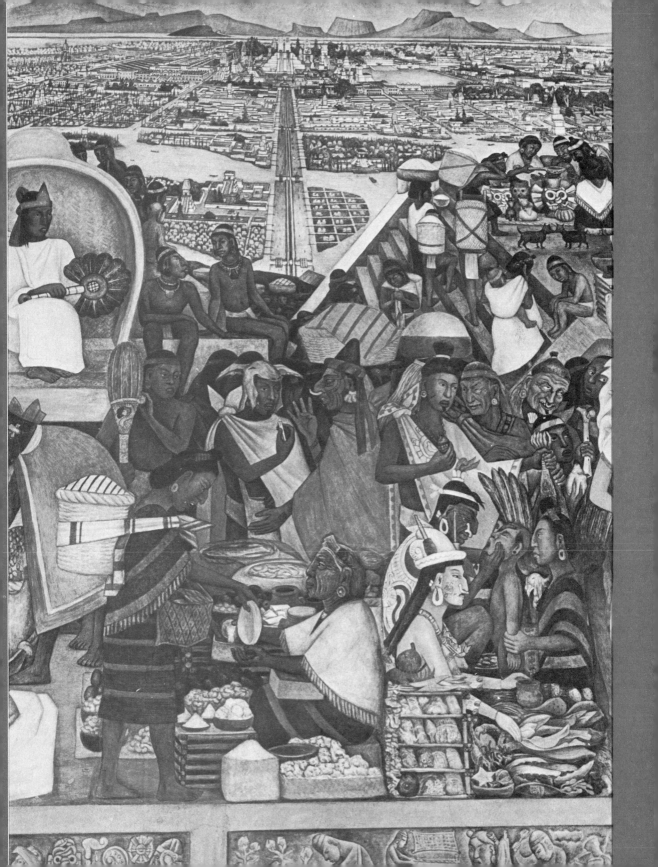

Present tense of regular -ir verbs

	VIVIR
yo	vivo
tú	vives
él, ella, usted	vive
nosotros, nosotras	vivimos
ellos, ellas, ustedes	viven

The present-tense endings of regular **-ir** and **-er** verbs are the same except for the **nosotros**-forms. Other regular **-ir** verbs that you have seen are **escribir** *(to write)*, and **cumplir**, as in **cumplir 15 años** *(to be 15 years old)*.

L   Ask a Mexican friend if the following people live near the Zócalo.

Personalize: *¿Quién vive cerca de aquí? ¿lejos? ¿Vives cerca del cine? ¿al lado del banco? detrás de la plaza?*

■▮▮   tú   *¿Vives cerca del Zócalo?*

1. ustedes
2. tus tíos
3. la Srta. Pacheco
4. Víctor y María
5. Javier
6. el Sr. García
7. Rosa y Manuel

M   Answer the following questions with *sí* or *no*. Be sure to use the correct endings for *-er* and *-ir* verbs.

■▮▮   ¿Corres en el parque?   *Sí, corro en el parque.*
        (No, no corro en el parque.)

1. ¿Viven sus padres en México?
2. ¿Aprendes español?
3. ¿Leen ustedes muchas novelas?
4. Tu hermana cumple diez años el sábado, ¿no?
5. ¿Ustedes escriben mucho?
6. ¿Escribes bien el español?
7. ¿Comprende tu padre español?
8. Ustedes viven cerca del colegio, ¿verdad?

¡vamos a hablar!

List familiar *-ar, -er,* and *-ir* verbs on board to aid students.

Ask your classmates about themselves or their activities.

¿Vives cerca del colegio?   Sí, vivo muy cerca.
¿Estudias francés y español?   No, sólo estudio español.

Present tense of **tener**

TENER	
yo	**tengo**
tú	**tienes**
él, ella, usted	**tiene**
nosotros, nosotras	**tenemos**
ellos, ellas, ustedes	**tienen**

You have already used the singular forms of **tener.** The forms of **tener** are irregular in the present tense.

¿Tienes que ir a casa?	Do you *have to* go home?
Tenemos que estudiar.	We *have to (must)* study.

A form of **tener que** + infinitive is used to express obligation.

N   Answer a new classmate's questions about your school.

■ıll   mucho trabajo   — *¿Tienen ustedes mucho trabajo?*
— *Sí, tenemos mucho trabajo.*
(No, no tenemos mucho trabajo.)

1. profesores buenos
2. muchos exámenes
3. libros interesantes
4. tiempo libre
5. clases difíciles
6. clase de música

O   Felipe wants to organize a bicycle trip, but no one is free. Explain to him why everyone is too busy to go.

Personalize: ¿Qué tienes que hacer esta tarde? ¿y mañana?

■ıll   Marta / trabajar   *Marta tiene que trabajar.*

1. nosotros / visitar a nuestros abuelos
2. Julio y Elena / ir a una clase
3. mis primos / ayudar a su papá
4. yo / llevar un paquete al correo
5. Álvaro / reparar su bicicleta
6. Cristina y Teresa / comprar unos regalos

¡vamos a hablar!   A friend suggests doing various activities. Decline and give her/him a logical excuse.

¿Quieres ir al parque?	No puedo. Estoy muy resfriado.
¿Quieres visitar a Juan?	Hoy no. Vive lejos y tengo que estar en casa a las cinco.

Lectura

Amigos por correspondencia

Comprehension check: Have students respond with books closed to oral questions: ¿Qué sabemos del chico? S¹: Es de México. S²: Tiene 15 años. S³: Vive cerca de la Embajada de los EE.UU. Can use as competition between teams.

Have class prepare a list of questions they might want to answer in letter: ¿Quién soy? ¿Cuántos años tengo? ¿Dónde vivo? ¿Cómo soy?

Optional: Have students select and write to pen pals in Spanish-speaking countries. *Hispania* has addresses of organizations which supply pen pal names.

30 de noviembre

Estimado° Robert: dear

Soy de México y tengo quince años. Vivo cerca
de la Embajada° de los Estados Unidos y del   embassy
centro de la ciudad.

5 Hablo un poco de inglés y quiero tener correspondencia con chicos y chicas norteameri-
canos, pues tengo planes de ir a estudiar en tu
país.

Colecciono timbres°, monedas y tarjetas pos-   stamps
10 tales° de muchos países. Tengo muchos discos   postcards
de música moderna y voy mucho al cine.

No soy ni alto ni bajo. Soy alegre y me gusta
bailar°. Tengo dos hermanos y una hermana   to dance
muy simpáticos. En mi próxima° carta te voy a   next
15 mandar una foto.

Tu amigo,

Fernando Ocampo

Río Rhin 214
México 6, D.F.

actividad   Respond to Fernando's letter with a letter of your own, describing yourself, your family, and your hobbies or activities. Use Fernando's letter as a model.

En resumen

Telling time (A, B)

¿Qué hora es?	**Es** la una.
¿A qué hora vas al cine?	**A las** nueve y media.

1. To tell time in Spanish, the verb form **es** is used with **una, mediodía,** and **medianoche.** The verb form **son** is used with plural hours.
2. The expression **¿Qué hora es?** is used to ask the time. **¿A qué hora?** is used to ask the time at which an event occurs.

Contractions **al** and **del** (C, D)

> a + el = al
> de + el = del

The prepositions **a** and **de** combine with the definite article **el** to form **al** and **del: ¿Quieres ir al parque? Está cerca del banco.**

La Mezquita, Córdoba, España. La Catedral de Guadalajara, México. Pescadores argentinos.

Present tense of ir (E, F)

Game for practice of *ir*. S¹: *Voy a México con mi abuela.* S²: *Voy a México con mi abuela y mi bolígrafo.* S³: *Voy a México con mi abuela, mi bolígrafo y mi cuaderno.* Each student adds an item beginning with the next letter of alphabet. Vary forms of *ir*.

IR	
yo	**voy**
tú	**vas**
él, ella, usted	**va**
nosotros, nosotras	**vamos**
vosotros, vosotras	vais
ellos, ellas, ustedes	**van**

Ser versus estar (G–I)

SER	
Physical and personality traits	Carmen **es** baja.
	Miguel **es** perezoso.
Occupation	Papá **es** obrero.
Telling time	**Son** las cinco.
Origin	**Soy** de Chicago.
Possession	Los discos **son** de Juan.

ESTAR	
Moods	**Estás** contento.
Health	Ana **está** resfriada.
Location	**Estamos** en México.

The verbs **ser** and **estar** are equivalent to English *to be,* but they cannot be used interchangeably.

Present tense of regular -er and -ir verbs (J–M)

Game: Play *Ta Te Ti* with *-er* and *-ir* verbs. See Teacher's Guide for instructions.

	COMPRENDER	ESCRIBIR
yo	compre**ndo**	escri**bo**
tú	compre**ndes**	escri**bes**
él, ella, usted	compre**nde**	escri**be**
nosotros, nosotras	comprend**emos**	escrib**imos**
vosotros, vosotras	comprend**éis**	escrib**ís**
ellos, ellas, ustedes	compre**nden**	escri**ben**

The present tense endings for regular **-er** and **-ir** verbs are alike except in the **nosotros-** and **vosotros-**forms.

Un lago en el parque Chapultepec.

Present tense of **tener** (N, O)

	TENER
yo	tengo
tú	tienes
él, ella, usted	tiene
nosotros, nosotras	tenemos
vosotros, vosotras	tenéis
ellos, ellas, ustedes	tienen

1. **Tener** is irregular in the present tense.
2. A form of **tener que** + infinitive is used to express obligation: **Pablo tiene que caminar al colegio.**

A   Make a logical statement about each of the persons, objects, or places in column 1. Use the correct form of *ser* or *estar* and an element from column 3.

1	2	3
1. los chicos		al lado de la casa
2. mi tío		alegre
3. la ciudad		en la clase
4. tu mamá	ser	a la izquierda
5. mis libros		enfermos
6. la entrada del metro	estar	lejos del museo
7. el hotel		muy cerca
8. yo		de Cuba
9. María y José Luis		muy interesante
		inteligente

■ⅲ   *Los chicos son de Cuba.*

B   Make complete sentences, using the cues provided.

■ⅲ   Diego / comprender bien / el inglés   *Diego comprende bien el inglés.*

1. Miguel / vivir / lejos de la ciudad
2. Luis y Anita / leer poco
3. yo / cumplir / dieciséis años hoy
4. tú / vivir / en México, ¿verdad?
5. Marta y yo / viajar / a Nueva York
6. Rosario / escribir / una carta
7. nosotros / aprender / tres idiomas
8. la profesora / comer / en el colegio

C   You're a detective recording your observations on a suspect you've been trailing. Tell what the suspect does at the indicated times.

■ⅲ   9:00   ir de su casa a la plaza   *A las nueve va de su casa a la plaza.*

9:30	ir al correo
10:00	llevar un paquete al metro
10:30	buscar otro paquete
12:00	tomar el almuerzo
1:00	hablar por teléfono
1:30	comprar un reloj
2:00	ir al banco

D   Tell where each person or object in the picture is located in relation to the first house on the left.

■Ⅲ   *El carro está detrás de la casa.*

E   Your family has friends from Mexico visiting for a week. For each day of the week, tell where you will go and at what time. Use the following place names: *parque, cine, colegio, iglesia, plaza, museo.*

■Ⅲ   *Vamos al cine el lunes a la una y media.*

F   Susana receives a phone call from a classmate who is new to the neighborhood and has a lot of questions to ask. Take Susana's role and reply with any logical response.

Personalize: Have students make large drawing of their own or an imaginary home and explain its location in relation to the *esquina, plaza, colegio, banco,* and *correo.*

1. ¿Dónde está tu casa?
2. ¿Vive tu familia al lado del parque?
3. Hay un cine enfrente del parque, ¿verdad?
4. Y la iglesia, ¿está cerca de tu casa?
5. ¿A qué hora tienes que ir al colegio?

G   Prepare a 4- to 6-line dialogue based on one of the following situations.

1. María gives Luisa a book that Luisa has wanted very much. What will Luisa say when she opens the package? How will María respond? Begin with Luisa's question: *¿Es un libro?*
2. A helpful young man has told you how to get back to your hotel and then walked with you to the subway stop. How will you thank him? How will he respond? Begin with: *Por favor, señor.*

Vocabulario

SUSTANTIVOS

el banco   bank
el bus (autobús)   bus
la calle   street
el cine   cinema, movie theater
la confusión   confusion
el correo   post office
la entrada   entrance
la esquina   street corner
la estación   station
el hotel   hotel
la iglesia   church
la información   information
la línea   route or line (transportation)
el mapa   map
la medianoche   midnight
el mediodía   noon
el mensajero, la mensajera   messenger
el metro   subway
el museo   museum
el paquete   package
el parque   park
la plaza   square, plaza

VERBOS

bajar   to descend
comprender   to understand
llegar   to arrive; to come
llevar   to bring; to carry
preguntar   to ask
repetir   to repeat
tomar   to take

OTRAS PALABRAS

a la derecha (de)   to the right
a la izquierda (de)   to the left
¿adónde?   where to?
al lado de   beside, next to
allí   there
cerca de   near
cerrado, -a   closed
despacio   slowly
detrás de   behind
enfrente de   in front of
lejos de   far from
más   more
tarde   late
ya   already, now

EXPRESIONES

¿a qué hora?   what time?
a [tres] cuadras   [three] blocks away
de nada   you're welcome
¡díos mío!   my goodness!, oh my!
eso es todo   that's all
hay que   it's necessary to; you must
[las dos] y media   half past [two]
no saben   they don't know
no se preocupe   don't worry
oiga   listen
perdón   excuse me, pardon
¿qué hago?   what shall I do?
¿qué hora es?   what time is it?
tener que *(+ inf.)*   to have to

El tiempo libre

Argentina is a nation with many sports enthusiasts. Whether as participants in a sport or as spectators at a sporting event, Argentinians are ardent fans of **fútbol** (soccer), auto racing, horse racing, polo, rugby, water sports, and skiing. Sports clubs often sponsor the country's professional leagues and teams in national and international competition.

La gran carrera

¡GRAN CIRCUITO MUNDIAL!

Precio de entradas		domingo
Oficiales	$200	15 noviembre
Mixto	200	13:30 horas
Generales	30	
Estacionamiento	10	

Autódromo Municipal de Buenos Aires
Avenida Roca esquina con Avenida General Paz

Locate Buenos Aires on map. Display photos of Argentina in class.

Assignment: Using the *gran circuito* poster as a model, have students make a poster of their favorite sporting event. (See sports in *Estudio de palabras,* p. 141.)

Have students discuss their posters and answer class questions about events. Display best posters on bulletin board.

El campeón mundial argentino, Juan Manuel Alfaro, organiza un gran circuito automovilístico en la ciudad de Buenos Aires. Todo el mundo lee con mucho interés las noticias sobre la gran carrera. Los participantes vienen de muchos países y manejan coches italianos, franceses y alemanes. El ganador de esta competencia va a recibir la Copa Mundial. Este trofeo representa mucho dinero y fama para el ganador.

comprensión

Answer the following questions, based on the poster and narrative.

1. ¿Qué anuncia el cartel?
2. ¿En qué ciudad es la carrera?
3. ¿Cuándo es el gran circuito?
4. ¿Dónde está el Autódromo Municipal de Buenos Aires?
5. ¿A qué hora es la carrera?
6. ¿Cuál es el precio de las entradas?
7. ¿Quién organiza la carrera?
8. ¿Qué recibe el ganador?

The Spanish
equivalent for
car has numerous re-
gional variations. It is
coche or *auto* in Argentina, *carro* in many
parts of Latin America,
and *coche* in Spain and
Mexico.

A. Ask a friend if he/she is going to the car race.

¿Vas a la carrera de carros? Sí, voy con unos amigos.
¡Claro! ¡Va a ser fantástica!
No puedo ir. No tengo dinero.
No me gusta ese deporte°.

B. You're discussing cars with some friends. Tell what kind of car you like.

¿Qué coche te gusta° más? Me gusta más un coche
deportivo°.
Prefiero un coche pequeño°.
Yo quiero un coche [alemán].
No sé. Me es igual°.

C. You're invited to a soccer game, but you don't want to go because you dislike the sport. Refuse the invitation.

V: Introduce sports,
p. 141. Ask question,
using other sports, and
have students accept or
refuse the invitation.

¿Quieres ir al partido° de fútbol°? No. Odio° el fútbol.
No. Es un deporte muy
aburrido.
No, gracias. No me
gusta el fútbol.

D. Inform a classmate whether or not you know how to drive a car.

¿Sabes° manejar? No. No sé manejar.
Sí, pero me falta práctica°.
Más o menos°.
¡Sí, claro!

¿Primavera en octubre?

En octubre es primavera en Buenos Aires. Es un mes maravilloso para jugar al tenis. Álvaro Ponti invita a su amiga Silvia Kaiser a jugar un partido.

ÁLVARO   Hola, Silvia, ¿quieres jugar al tenis el sábado por la mañana?
SILVIA   Gracias, Álvaro, pero no puedo ir.
ÁLVARO   ¿Por qué? ¿Qué haces?
SILVIA   Voy a practicar la guitarra con Luisa.
ÁLVARO   Si prefieres, jugamos por la tarde.
SILVIA   ¡Magnífico! Entonces, acepto tu invitación. ¿A qué hora?
ÁLVARO   ¿A las tres?
SILVIA   Sí. De acuerdo. ¡Chao, Álvaro!

Durante el juego

SILVIA   ¿Cuarenta quince a tu favor? ¡Haces trampa!
ÁLVARO   Yo no hago trampa. Es que sé jugar mejor que tú.
SILVIA   ¿Mejor que yo? ¡Estás loco! Hoy tienes suerte. Eso es todo.
ÁLVARO   Y tú no sabes perder. Bueno, ¿quieres ir a tomar un refresco?

comprensión

Decide whether the following statements are true or false, according to the dialogue. Use *sí* or *no* and correct any false statements.

1. En octubre es primavera en Buenos Aires.
2. Silvia practica la guitarra con Álvaro.
3. Álvaro quiere jugar al tenis.
4. Silvia y Álvaro van a jugar por la mañana.
5. Álvaro hace trampa.

extensión

A.   A friend invites you to play soccer. Accept or refuse the invitation.

   ¿Quieres jugar al fútbol   Sí, de acuerdo. ¿A qué hora?
   el sábado?   No puedo. Tengo que [estudiar].
                                   Prefiero jugar al béisbol°.

B.   How well or how poorly do you play the guitar?

   ¿Sabes tocar° la guitarra?   Sí, toco bastante° bien.
                                     Un poco. Me falta práctica.
                                     No, pero quiero aprender.

C.   Every time you play tennis with María you lose. How do you react?

   ¡Voy a ganar otra vez°!   ¡Odio este juego!
                                       ¡Tú haces trampa!
                                       Sólo tienes suerte.
                                       ¡Caramba! Siempre pierdo°.

Estudio de palabras

Deportes

el vólibol

el fútbol

el fútbol americano

el esquí/esquiar

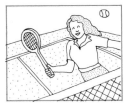
el tenis

el básquetbol

el béisbol

la natación/nadar

A   Tell a classmate what sport you like to play during different months of the year. Choose from the sports listed above.

▪‖   ¿Qué deporte te gusta jugar en mayo?   *En mayo me gusta jugar al béisbol.*

Las estaciones del año

el invierno

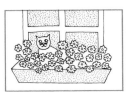
la primavera

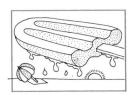
el verano

el otoño

B   Which months of the year are associated with each season where you live?

▪‖   *Junio, julio y agosto son los meses de . . .*

C   Which months of the year are associated with each season in Argentina?

▪‖   *En Argentina, junio . . .*

Instrumentos musicales

Use flash cards to introduce instruments. Refer students to supplementary list in Appendix C.

1 el clarinete
2 la guitarra
3 el piano
4 el tambor
5 la trompeta
6 el violín

D You're looking for some musicians to form a band. Ask various friends if they can play the instruments needed.

Assignment: Have students bring in photos or names of famous Spanish-speaking musicians.

■ ¿Tocas [el clarinete]? *Sí, toco [el clarinete].*
(No, pero toco [el piano].)

Pronunciación y ortografía

palabras claves

[H]	joven, gente
hard [g]	ganar, guitarra
soft [g̸]	amigo

In Spanish, the [H] sound or **jota** has no English equivalent. It is pronounced at the back of the throat, by forcing air through a narrow opening. The **jota** sound is spelled **j** before **a, o,** or **u.** It is spelled **j** or **g** before **e** or **i.**

A Listen and repeat the following words after your teacher.

joven	lejos	hijo	gente	ingeniero
jugar	manejar	viaje	colegio	argentino
jueves	mensajero	tarjeta	álgebra	inteligente

B   Read aloud the following sentences to practice the [H] sound.

Use sentences for dictation.

1. Juan juega al tenis el jueves.
2. El argentino se llama Jorge.
3. Mi hija es ingeniera.
4. Estudio álgebra en el colegio.

The Spanish hard [g] sound is similar to English [g] in *go,* and occurs at the beginning of a word and after **n.** The soft [ǥ] sound is similar to English [ǥ] in *egg,* and occurs after a vowel and after consonants other than **n.** Both hard [g] and soft [ǥ] are spelled **g** before **a, o,** and **u.** Before **e** and **i,** a silent **u** after the **g** indicates the hard [g] sound.

C   Listen and repeat the following words after your teacher.

hard [g]		soft [ǥ]	
ganar	gracias	amigo	agosto
gusto	inglés	iglesia	organizar
gran	guitarra	alegre	regalo

D   Read aloud each sentence. The soft [ǥ] sounds are printed with boldface letters.

1. Gonzalo organiza un gran circuito.
2. ¡Magnífico! Yo gano el juego.
3. Me es igual. Jugamos el domingo.
4. Me gusta tocar la guitarra.

Cada oveja con su pareja.

Proverb: Birds of a feather flock together.

Gramática

More on telling time

Review hours and half hours briefly.

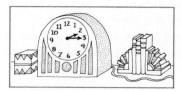

Son las dos **y cuarto.**

Son las dos **menos quince.**

Son las tres **y veinte.**

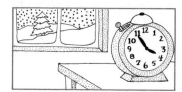

Son las cuatro **menos cinco.**

The quarter hours may be expressed with **cuarto** or **quince.** From the full hour to the half hour, minutes are added to the hour. From the half hour to the next full hour, minutes are subtracted.

A   Tell what time it is, according to the cues.

■ǁ   3:15   *Son las tres y quince.*

1. 12:45
2. 4:25
3. 1:55
4. 1:15

5. 10:10
6. 6:40
7. 8:45
8. 3:05

In Spanish, A.M. is expressed with the phrase **de la mañana.** P.M. is expressed with **de la tarde** or **de la noche.** **De la tarde** refers to afternoon and early evening. **De la noche** refers to late evening or after dark. Usage varies from country to country.

B   Specify what time of day it is, using *de la mañana, de la tarde,* or *de la noche.*

Game: ¿Qué hora es?
See p. 120 for instructions.

■ǁ   10:00 A.M.   *Son las diez de la mañana.*

1. 11:10 A.M.
2. 9:15 P.M.
3. 8:05 A.M.
4. 3:30 P.M.

5. 7:45 A.M.
6. 9:50 P.M.
7. 5:15 P.M.
8. 11:20 A.M.

The twenty-four hour clock system is widely used in Hispanic countries on time schedules for buses, trains, planes, theaters, television, and many public functions. The hours 1 to 12 correspond to A.M., and the hours 12 to 24 correspond to P.M. For example, at a bus terminal or airport, a departure time for **16 horas** corresponds to 4:00 P.M., and **22:30 horas** corresponds to 10:30 P.M.

VIERNES	30

noche

21.00	TELEDIARIO (color).
21.35	EL HOMBRE Y LA TIERRA (color).
22.00	EL NIDO DE ROBIN: "El caso de las siete libras" (color).
22.30	GRANDES RELATOS: "King" (color).
23.35	ULTIMAS NOTICIAS (color).
23.55	BUENAS NOCHES (color).
24.00	DESPEDIDA Y CIERRE (color).

Present tense of **jugar**

	JUGAR
yo	ju**e**go
tú	ju**e**gas
él, ella, usted	ju**e**ga
nosotros, nosotras	jugamos
ellos, ellas, ustedes	ju**e**gan

The verb **jugar** means *to play* a sport or game. The stem vowel **u** changes to **ue** in most forms of **jugar**. There is no stem change in the **nosotros-**form. The verb **jugar** takes the endings of regular **-ar** verbs.

C

Redo Ex. D, using assignment, p. 141. Student shows photo: *Manuel Orantes juega al tenis. Lee Trevino y Nancy Lopez juegan al golf. Pele: fútbol. Guillermo Vilas: tenis. Luis Tiant: béisbol.*

Beatriz is in charge of reserving the basketball court. Check with her about the time you and a friend are scheduled to play.

■□□ María Tú: *¿Jugamos María y yo [a las dos]?*
Beatriz: *Sí, ustedes juegan [a las dos].*
(No, juegan [a las dos y media].)

1. Eduardo
2. Julio
3. Ana

4. Rosa
5. José
6. Gabriel

D

Tell what sport the following people play well.

■□□ mi hermano / fútbol *Mi hermano juega bien al fútbol.*

1. Daniel / tenis
2. tú / vólibol
3. Papá / básquetbol
4. yo / béisbol

5. Toño / fútbol americano
6. mamá y yo / tenis
7. mis primos / fútbol
8. ustedes / básquetbol

Jugar and tocar

Explain that *tocar* is regular. *Tocar* means *to play* (instruments) or *to touch.*

¿**Juegas** al tenis?   *Do you play* tennis?
Toco el piano.   *I play* the piano.

Jugar means *to play* a sport or game. **Tocar** means *to play* a musical instrument.

E   Carlos wants to know what kinds of things you do in your spare time. Indicate which sports and instruments you do or don't play.

Use assignment, p. 142, to practice *tocar.* *Andrés Segovia y Carlos Montoya tocan la guitarra clásica. Las Mocedades es un conjunto de España. Cantan y tocan. Vikki Carr canta. José Feliciano toca la guitarra y canta.*

   el violín   Carlos: *¿Tocas el violín?*
                  Tú: *Sí, toco el violín.*
                     (No, no toco el violín.)

1. el tenis
2. la guitarra
3. el piano
4. el fútbol
5. el béisbol
6. la trompeta
7. el básquetbol
8. el clarinete

¡vamos a hablar!

V: Student mimes or shows photo and names classmate. Class: *Ana toca el piano. Jaime juega al tenis.*

Find out whether or not several of your friends play various instruments or sports well.

¿Juegas bien al vólibol?   No muy bien. Me falta práctica.
¿Tocas bien la guitarra?   Sí. Más o menos.

Me gusta and te gusta

Me gusta la música.   *I like* music.
No **me gusta** el tenis.   *I don't like* tennis.
¿**Te gusta** nadar?   *Do you like* to swim?

In Spanish, **me gusta** and **te gusta** are used to express likes and dislikes. **Me gusta** or **te gusta** may be followed by a singular noun or by an infinitive.

F   Tell whether or not you like the following things or activities.

   trabajar mucho   *Me gusta trabajar mucho.*
                      (No me gusta trabajar mucho.)

1. leer
2. el béisbol
3. el colegio
4. tocar la guitarra
5. la primavera
6. esquiar
7. escuchar discos
8. la música

G Take a poll to determine whether or not some of your classmates like the following activities.

Add-an-element to practice *gustar*: T: *Me gusta estudiar.* S¹: *Me gusta estudiar y jugar al tenis.* S²: *Me gusta . . .* Repeat, using nouns.

▪▥ ir al cine   — *¿Te gusta ir al cine?*
                  — *Sí, me gusta ir al cine.*
                  (No, no me gusta ir al cine.)

1. viajar a otros países
2. mirar televisión
3. estudiar biología
4. jugar con los amigos

5. aprender español
6. escribir cartas
7. ganar mucho dinero
8. ir a las carreras

¡vamos a hablar! Tell a friend whether or not you like different things or activities. If you can, tell her/him why.

¿Te gusta el invierno?   Sí, me gusta mucho porque me gusta esquiar.

¿Te gusta ir a museos?   No, no me gusta. Es aburrido.

Soccer is by far the most popular sport played in Spanish-speaking countries. Although interscholastic sports are less common than in the United States, students are ready for a soccer game as long as two or more players and a ball are available. Young and old enthusiastically support professional teams and closely follow games held among the country's teams. Considerable rivalry often develops between proud fans of opposing teams, especially in national competitions between countries.

Jai alai, juego popular de origen vasco.

Present tense of **saber**

Trabalenguas using *saber: Yo solo sé una cosa, solo sé que no sé nada.* (I know only one thing, only that I know nothing.)

	SABER
yo	**sé**
tú	sabes
él, ella, usted	sabe
nosotros, nosotras	sabemos
ellos, ellas, ustedes	saben

The **yo**-form of **saber** is irregular in the present tense. All other forms follow the pattern of regular **-er** verbs.

H A neighbor's five-year-old child is always asking you questions. You patiently answer them.

　　　■ⅲ　qué hora es　　Niño/a: *¿Sabes qué hora es?*
　　　　　　　　　　　　　　　Tú: *Sí, sé qué hora es.*
　　　　　　　　　　　　　　　　　(No, no sé qué hora es.)

Optional: Teach gesture for *no sé.* Shrug shoulders, turn down corners of mouth, wrinkle brow, extend palms of hands forward with arms bent at elbow.

1. hablar francés
2. jugar al básquetbol
3. dónde vive mi amiga Sara
4. dónde trabaja mi papá
5. tocar el piano
6. escribir el español
7. nadar bien

I   Tell what the following people know how to do.

■‖   David y Antonio / jugar al tenis   *David y Antonio saben jugar al tenis.*

1. nosotros / hablar inglés
2. Daniel / tocar la trompeta
3. yo / manejar un carro

4. Álvaro y Teresa / reparar bicicletas
5. mis padres / esquiar muy bien
6. Uds. / nadar bien

Expressing the future with **ir a**

Review present of *ir* before discussing *ir a*.

Voy a tocar el clarinete.
¿Vamos a jugar al tenis el sábado?

I'm going to play the clarinet.
Are we going to play tennis on Saturday?

A form of the verb **ir a** + infinitive is used to express an action planned for the future.

J   What are the following people going to do this afternoon?

Chain drill: S¹: *nadar.* S²: *¿Cuándo vamos a nadar?* S³: *Vamos a nadar mañana.* S⁴: *¡Fantástico! ¿A qué hora?* S⁵: *Vamos a nadar mañana a las siete.*

■‖   nosotros / esquiar   *Vamos a esquiar.*

1. la profesora / nadar
2. yo / jugar al tenis
3. tú / comprar una bicicleta
4. Pilar y Carmen / buscar empleo
5. Antonio / visitar a Marta en el hospital
6. ustedes / ayudar a José Luis
7. nosotras / mirar televisión
8. los abuelos / escuchar música

K   Confirm what the people mentioned are going to do today.

■‖   Manuel llama a Diego, ¿verdad?   *Sí, va a llamar a Diego.*

1. Susana invita a sus primos a la fiesta, ¿no?
2. Ustedes buscan entradas para la carrera, ¿no?
3. Tú hablas con el profesor, ¿verdad?
4. Juan y Elena aprenden a nadar, ¿no?
5. Papá lleva el carro al garaje, ¿verdad?
6. Nosotros compramos un regalo para José, ¿no?

¡vamos a hablar!   Ask your friends about their plans for the coming weekend.

¿Vas a ir al partido de tenis?
¿Vas a estudiar?

No sé. ¿Quién va a ir?
Un poco. Tengo examen el lunes.

Telling time (A, B)

> Son las diez **y** cuarto de la mañana.
> Son las once **menos** cinco.

1. In telling time in Spanish, from the full hour to the half hour, minutes are added to the hour. From the half hour to the next full hour, minutes are subtracted.
2. The phrase **de la mañana** is used to express A.M. **De la tarde** and **de la noche** are used to express P.M.

Jugar and tocar (C–E)

	JUGAR (u > ue)
yo	juego
tú	juegas
él, ella, usted	juega
nosotros, nosotras	jugamos
vosotros, vosotras	jugáis
ellos, ellas, ustedes	juegan

1. The verb **jugar** takes the regular **-ar** verb endings. The stem vowel changes from **u** to **ue** in all forms except the **nosotros-** and **vosotros-** forms.
2. Remember that the verb **jugar** means to play a game or a sport, and **tocar** means to play a musical instrument: **Jugamos al tenis. ¿Tocas el violín?**

Me gusta and te gusta (F, G)

> **Me gusta** tocar la guitarra.
> No **te gusta** el invierno, ¿verdad?

Me gusta and **te gusta** are used to express likes and dislikes. They can be followed by an infinitive or a singular noun.

Present tense of **saber** (H, I)

	SABER
yo	**sé**
tú	sabes
él, ella, usted	sabe
nosotros, nosotras	sabemos
vosotros, vosotras	sabéis
ellos, ellas, ustedes	saben

1. The **yo**-form of **saber** is irregular in the present tense.
2. **Saber** means to know the facts or information. A form of **saber** + infinitive means to know how to do something: **Sé nadar.**

Future with **ir a** (J, K)

> **¿Vas a nadar** hoy?
> **Van a comprar** un carro nuevo.

A form of the verb **ir a** + infinitive may be used to express an action planned for the future.

Conjunto boliviano de música folklórica.

Repaso

A   Tell which sport you prefer in each of the months listed. Choose from *jugar al béisbol, nadar, jugar al tenis, esquiar, jugar al básquetbol.*

■‖   diciembre   *En diciembre prefiero jugar al básquetbol.*

1.   marzo   3.   mayo   5.   septiembre
2.   abril   4.   agosto   6.   enero

B   Try to out-do a classmate by adding one more activity that you can do.

■‖   Toco la guitarra.   *Yo toco la guitarra y el tambor.*

1.   Toco el piano.   4.   Juego al fútbol.
2.   Hablo francés.   5.   Sé nadar.
3.   Toco la trompeta.   6.   Juego al vólibol.

C   Complete the sentences with a form of *ir a* to tell what is going to happen.

■‖   Ramón ___ aprender a manejar.   *Ramón va a aprender a manejar.*

1.   Yo ___ tomar el metro.
2.   Mis tíos ___ vivir cerca de aquí.
3.   Juan y Teresa ___ cumplir quince años.
4.   Tú ___ estar en México en abril.
5.   Papá y yo ___ esquiar.
6.   Uds. ___ ir a California, ¿verdad?
7.   Nosotras ___ sacar unas fotos del partido.

D   Say whether you like or dislike each of the activities pictured below.

■‖   *No me gusta mirar televisión.*

E Pick out the three words from each group that best fit into one category.

1. autódromo, cartel, carrera, música
2. invierno, otoño, morena, primavera
3. manejar, nadar, jugar al tenis, esquiar
4. intérprete, mecánico, enfermera, ganador
5. perezoso, argentino, italiano, francés
6. perro, abuelo, madre, tía

F React to each of the following sentences by choosing a logical response from the list given on the right.

1. ¿Quién va al partido?   Sí, siempre gano.
2. ¡Haces trampa!   Todo el mundo.
3. ¿Tocas bien el piano?   No. Está lejos.
4. Tienes mucha suerte.   ¡Estás loco!
5. ¿Está cerca el cine?   No, me falta práctica.
6. No puedo ir.   Me es igual.
                                  Lo siento. ¿Mañana, quizás?

G   Complete the following dialogue with the correct forms of *saber*.

Mónica: ¿____ quién es ese chico?
  Pedro: Sí, es Miguel Santos.
Mónica: ¿____ dónde vive?
  Pedro: No, no ____. Pero sé que Miguel ____ jugar al tenis. Juega con mi hermano los fines de semana. Ellos ____ jugar muy bien. No juego con ellos porque yo no ____ jugar bastante bien.

Answer the following questions based on the preceding dialogue between Pedro and Mónica.

1. ¿Sabe Mónica dónde vive Miguel?
2. ¿Con quién juega al tenis Miguel?
3. ¿Cuándo juega al tenis?
4. ¿Quién juega bien?

Culminating activity: Play *béisbol*, *fútbol*, or *básquetbol* in season. (See Teacher's Guide for instructions.) Use any of Chapter 7 activities for questions.

Vocabulario

SUSTANTIVOS

el argentino, la argentina Argentinian
el básquetbol basketball
el béisbol baseball
el campeón champion
la carrera race
el carro deportivo sports car
el cartel poster
el clarinete clarinet
el coche car
la competencia competition
el deporte sport
la entrada admission
el esquí skiing
la estación season
la fama fame
el fútbol soccer
el fútbol americano football
el ganador, la ganadora winner
la guitarra guitar
el instrumento instrument
el invierno winter
la invitación invitation
el juego game
la natación swimming
las noticias news
el otoño autumn
el partido game, match
el piano piano
la práctica practice
el precio price
la primavera spring
el refresco refreshment, soft drink
el tambor drum
el tenis tennis

el trofeo trophy
la trompeta trumpet
el verano summer
el violín violin
el vólibol volleyball

VERBOS

aceptar to accept
anunciar to announce
esquiar to ski
invitar to invite
ir to go
jugar (ue) to play (a sport or game)
manejar to drive
nadar to swim
odiar to hate
organizar to organize
perder to lose; **pierdo** I lose
practicar to practice
recibir to receive
saber to know
tocar to play (an instrument)

EXPRESIONES

a tu favor in your favor
bastante bien quite well
chao good-by
de la mañana (tarde, noche) A.M. (P.M.)
hago/haces trampa I am/you are cheating
más o menos more or less
me es igual it's all the same to me
me falta [práctica] I need [practice]
otra vez again
te gusta you like
tener suerte to be lucky
todo el mundo everybody
vienen they come, they're coming

OTRAS PALABRAS

alemán, alemana German
bastante quite, enough
bueno all right; well
cuarto 1/4 (hour)
durante during
francés, francesa French
gran great
italiano, -a Italian
loco, -a crazy
magnífico, -a magnificent, great
maravilloso, -a marvelous
menos less, minus
mundial worldwide
pequeño, -a little, small
según according to
si if
sobre about, concerning

De vacaciones

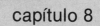 Colombia, located in the northwestern part of South America, is a country of great geographical diversity. It has long coastlines on both the Caribbean Sea and the Pacific Ocean, deep tropical valleys, windswept plateaus, jungles, lowland plains, and mountain ranges that form part of the Andes. Because Colombia is located close to the equator, climate and temperature depend in large part on altitude.

Una excursión a Monserrate

Locate Colombia and Bogotá on map.

Warm-up: Ask questions, reviewing structures from Chapter 7.

Leonor y Margarita visitan a su primo Ernesto. Ellas son de la costa atlántica y éste es su primer viaje a Bogotá. Ernesto sugiere subir a Monserrate en funicular. Los chicos llegan a la cima de la montaña a mediodía.

LEONOR	¡Qué vista tan hermosa! ¡Qué aire tan puro!
MARGARITA	Sí, chica, pero ¡qué frío hace aquí arriba! Hay mucha diferencia con la temperatura de la costa.
ERNESTO	Para Bogotá, hace buen tiempo hoy. ¿Por qué no bajamos la montaña a pie? Es un ejercicio excelente.
MARGARITA	¡Magnífica idea! Yo tengo mucho frío.
LEONOR	¿No es peligroso? Tengo miedo de un atraco.
ERNESTO	¡Qué tonta eres! Ven con nosotros. Durante el día no hay peligro.
LEONOR	Bueno ... de acuerdo. Si insistes.

Después de caminar toda la tarde, las chicas ven que están perdidos.

LEONOR	¡Ernesto! ¡Estamos perdidos!
ERNESTO	¿Perdidos? Yo sé muy bien el camino.
MARGARITA	¿Estás seguro?
ERNESTO	Pues, ahora no estoy seguro.
LEONOR	¡Qué miedo! ¡Y ya casi es de noche!
ERNESTO	No te preocupes. Yo sé volver. ¡Mira! Allí están ya las primeras casas de la ciudad.

comprensión

After introducing dialogue, play taped version. Assign roles and have class read along. Then act out.

Game to check comprehension: Prepare simple questions about dialogue and play *College Bowl*. See Teacher's Guide for instructions.

Retell the outing to Monserrate from Leonor's point of view.

▪ Mi hermana y yo ...   Mi hermana y yo visitamos Bogotá.

1. Somos de ...
2. Nuestro primo Ernesto sugiere subir ...
3. En la cima ...
4. Ernesto quiere ...
5. Tengo miedo ...
6. Ernesto está seguro ..., pero ...
7. Finalmente, podemos ver ...

extensión

A. Ask several classmates where each one plans to go on vacation.

▪ ¿Adónde piensas° ir de vacaciones°?   A las montañas.
A la playa°, quizás.
Pienso [estar aquí].
No sé todavía.

Bogotá y el teleférico a Monserrate.

B. During a hiking expedition, your group leader loses the way. Reassure a frightened hiker that everything's all right.

▪▥ ¡Tengo miedo! ¡Estamos perdidos!   Estoy seguro/segura que no.
No te preocupes.
Yo sé el camino.

C. Express your likes and dislikes or your moods in various situations by combining elements from the two columns.

1	2
Me gusta mucho	la ciudad de Bogotá
No me gusta	estar perdido/perdida
Tengo miedo de	subir montañas
Es aburrido	el aire puro
Odio	tener frío
	hacer ejercicio
	un atraco

▪▥ No me gusta hacer ejercicio.

Bogotá, the capital of Colombia, is located on a plateau at an altitude of over 2600 meters. In spite of its proximity to the equator, the city enjoys cool temperatures all year round, averaging between 12 to 15 degrees Celsius. On top of Monserrate, a mountain that rises more than 300 meters above Bogotá, the temperature drops to about 5 degrees Celsius. In the coastal areas the climate is hot and humid, with little more than a few degrees difference between the hottest and coolest months.

Photo: View of Bogotá from Monserrate.

La tierra caliente

Melgar is a resort area near Bogotá.

Hotel Melgar

Favor enviar su reservación a las oficinas del hotel.
Melgar, Tolima
Teléfonos: 55 20 55   52 21 00

¡¡¡5 razones para venir al Hotel Melgar a pasar sus vacaciones!!!

¿Un clima ideal?
¡Lo tenemos!

¿Precios económicos?
¡Aquí los encuentra!

¿Piscina privada?
¡La tenemos!

¿Habitaciones confortables?
¡Nosotros las tenemos!

¿Discoteca y restaurante?
¡Aquí los hay!

comprensión

Assignment: Have students make ads similar to the *Hotel Melgar* ad, stressing important aspects of the resort. Best ads may be displayed on bulletin board.

Check your understanding of the advertisement by correcting the statements below.

▣▥ El anuncio describe unas oficinas.   No. Describe un hotel.

1. El hotel se llama Tierra Caliente.
2. Hay cinco vacaciones.
3. El hotel tiene un clima privado.
4. Los precios son confortables.
5. Las habitaciones son calientes.
6. Hay que enviar su reservación a la discoteca.
7. No hay restaurante.

extensión

V: Students select place to which they seek directions: *las montañas, el hotel, la discoteca, el restaurante.*

The word *finca*, in Colombia, means farm or ranch. In other countries these might be called *estancias* or *haciendas*.

In Colombia, *el radio* is often used to refer to a radio set; *la radio* refers to a broadcast. In other countries, *la radio* is generally used for both meanings.

A. You and a friend have wandered off from the farm where you're spending your vacation. Convince her/him that you know how to get back.

■III ¿Sabes volver° a la finca°?

¡Claro! Es fácil.
Estoy seguro que es [a la derecha].
Sé el camino de memoria°.

B. Tell a classmate what you do on weekends during the summer.

■III En verano, ¿qué haces los fines de semana?

A veces° voy a la piscina.
Voy a merendar° al campo°.
Voy a [montar a caballo°].
Muy poco.

C. You and your friends are setting off for an all-day picnic. Ask if everything is ready.

■III ¿Está todo listo°?

Creo que sí°.
Casi, pero no encuentro° mi cámara°.
Sí, todo está listo.
Me falta mi radio°.

Santa Marta, en la costa atlántica colombiana.

Estudio de palabras

¿Qué tiempo hace?

Optional: If foreign weather reports are available, discuss weather abroad. Have students locate cities on map as they report.

Hace buen tiempo.
Hace sol.
Hace calor.

Hace mal tiempo.
Hace viento.
Hace fresco.
Llueve.
Está nublado.

Hace frío.
Nieva.

GRADOS	
F	C
122	50
113	45
104	40
95	35
86	30
77	25
68	20
59	15
50	10
41	5
▸32	0◂
23	−5
14	−10
5	−15
−4	−20
−13	−25

A Imagine what the weather is like in the following cities, based on the temperature given. Use the thermometer as a guide.

- Buenos Aires: 17°C   *Hace fresco y está nublado.*
- Anchorage: −22°C   *Hace mucho frío y hace viento.*

1. París: 5°C
2. México: 21°C
3. La Habana: 40°C
4. Londres: 8°C

5. Bogotá: 15°C
6. Boston: −10°C
7. Caracas: 29°C
8. Tokio: 12°C

B Explain to an exchange student from Colombia what the weather is like in your town during each season of the year.

- ¿Qué tiempo hace en invierno?   *Hace mucho frío y nieva.*

Chain drill combining weather and months: S¹: ¿Qué tiempo hace en enero? S²: Hace frío. Y en febrero, ¿qué tiempo hace? S³: Hace fresco. Y en marzo. . . .

Optional: Assign a date to each student for current month. Student must write and give weather report for the day. Students assigned to weekends give their reports on Mondays, using *hacía*.

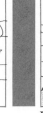

Spending a few days in **tierra caliente** (hot country) is a welcome change for residents of cities located in the mountains. **Tierra caliente** is a term used to refer to low altitude areas where the climate is always warm. **Tierra fría** (cold country) refers to regions at high altitudes where temperatures are always cool. Bogotá is in **tierra fría,** while Melgar, near Bogotá, is in **tierra caliente.**

Expresiones con **tener**

Marcos tiene sueño.

Cristina tiene calor.

Daniel tiene frío.

Tere tiene prisa.

Carlota y Adolfo tienen miedo.

Anita tiene razón y Manuel no tiene razón.

C   Describe to a classmate a situation in which you're sleepy, hot, cold, in a hurry, afraid, and right or wrong.

Optional: Practice *tener* expressions, books closed, before doing exercise. Have students mime gestures for classmates to describe.

- ◼‖ ¿Cuándo tienes prisa?   *Tengo prisa cuando voy al colegio.*
- ◼‖ ¿Cuándo tienes miedo?   *Tengo miedo cuando tengo examen.*

Pronunciación y ortografía

palabras claves ‖ **flap** [r]   mira
trilled [rr]   carro, rubio

In Spanish, the flap [r] sound is similar to the sound of *dd* in English *ladder* or *tt* in *letter*. The tip of the tongue makes a single flap against the gum ridge behind the upper front teeth. The flap [r] sound is spelled **r.**

A   Listen and repeat the following words after your teacher.

pero	primo	tarjeta	obrero
hora	fresco	moderno	enfermera
mira	gran	interés	profesor
puro	trabaja	verano	por favor

B Read the following sentences aloud. Pay special attention to the flap [r] sound.

1. ¡Qué aire tan puro!
2. Ernesto sugiere subir en funicular.
3. Por favor, ¿está cerca el parque?

Suggest that students probably made lots of trilled [rr] sounds in imitation of planes, cars, telephones when they were younger.

The trilled [rr] is pronounced with the tip of the tongue in the same position as for the flap [r], but the tip of the tongue vibrates against the gum ridge. The trilled [rr] sound is spelled **rr** between vowels and **r** at the beginning of a word and after **l, n,** or **s (alrededor, Enrique, Israel).**

C Listen and repeat after your teacher the following words containing the trilled [rr] sound.

carro	arriba	razón	refresco
perro	pizarra	restaurante	regular
correo	guitarra	repetir	resfriado
carrera	horror	reparar	recibe

D Read the following sentences aloud. Pay careful attention to the trilled [rr] sound.

Trabalenguas: Erre con erre, cigarro. Erre con erre, barril. Rápido corren los carros, los carros del ferrocarril.

1. Enrique va a Monserrate en carro.
2. Raquel toma un refresco.
3. ¡Qué horror! Esta carrera es muy aburrida.

For better retention of proverbs, make poster of each for classroom display.

Perro que ladra no muerde.

Gramática

Stem-changing verbs: e to ie

Optional: Review present tense of -ar, -er, and -ir verbs before introducing stem-changing verbs. Explain that it is the stress on the stem vowel that causes it to change. The stem vowel of the nosotros-form has no stress, therefore it does not change. Emphasize that endings remain the same.

	PENSAR
yo	pienso
tú	piensas
él, ella, usted	piensa
nosotros, nosotras	pensamos
ellos, ellas, ustedes	piensan

The verb **pensar** (to think; to intend) has a change from **e** to **ie** in the stem vowel in the present tense. The stem does not change in the **nosotros-**form. The endings of **pensar** are regular.

Other verbs with a stem change **e>ie** are **perder** (to lose), **querer** (to want), **preferir** (to prefer), and **sugerir** (to suggest).

A Next week is a busy one for everybody. Say what the following people are planning to do.

Optional: Have students cue original activities with pictures or actions. Others must give sentence.

■ꜱ Anita / esquiar   *Anita piensa esquiar.*

1. yo / ir de compras
2. papá y yo / trabajar en casa
3. Daniel / jugar al básquetbol
4. tú / estudiar para un examen
5. usted / escribir cartas
6. mamá / visitar a mi abuela
7. mis hermanos / tocar el piano
8. ustedes / aprender francés

B Inform your teacher of your group's suggestions and preferences concerning activities for a Spanish Club trip.

■ꜱ ¿Cómo prefieren ir al campo?   (en carro)   *Preferimos ir en carro.*

1. ¿Dónde quieren merendar?   (cerca de la piscina)
2. ¿Adónde sugieren ir por la noche?   (una discoteca)
3. ¿Cómo quieren subir la montaña?   (a pie)
4. ¿Cuándo prefieren nadar?   (por la tarde)
5. ¿Qué quieren hacer por la mañana?   (jugar al béisbol)
6. ¿A qué hora sugieren volver?   (a las cinco)
7. ¿Cuándo quieren montar a caballo?   (por la mañana)

¡vamos a hablar! Ask your classmates their preferences concerning various activities and things.

¿Prefieres las montañas o la playa?   Prefiero la playa. ¿Y tú?

¿Prefieres jugar al tenis o al vólibol?   Al vólibol. Siempre pierdo cuando juego al tenis.

Stem-changing verbs: o to ue

	PODER
yo	puedo
tú	puedes
él, ella, usted	puede
nosotros, nosotras	podemos
ellos, ellas, ustedes	pueden

The verb **poder** *(to be able, can)* has a stem-vowel change from **o** to **ue** in the present tense. The stem of the **nosotros**-form does not change. **Poder** takes the regular endings for **-er** verbs.

Other verbs with a stem change **o** > **ue** are **encontrar** *(to find)*, **recordar** *(to remember)*, and **volver** *(to return)*.

C You're trying to organize a volleyball game. Say that the people indicated can play today but not tomorrow.

■ıı   Daniel   *Daniel puede jugar hoy, pero mañana, no.*

1. yo
2. Rosa
3. tu primo
4. ustedes

5. tú
6. Alberto
7. Silvia y yo
8. Carmen y Pablo

D It's Saturday and everyone is going to be out or away. Tell a friend when the following people will return home. Use a time reference or day of the week in your response.

■ıı   Elisa   — *¿Cuándo vuelve Elisa?*
— *Vuelve a las doce.*

1. Raquel y yo
2. yo
3. Javier
4. tú
5. Ignacio y sus padres
6. Anita y Carmen

E   The following people are very forgetful. Explain what things they can't find or remember.

For added practice with stem-changing verbs, play *Ta Te Ti*.

■⫶   yo / encontrar / reloj   *Yo no encuentro mi reloj.*

1. María / recordar / su número de teléfono
2. ustedes / encontrar / sus libros
3. tú / encontrar / tu radio
4. Julio / recordar / el cumpleaños de su hermano
5. mis primos / encontrar / sus instrumentos
6. nosotros / recordar / cómo ir a la finca

Personal a

Optional: Elicit explanation of what direct objects are before introducing personal *a*.

Explain that the personal *a* used with *el* contracts to *al*.

Pienso visitar **a** mis amigos.	I plan to visit my friends.
Tengo que llamar **a** mi padre.	I have to call my father.
No quiero invitar **a** Carmen a la fiesta.	I don't want to invite Carmen to the party.

The preposition **a** is used before a direct-object noun that refers to a person. Personal **a** has no English equivalent.

F   You're moving to another city and want to phone some friends to say good-by. Whom are you going to call?

■⫶   David   *Voy a llamar a David.*

1. Anita y Julia
2. Carmen
3. José
4. Daniel y Roberto
5. Marcos y Sara
6. tu prima

G   You're trying to remember whom you have to see, help, or contact today. State what you have to do.

■⫶   llamar / el profesor   *Tengo que llamar al profesor.*

1. invitar / Juan a merendar
2. ayudar / mi hermana
3. llamar / mis abuelos
4. llevar / Elena al dentista
5. visitar / la señora Ruiz
6. invitar / los primos a la finca
7. ayudar / Ricardo

Direct-object pronouns **lo, la, los, las**

Optional: Before drilling object pronouns in complete sentences, give quick drill of pronouns alone, cueing with objects or flashcards: *el libro > lo; la silla > la; los cuadernos > los; las chicas > las.*

¿Buscas **el correo?**	Sí, **lo** busco.
¿Escuchas **la música?**	Sí, **la** escucho.
¿Tienes **tus libros?**	Sí, **los** tengo.
¿Invitas **a tus primas?**	Sí, **las** invito.

A direct-object pronoun replaces a direct-object noun or noun phrase. The pronouns **lo, la, los,** and **las** agree in number and gender with the noun they replace. In Spanish, a direct-object pronoun generally precedes a conjugated verb.

SINGULAR	
lo	him, it, you *(formal)*
la	her, it, you *(formal)*

PLURAL	
los	them, you *(formal and familiar)*
las	them, you *(formal and familiar)*

The direct-object pronouns **lo, la, los,** and **las** have several English equivalents.

H Absent-minded Alberto is looking for some missing possessions and asks you if you have them. Tell him whether or not you do.

Chain drill to combine practice of *tener* and pronouns. S¹: *¿Tienes mi libro?* S²: *No, no lo tengo, pero Claudia lo tiene. ¿Tienes mis lentes? S³: No, no los tengo, pero Cristina los tiene,* etc.

■III   mi libro   Alberto: *¿Tienes mi libro?*
　　　　　　　　　　　　Tú: *Sí, lo tengo.*
　　　　　　　　　　　　(No, no lo tengo.)

1. mi cuaderno
2. mi bicicleta
3. mis papeles
4. mi guitarra
5. mis discos
6. mis lápices
7. mi trompeta
8. mis cartas

I Pedro is joining you and your family for a weekend at a resort. Assure him that there are all the attractions he asks about.

■III   caballos   Pedro: *¿Hay caballos?*
　　　　　　　　　　　　Tú: *Sí, los hay.*

1. discoteca
2. piscinas
3. tenis
4. fiestas
5. restaurante
6. vistas bonitas
7. televisión
8. habitaciones confortables
9. partidos de fútbol

Direct-object pronouns with infinitives

Optional: Explain that a direct-object pronoun may also precede the conjugated verb in double verb constructions: *Lo sé tocar.*

Sé tocar el piano.   Sé **tocarlo.**
Quiero visitar a Elena.   Quiero **visitarla.**

When a conjugated verb is followed by an infinitive, a direct-object pronoun usually follows and is attached to the infinitive.

J   Pilar asks who's coming to your party. Tell her you plan to invite the following people today.

V: S¹: *¿Sabes tocar el piano?* S²: *Sí, sé to-carlo. (No, . . .)*

■ⅲ   ¿Va David?   *Hoy pienso invitarlo.*

1. ¿Van Anita y Julia?   5. ¿Daniel y Roberto van?
2. ¿Carmen va?   6. ¿Va tu prima?
3. José va, ¿verdad?   7. ¿Van tus hermanas?
4. ¿Van Marcos y Sara?   8. Pedro y Rosa van, ¿no?

Direct-object pronouns **me, te, nos**

¿**Me** llamas?   Are you calling *me*?
No **te** comprendo.   I don't understand *you*.
Juan quiere llevar**nos** al cine.   Juan wants to take *us* to the movies.

The direct-object pronouns **me, te,** and **nos** precede a conjugated verb. They usually follow and are attached to an infinitive.

K   Reassure various friends that you'll do or are doing what each one asks.

■ⅲ   ¿Me invitas a la fiesta?   *¡Claro que te invito a la fiesta!*

1. ¿Me ayudas a estudiar?
2. ¿Me escuchas ahora?
3. ¿Me llamas por teléfono esta tarde?
4. ¿Me llevas a casa?
5. ¿Me llevas a la piscina?

L   Your grandparents called while your family was out. Give your parents their messages, using the cues provided.

■ⅲ   llamar por teléfono mañana   *Van a llamarnos por teléfono mañana.*

1. ayudar a buscar una casa
2. visitar en junio
3. invitar a su casa
4. llevar a una finca
5. invitar a un restaurante

Danzas populares, Cali, Colombia.

Me gustan and te gustan

Me gustan los domingos.	*I like* Sundays.
No **me gustan** los viajes.	*I don't like* trips.
¿**Te gustan** los deportes?	*Do you like* sports?

In *Capítulo 7* (page 146), you learned that **me gusta** and **te gusta** are used with infinitives and singular nouns to express likes and dislikes. The forms **me gustan** and **te gustan** are used with plural nouns.

M

Ask a classmate if he/she likes the following things. Use *me gusta(n)* and *te gusta(n)*, as appropriate.

> ▪‖‖ las vacaciones — ¿*Te gustan las vacaciones?*
> — *Sí, me gustan* [*mucho*].
>   (*No, no me gustan.*)

1. los caballos
2. el invierno
3. nadar
4. las montañas

5. los deportes
6. las fiestas
7. el béisbol
8. ir al colegio

Game: Each student writes 5 sentences about what he/she likes or dislikes. Read one student's sentences and ask, ¿Quién es? S¹: Eres tú, María, porque [te gustan los tacos]. María: Sí (No) . . . Winner reads next sentence.

Lectura

¡Fútbol! El deporte número uno

¡GOL! Es el grito° entusiasmado de todos los espectadores cuando entra el
balón° en la portería°. El estadio de Bogotá está lleno°. Hace un día fresco
e ideal para un partido de fútbol.

   ¿Y qué deporte es el fútbol que vuelve locos° a jóvenes y a viejos°? Es un
deporte de mucho dinamismo, agilidad y estrategia, en el que dos equipos°
luchan° por llevar el balón a la portería contraria. Un equipo tiene diez
jugadores° y un portero° y todos tienen una posición que defender. En este
juego los jugadores pueden usar los pies° y la cabeza, pero no pueden usar
las manos°.

shout
ball/goal/full

drives crazy/old (persons)
teams
struggle
players/goalkeeper
feet
hands

actividades

Help students pick out
cognates. List on
board, and elicit equiva-
lents. Alert students to
false cognates: *portero*
is not porter, *equipo* is
not equipment in con-
text of reading.

A. Find five cognates in the reading and give their English equivalents.

B. Answer the following questions about sports.

    1. ¿Te vuelve loco/loca el fútbol?
    2. ¿Piensas que el béisbol es un deporte de dinamismo y estrategia?
       ¿el básquetbol?
    3. ¿Cuántos jugadores hay en un equipo de béisbol? ¿de básquetbol?
       ¿de vólibol?

Stem-changing verbs **e** to **ie** and **o** to **ue**   (A–E)

	PREFERIR (e>ie)	VOLVER (o>ue)
yo	prefiero	vuelvo
tú	prefieres	vuelves
él, ella, usted	prefiere	vuelve
nosotros, nosotras	preferimos	volvemos
vosotros, vosotras	preferís	volvéis
ellos, ellas, ustedes	prefieren	vuelven

1. Some **-ar, -er,** and **-ir** verbs have a stem change from **e** to **ie** or from **o** to **ue** in the present tense. The change occurs in all forms except the **nosotros-** and **vosotros-**forms.
2. Stem change **e>ie: pensar; perder, querer; preferir, sugerir.**
   Stem change **o>ue: encontrar, recordar; poder, volver.**

Personal **a**   (F, G)

> Voy a buscar **a** Daniel.
> Voy a buscar un mapa.

The preposition **a** is used before a direct-object noun that refers to a person. Personal **a** has no English equivalent.

Direct-object pronouns   (H–L)

SINGULAR	
me	me
te	you *(familiar)*
lo	him, it, you *(formal)*
la	her, it, you *(formal)*

PLURAL	
nos	we
os	you *(familiar in Spain)*
los	them *(m.)*, you *(formal, familiar)*
las	them *(f.)*, you *(formal, familiar)*

1. In Spanish, a direct-object pronoun precedes a conjugated verb. It often follows and is attached to an infinitive: **Lo juego bien; Sé tocarlo.**
2. The direct-object pronouns **lo, la, los,** and **las** agree in number and gender with the noun they replace: **¿Escuchas el disco? Sí, lo escucho.**

Me gusta(n) and te gusta(n) (M)

SINGULAR	PLURAL
Me gusta el otoño.	No me gustan los perros.
¿Te gusta nadar?	¿Te gustan los viajes?

Me gusta and **te gusta** are used with a singular noun or an infinitive. **Me gustan** and **te gustan** are used with a plural noun.

Repaso

A Describe the weather and say what the people are doing or can't do. Make three or four statements about each scene.

■||| *Hace buen tiempo . . . Los chicos no pueden . . .*

B Make an assumption about the following people, choosing an expression from the list below.

Tiene sueño.   **Tiene frío.**   **Tiene prisa.**
Tiene calor.   **Tiene miedo.**   **(No) tiene razón.**

Assignment: Have students draw scenes illustrating weather and activities. Display in next class and have students describe. Have students bring in pictures illustrating *tener* expressions, with appropriate labels. Display on bulletin board.

■||| Miguel piensa que Bogotá está en Colombia.   *Tiene razón.*

1. Es verano y hace sol. Claudia juega al tenis.
2. Daniel vuelve a casa. Nieva y hace viento.
3. Ernesto piensa que Bogotá es la capital de México.
4. Es medianoche y Rosario estudia todavía.
5. Lourdes corre a casa porque no quiere llegar tarde.
6. ¡Ricardo está perdido! No sabe el camino a casa.

C   Adela and Mario plan a tennis match. Complete their dialogue with the correct forms of the verbs in parentheses. Then answer the questions that follow.

Adela: Alberto *(pensar)* jugar al tenis el sábado. Leonor y Margarita *(poder)* jugar el domingo.

Mario: Y Daniel, ¿cuándo *(querer)* jugar? Mañana, ¿verdad?

Adela: Sí, y Silvia y yo *(pensar)* jugar mañana también. Y tú, ¿cuándo *(querer)* jugar?

Mario: Mañana o el sábado, me es igual.

1. ¿Cuándo va a jugar Daniel?
2. ¿Con quién va a jugar Silvia?
3. ¿Cuándo quiere jugar Mario?

D   As your band prepares to leave for a concert, the director checks to see that the group has all the instruments and equipment. Answer his questions with the correct direct-object pronouns.

▪ɪɪɪ   ¿Tienen las guitarras?   *Sí, las tenemos.*
(No, no las tenemos.)

1. ¿Tienen las trompetas?
2. Marta, ¿tienes tu violín?
3. ¿Tienen ustedes los clarinetes?
4. Pedro, ¿tienes tu tambor?
5. Fernando, ¿tienes la grabadora?

E   Help Felipe, an exchange student from Bogotá, say what he likes and dislikes about the United States.

▪ɪɪɪ   los discos   *Me gustan los discos.*
(No me gustan los discos.)

1. los deportes
2. las playas de Miami
3. practicar inglés
4. las montañas de Colorado
5. la música
6. las ciudades grandes
7. el otoño
8. los amigos que tengo aquí

F   Create a six-line conversation in which you arrange to go to the swimming pool with Javier and Susana. Use the following guidelines.

1. Ask Javier and Susana if they want to go to the pool.
2. They answer that they can't go in the morning because they plan to go horseback riding.
3. Ask them what time they'll return.
4. They reply that they'll return at noon.
5. Tell them that, if they prefer, you can all go in the afternoon.
6. They answer, "Great! See you later."

capítulo 8   **173**

G   You're vacationing in Colombia and telephone your parents in the United States. Show them how much Spanish you've learned by describing the view from Monserrate, and by telling them what you like or dislike about your trip.

■III   *La vista es . . .*

H   Mr. Durán is a visitor in your town and asks about the weather in your area at different times of the year. Describe it for him.

Using Ex. G as model, students send post-cards describing view from Grand Canyon, Golden Gate Bridge, Rocky Mountains, World Trade Center, Key West, Florida, or other scenic spots students are familiar with.

Optional: Suggest research on Gold Museum or other place that students might like to visit in Colombia.

1. ¿Qué tiempo hace en octubre?
2. ¿Y en diciembre?
3. ¿Y en marzo?
4. ¿Qué tiempo hace en junio?

Artefactos precolombinos, Museo del Oro de Bogotá.

Vocabulario

SUSTANTIVOS

el atraco   holdup
el caballo   horse
la cámara   camera
el camino   road
el campo   country
la cima   summit
el clima   climate
la costa   coast
la discoteca   discotheque
el ejercicio   exercise
la excursión   excursion
la finca   farm, ranch
el funicular   cable railway
la habitación   room
la montaña   mountain
el peligro   danger
la piscina   swimming pool
la playa   beach
el radio   radio
el restaurante   restaurant
la temperatura   temperature
el tiempo   weather
la tierra   land, soil
las vacaciones   vacation
el viaje   trip
la vista   view

OTRAS PALABRAS

arriba   above, up
caliente   hot
confortable   comfortable
después (de)   after
económico, -a   economical
excelente   excellent
hermoso, -a   beautiful
listo, -a   ready
peligroso, -a   dangerous
perdido, -a   lost
seguro, -a   sure
tan   so

VERBOS

caminar   to walk
encontrar (ue)   to find
enviar   to send
insistir   to insist
merendar (ie)   to picnic
pasar   to spend (time)
pensar (ie)   to think; to intend
poder (ue)   to be able, can
recordar (ue)   to remember
subir   to ascend, climb
sugerir (ie)   to suggest
venir   to come
ver   to see; **ven**   they see
volver (ue)   to return

¿QUÉ TIEMPO HACE?

está nublado   it's cloudy
hace buen tiempo   the weather's nice
hace calor   it's warm
hace fresco   it's cool
hace frío   it's cold
hace mal tiempo   the weather's bad
hace sol   it's sunny
hace viento   it's windy
llueve   it's raining
nieva   it's snowing
¿qué tiempo hace?   what's the weather like?

EXPRESIONES

a pie   on foot
a veces   sometimes
creo que sí   I believe so
de memoria   by heart
hacer ejercicio   to exercise
montar a caballo   to ride horseback
no tener razón   to be wrong
tener calor   to be hot
tener frío   to be cold
tener miedo   to be afraid
tener prisa   to be in a hurry
tener razón   to be right
tener sueño   to be sleepy
ven [con nosotros]   come [with us]

capítulo 9

¡A comer!

Spain, separated from Europe by the Pyrenees and nearly surrounded by the Mediterranean Sea and the Atlantic Ocean, is marked by its diversity in geography, climate, and regional traditions. Each region prides itself for its own customs, language, and excellent foods. Among the many regional specialties enjoyed by Spaniards and visitors are **gazpacho, paella,** roast suckling pig, and varied seafood and fish dishes.

¿Adónde vamos a cenar?

Luz María y Ricardo, dos estudiantes universitarios de Madrid, pasan todo el sábado en la biblioteca. Son las 9:30 de la noche.

LUZ MARÍA	Acabo de terminar mi trabajo. ¡Me muero de hambre!
RICARDO	Yo también. Además estoy cansado.
LUZ MARÍA	Vamos a la cafetería a ver qué hay de comer.
RICARDO	Filetes, tortilla española, sandwiches . . . Ya sabes, nada nuevo.
LUZ MARÍA	¿Por qué no vamos a un restaurante?
RICARDO	¡Buena idea! Pero no tengo suficiente dinero.
LUZ MARÍA	No importa. Yo tengo bastante. Me pagas después.
RICARDO	De acuerdo. Vamos al Bodegón Español. Allí sirven unas comidas deliciosas y no muy caras.
LUZ MARÍA	¡Fantástico! Vamos, entonces.

extensión

A. You've worked all day and are exhausted and hungry. A friend suggests going to the cafeteria, but the menu doesn't appeal to you. Express your discontent or suggest going elsewhere.

◼▮ ¿Vamos a la cafetería?　　No. Siempre sirven [hamburguesas°].
La comida es barata°, pero no me gusta.
La comida es horrible allí.
¿Por qué no vamos a un restaurante?

B. You and a friend want to get something to eat, but you need some money. Ask to borrow $3.00.

◼▮ ¿Puedes prestarme tres dólares?　　Lo siento. Hoy no tengo dinero.
Sí, me pagas después.
Si llevo suficiente dinero.

C. It's the end of a long day. Explain to a friend what you've just done and how you feel or what you do or don't want to do. Use some of the following phrases.

Acabo de . . .　　　No quiero . . .
Quiero . . .　　　　Me muero de . . .
Estoy . . .　　　　 Tengo . . .

◼▮ ¿Qué tal?　　¡Acabo de terminar mi trabajo!
Me muero de sueño.

En el restaurante

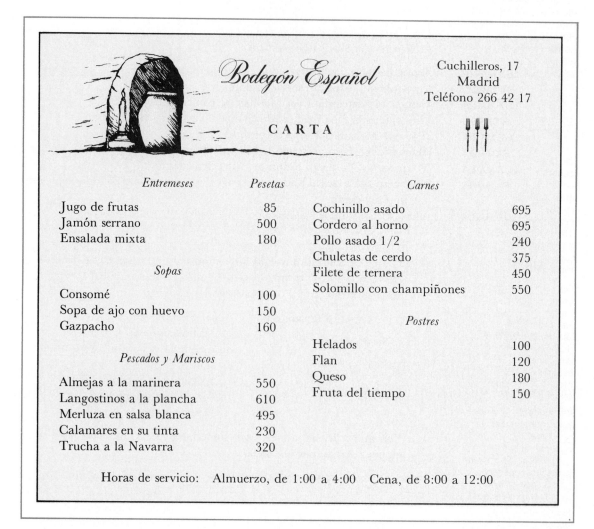

Bodegón Español

Cuchilleros, 17
Madrid
Teléfono 266 42 17

CARTA

Entremeses	Pesetas
Jugo de frutas	85
Jamón serrano	500
Ensalada mixta	180

Sopas

Consomé	100
Sopa de ajo con huevo	150
Gazpacho	160

Pescados y Mariscos

Almejas a la marinera	550
Langostinos a la plancha	610
Merluza en salsa blanca	495
Calamares en su tinta	230
Trucha a la Navarra	320

Carnes

Cochinillo asado	695
Cordero al horno	695
Pollo asado 1/2	240
Chuletas de cerdo	375
Filete de ternera	450
Solomillo con champiñones	550

Postres

Helados	100
Flan	120
Queso	180
Fruta del tiempo	150

Horas de servicio: Almuerzo, de 1:00 a 4:00   Cena, de 8:00 a 12:00

Compare *tener sed* / *hambre* to *tener sueño* / *frío*, etc.

Luz María y Ricardo llegan al Bodegón Español. Después de decidir lo que quieren, piden la cena.

CAMARERO	Buenas noches, señores. ¿Qué desean para cenar?
LUZ MARÍA	Para mí una ensalada y la merluza.
RICARDO	Y para mí un gazpacho y el solomillo con champiñones.
CAMARERO	Muy bien. Para beber, ¿qué desean?
LUZ MARÍA	Vino blanco, por favor.
RICARDO	Para mí también, y agua, por favor. Tengo mucha sed.

Students are not expected to master entire contents of menu. Drill only most common items or those which most interest students. The selection illustrates a typical Spanish menu. (See Appendix B for menu equivalents.)

Optional: Have small groups act out a restaurant scene with one waiter and four diners. Dialogue might include discussion of where to dine, arrival and being seated, reading menu, ordering, commenting on food, asking for and paying bill.

Both *ser* and *estar* may be used with certain adjectives. With food, *ser* + adj. generally describes normal or inherent characteristics. Use of *estar* indicates a subjective appraisal of the appearance or taste of a dish at a given moment.

Possible responses: 1) ¡Claro que sí! 2) ¡Qué ricos! Muchas gracias. / ¡Uy! ¡Los odio! 3) No quiero postre, gracias. 4) Me es igual, gracias.

Tell whether the following statements are true *(sí)* or false *(no)*. Correct any wrong information.

1. Los chicos van a la cafetería universitaria.
2. El restaurante sólo sirve la cena a las 9:30 de la noche.
3. El Bodegón Español está en Madrid.
4. Luz María quiere sopa de ajo y vino blanco.
5. Ricardo pide el solomillo.

A. You're at the Bodegón Español and have 900 *pesetas*. Look at the menu on page 178 and order a meal.

◼▥ Camarero: ¿Qué desea, [señor]?   Tú: [Solomillo], por favor.
   ¿Y para beber?   Para beber quiero . . .
   ¿Algo° más?   De postre . . .

B. It's Soledad's birthday. You and your friend Alejandro are taking her out to dinner. Order a meal for the three of you, based on the menu on page 178.

◼▥ ¿Qué desean los señores?   Para la señorita . . .
                                        Para el señor . . .
                                        Para mí . . .

C. You're dining out and have finished the main course. Your waitress asks you if that's all you would like.

◼▥ ¿Es todo, [señorita]?   Sí, gracias.
                                     La cuenta°, por favor.
                                     Quiero [un café°].

D. Imagine that you are tasting a food for the first time. Express your opinion of it, using one of the statements on the right.

◼▥ ¿Qué tal [el jamón serrano]?   No me gusta.
                                            ¡Uy! ¡Es horrible!
                                            Me gusta mucho.
                                            Es muy rico°.

E. React to the following suggestions. Accept or decline politely, make a choice, or express your like or dislike for the food offered to you.

◼▥ ¿Quieres más pescado?   Es delicioso, pero no puedo
                                     comer más.

1. ¿Quieres helado?
2. Hay calamares para la cena.
3. De postre, hay fruta.
4. ¿Prefiere un vaso° de agua o
   un jugo de frutas?

¿Qué quieres comer?

Introduce, using food flashcards. See Appendix C for additional foods and utensils.

Extend Ex. A: Order various *sopas (sopa de pollo, tomate, pescado)*, *ensaladas (pollo, fruta, jamón)*, or *sandwiches (jamón, pollo, huevo, bistec, lechuga y tomate)*.

la ensalada	salad
la lechuga	lettuce
el tomate	tomato
la sopa	soup
la carne	meat
el pollo	chicken
el jamón	ham
el bistec	steak
el pescado	fish
los huevos	eggs

la verdura	vegetable
la patata (la papa)	potato
la fruta	fruit
la manzana	apple
la naranja	orange
la bebida	drink
la leche	milk
el refresco	soft drink
el pan	bread
el postre	dessert

A   You're very hungry today. Order a meal from the foods listed above. Begin with *para mí* or *quiero*.

■||| *Para mí, una ensalada, una sopa de tomate, un bistec con patatas y una manzana, por favor.*

Assignment: Have students bring in 5 pictures of food and state likes / dislikes.

B   You're preparing dinner for your brothers and sisters while your parents are away. Announce what you're serving, based on the illustration above.

■||| *Para la cena, hay . . .*

Los números de 100 a 1.000

Review numbers from zero to ninety-nine before introducing higher numbers.

Optional: Teach year dates: 1982 = *mil novecientos ochenta y dos.*

100 = cien (ciento)		600 = seiscientos, -as	
200 = doscientos, -as		700 = setecientos, -as	
300 = trescientos, -as		800 = ochocientos, -as	
400 = cuatrocientos, -as		900 = novecientos, -as	
500 = quinientos, -as		1.000 = mil	

1. **Cien** is used before nouns, and **ciento** is used before other numbers: **cien casas, ciento trece carros.**
2. Numbers from 200 through 999 agree in gender with the noun they modify: **cuatrocientas pesetas.**
3. **Y** is used between units of tens and ones, but not between tens and hundreds: **ochocientos setenta y ocho.**

E Say how many calories each food has.

un helado	248	patatas	470
pescado	173	jugo de naranja	100
una hamburguesa	548	bistec, ensalada y papas	983
un vaso de leche	180	un sandwich de queso	315
un sandwich de jamón	362	ensalada de mariscos	705

Assignment: Using calorie charts, students prepare diet menu for *desayuno, almuerzo,* and *cena,* listing calories for each item and for whole meal. Write out figures.

■ *Un vaso de leche tiene ciento ochenta calorías.*

F You're helping to count ballots for the student council elections. Say how many votes each candidate for president received.

■ Jaime: 348 *Jaime tiene trescientos cuarenta y ocho.*

1. Juan: 563
2. Rosa: 718
3. Antonio: 391
4. Dolores: 207
5. Gloria: 872
6. David: 950

Good table manners are considered important by most Spanish-speaking people, though customs vary depending on the socioeconomic level of the family. In Spain, for example, as in many countries in Latin America and in Europe, it is considered polite to rest one's forearms lightly on the edge of the table while eating. It is also customary to keep the fork in the left hand and the knife in the right, instead of switching back and forth, as most Americans do. Some people use a knife and fork to eat a sandwich, and a knife to peel and slice fruit before eating it with a fork.

Pronunciación y ortografía

palabras claves
[p]	**pan**
[t]	tomate
[ñ]	se**ñ**or

The Spanish [p] sound is similar to English [p] sound except that it is pronounced without a puff of air. The [p] sound is always spelled **p.** The Spanish [t] sound is also pronounced without a puff of air. It is produced with the tip of the tongue touching the back of the upper front teeth. The [t] sound is always spelled **t.**

A Listen and repeat the following words after your teacher. Hold the back of your hand close to your mouth to be sure you pronounce the [p] and [t] sounds without a puff of air.

Trabalenguas: Pedro Pablo Pérez Peña, pintor portugués. Pinta paisajes por poco precio para poder pasar pronto para París.

[p]		[t]	
pan	papel	tener	bastante
postre	lápiz	tortilla	restaurante
pollo	después	tomate	barato
pescado	siempre	trescientos	bistec

B Say the following words aloud to practice the [p] and [t] sounds.

postre	deporte	intérprete	capítulo
patata	importa	trompeta	impaciente
prestar	simpático	tiempo	temperatura

El buen apetito es la salsa más sabrosa.

182   spanish today, one   Proverb: A good appetite is the best sauce.

C Read aloud the following sentences. Be sure that no puff of air leaves your mouth when you pronounce the [p] and [t] sounds.

1. Pedro pide una tortilla de patatas.
2. De postre quiero fruta, por favor.
3. Trescientas pesetas por un bistec es barato.
4. Siempre tengo tiempo para un partido de fútbol.

In Spanish, the [ñ] sound is very similar to the sound of **ny** in English *canyon*. The letter **ñ** is a separate letter of the alphabet and follows **n** in vocabularies and dictionaries.

D Read aloud the following words. Then form two sentences, using two words with **ñ** in each sentence.

señor	español	año
señora	mañana	pequeño

Gramática

Affirmative **tú**-commands

¡**Juega** con tu hermano!	*Play* with your brother!
¡**Come** la sopa!	*Eat* your soup!
¡**Escribe** la carta!	*Write* the letter!

Affirmative **tú**-commands of regular verbs are formed by dropping the **-s** from the **tú**-form of the present tense. **Tú**-commands are used to tell a person you address as **tú** to do something.

A You're a group leader at a summer camp. Give the following orders to various children in your group.

■▥ beber la leche   *¡Bebe la leche!*

1. volver a las dos
2. terminar la comida
3. buscar el mapa
4. comer el sandwich
5. ayudar a tu amigo
6. mirar el paisaje
7. nadar más cerca
8. sugerir un juego

B   You're taking care of ten-year-old Daniel. Give him permission to do the following things, using an affirmative *tú*-command.

■⫾⫾   mirar televisión   Daniel: *¿Puedo mirar televisión?*
                               Tú: *Sí, mira televisión.*

1. jugar al béisbol
2. leer el libro
3. comer una naranja

4. escribir en el papel
5. llamar a papá
6. llevar el perro al parque

Vamos a + infinitive

Optional: Explain *vamos a* + noun phrase. *Vamos al cine* = Let's go to the movies.

¡**Vamos a** comer!   *Let's* eat!
¡**Vamos a** nadar!   *Let's* swim!

Vamos a + infinitive expresses *let's* in Spanish. Remember that a form of **ir a** + infinitive is also used to express an activity planned for the future.

C   Suggest to some friends that you do the following things.

V: Students give commands using *vamos a*. Others give exclamations. S¹: *Vamos a estudiar.* S²: *¡Uy! No quiero.* S³: *Vamos a comer.* S⁴: *¡Qué bueno!*

■⫾⫾   cenar al restaurante   *¡Vamos a cenar al restaurante!*

1. ver la carrera
2. llamar a David
3. jugar al tenis
4. comer algo

5. montar a caballo
6. escuchar música
7. comprar helado
8. subir la montaña

Acabar de + infinitive

Acabo de volver del cine.   *I have just* returned from the movies.

Acabamos de comer.   *We have just* eaten.

The expression **acabar de** + infinitive means to have just done something. **Acabar** is a regular **-ar** verb.

D   A friend asks if you want something to eat or drink. Decline and explain that you have just had the items indicated.

Expand: S¹: *¿Quieres jugar al tenis?* S²: *No, acabo de jugar.* S³: *¿Quieres estudiar un poco?* S⁴: *No, acabo de estudiar. Tengo examen mañana.*

■⫾⫾   un sandwich de pollo   —*¿Quieres tomar algo?*
                              —*No, gracias. Acabo de comer un sandwich de pollo.*

1. un postre
2. un vaso de leche
3. una ensalada

4. un refresco
5. una hamburguesa
6. un café

E Say what the following people have just finished doing.

  ▪▥ tú / tocar el piano   *Acabas de tocar el piano.*

1. yo / ir de compras
2. ustedes / jugar al tenis
3. Marcos / cenar
4. mis hermanos / volver de Madrid

5. Mamá / ir a Puerto Rico
6. mi amiga y yo / nadar
7. tú / comer un helado
8. yo / ver a Sara

Present tense of ver

	VER
yo	**veo**
tú	ves
él, ella, usted	ve
nosotros, nosotras	vemos
ellos, ellas, ustedes	ven

The verb **ver** *(to see)* is irregular in the **yo**-form of the present tense.

F Help your mother sort out the groceries. Tell her whether or not you see the following items among the packages.

  ▪▥ los tomates   Mamá: *¿Ves los tomates?*
    Tú: *Sí, los veo. Aquí están.*
       (No, no los veo.)

1. la leche
2. el pollo

3. las naranjas
4. las verduras

5. el pan
6. la lechuga

G Help your teacher locate members of your class who have become separated from your group on a trip. Tell her/him who sees whom.

  ▪▥ Roberto / Carmen   [*Señorita*], *Roberto ve a Carmen.*

1. Diego y Ana / Daniel
2. nosotras / Marta
3. Susana / Jesús
4. Rosa y Teresa / Carlos

5. yo / Fernando
6. Luis / Alejandro
7. José María / Elena
8. Sara y yo / Ricardo

V: S¹: *¿Quién ve a Roberto?* S²: *Carmen lo ve.*

¡vamos a hablar! A friend suggests an activity. Reply, telling whether or not you want to join her/him, or what you prefer to do.

Vamos a ver el partido.
Vamos a mirar televisión.

Sí. ¡Buena idea!
No quiero. Prefiero ir al parque.

Pescadores en el Cantábrico. Puesto con
chorizos en un mercado de Madrid. Paella,
la especialidad valenciana.

Prepositional pronouns

El regalo es para **ti**.　　The gift is for *you*.
Tengo una carta de **él**.　　I have a letter from *him*.
Miguel está con **nosotros**.　　Miguel is with *us*.

Prepositional pronouns are used after prepositions, such as **para, a, de,** and **con.**

SINGULAR	
mí	me
ti	you *(familiar)*
usted	you *(formal)*
él, ella	him, her

PLURAL	
nosotros, nosotras	us
ustedes	you *(familiar or formal)*
ellos, ellas	them

Prepositional pronouns are the same as the subject pronouns except for **mí** and **ti.**

¿Vas **conmigo**?　　Are you going *with me?*
Sí, voy **contigo**.　　Yes, I'm going *with you.*

The prepositional pronouns **mí** and **ti** combine with **con** to form **conmigo** and **contigo.**

H　There's a big game tonight. Tell a friend with whom you're going.

　■⫶　Víctor　　Amigo/a: *¿Con quién vas? ¿Con Víctor?*
　　　　　　　　　Tú: *Sí, voy con él.*

1. Luis y Cristina
2. Toño y Marcos
3. Elena
4. Alicia y Carmen
5. tu hermano
6. David

I　You're at a restaurant with a group of friends. Help the waiter by pointing out the person who has ordered each dish.

　■⫶　el café / Pablo　　Camarero: *¿Para quién es el café?*
　　　　　　　　　　　　Tú: *Es para él.*

1. el postre / Manolo y Vicente
2. el sandwich / Joaquín
3. la ensalada / yo
4. el bistec / Claudia
5. las sopas / Felipe y Teresa
6. los refrescos / Soledad y yo

V: S¹: *Tengo un regalo.* S²: *¿Para quién es?* S³: (pointing to girl) *Es para ella.* S⁴: (pointing to boy) *No es para mí. Es para él.* Etc.

¡vamos a hablar!　Find out from a friend with whom he/she does various activities.

¿Estudias con Gloria?　　No, no estudio con ella.
¿Juegas al fútbol con Federico?　　Sí, juego con él.

Definite articles with titles

Buenas tardes, **señora Ruiz.**　　　*Good afternoon, Mrs. Ruiz.*
La señora Ruiz es mi profesora.　　*Mrs. Ruiz is my teacher.*

In Spanish, a definite article (**el, la, los,** and **las**) is used before a courtesy title, except in direct address.

J　You're a receptionist in a large office. Answer the phone and notify the person requested that he/she has a call.

◼ ‖　Sr. Márquez　Una persona: *¿Está el Sr. Márquez?*
　　　　　　　　　　　　　Tú: *Sr. Márquez, es para usted.*

1. Sra. Cuevas
2. Srta. Arias
3. Srta. de la Fuente

4. Sr. Gallegos
5. Sr. Moreno
6. Sr. Suárez

Stem-changing verbs: e to i

	PEDIR
yo	pido
tú	pides
él, ella, usted	pide
nosotros, nosotras	pedimos
ellos, ellas, ustedes	piden

Optional: Review present tense of *vivir* before introducing *pedir.*

In some **-ir** verbs, like **pedir** *(to ask for),* the stem vowel **e** changes to **i** in the present tense. There is no stem change in the **nosotros-**form. **Pedir** takes the endings of regular **-ir** verbs.

Other verbs like **pedir** are **repetir** *(to repeat),* and **servir** *(to serve).*

K　Say what each person is ordering for dinner.

◼ ‖　tú / jamón　*Pides jamón.*

1. yo / un sandwich de pollo
2. ustedes / una ensalada de mariscos
3. mamá y yo / un postre
4. usted / un refresco
5. Joaquín / un café
6. Amalia y Lourdes / fruta fresca
7. tía Isabel / una tortilla de jamón

L Tomás is a judge for a class cooking contest and wants to know what dishes he'll have to test. Tell him what you and your friends are serving.

■III Alicia / una tortilla Tomás: *¿Qué sirve Alicia?*
Tú: *Sirve una tortilla.*

1. Roberto / sopa de verduras
2. Anita y Julia / una ensalada
3. tú / huevos con jamón

4. Enrique / pollo asado
5. David y yo / un postre
6. la profesora / helado

If you happen to eat in a Spanish-speaking restaurant, a waiter might say to you **Buen provecho** as he sets the main meal in front of you. This expression is equivalent to "Enjoy your food." It is often said in homes, especially when guests are invited to join the family group for lunch or dinner. If you should travel in a train or bus, and are invited to share the food being eaten by a fellow passenger, you should decline courteously by responding politely **Gracias, que le aproveche** (Thank you, go ahead and enjoy your food).

En resumen

Affirmative tú-commands (A, B)

	TÚ-FORM	COMMAND
-ar	hablas	¡**Habla** conmigo!
-er	lees	¡**Lee** la carta!
-ir	pides	¡**Pide** un postre!

Affirmative **tú**-commands of regular verbs are formed by dropping the **-s** from the **tú**-form of the present tense.

Vamos a + infinitive (C)

Vamos a ver a Juan.
Vamos a jugar al básquetbol.

Vamos a + infinitive is equivalent to English *let's* + verb.

Acabar de + infinitive (D, E)

Acabo de pedir una sopa.
Acaban de pagar la cuenta.

Acabar de + infinitive is used to express *to have just done something*.

Present tense of ver (F, G)

	VER
yo	**veo**
tú	ves
él, ella, usted	ve
nosotros, nosotras	vemos
vosotros, vosotras	veis
ellos, ellas, ustedes	ven

The verb **ver** is irregular in the **yo**-form in the present tense.

Prepositional pronouns (H, I)

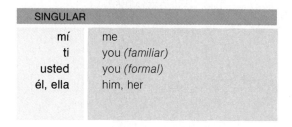

SINGULAR	
mí	me
ti	you *(familiar)*
usted	you *(formal)*
él, ella	him, her

PLURAL	
nosotros, nosotras	us
vosotros, vosotras	you *(familiar)*
ustedes	you *(familiar and formal)*
ellos, ellas	them

1. Prepositional pronouns are used after prepositions such as **para, a, de,** and **con.**
2. **Mí** and **ti** combine with **con** to form **conmigo** and **contigo.**

Definite articles with titles (J)

La Sra. Oliveros está en casa.   Buenos días, **Sra. Oliveros.**

A definite article is used before a courtesy title except in direct address.

Stem-changing verbs: **e** to **i**   (K, L)

	SERVIR (e>i)
yo	sirvo
tú	sirves
él, ella, usted	sirve
nosotros, nosotras	servimos
vosotros, vosotras	servís
ellos, ellas, ustedes	sirven

1. Some **-ir** verbs have a stem change from **e** to **i** in the present tense in all forms but the **nosotros-** and **vosotros-**forms.
2. Other verbs with the stem change **e** > **i**: **pedir, repetir.**

Lunch at two and dinner at ten may seem late to many Americans. In Spain, many businesses close between one or two and four o'clock for the main meal of the day. Dinner may begin anywhere from nine to eleven. A **merienda** of coffee and pastry in the late afternoon, or other snacks in the evening give people a chance to socialize with friends before going home for dinner. Common snacks, called **tapas** or **pinchos,** are bite-size servings of meats, fish, vegetables, or **tortilla.**

Photo: Barcelona, Spain.

Repaso

A   Prepare a four to six-line dialogue for each scene below. Tell what each person is saying about the food or restaurant shown.

◼‖   1. Sra.: *Vamos a comer en ese restaurante.*   Sr.: . . .

B   Mrs. Valencia informs her husband about the family's busy day. Say what each person has just finished doing, choosing from the activities listed on the right.

◼‖   tu hermana   *Tu hermana acaba de ver a tus padres.*

1. Héctor
2. yo
3. Beatriz y Diego
4. tu madre
5. Alberto y Miguel
6. Sara y yo

jugar al tenis
llamar a tu oficina
comprar un carro
ir al Bodegón Español
volver del colegio
comer una tortilla

C   Each of the following persons needs something different. Explain what they ask for, choosing from the list on the right. Use an appropriate form of *pedir*.

◼‖   Felipe   *Felipe pide la cuenta.*

1. yo
2. Ana
3. nosotros
4. tú
5. Alberto y Francisco
6. Laura
7. ustedes

la cuenta
más agua
un mapa del metro
dinero a papá
un clarinete nuevo
información
entradas para el cine
carne para la cena

D

Expand Ex. D by having students add what they would like to eat or drink: *Tengo sed. Voy a tomar una taza de café. Tengo hambre. Voy a comer un sandwich.*

Decide whether the following people are hungry, thirsty, hot, cold, or tired, according to the situation described.

■║ Hace sol y acabas de jugar al tenis. *Tienes sed.*

■║ Ya son las ocho y quiero cenar. *Tengo hambre.*

1. Acabamos de jugar al fútbol.
2. Para mí, una tortilla, un bistec y pan.
3. Hace mucho sol y Ernesto acaba de subir la montaña.
4. Hace mal tiempo y nieva. Acabas de llegar a casa.
5. Raúl y Sara no quieren estudiar más.
6. Cristina y yo vamos a tomar un refresco.
7. Vamos a la piscina. Hace fresco allí.

E

You have lots of work to do and daydream of having a genie to do it for you. Command the genie to do the following things.

■║ servir la cena *¡Sirve la cena!*

1. estudiar español
2. escribir una carta a mi tía
3. reparar mi radio
4. practicar la trompeta
5. llevar el perro al parque
6. comprar un regalo para papá

F

Your grandparents visit once a year and always bring gifts for the whole family. Ask them to verify who is to receive each item.

■║ el reloj / Pedro Tú: *¿El reloj es para Pedro?*
Abuelos: *Sí, es para él.*

1. los discos / Raquel
2. la cámara / mamá y papá
3. la grabadora / mí
4. la guitarra / nosotros
5. los libros / los tíos
6. las fotos / todos nosotros

G

Game for review of foods: Acrostic using *almuerzo* for one team and *desayuno* for other. (See Teacher's Guide.)

Optional: Distribute dittoed copies of sample Spanish menus for discussion of prices: *¿Cuánto cuesta la sopa de ajo? ¿Y la ensalada de frutas? ¿Cuál es más cara?*

You're helping a restaurant owner determine how often certain dishes are ordered by customers. Put the week's results in Spanish.

■║ Thursday: 532 soft drinks *El jueves: quinientos treinta y dos refrescos*

1. Monday: 285 salads
2. Tuesday: 874 soups
3. Wednesday: 989 hamburgers
4. Thursday: 100 desserts
5. Friday: 456 sandwiches
6. Saturday: 223 tortillas
7. Sunday: 162 chickens

H Your friends José and Carmen join you for lunch at a local cafeteria. Prepare a dialogue in Spanish to express the following ideas.

1. Tell the hostess you want a table for three.
2. The waiter asks what you wish to order.
3. Order 2 soft drinks, 3 hamburgers, and ice cream.
4. Explain that you are very thirsty.
5. Ask the waiter to bring you a glass of water.
6. Ask for the check.

Café en la Plaza Mayor de Madrid.

Activity: Class prepares Spanish meal. Typical menu might include *gazpacho, paella, tortilla, flan.* Encourage students to eat with hands resting lightly on table, fork in left hand. Conversation must be in Spanish. Exchange students may be invited as special guests.

Vocabulario

SUSTANTIVOS

el agua *(f.)* water
la bebida drink
la biblioteca library
el bistec beefsteak
el café coffee
la cafetería cafeteria
el calamar squid
la camarera waitress
el camarero waiter
la carne meat
la cena dinner
la comida meal
la cuenta bill
el champiñón mushroom
la ensalada salad
el filete steak
la fruta fruit
la hamburguesa hamburger
el helado ice cream
el huevo egg
el jamón ham
el jugo juice
la leche milk
la lechuga lettuce
la manzana apple
el marisco shellfish
la merluza hake
la naranja orange
el pan bread
la patata (la papa) potato
el pescado fish
el pollo chicken

el postre dessert
el sandwich sandwich
el solomillo sirloin
la sopa soup
el tomate tomato
la tortilla omelette
el vaso glass
el vino wine
la verdura vegetable

VERBOS

acabar de *(+ inf.)* to have just
beber to drink
cenar to eat dinner
comer to eat
decidir to decide
desear to desire, wish
pagar to pay
pedir (i) to ask for; to order
servir (i) to serve
terminar to finish
tomar to eat or drink

EXPRESIONES

del tiempo in season
me muero de hambre I am dying of hunger
tener hambre to be hungry
tener sed to be thirsty

OTRAS PALABRAS

además besides
algo something
barato, -a cheap, inexpensive
blanco, -a white
caro, -a expensive
conmigo with me
delicioso, -a delicious
horrible horrible
rico, -a rich; delicious
suficiente sufficient

LOS NÚMEROS DE 100 A 1.000

cien (ciento) 100
doscientos 200
trescientos 300
cuatrocientos 400
quinientos 500
seiscientos 600
setecientos 700
ochocientos 800
novecientos 900
mil 1.000

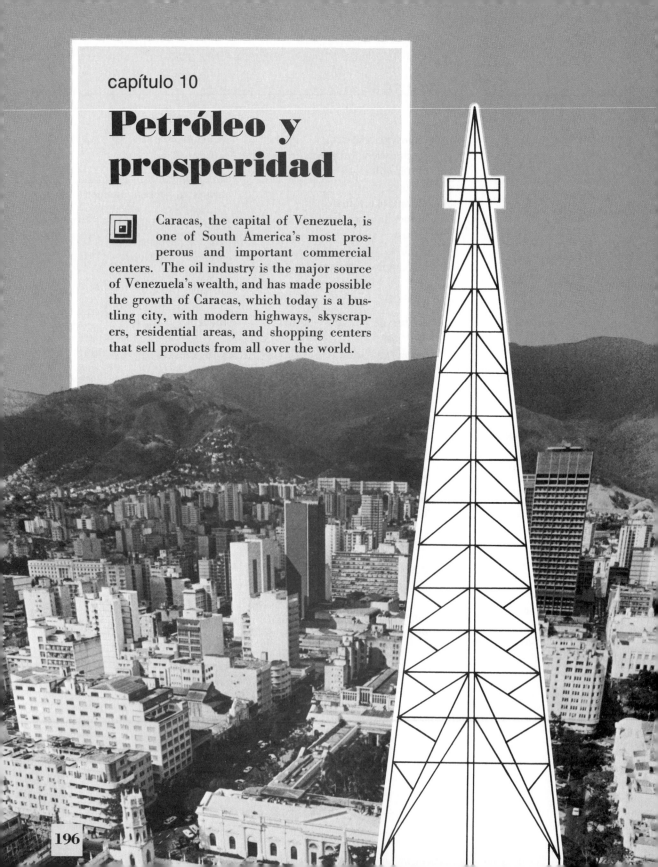

Petróleo y prosperidad

Caracas, the capital of Venezuela, is one of South America's most prosperous and important commercial centers. The oil industry is the major source of Venezuela's wealth, and has made possible the growth of Caracas, which today is a bustling city, with modern highways, skyscrapers, residential areas, and shopping centers that sell products from all over the world.

¡Todos a Miami!

Using map, locate *Venezuela, Caracas,* and *Isla de Margarita.*

Warm up: *¿Qué acabas de hacer? ¿Qué vas a comer hoy? ¿Te gusta la comida de la cafetería?*

The *Isla de Margarita* is a Venezuelan possession, located north of Venezuela, in the Caribbean Sea. The tropical island is a favorite weekend resort area for *caraqueños,* who go to enjoy its beaches and water sports. The island is also known for its pearl-bearing clams. See photo, p. 213.

Explain that *don* and *doña* are used with first names. *Don* is a title for a gentleman. *Doña* is used for married women and widows.

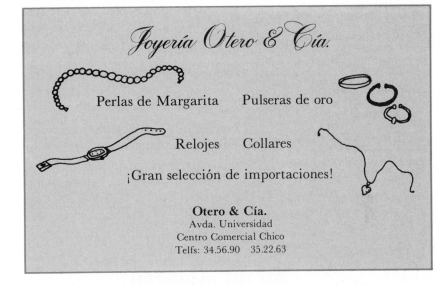

Joyería Otero & Cía.

Perlas de Margarita   Pulseras de oro

Relojes   Collares

¡Gran selección de importaciones!

Otero & Cía.
Avda. Universidad
Centro Comercial Chico
Telfs: 34.56.90   35.22.63

Los Jiménez, una familia caraqueña bastante acomodada, se preparan para ir a Miami a visitar a sus parientes, los Mendoza. Van a pasar un mes allí y quieren llevarles unos regalos.

Antes de ir de compras, doña Sofía busca en el periódico a ver qué anuncian. Encuentra el aviso de una joyería que vende perlas de la Isla de Margarita y otras joyas de oro. Decide darle a su hermana un collar de perlas.

Don Guillermo prefiere ir a un almacén grande, pues quiere buscar un juego de ajedrez para su cuñado. Su hija Lola quiere buscar un disco para su primo Julio, y para su prima Ana, una pulsera.

comprensión

A. Answer the following questions, based on the advertisement and narrative.

1. ¿De qué ciudad son los Jiménez?
2. ¿A quién van a visitar? ¿Dónde viven?
3. ¿Qué vende la joyería?
4. ¿Qué quiere comprar doña Sofía? ¿don Guillermo? ¿Lola?

B. Correct the following information, based on the advertisement and narrative.

1. La joyería vende discos.
2. Doña Sofía quiere comprar una pulsera.
3. Los Mendoza van a Caracas a visitar a sus parientes.
4. Lola quiere comprar un collar para su prima.

A. You're a clerk in a department store. A customer asks you for an appropriate gift for a 15-year-old girl. What would you recommend?

Repeat, requesting gifts for a 15-year-old boy. Encourage variation of responses.

■ ¿Qué regalo sugiere para una chica de 15 años?

Le sugiero un juego.
Un disco, quizás.
Hay pulseras a buen precio.

Explain *tocadiscos* (play records). Introduce *el estéreo*.

B. Try to persuade your parents to buy you a new record player.

■ ¿Otro tocadiscos°?

Por favor, están en rebaja°.
El viejo° no sirve.
Yo ayudo a pagarlo.

Assign 3-member teams to change narrative on p. 197 to dialogue. Each member writes one part (*Lola, doña Sofía,* or *don Guillermo*). Team presents orally.

C. Ask a classmate to evaluate the advantages or disadvantages of a gift you're thinking of buying.

■ ¿Qué piensas de este [reloj]?

¡Parece° muy fino°!
Me gusta.
Es demasiado caro, ¿no?
No es práctico°.

En un almacén

Warm-up: ¿Te gusta ir de compras? ¿Prefieres ir solo/sola o con un/a amigo/a?

Hoy los Jiménez están de compras por Sabanagrande, un barrio central de Caracas. Doña Sofía va a la joyería mientras Lola y don Guillermo van a un almacén. Lola busca la sección de discos en el primer piso.

LOLA	¿Cuál es el último disco de los *Melódicos?*
DEPENDIENTE	Perdón, señorita. ¿Qué dice? No le oigo.
LOLA	¿Puede bajar el volumen?
DEPENDIENTE	Por supuesto.
LOLA	Le pregunto que cuál es el último disco de los *Melódicos.*
DEPENDIENTE	Hay varios, señorita. Puede mirar los que tenemos. Hoy hay dos por el precio de uno.

Lola escoge dos discos y los lleva a la caja.

The *bolívar* is the monetary unit of Venezuela, named after the national hero, *Símón Bolívar.* Each *bolívar* contains 100 *centavos.* Have students check current value.

DEPENDIENTE	¿Es todo? Son 40 bolívares.
LOLA	Aquí tiene usted. Gracias.

Retell the shopping trip from Lola's point of view.

■ Papá, mamá y yo estamos . . .   Estamos de compras por Sabanagrande.

1. Mientras mamá va . . .
2. Busco un . . .
3. El dependiente no oye porque . . .
4. Yo le pregunto . . .
5. El dependiente me dice . . .
6. Compro dos . . .

Optional: Bring in records of current Spanish-speaking *conjuntos.* Play sample songs or make bulletin board display of record jackets. Discuss price of records, likes and dislikes, favorite groups.

A. You're at a party where the music is very loud. Ask the person you are talking to what he/she is saying.

■ı ¡Este disco de los *Melódicos* es fantástico!

Perdón, ¿qué dices?
Lo siento. No te oigo.
¿Quieres repetir, por favor?
¿Cómo dices?

B. A classmate of yours works weekends in a department store. Ask her/him about the location of a department where you want to shop.

■ı ¿Venden [zapatos°] aquí?

Sí, en el [primer] piso.
Sí. Al lado de [la sección de niños°].
Debes subir hasta el último piso.
No. Aquí no hay [zapatos].

C. You're shopping for a record player. Determine whether or not the price is within your range and tell the salesperson your decision.

■ı ¿Le gusta este tocadiscos?

Voy a pensarlo. ¿Puedo ver otro?
No, gracias. Cuesta° mucho.
Me gusta. Lo llevo.
Es una ganga°.

In Spanish-speaking countries, many people favor unhurried shopping at local specialty stores rather than at larger department stores or shopping centers. For example, they go to the **zapatería** for shoes, to the **librería** for books, and to a **joyería** for jewelry. To purchase special food items a shopper may go to the **panadería** (bakery) or to a **mercado** (market) where fruits, meat or vegetables are sold at separate stands.

Photo: Shop in Mexico City.

Estudio de palabras

Números ordinales

Tell students that *ordinal* is a cognate of *order.* Mention *Felipe Segundo* and *Carlos Quinto* of Spain; *Enrique Octavo* of England. Indicate that after *décimo,* cardinal numbers are used to indicate order: *Alfonso Trece* of Spain.

See note, p. 201, on numbering of floors, and photo, p. 205.

primero, -a	first		**sexto, -a**	sixth
segundo, -a	second		**séptimo, -a**	seventh
tercero, -a	third		**octavo, -a**	eighth
cuarto, -a	fourth		**noveno, -a**	ninth
quinto, -a	fifth		**décimo, -a**	tenth

el **primer** piso — the *first* floor
el **tercer** capítulo — the *third* chapter

Ordinal numbers are used to indicate the order of objects or persons in a series. An ordinal number usually precedes the noun. Both **primero** and **tercero** drop the **-o** when they precede a masculine singular noun.

la **quinta** clase — las **primeras** chicas
el **cuarto** mes — los **primeros** anuncios

An ordinal number agrees in number and gender with the noun it modifies.

A Tell the elevator operator of a ten-floor office building what floor you want.

▪️▥ ¿Qué piso quiere usted? — [*El cuarto*] *piso, por favor.*

B You're the captain for a baseball game. Announce the batting order of the players on your team.

▪️▥ Mariana — *Mariana es la primera.*

1. Daniel
2. Marcos
3. Lucía
4. Anita
5. José
6. David
7. Antonio
8. Marta
9. Carmen

Preposiciones

Game: Play *Concentración* using pairs of prepositions. (See Teacher's Guide for instructions.) Possible pairs: *sin / con; lejos de / cerca de; delante de / detrás de; a la izquierda / a la derecha.*

hacia	toward		**antes de**	before
desde	since, from		**después de**	after
sin	without		**delante de**	in front of
sobre	on, about		**en vez de**	instead of
según	according to		**encima de**	on top of
			debajo de	under

Prepositions are frequently used to show the relationship of objects or persons to each other.

200 spanish today, one

C   Complete the information in the following sentences with an appropriate preposition from the list on page 200.

preposition from the list on page 200.

    ▪▥   Estoy en clase _____ las ocho.   *Estoy en clase desde las ocho.*

1. Julio va _____ el parque.
2. Prefiero comer en casa _____ ir al restaurante.
3. ¿Quién quiere escribir algo _____ Caracas?
4. _____ María, David hace trampa cuando juegan al vólibol.
5. ¿De quién es el carro que está _____ el banco?
6. No veo mis papeles. Ah, están _____ mi libro.
7. No quiero ir _____ ti.

Game for practice of prepositions: Have students complete an acrostic using the word *preposiciones.* (See Teacher's Guide.)

D   Contradict the following statements by using a preposition opposite in meaning to the one indicated.

1. El lápiz está *debajo de* la mesa.
2. Jugamos al tenis *después de* las dos.
3. Ricardo está *detrás de* Mónica.
4. Carmen siempre va a clase *con* sus libros.
5. El profesor llega *antes de* los estudiantes.

In Spanish-speaking countries, the ground floor is usually called the **piso bajo** or **planta baja,** and the first floor is the one directly above it. Many buildings skip thirteen in the numbering system because of superstition, just as in the United States.

Pronunciación y ortografía

palabras claves

stop [d]	disco, grande
fricative [ø]	todo

The Spanish letter **d** represents two sounds. The stop [d] sound is pronounced with the tip of the tongue touching lightly the back of the upper front teeth. Stop [d] occurs at the beginning of a word and after **n** and **l.**

A   Pronounce the following words to practice the stop [d] sound.

disco	gran**d**e
décimo	ven**d**e
domingo	segun**d**o
deportes	cal**d**o

Spanish fricative [đ] is similar to the sound of *th* in English *they*. The fricative [đ] sound is pronounced with the tip of the tongue protruding slightly between the teeth. Fricative [đ] occurs after or between vowels, after consonants other than **n** or **l**, and at the end of a word.

B Listen and repeat the following words after your teacher to practice the fricative [đ] sound.

to**d**o	cuña**d**o	uste**d**
na**d**a	sába**d**o	ciu**d**a**d**
mie**d**o	aboga**d**o	des**d**e
ra**d**io	acomo**d**a**d**o	orden

C Read the following sentences aloud. The fricative [đ] sounds are indicated with boldface letters.

1. Estu**d**io con Daniel des**d**e las diez.
2. ¿De qué ciu**d**a**d** son los Delga**d**o?
3. ¿Dónde están los discos?
4. El sába**d**o jugamos to**d**o el día.

V: Show sentences on board or transparency. Have several students underline [đ], others circle [d]. Class reads, stressing the two sounds of *d*.

D Create a sentence, using words that contain the letter *d*. Read it to a classmate, and have her/him check your pronunciation.

Dime con quién andas y te diré quién eres.

Proverb: We are known by the company we keep.

Gramática

Para and por

El disco es **para** Daniel.
¿Estudias **para** un examen?
Voy de compras **para** buscar un regalo.

The record is *for* Daniel.
Are you studying *for* an exam?
I'm going shopping (*in order*) *to* look for a gift.

The preposition **para** means *for* when it expresses *destined for* or *directed toward* another person, item, or action. **Para** frequently means *in order to*.

A

Your inquisitive sister Alicia asks who's getting all the presents you're wrapping. Answer her according to the cues.

V: Re-enter preposi-
tional pronouns. S¹:
*¿Es para Marcos el
juego?* S²: *Sí, es para
él.*

■⫶ el juego / Marcos   Alicia: *¿Para quién es el juego?*
                 Tú: *Es para Marcos.*

1. el collar / tía Isabel
2. los discos / nuestros primos
3. los zapatos / papá
4. la novela / mamá

5. el tambor / David
6. los vasos / los abuelos
7. la grabadora / nuestros padres
8. la pulsera / una amiga

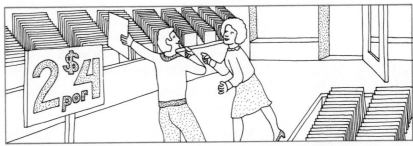

Venden dos discos **por** cuatro dólares.

They're selling two records *for* four dollars.

Por is often equivalent to *for* when it is used in the sense of *in exchange for*.

B Your favorite department store is having a half-price sale. Tell a friend about it.

▣ *Oye, [Pedro]. Venden dos cuadernos por tres dólares.*

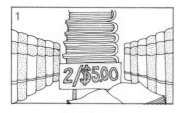  

 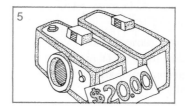 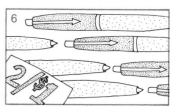

C Complete the following sentences with *por* or *para,* as appropriate.

▣ Diego vende su bicicleta / $50   *Diego vende su bicicleta por $50.*

1. te cambio un disco / un libro
2. tengo que estudiar / un examen
3. ¿quieres comprar entradas / el partido?
4. allí hay comidas deliciosas / poco dinero
5. ¿me prestas tu bicicleta / la carrera?

Indirect-object pronouns

Escribo una carta **a Carmen.**	**Le** escribo una carta.
Juan vende su carro **a los Delgado.**	Juan **les** vende su carro.
Compra un helado **para nosotros.**	**Nos** compra un helado.

An indirect-object pronoun replaces a noun or phrase telling *to whom* or *for whom* something is done.

An indirect-object pronoun may also precede the conjugated verb in double verb constructions: *¿Me quieres dar el libro?*

Miguel **me** da el libro.	Miguel gives *me* the book.
¿Quieres dar**me** el libro?	Do you want to give *me* the book?

Like a direct-object pronoun, an indirect-object pronoun precedes a conjugated verb, and usually follows and is attached to an infinitive.

Practice indirect-object
pronouns: Point to *Ana,*
class responds *le; Ana*
and *Pablo, les;* yourself
and another, *nos.*

SINGULAR	
me	me
te	you *(familiar)*
le	him, her, you *(formal)*

PLURAL	
nos	us
les	them, you

Note that the indirect-object pronouns **me, te,** and **nos** are the same in form as the direct-object pronouns.

D　Announce that your sister is buying dessert for everyone.

　　　■ꐦ　para Carlos　　*Le compra un postre.*

1. para ti
2. para Uds.
3. para nosotros
4. para Daniel
5. para mí
6. para Anita
7. para mis papás
8. para Susana y Jesús

E　Amalia plans to remind everyone of tomorrow's class meeting. Say when she plans to speak to each of her friends.

　　　■ꐦ　José / a las seis　　*Amalia piensa hablarle a las seis.*

1. ti / a las diez
2. mis hermanos / a las dos y media
3. Margarita / a las cuatro
4. mí / antes de las cinco
5. Ud. / después de las cuatro
6. nosotros / a las siete
7. Ricardo / a las cinco

De compras en un almacén de Madrid.

Present tense of **dar**

	DAR
yo	**doy**
tú	das
él, ella, usted	da
nosotros, nosotras	damos
ellos, ellas, ustedes	dan

The verb **dar** *(to give)* is irregular in the **yo**-form of the present tense.

F Jorge is gathering coins for his collection from his friends. Tell who gives him some coins.

◼⫿ Mariana *Mariana le da unas monedas.*

1. Marta y yo
2. yo
3. mamá
4. tú
5. Uds.
6. Roberto y yo
7. Ud.
8. Francisco

G Ask a classmate what he/she will give you in exchange for something of yours. Use the cues provided.

◼⫿ mi radio / mi grabadora Compañero/a: *¿Qué me das por mi radio?*
Tú: *Te doy mi grabadora.*

1. mi cuaderno / mi bolígrafo
2. mi bicicleta / treinta dólares
3. mi sandwich / mi manzana
4. dos discos viejos / un disco de los *Melódicos*
5. mi collar / mi pulsera

Indirect-object pronouns with **gustar**

Me gusta la música.	I like music.
Les gustan los deportes.	They like sports.
No **nos** gusta ese almacén.	We don't like that store.

You have been using the indirect-object pronouns **me** and **te** with **gusta** and **gustan** to express likes and dislikes. The indirect-object pronouns **le, les,** and **nos** are also used with a form of **gustar.**

H   Ask Jaime if the following people play chess. He answers enthusiastically.

V: Repeat with negative responses: S¹: *Alicia juega al ajedrez, ¿no?* S²: *¡Imposible! No le gusta.*

■||| Alicia   Tú: *Alicia juega al ajedrez, ¿no?*
                  Jaime: *Sí, le gusta mucho.*

1. Roberto y Carlos
2. tú
3. tu abuelo
4. Cristina

5. tus papás
6. Marcos
7. tú y tu hermana
8. Susana y Adolfo

Photo: Chichicastenango, Guatemala.

It is customary in many Spanish-speaking countries to bargain for items sold in open-air markets. The seller does not expect the buyer to pay the first price mentioned, and the buyer in turn does not expect to pay the asking price. After considerable conversation (enjoyed by both parties), and bargaining back and forth, buyer and seller usually come to an agreement that satisfies both, even though they may try not to show their satisfaction. In shops and department stores, however, prices are usually fixed, and customers are expected to pay the posted price (**el precio fijo**) without bargaining.

Prepositional phrases for emphasis or clarification

A mí me gusta mucho el pescado.
I like fish very much.

Le doy un juego a mi hermano.
I'm giving my brother a game.

The prepositional phrase **a** + a prepositional pronoun or a noun may be used to *emphasize* the indirect-object pronoun or to *clarify* the person referred to by the indirect-object pronoun.

I

Re-do Ex. F, p. 206, adding prepositional phrases. Change sentence so that Jorge is giving the coins to the persons indicated: *Jorge le da a Mariana unas monedas.*

Stress that the following people don't like certain activities or things.

▮▯▯ A Ana le gusta esquiar, ¿no?   *No, a ella no le gusta esquiar.*

1. A ustedes les gusta leer, ¿verdad?
2. A Marta y Elena les gusta el tenis, ¿no?
3. A David le gusta el béisbol, ¿verdad?
4. A tus papás les gustan los mariscos, ¿no?
5. A usted le gusta jugar al vólibol, ¿no?
6. A ti te gustan los deportes, ¿verdad?

¡vamos a hablar!

Tell a friend what gifts you're planning to give different members of your family. Here are some ideas to get you started.

un collar   una pulsera   un juego de ajedrez
un disco   un libro   un radio

¿Qué le das a Marta?   A Marta le doy una pulsera.

Using adjectives as nouns

Drill changing of adjectives to nouns before doing Ex. J. S¹ (gives article): *la.* S² (gives noun): *lección.* S³ (gives adjective): *difícil.* S⁴ (forms noun phrase): *la difícil.*

¿Dónde está **el bolígrafo nuevo?**   ¿**El nuevo?** Está en la mesa.
¿Quién es **la chica alta?**   **La alta** es mi prima.

A noun modified by an adjective is often omitted in conversation when the noun is clearly understood. The article and adjective that remain function as a noun phrase.

J   Help Luisa find what she is looking for. Answer according to the model.

▪‖   el libro nuevo   Luisa: *¿Dónde está mi libro nuevo?*
Tú: *¿El nuevo? Aquí está.*

1. los cuadernos pequeños
2. el collar nuevo
3. el lápiz grande

4. las monedas españolas
5. los discos viejos
6. la cámara nueva

Shortened forms **gran** and **buen**

Es un estudiante **bueno.**   He's a *good* student.
Es un **buen** estudiante.   He's a *good* student.

The adjective **bueno** may be used before or after a masculine singular noun. When it precedes a masculine singular noun, **bueno** is shortened to **buen.**

Tenemos una casa **grande.**   We have a *big* house.
Es una **gran** casa.   It's a *magnificent* house.
Es un **gran** pintor.   He's a *great* painter.
Son unos **grandes** pintores.   They are *great* painters.

The adjective **grande** changes in form and meaning when it precedes a singular noun. **Grande** is shortened to **gran** before a masculine or feminine singular noun. When **gran** or **grandes** is used before a noun, it means *great* or *magnificent.*

K   Restate the following sentences, according to the cues. Make all necessary changes in adjectives and nouns.

▪‖   Marta es una buena profesora. (Daniel)   *Daniel es un buen profesor.*

1. Es una buena semana. (día)
2. Elena es una buena estudiante. (Rafael)
3. Tengo un buen carro. (bicicleta)
4. Tienes un buen hermano. (hermana)
5. Son unos buenos médicos. (mecánicos)
6. ¿Quieres un buen sandwich? (postre)
7. Quiero leer una buena novela. (periódico)

Present tense of decir and oír

	DECIR	OÍR
yo	digo	oigo
tú	dices	oyes
él, ella, usted	dice	oye
nosotros, nosotras	decimos	oímos
ellos, ellas, ustedes	dicen	oyen

Ask students what other verb they know with the yo-form ending -go: (tengo).

The verbs **decir** *(to say)* and **oír** *(to hear)* are irregular in most forms of the present tense. The **nosotros-**form of **decir** is regular. The **nosotros-**form of **oír** has a written accent on the **i.**

L   Marta can't hear because of the noise in the school cafeteria. Repeat for her what each person is saying.

Introduce ¿Qué dices? No oigo bien. Have students use these expressions to elicit responses for Ex. L.

■ⅲ   Daniel / tiene fiebre   *Daniel dice que tiene fiebre.*

1. la profesora / hay que ir a clase
2. mis hermanos / van a jugar
3. ellas / hace calor
4. Elena / vuelve más tarde
5. yo / la comida es horrible
6. Rafael y yo / vamos al partido a las seis
7. tú / no oyes bien

M   You're adjusting the microphones in the auditorium. Find out if everyone can hear the music.

■ⅲ   ¿La oyes ya?   *Sí, la oigo ya.*

1. ¿La oyen ahora?
2. ¿La oye Daniel?
3. ¿La oyen ustedes?
4. ¿La oyes bien?
5. ¿La oye Elena?
6. ¿La oyen tú y Pedro?

¡vamos a hablar!   Tell a classmate the latest news about your family or friends.

Mis padres dicen que vamos   ¡Qué bueno!
a ir a México.

Raúl dice que va a comprar   ¡No me digas! ¡Qué suerte!
un carro.

Futuro de un país

Photo: Lake Maracaibo, Venezuela.

El petróleo no es una industria nueva en Venezuela. La explotación del petróleo se inició° en 1922 con el descubrimiento° de una enorme riqueza° en el subsuelo° del lago° de Maracaibo. Venezuela es hoy conocida como la "Arabia de las Américas". La prosperidad inesperada° del país empezó°
5 en 1973 con la subida de los precios del petróleo a cuatro veces su valor original. En 1976 Venezuela nacionalizó la industria petrolífera y adquirió° control económico completo.

   ¿Cómo afecta esta riqueza al venezolano corriente°? Caracas, donde vive aproximadamente el 20% de la población del país, ha conocido° una gran
10 expansión industrial y comercial. Sin embargo°, la gente° de las clases altas vive con mucho lujo° mientras que muchos viven en la pobreza.

   El gobierno° trata de° solucionar el problema de desigualdad° comprando equipo y materiales para proyectos públicos que, a su vez, aumentan° el número de empleos. De esta forma, aunque° indirectamente, la
15 riqueza producida por el petróleo beneficia° a la gente corriente.

   El gobierno ha puesto° sus esperanzas° en la educación de la juventud° y ha establecido un programa de becas° para darles mayores oportunidades a los jóvenes, futuros administradores de la economía de su país.

began/discovery/wealth
subsoil/lake
unexpected/began

acquired

common

has experienced

nevertheless/people

luxury

government/tries to/
  inequality

increase/although

benefits

has placed/hopes/youth

scholarships

Check comprehension by asking questions on the reading. List useful vocabulary on board for activities. Reports (B) may be given in English.

Optional: Help students list reasons for importance of oil.

A. Answer the following questions concerning some economic aspects of the United States.

1. ¿Cuál es la industria más importante en tu pueblo, ciudad o estado?
2. ¿Hay mucha igualdad o desigualdad económica entre la gente de los Estados Unidos?
3. ¿Tiene su pueblo, ciudad o estado proyectos públicos para aumentar el número de empleos?

B. Gather information from the library and photographs from magazines on Venezuela's resources. Report your findings briefly to the class.

En resumen

Para and por (A–C)

PARA	POR
El libro es **para** Pilar. Se preparan **para** ir a Miami.	Vendo el libro **por** dos dólares.

1. The preposition **para** frequently means *for,* in the sense of *destined for* or *directed toward,* and *in order to.*
2. The preposition **por** means *for* when used to express *in exchange for.*

Indirect-object pronouns (D, E, H, I)

SINGULAR		PLURAL	
me	me	nos	us
te	you (*familiar*)	os	you (*familiar*)
le	him, her, you (*formal*)	les	them, you (*familiar and formal*)

1. An indirect-object pronoun is used to tell *to whom* or *for whom* something is done: **¿Me das el papel?**
2. An indirect-object pronoun precedes a conjugated verb. It usually follows and is attached to an infinitive: **¿Quiere leernos la carta?**
3. The prepositional phrase **a** + noun or prepositional pronoun is often used with an indirect-object pronoun for emphasis or to clarify the person referred to: **A Enrique le gusta el helado.**

Using adjectives as nouns (J)

¿Para quién es la manzana grande?   **¿La grande?** Es para ti.

A noun modified by an adjective may be omitted when the noun referred to is clearly understood. The article and adjective function as a noun phrase.

Shortened forms **gran** and **buen** (K)

Es un piloto **bueno.**   Es un **buen** piloto.
Es una casa **grande.**   Es una **gran** casa.
Es un chico **grande.**   Es un **gran** chico.

1. **Bueno** is shortened to **buen** before a masculine singular noun. **Grande** is shortened to **gran** before a feminine or masculine singular noun.
2. **Grande** means *big* or *large* when it follows a noun. It means *great* or *magnificent* when it precedes a noun.

Present tense of **dar, decir, oír** (F, G, L, M)

	DAR	DECIR	OÍR
yo	doy	digo	oigo
tú	das	dices	oyes
él, ella, usted	da	dice	oye
nosotros, nosotras	damos	decimos	oímos
vosotros, vosotras	dais	decís	oís
ellos, ellas, ustedes	dan	dicen	oyen

Puerto Juan Griego en la Isla de Margarita.

ARSH 1343

213

Repaso

A Elena and Álvaro are shopping for gifts. Complete their dialogue with *para* or *por,* as appropriate. Then answer the questions that follow.

> Elena: Tengo que comprar regalos ＿＿ mi familia, y en este almacén tienen muchas cosas. ¡Mira! Aquí hay tres libros ＿＿ quince dólares.
>
> Álvaro: Sí, pero aquí hay un collar ＿＿ diez dólares. ¿Te gusta ＿＿ tu mamá?
>
> Elena: ¿＿＿ quién? Ah, ＿＿ mi mamá. Sí, es muy bonito. Pero ¿qué puedo comprar ＿＿ mi papá? Vamos a buscar un libro.

1. ¿Dónde están Elena y Álvaro?
2. ¿Qué quiere comprar Elena?
3. ¿Qué regalo sugiere Álvaro para la madre de Elena?
4. ¿Cuánto cuesta el collar que Álvaro ve?
5. ¿Qué piensa comprar Elena para su padre?

B Decide what gifts various members of the Jiménez family are giving to each other. Use an indirect-object pronoun in each statement.

Divide exercise into segments. Practice *dar* with each subject, then the i.o. pronoun for the persons listed in column 3, finally, combine into sentences.

Have students redo Ex. B, using prepositional pronouns: *Guillermo le da una pulsera a ella.*

1	2	3	4
1. don Guillermo	dar	Paco	unos discos
2. tú		don Guillermo	una novela
3. yo		doña Sofía	un juego
4. nosotros		los hijos	un tocadiscos
5. doña Sofía		Lola	una pulsera
6. los hijos		nosotros	un radio
7. los abuelos		Paco y María	un perro

▪▥ *Don Guillermo le da a Lola una pulsera.*

C Mr. Jiménez thinks the gift choices are excellent. Take his role and say that the following people are going to like their gifts very much.

1	2	3
1. Paco	ir a gustar mucho	los discos
2. don Guillermo		la novela
3. doña Sofía		el juego
4. los hijos		el tocadiscos
5. Lola		la pulsera
6. nosotros		el perro
7. Paco y María		

▪▥ Paco   *A él le va a gustar mucho el perro.*

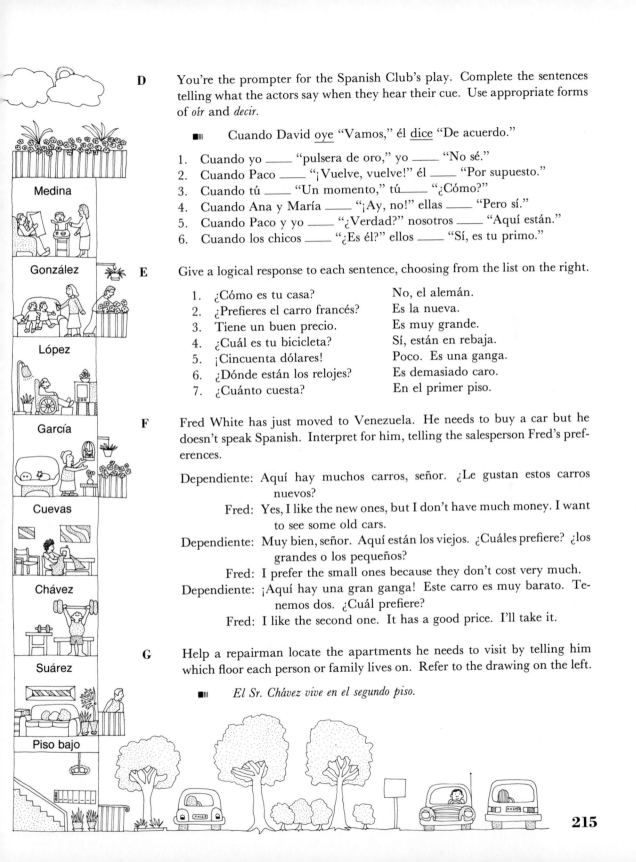

D You're the prompter for the Spanish Club's play. Complete the sentences telling what the actors say when they hear their cue. Use appropriate forms of *oír* and *decir*.

■‖ Cuando David <u>oye</u> "Vamos," él <u>dice</u> "De acuerdo."

1. Cuando yo ＿＿＿ "pulsera de oro," yo ＿＿＿ "No sé."
2. Cuando Paco ＿＿＿ "¡Vuelve, vuelve!" él ＿＿＿ "Por supuesto."
3. Cuando tú ＿＿＿ "Un momento," tú＿＿＿ "¿Cómo?"
4. Cuando Ana y María ＿＿＿ "¡Ay, no!" ellas ＿＿＿ "Pero sí."
5. Cuando Paco y yo ＿＿＿ "¿Verdad?" nosotros ＿＿＿ "Aquí están."
6. Cuando los chicos ＿＿＿ "¿Es él?" ellos ＿＿＿ "Sí, es tu primo."

E Give a logical response to each sentence, choosing from the list on the right.

1. ¿Cómo es tu casa?   No, el alemán.
2. ¿Prefieres el carro francés? Es la nueva.
3. Tiene un buen precio.   Es muy grande.
4. ¿Cuál es tu bicicleta?   Sí, están en rebaja.
5. ¡Cincuenta dólares!   Poco. Es una ganga.
6. ¿Dónde están los relojes?   Es demasiado caro.
7. ¿Cuánto cuesta?   En el primer piso.

F Fred White has just moved to Venezuela. He needs to buy a car but he doesn't speak Spanish. Interpret for him, telling the salesperson Fred's preferences.

Dependiente: Aquí hay muchos carros, señor. ¿Le gustan estos carros nuevos?

Fred: Yes, I like the new ones, but I don't have much money. I want to see some old cars.

Dependiente: Muy bien, señor. Aquí están los viejos. ¿Cuáles prefiere? ¿los grandes o los pequeños?

Fred: I prefer the small ones because they don't cost very much.

Dependiente: ¡Aquí hay una gran ganga! Este carro es muy barato. Tenemos dos. ¿Cuál prefiere?

Fred: I like the second one. It has a good price. I'll take it.

G Help a repairman locate the apartments he needs to visit by telling him which floor each person or family lives on. Refer to the drawing on the left.

■‖ *El Sr. Chávez vive en el segundo piso.*

Medina

González

López

García

Cuevas

Chávez

Suárez

Piso bajo

215

Vocabulario

SUSTANTIVOS

el ajedrez chess
el almacén store, department store
el aviso advertisement
el barrio district
la caja cash register
el collar necklace
el cuñado brother-in-law
el dependiente clerk
la ganga bargain
la joya jewel
la joyería jewelry store
el niño, la niña child
el oro gold
el pariente relative
el periódico newspaper
la perla pearl
el piso floor, story
la pulsera bracelet
la rebaja discount
el tocadiscos record player
el volumen volume
el zapato shoe

VERBOS

bajar to lower, turn down
costar (ue) to cost
dar to give
decir to say
escoger to choose
oír to hear
parecer to appear, seem
vender to sell

OTRAS PALABRAS

acomodado, -a well-to-do
antes de before
caraqueño, -a from Caracas
debajo de under
delante de in front of
desde since, from
en vez de instead of, in place of
encima de above, over
fino, -a fine
grande large, great
hacia toward
mientras while, during
por for (in exchange for)
práctico, -a practical
sin without
último, -a last, latest
varios, -as various, several
viejo, -a old

EXPRESIONES

ir de compras to go shopping
los que the ones that
por supuesto of course
se preparan they get ready, they're getting
  ready

NÚMEROS ORDINALES

primero first
segundo second
tercero third
cuarto fourth
quinto fifth
sexto sixth
séptimo seventh
octavo eighth
noveno ninth
décimo tenth

Playa salvadoreña en el Pacífico.

Una casa en el lago

El Salvador is Central America's smallest, most densely populated, and most industrialized country. Its Pacific beaches attract visitors from all parts of the hemisphere. Lake Ilopango, about 15 kilometers from the capital city of San Salvador, is a picturesque vacation site for residents of the capital. Set in the crater of an extinct volcano, Lake Ilopango is an ideal recreational area for boating, swimming, water skiing, fishing, and camping.

Una invitación oportuna

Locate *El Salvador* and *Lago Ilopango* on map. Tell class that name means "The Saviour."

Pedro e Inés Castillo, dos chicos de San Salvador, no saben qué hacer para el fin de semana. De pronto, el teléfono suena. Pedro contesta.

PEDRO	¿Aló?
VOZ DE HOMBRE	¿Con quién hablo? ¿Con Pedro?
PEDRO	Sí. ¿Tío Arturo? ¡Qué sorpresa!
TÍO ARTURO	¿Está tu mamá?
PEDRO	No, no está. Lo siento, tío.
TÍO ARTURO	Entonces dile que quiero invitarlos a conocer la casa nueva cerca del lago.
PEDRO	¡Ay! ¡Qué bueno!
TÍO ARTURO	Dile a tu mamá que debe llamarme si pueden venir este fin de semana.
PEDRO	Sí, tío. Con mucho gusto. Hasta pronto.

comprensión

Act out dialogue, using real or toy telephones.

Take Pedro's role and retell your conversation with Uncle Arturo.

■III   De pronto . . .   De pronto el teléfono suena.

1. Yo contesto. Es . . .
2. Él quiere hablar . . .
3. Nos quiere invitar . . .
4. Mamá debe . . .

extensión

A. The phone rings. Answer it and give the information requested.

■III   ¿Está [Isabel]?   No. No está.
Un momento, no sé.
Sí, voy a llamarla.
¿De parte de quién?°

B. You're invited to a friend's vacation home. Let her/him know how you feel and whether or not you can go.

■III   ¿Puedes venir el domingo a   ¡Qué bueno!
nuestra casa de verano?   Sí. ¡Fantástico!
¡Qué lástima! No puedo ir.
Lo siento. Quizás otro día.

Remind students that *¡Aló!, ¡Oiga!, ¡Bueno!, ¡Diga!,* and *¡Dígame!* are all used in answering telephone.

C. You call up a friend to ask about tomorrow's assignment, but he/she is not at home. Act out the conversation with a classmate.

Have pairs of students prepare original telephone conversations and act out.

■III   ¿Aló? Casa de la familia [Cortés].   ¿Está. . .
Lo siento. No . . .   Por favor, dile que . . .
De acuerdo. Llega . . .   Gracias. Llamo . . .

A orillas del lago

La familia Castillo llega a la casa que el tío Arturo tiene a orillas del lago Ilopango. Es una casa grande y tiene alrededor muchos árboles.

TÍO ARTURO	¡Bienvenidos a casa!
SRA. DE CASTILLO	Es un lugar muy hermoso, Arturo. Los chicos van a estar muy contentos.
TÍO ARTURO	Sí, aquí ellos pueden nadar, pasear en bote o pescar.
INÉS	¿Tienes un bote, tío?
TÍO ARTURO	Yo no, pero conozco unos vecinos que tienen uno. A ver si podemos salir con ellos mañana.
INÉS	¡Fantástico!

comprensión

Play College Bowl to check comprehension. (See Teacher's Guide.) Use activity questions and original questions on dialogue.

Correct the following statements, based on the dialogue.

1. Don Arturo llega a la casa del lago.
2. Es un lugar hermoso, pero no tiene árboles.
3. Los chicos no deben nadar o pasear en bote.
4. El tío Arturo les dice a todos "Adiós."

extensión

A. Uncle Arturo welcomes you to his house. Compliment him on the house and its location.

■||| ¡Bienvenidos a casa!   Gracias. ¡Qué grande es!
Es un lugar muy hermoso.
¡Qué bonita es!

Lago Ilopango, El Salvador. Al fondo, el volcán San Vicente.

219

B. Ask a classmate what her/his house is like.

   ▪▥   ¿Cómo es tu casa?   Es [pequeña].

                                                Es más pequeña que° tu
casa.

                                                Ni grande ni° pequeña.

C. What kinds of activities do you generally do when you go to a lake?

   ▪▥   ¿Qué haces cuando vas a un lago?   Voy a [pescar].

                                                Me gusta [nadar].

En busca de una casa

Patricia y Julio Rodríguez, dos jóvenes de San Salvador, leen la sección de avisos del periódico. Sus padres quieren comprar una casa cerca del lago Ilopango. Patricia encuentra el siguiente aviso.

> EL LAGO, amplia, sala, comedor, 3 alcobas, 2 baños, patio, jardín, estacionamiento. Tel. 23-9264

comprensión

Answer the following questions based on the information above.

1. ¿Qué quieren comprar los Rodríguez?
2. ¿Qué sección del periódico miran Patricia y Julio?
3. ¿Es grande o pequeña la casa del aviso?
4. ¿Cuántas alcobas tiene?
5. ¿Hay lugar para el carro?

extensión

A. You've just bought a second-hand bicycle through an ad in the local paper. Describe the bicycle's qualities or defects to a friend.

   ▪▥   ¿Qué tal la bicicleta?   Es buena. Corre mucho.

                                                  Necesito° repararla.

                                                Es más [grande] que la vieja.

B. Your parents want to buy a larger house. A real estate agent has just shown one to your family. Give your parents your opinion of it.

   ▪▥   ¿Qué piensas de esta casa,   Me gusta mucho. Tiene un
          [Emilio]?   jardín grande.

                                                  Las alcobas son pequeñas.

                                                  Es bonita, pero está lejos de
todo.

Una casa de estilo español

Introduce *Estudio de palabras*,
using doll house or transparency
of floor plan.

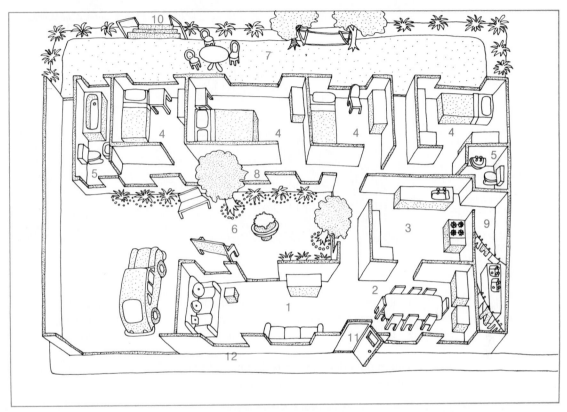

1	**la sala** living room	5	**el cuarto de baño** bathroom	9	**el lavadero** laundry area
2	**el comedor** dining room	6	**el patio** courtyard, patio	10	**la escalera** stairs
3	**la cocina** kitchen	7	**la terraza** terrace	11	**la puerta** door
4	**la alcoba** bedroom	8	**el pasillo** hallway	12	**la ventana** window

A   You're interested in buying the house shown above. Question the realtor about the number of rooms and what they're like.

Have students prepare floor plan of dream home on large paper or transparency for use in oral presentation.

- ■||| ¿Cuántas alcobas hay?   *Hay cuatro.*
- ■||| ¿Cómo es la sala?   *Es muy amplia.*

B   Describe your own house or your dream house. Be sure to say something about each room.

Have students ask questions about features of others' dream homes.

- ■||| *Mi casa es bastante grande. Tiene cuatro alcobas . . .*

Muebles de una alcoba

Optional: Introduce other furniture from list in Appendix C.

Using doll house, board, or transparency of house, have students place furniture in bedroom and explain their actions: *Pongo (poner:* to put) *la cama en la alcoba. Pongo el sillón al lado de la lámpara.*

1 la cama	4 la lámpara	7 el escritorio
2 la mesita de noche	5 la silla	8 el estante
3 la alfombra	6 el sillón	9 el tocador

C   You're remodeling your bedroom and plan to buy new furniture. What do you need? Refer to the preceding display.

  ■▥   *Necesito [una alfombra pequeña].*

  ■▥   *Quiero [dos sillones].*

If you are invited into the home of a Spanish speaker, your host or hostess may say to you **Mi casa es su (tu) casa** or **Está(s) en su (tu) casa.** These courtesy expressions are meant to put guests at ease, to make them feel as comfortable as though they were in their own homes. A similar courtesy expression is often used when a Spanish speaker gives a friend her or his address and says, for example, **Vivo en la calle 17, número 202, donde tienes tu casa.**

Pronunciación y ortografía

Remind students that the letters *k* and *w* appear only in foreign words.

The following chart shows the letters of the Spanish alphabet and their names.

a	a	**j**	jota	**r**	ere
b	be	**k**	ka	**rr**	erre
c	ce	**l**	ele	**s**	ese
ch	che	**ll**	elle	**t**	te
d	de	**m**	eme	**u**	u
e	e	**n**	ene	**v**	ve (uve)
f	efe	**ñ**	eñe	**w**	doble ve (doble u)
g	ge	**o**	o	**x**	equis
h	hache	**p**	pe	**y**	i griega (ye)
i	i	**q**	cu	**z**	zeta

The Spanish alphabet has thirty letters, four more than the English alphabet: **ch, ll, ñ, rr.** All letters are feminine in gender. The letters **ch, ll,** and **ñ** are treated as single letters and follow **c, l,** and **n** respectively in vocabularies and dictionaries. The letter **rr** occurs only within words and is alphabetized as in English.

A Alphabetize the following groups of words, and then read them aloud.

1. carta, carro, chico, cuaderno, champiñón
2. lago, llegar, llamar, lugar, luego
3. señorita, silla, suerte, sin, salir
4. para, perro, parque, pero, papel

Quien no se aventura no pasa el mar.

In spelling aloud, **mayúscula** indicates a capital letter and **minúscula** indicates a small letter: **A** = **a mayúscula**; a = **a minúscula**. The expression **con acento** is used to indicate a written accent: **é** = **e con acento**.

B

Dictate to a classmate the following words in Spanish, spelling each word letter by letter.

Have students call *Información* for a number, and spell name they request. Act out in pairs.

1. your first and last name
2. your favorite season of the year
3. the name of your favorite television program

conjunctions

The conjunction **y** becomes **e** before a word beginning with the [i] sound. The conjunction **o** becomes **u** before a word beginning with the [o] sound.

C

Complete the following paragraph with *y* or *e*, and *o* or *u*.

Elicit meaning of *y* and *o*. Ask why *y* becomes *e* before words beginning with [i] sound. Ask why *o* becomes *u* before words beginning with [o] sound.

Pedro _____ Inés Castillo miran los avisos del periódico. Buscan una casa de campo _____ un apartamento cerca del lago. Necesitan una casa con siete _____ ocho habitaciones _____ dos baños. Quieren una casa amplia con jardín para poder jugar _____ invitar a sus parientes _____ amigos.

Gramática

Present tense of **salir**

	SALIR
yo	**salgo**
tú	sales
él, ella, usted	sale
nosotros, nosotras	salimos
ellos, ellas, ustedes	salen

Elicit other *yo*-forms ending in *-go: (tengo, vengo, digo, oigo).*

The verb **salir** (*to leave, go out*) is irregular in the **yo**-form of the present tense.

A

Say that the following people will leave for the lake at six o'clock.

▪||| ustedes   *Salen para el lago a las seis.*

1. yo
2. Adolfo
3. Pablo y Teresa
4. tú

5. Vicente y yo
6. Carmen
7. las señoras
8. usted

B   Tell what time the following people leave their jobs or activities. Use any logical time in your responses.

Have students question each other: *¿A qué hora sales de casa? ¿de la escuela? ¿de la clase de español? ¿de la cafetería?*

∎⫿   tu papá / del trabajo   —*¿A qué hora sale tu papá del trabajo?*
—*Sale a [las cinco].*

1. los López / de casa
2. David / del banco
3. tú / de casa
4. tu mamá / del correo

5. el Sr. Medina / del restaurante
6. tus hermanas / del colegio
7. Marcos y Julia / del museo
8. tú / del cine

The patio originated among the Moors, who ruled Spain for nearly eight hundred years. Their houses were usually constructed so that the central portion was open, thus allowing air to circulate freely. A fountain often provided the soothing sound of cool running water in the hot, dry climate of southern Spain, where many Moors settled. Patios are very common in homes in many Spanish-speaking countries today. In cities and towns, houses may be built close to the sidewalk or street, with no lawns or yards. Inside these houses, however, there may be one or more patios, often decorated with plants and sometimes with tiles. They provide privacy for the family with a minimum of space.

Present tense of **venir**

	VENIR
yo	vengo
tú	vienes
él, ella, usted	viene
nosotros, nosotras	venimos
ellos, ellas, ustedes	vienen

The verb **venir** *(to come)* is irregular in the present tense. The **yo**-form ends in **-go** and certain other forms have a stem change from **e** to **ie.**

¿**Vienes** a mi casa?   *Are you coming* to my house?
Sí, **voy** a tu casa.   Yes, *I'm coming* to your house.

The verb **venir** is used to indicate direction *toward* the person speaking. The verb **ir** is used to indicate direction *away from* the speaker.

Barrio antiguo de Granada, España.

C You're at a Spanish Club party. Inform the club president that the following people aren't coming to it.

> ▪ꓲꓲ   el Sr. Martínez   *El Sr. Martínez no viene a la fiesta.*

Expand: S¹: ¿Viene el
Sr. Martínez? S²: Sí,
(No) . . .

1. tú
2. ustedes
3. Ana

4. Miguel
5. los profesores de francés
6. el estudiante argentino

D You and your friends are returning from a long weekend. Tell where the following people are coming from.

> ▪ꓲꓲ   Alberto / la playa   *Alberto viene de la playa.*

1. yo / el lago
2. ustedes / su casa de campo
3. Cristina / una excursión
4. tú / las montañas
5. David y Antonio / la costa
6. mi familia y yo / nuestra finca
7. mis primos / casa de los abuelos

Present tense of **hacer**

	HACER
yo	**hago**
tú	haces
él, ella, usted	hace
nosotros, nosotras	hacemos
ellos, ellas, ustedes	hacen

Review weather expres-
sions, chapter 8, before
introducing *hacer*.

The verb **hacer** *(to do, make)* is irregular in the **yo**-form of the present tense.

E Everyone in your family is helping with supper. Say what the following people are making, according to the cues.

> ▪ꓲꓲ   Marta / el postre   *Marta hace el postre.*

1. los tíos / los sandwiches
2. ustedes / el café
3. la abuela / una ensalada
4. mamá y yo / las patatas
5. papá / la sopa
6. mi hermano menor / las hamburguesas
7. yo / la bebida

Demonstrative adjectives

Equate demonstrative adjectives with subject pronouns: If item discussed is near speaker (*yo*), use *este;* if near person(s) spoken to (*tú, usted, ustedes*), use *ese;* if near person(s) spoken about (*él, ella, ellos, ellas*), use *aquel*, or forms thereof.

The demonstrative adjectives **este, ese,** and **aquel** are used to point out an object, place, or person. A demonstrative adjective has four forms and agrees in number and gender with the noun it modifies.

SINGULAR		PLURAL	
este libro	*this* book	**estos** libros	*these* books
esta silla	*this* chair	**estas** sillas	*these* chairs

The **este**-group is generally used to refer to something close at hand to the speaker.

SINGULAR		PLURAL	
ese, aquel lago	*that* lake	**esos, aquellos** lagos	*those* lakes
esa, aquella montaña	*that* mountain	**esas, aquellas** montañas	*those* mountains

The **ese**-group is used to refer to something near the person spoken to. The **aquel**-group refers to people or objects in the distance or not associated with the speaker.

F   You and your friend Rosa are shopping in a department store. Point out to her some bargain items. Use an appropriate form of *este* or *ese.*

■▯▯   radios   *Mira esos radios. Son una ganga.*

1. lámparas
2. estante
3. tocadiscos
4. discos
5. alfombra
6. zapatos
7. grabadora
8. reloj

G   Point out to a guest at your lakeside home several items or places of interest. Use an appropriate form of *aquel.*

■▯▯   La montaña es hermosa.   *Aquella montaña es hermosa.*

1. La discoteca es muy buena.
2. Podemos pescar en la playa.
3. Los botes son del club del lago.
4. Las casas enfrente son nuevas.
5. Podemos montar a caballo en el parque.
6. El bote grande es de mi tío.
7. A veces cenamos en el hotel.

Present tense of conocer

	CONOCER
yo	**conozco**
tú	conoces
él, ella, usted	conoce
nosotros, nosotras	conocemos
ellos, ellas, ustedes	conocen

The verb **conocer** is irregular in the **yo-**form of the present tense.

¿Conoces a mi primo?	*Do you know* my cousin?
Conocen bien el lago Ilopango.	*They know* Lake Ilopango well.
No **conocemos** ese libro.	*We* don't *know* that book.

Conocer means *to know* or *to be acquainted with* people, places, or things.

H   Tell what persons, places, or things the following people know or don't know. Remember to use *a* before words referring to people.

■⫶   tú / Carlos   *Tú conoces a Carlos.*
                        (No conoces a Carlos.)

1. yo / tu primo
2. mi papá / tu papá
3. ustedes / la casa del lago
4. tú / los Medina
5. Marta y José / tío Ignacio
6. el Sr. Galindo / Madrid
7. Alicia y yo / tu hermana
8. el profesor / ese libro

I   Luis wants to know if you are acquainted with certain people, places, or things. Answer that you do or don't know them well.

■⫶   el Sr. Sánchez   Luis: *¿Conoces al Sr. Sánchez?*
                        Tú: *Sí, lo conozco bien.*
                            (No, no lo conozco bien.)

1. El Salvador
2. Mariana López
3. la plaza de Bolívar
4. el profesor de español
5. los discos de los *Melódicos*
6. las hermanas de José
7. la Srta. Martínez

Uses of **conocer** and **saber**

CONOCER	
(No) Conozco	a Carmen. San Salvador. esa ciudad.

SABER	
(No) Sé	nadar. cómo se llama. tu número de teléfono.

Review forms of *saber*.

Saber and **conocer** both mean *to know,* but they are used differently. **Conocer** means *to know* or *to be acquainted with* people, places, or things. **Saber** means *to know* facts or information. **Saber** + infinitive expresses *to know how to* do something.

J Say that you know the following people, places, or information, or how to do certain things. Use a form of *saber* or *conocer,* as appropriate.

Have students ask and answer original questions, using *conocer* and *saber.*

▪▥ Eduardo *Conozco a Eduardo.*

▪▥ dónde vives *Sé dónde vives.*

1. dónde está tu oficina
2. tus hermanas
3. Gregorio
4. esquiar

5. qué día es tu cumpleaños
6. hablar español
7. San Francisco
8. una buena cafetería

¡vamos a hablar!

Tell a classmate what you, your father, or your friends do or don't know, using one of the following phrases. Ask your classmate if the same is true for her/him.

Sé (que) . . .   **Mis amigos saben . . .**   **No sé . . .**
Mi padre conoce . . .   **Conozco bien . . .**   **No conozco . . .**

Remind students to use *No sé* gesture when appropriate. (See chapter 7, p. 148.)

Sé hacer tortillas. ¿Y tú?
No conozco San Francisco. ¿Y tú?

Comparisons of inequality

Explain that a subject pronoun is used after *más . . . que* and *menos . . . que* in comparisons between two persons or groups of persons.

Ricardo es **más alto que** tú.
La televisión es **menos interesante que** el cine.
Tú corres **más despacio que** yo.

Ricardo is *taller than* you.
Television is *less interesting than* the movies.
You run *more slowly than* I.

In Spanish, the patterns **más . . . que** and **menos . . . que** are used with adjectives and adverbs to compare two persons or items, or two groups that are unlike each other. An adjective must agree with the noun it modifies.

Una familia asomada al balcón en Sevilla, España.

K   Decide whether the first item of each pair is more or less expensive than the second.

        ▪ⅲ   esa finca / esa casa   *Esa finca es [menos] cara que esa casa.*

    1. este carro / ese carro
    2. esta bicicleta / aquella bicicleta
    3. el pollo / el jamón
    4. las camas / los sillones
    5. el autobús / el metro
    6. este radio / este tocadiscos

L   Which of the following activities or things is more popular? Give your opinion, based on your own experience at your school.

        ▪ⅲ   el béisbol o el fútbol   *El béisbol es [más] popular que el fútbol.*

    1. el esquí o la natación   4. el campo o la playa
    2. la trompeta o la guitarra   5. el cine o la televisión
    3. la biología o la historia   6. los carros o las bicicletas

Pueblo cerca de Quito, Ecuador.

Comparisons of equality

Mi casa es **tan grande como** esa casa.

My house is *as large as* that house.

El lago está **tan lejos como** aquella montaña.

The lake is *as far away as* that mountain.

The pattern **tan . . . como** is used with adjectives and adverbs in comparisons of equality. An adjective must agree with the noun it modifies.

M Compare the following items, saying that the first item in each pair is as good as the second.

■III las verduras / las frutas *Las verduras son tan buenas como las frutas.*

1. la silla / el sillón
2. este reloj / ese reloj
3. los sandwiches / las hamburguesas
4. esa cama / aquella cama
5. las pulseras / los collares
6. ese parque / aquel parque
7. el bistec / el jamón

¡vamos a hablar!

Have students bring pictures of items for comparison.

Compare two of your classmates, using any of the following adjectives.

inteligente	**alegre**	**alto,-a**
simpático,-a	**perezoso,-a**	**creador,-a**

Inés es más alegre que Teresa.
Paco es tan inteligente como Enrique.

—————— En resumen ——————

Present tense of **salir, venir, hacer** (A–E)

Game: *Ta Te Ti* using *salir, oír, decir, venir, tener, saber, conocer, ser, estar.* (See Teacher's Guide.)

	VENIR	SALIR	HACER
yo	**vengo**	**salgo**	**hago**
tú	**vienes**	sales	haces
él, ella, usted	**viene**	sale	hace
nosotros, nosotras	venimos	salimos	hacemos
vosotros, vosotras	venís	salís	hacéis
ellos, ellas, ustedes	**vienen**	salen	hacen

Demonstrative adjectives (F, G)

	SINGULAR	PLURAL
Masculine	**este** libro	**estos** libros
Feminine	**esta** casa	**estas** casas
Masculine	**ese** papel	**esos** papeles
Feminine	**esa** cama	**esas** camas
Masculine	**aquel** chico	**aquellos** chicos
Feminine	**aquella** profesora	**aquellas** profesoras

1. The demonstrative adjectives **este, ese,** and **aquel** agree in number and gender with the nouns they modify.
2. **Este** and **esta** mean *this;* **estos** and **estas** mean *these.* They are used to refer to people or objects close to the speaker.
3. The singular forms of **ese** and **aquel** mean *that.* The plural forms mean *those.* **Ese** refers to people or objects near the person spoken to. **Aquel** refers to people or objects in the distance or not associated with the speaker.

Conocer and saber (H–J)

	SABER	CONOCER
yo	**sé**	**conozco**
tú	sabes	conoces
él, ella, usted	sabe	conoce
nosotros, nosotras	sabemos	conocemos
vosotros, vosotras	sabéis	conocéis
ellos, ellas, ustedes	saben	conocen

1. **Saber** means *to know* facts or information. **Saber** + infinitive means *to know how to* do something: **Sé su nombre; Sabe jugar al ajedrez.**
2. **Conocer** means *to know* or *to be acquainted with* people, places, or things: **No conozco a Elena.**

Comparisons of equality and inequality (K–M)

Equality	**tan** + adjective / adverb + **como**	*as . . . as*
Inequality	**más** / **menos** + adjective / adverb + **que**	*more . . . than* / *less . . . than*

Casa en una zona residencial de San Salvador.

A   Tell about the activities of the following people by combining elements from each column. Make two statements about each subject.

1. yo
2. Adolfo
3. Vicente y yo
4. tus primos

salir a las seis de la tarde
venir aquí los fines de semana
hacer las invitaciones para la fiesta

   ▪ⅲ   *Yo salgo a las seis de la tarde.*

B   Pick out from each group the three words that best fit into one category.

Assignment: Students list sets of words, each set with one non-conforming item. In class, they read list and others must pick out odd item.

1. nadar, pasear, lugar, pescar
2. comedor, orilla, sala, alcoba
3. árbol, perezoso, alegre, feo
4. lago, cerca, montaña, playa
5. empleo, postre, pescado, sopa
6. enfermo, aburrido, cansado, amplio
7. sala, sillón, estante, tocador

C   Complete the sentences with the correct forms of *saber* or *conocer*.

1. ¿Quién _____ a Pilar Santos?
2. Yo no la _____.
3. ¿Quién _____ dónde vive Pilar?
4. Yo no _____ dónde vive.
5. Y tú, ¿_____ dónde vive Pilar?
6. Yo _____ que Pilar vive en Acapulco.
7. Yo no _____ bien la ciudad.
8. Quiero ir a Acapulco porque ahora _____ hablar español.
9. ¿Y tú? ¿_____ Acapulco?

D   State your preferences, based on the following situations, and tell why you make each choice.

1. Buscas un cuaderno porque tienes mucho trabajo. Aquí hay un cuaderno con veinte páginas. Hay otro con doscientas páginas. ¿Cuál prefieres? ¿por qué?
2. Buscas un tocadiscos y no tienes mucho dinero. Hay un tocadiscos que cuesta cincuenta dólares. Hay otro que cuesta cien dólares. ¿Cuál prefieres? ¿por qué?
3. Buscas una casa nueva. Hay diez personas en tu familia. Hay una casa que no es muy amplia. Hay otra casa que tiene seis alcobas. ¿Cuál prefieres? ¿por qué?

E Compare the first item shown to the second, using *más . . . que, menos . . . que,* or *tan . . . como,* and one of the following adjectives: *grande, pequeño, caro,* or *barato.*

Let students draw stick figures for expansion of Ex. E. Each shows one drawing and queries class.

Esta mesa es más grande que aquella mesa.

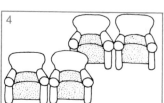

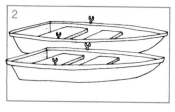

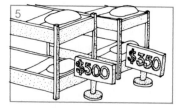

F What would you say in each of the following situations?

Acrostic to review rooms and furniture: Use *pasillo* and *comedor.*

Vary Ex. G to practice questions. Each student interviews another for school newspaper. Interviewer then prepares a short article with photo of interviewee. Post best articles under *Chicos de la semana.*

1. Greet your neighbor, Mr. Castañeda, after school.
2. Say good-by to your Aunt Mónica after a visit.
3. A friend shows you her new pearl necklace.
4. You're offered a second helping of *paella,* which you like very much.
5. A friend asks whether he/she should buy a new bicycle that is very expensive, or an old one that costs less.
6. Your teacher asks how you're feeling.
7. A new friend asks if you'd like to play tennis tomorrow.
8. A friend calling long distance asks you what the weather's like where you live.
9. The school principal asks if your house is big enough to have four students from El Salvador for the weekend.

G See how much you've learned to say about yourself in Spanish since *capítulo uno.* Prepare an autobiography of at least ten lines, using some of the ideas below.

Me llamo . . .   Los fines de semana . . .
Tengo . . . años. Mi cumpleaños . . .   Me gusta . . .
En mi familia . . .   No me gusta . . .
Mi casa . . .   En el verano . . .

Vocabulario

SUSTANTIVOS

la alcoba bedroom
la alfombra carpet
el árbol tree
el bote rowboat
la cama bed
la cocina kitchen
el comedor dining room
el cuarto de baño bathroom
la escalera staircase, stairs
el escritorio desk
el estacionamiento parking
el estante bookcase
el jardín garden
el lago lake
la lámpara lamp
el lavadero laundry area
el lugar place
la mesita small table; **la mesita de noche**
  night table
el mueble piece of furniture
la orilla bank (river, lake)
el pasillo hallway
el patio courtyard
la puerta door
la sala living room
el sillón armchair
la terraza terrace
el tocador dresser
el vecino, -a neighbor
la ventana window

VERBOS

conocer to know, to be acquainted with
contestar to answer
deber to be obligated to, ought
necesitar to need
pasear to go for a walk (drive, ride)
pescar to fish
salir to leave
sonar (ue) to ring

OTRAS PALABRAS

alrededor around
amplio, -a ample, spacious
aquel, aquella that
de pronto suddenly
siguiente following, successive

EXPRESIONES

bienvenidos welcome
¿de parte de quién? who's calling?
dile tell her/him
más ... que more ... than
menos ... que less ... than
ni ... ni neither ... nor
tan ... como as ... as

algo más

A **Una invitación.** Invite a classmate to your home or to the movies. Draw a map showing the route from school to your house or to the theater. Draw any important landmarks and include street names. Using the map, explain in Spanish how to get to your house or to the theater. Answer any questions your classmate has about the route.

B **Noticias escolares.** With three or four classmates, prepare a newscast of real or fictional announcements about upcoming school events and activities. You might include items about sports or musical events, a class trip, a meal at a Spanish or Mexican restaurant, a club meeting, a Hispanic holiday celebration, or teachers and students in the news. Compete with other groups in your class for the best newscast.

C **De compras.** Form a group of three to six people and prepare a skit related to shopping. Possible settings are a department store, a small specialty shop, a food market, a furniture store, or an automobile showroom. Use props and add lively situations, such as complaints, inefficient or overenthusiastic salespersons, or an argument between two people about what to buy. Act out the skit in class.

D **En el restaurante.** Act out a scene in a restaurant with several classmates. Take the roles of diners, waiters and waitresses, and a cashier. Order from the menu on page 178 or from an actual Spanish menu. Your scene should include serving, eating, and paying for the meal. During the meal, the diners can talk about the food and service, while the restaurant personnel comment on the diners.

E **Agencia de viajes.** Select one of the countries mentioned in Chapters 6 through 11 and prepare a travel brochure highlighting the country's points of interest. Use photos or drawings and provide descriptive captions. Refer to the cultural notes and photographs in the text and add information that you find in the library, a newspaper travel section, or magazines. Try to interest your classmates in a trip to the country you have chosen. Show them your brochure and describe the sights you've illustrated.

Información meteorológica. For a week, consult a newspaper containing information on the weather in major foreign cities. Keep a journal describing the weather in your area and in a Spanish-speaking country. Then prepare a summary in Spanish comparing the weather in the two locations. Give as many details as possible for each day of the week and report your findings to the class.

En busca de una casa. With two or three classmates, prepare a dialogue related to buying a house or renting an apartment. One student takes the role of a real estate agent and the others portray a family. The clients should describe what they want and find out whether or not schools, shopping facilities, and public transportation are near by. The real estate agent should show the clients a house or apartment and convince them that it meets all their needs.

Álbum. Here are some ideas for additions to the album described in the **algo más** section of Stage One. Draw a simplified, illustrated map of your community, showing the places you go most often. Include a floor plan of your dream house and its furnishings, tickets and fliers for sports, musical or other events, and a menu from your favorite snack bar or cafeteria. Be sure to write a caption or brief description in Spanish of the items you include.

El regateo. Act out a market scene in your class. Bring in objects or magazine clippings of items you want to sell and use foreign currency if it's available. Take turns acting as venders and buyers. As a vender, you must try to obtain the highest possible price for each item you sell, convincing the buyer of its worth. As a buyer, you must bargain to obtain as low a price as possible.

La vida diaria. Look at the color photographs on pages 105–112. Select the setting and person that interest you the most and imagine yourself in that person's place. Describe where you are, why, and what you are doing. Create a dialogue that might take place between you and another person in the setting you choose.

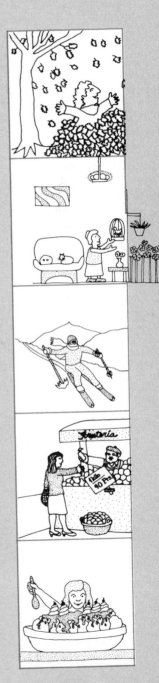

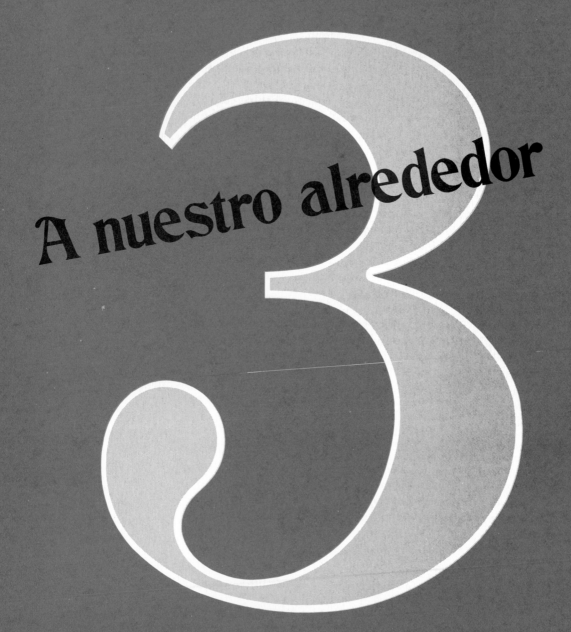

A nuestro alrededor

3

247

¡A divertirnos!

Locate Guadalajara on map.

Guadalajara, Mexico's second largest city, is an important university, sports and cultural center. The Degollado Theater features concerts performed by the city's orchestra and by guest orchestras, as well as plays and operas. Mariachi music played by traditional street musicians, **charreadas** (rodeos), soccer, baseball, and bullfights are especially popular in and around Guadalajara.

¡Vamos al concierto!

Warm-up: ¿Te gusta ir al cine? ¿a los partidos de [fútbol]? ¿Te gusta la música [clásica]?

Mónica, una estudiante de Guadalajara, cumple dieciséis años el domingo. Sus amigos Laura y Diego quieren invitarla a salir para celebrar su cumpleaños. Los tres chicos miran la sección de atracciones del periódico en casa de Mónica y discuten qué hacer.

LAURA	¿Te gustaría ir al cine con nosotros? Dan una película de terror muy buena.
MÓNICA	¿Cuál ... *Tigre?* Ya la vi. Me gustó mucho.
DIEGO	Entonces, ¿quieres ir al fútbol?
MÓNICA	No, gracias. Fui la semana pasada ... ¡Mira aquí! La Orquesta Sinfónica de Xalapa tiene un programa excelente. ¿Qué dicen?
LAURA	¡Magnífico! Vamos a la sinfónica. Diego y yo compramos los boletos para los tres.
DIEGO	El concierto empieza a las 9:30. Laura y yo venimos a buscarte a las 8:30. ¿De acuerdo?
MÓNICA	Sí, y mil gracias, chicos. Promete ser un cumpleaños maravilloso.

comprensión

A. Indicate which statements are true and which are false, according to the preceding dialogue. Use *sí* or *no* and correct any false statements.

1. Los chicos miran televisión.
2. Mónica cumple diecisiete años.
3. Mónica ya vio la película *Tigre.*
4. Todos quieren ir al partido de fútbol.
5. Laura dice que le gustaría oír la Sinfónica de Xalapa.
6. El concierto empieza a las 8:30 de la noche.
7. Mónica va a comprar los boletos.

B. Supply the information requested, based on the newspaper ad for the concert.

Nombre del teatro   Una de las selecciones del programa
Hora del concierto   Precio de los boletos
Nombre de la orquesta   Nombre del director

música

TEATRO DEGOLLADO
En colaboración con **LA EMBAJADA DE LA REPUBLICA POPULAR DE POLONIA**, **SECRETARIA DE RELACIONES EXTERIORES Y EL INBA**
domingo 15, 21:30 hrs.

ORQUESTA SINFONICA DE XALAPA
de la Universidad Veracruzana
director huésped, **Manuel de Elías**
solista, **Oscar Tarrago**

PROGRAMA
Obertura "Bajka" (cuento de invierno) — **Moniuszko**
Concierto Núm. 1, para piano y orquesta — **Chopin**
Krzesany, Poema Sinfónico — **Kilar**
Step (la estepa), Poema Sinfónico — **Noskowski**

boletos de $30.00 a $100.00 en las taquillas del teatro.

extensión

A. A friend invites you to go to the movies. Accept her/his invitation.

◼ ¿Te gustaría ir al cine?   Sí, gracias. ¿A qué hora?
                                 ¡Buena idea! ¿Qué dan?
                                 Por supuesto. Me encanta° el cine.
                                 Sí. ¿Por qué no?

B. Politely refuse a friend's invitation to a dance.

◼ ¿Quieres ir a bailar°   Lo siento. Estoy ocupado/a°.
  esta noche?   Muchas gracias, pero no puedo ir.
                                 ¡Ay, qué lástima! No puedo.
                                 No, gracias. Otro día, quizás.

C. Express to a friend your opinion of a movie you saw yesterday.

◼ ¿Cómo fue la película ayer°?   Me gustó mucho.
                                       Fue [mala°].
                                       Así así°.

D. How do you react when a friend rejects an invitation to a game?

◼ No puedo ir.   Otro día, entonces.
                   ¡Caramba! Nunca quieres salir.
                   ¿Por qué? Va a ser fantástico.

En el teatro

El domingo Laura, Diego y Mónica van al teatro. Llegan a las 9:25 en punto y Laura, con gran prisa, compra los boletos en la taquilla del teatro.

LAURA	Déme tres boletos de $30 pesos, por favor.
TAQUILLERA	Ya no quedan. Sólo hay en platea y en palco. Cuestan $50 y $75 pesos.
LAURA	Entonces, déme tres en platea.
TAQUILLERA	Son $150 pesos, por favor.
LAURA	Aquí tiene usted. Gracias.

Al entrar los chicos en el teatro, el acomodador les da los programas y los acompaña a sus asientos.

ACOMODADOR	Sus asientos están aquí en la fila RR. Son los números 7, 9 y 11.
DIEGO	Gracias. ¡Rápido, chicas, que ya va a empezar!
UNA SEÑORA	¡Ay, mi pie! ¡Cuidado, joven!
DIEGO	Perdone usted, señora. ¡Cómo lo siento!
MÓNICA	¡Qué vergüenza! Tenemos la culpa por no llegar más temprano.

extensión

A. You've invited a friend to the theater. Explain to her/him your plans for the evening by combining elements from the two columns.

Quiero . . .   buscarte a las ocho.
Pienso . . .   llegar temprano al teatro.
Voy a . . .   comprar los boletos primero.
Prefiero . . .   ir a comer después.
                   invitar a Julio y a Ana también.

Teatro Degollado en Guadalajara.

B. You're trying to get to your seat in a train and accidentally step on someone's toe. Apologize to her/him.

◼▥ ¡Ay, mi pie!   Perdone usted, [señor].
                    ¡Cómo lo siento!

C. You want to buy tickets for a concert. Make up a dialogue with at least four conversational exchanges and act out the scene with a classmate.

¿Hay boletos para hoy?	Lo siento, [señor]. No hay. Ya no quedan. Sí. ¿Cuántos necesita?
¿Cuánto cuestan?	Hay boletos de $30 a $100 pesos. Sólo hay de [$50] pesos.
Déme tres boletos de [$50], por favor.	Aquí los tiene. Son [$150] pesos, por favor.
Gracias. ¿Dónde están los asientos?	Los de [$50] están en platea. Sus asientos están en la fila [RR].

D. Invite a friend to go out. Your friend should accept or decline the invitation. Agree on an alternate activity if your friend declines.

ir al cine	salir a cenar a un restaurante
ir al partido de fútbol	oír música rock°
ir al teatro el domingo	ir a un baile°

--------------- Estudio de palabras ---------------

Diminutivos

Mention that students may already know the diminutive forms of some proper names: *Juanito, Carlitos, Anita, Rosita,* etc. Discuss meaning.

Miguelito tiene dos años.	*Mickey* is two years old.
Tu libro está en **la mesita.**	Your book is on the *small table.*
Un **cafecito,** por favor.	A *little* (cup of) *coffee,* please.
Luisa tiene fiebre. **¡Pobrecita!**	Luisa has a fever. *Poor thing!*

In Spanish, diminutive endings are often used with nouns and sometimes with adjectives to indicate smallness in size and to express affection. Common diminutive endings are **-ito, -ita, -cito** and **-cita.**

The endings **-ito** and **-ita** are usually added to words ending in **-o, -a,** or **-l.** A final vowel is dropped before the ending is added. The endings **-cito** and **-cita** are usually added to words ending in **-e** or **-n.**

Diminutives should be used very carefully because their meaning and use varies considerably from one Spanish-speaking area to another.

A Answer the following questions affirmatively. Use a diminutive to show affection or to indicate the smallness of each person, animal, or object.

◼▥ ¿Tienes una *casa* de campo?   *Sí, tengo una casita de campo.*

1. Esta niña es tu *hermana,* ¿verdad?
2. ¿Es inteligente ese *joven?*
3. *¡Pobre!* Está muy enfermo, ¿no?
4. ¿Fue un *viaje* interesante?
5. ¿Es del profesor ese *perro?*
6. *Carmen* es muy bonita, ¿no?

Expresiones de cortesía

Con permiso.

Perdón.
Perdone usted.

Gracias.
De nada.

Pasa.
Pase usted.

Buen provecho.

Lo siento.
¡Cómo lo siento!

B Respond to each situation with an appropriate expression from above.

◼▥ Un señor te dice "¡Ay! ¡Mi pie!"   *Perdón.*

1. Estás con tu familia. Acabas de comer y quieres ir a tu alcoba.
2. Acabas de servir una tortilla española a unos amigos.
3. Tienes que pasar delante de varias personas para llegar a tu asiento.
4. Tú y la profesora están a la puerta de la clase. Crees que ella debe entrar primero.
5. Le das un regalo de cumpleaños a un amigo. Te dice "Gracias."
6. Hablas cuando no debes, mientras habla tu tío.
7. No encuentras el cassette que te prestó tu hermana.

Expand Ex. B by having students act out each situation.

Optional: Have students make posters that illustrate courtesy expressions. Display the posters on bulletin board.

Pronunciación y ortografía

strong vowels

The letters **a**, **e**, and **o** are traditionally called strong vowels. When two strong vowels occur in sequence, each one is pronounced as a separate syllable.

A   Listen and repeat the following words after your teacher. Be sure you pronounce each strong vowel as a separate syllable.

feo	teatro	poeta	cacao
creo	museo	cumpleaños	toalla
leer	pasear	platea	cooperar

B   Read the following sentences aloud to practice strong vowel combinations.

Review the vowel sounds. Stress the importance of sharp, clear sounds. Use a rhyme for drill: Ba, be, bi, bo, bu, el burro sabe más que tú.

1. El cumpleaños de Rafael es mañana.
2. Creo que vamos al teatro en vez del museo.
3. Dar un paseo es una buena idea.
4. Ese poeta es norteamericano.
5. Beatriz quiere buscar empleo.
6. Joaquín lee el periódico.

De músico, poeta y loco,
todos tenemos un poco.

Proverb: Everyone is a bit crazy, musical, and poetic.

Gramática

Preterit tense of regular -ar verbs

Point out the importance of stress and accents in the preterit tense. Contrast the *yo*-present tense form and the *él/ella/usted*-preterit tense form: *miro/miró, hablo/habló, preparo/preparó*.

Escuché las noticias anoche.   *I listened to* the news last night.
¿Estudiaste mucho ayer?   *Did you study* a lot yesterday?
Tomás **trabajó** en México dos años.   Tomás *worked* in Mexico for two years.

The preterit is usually used to describe an action or event that began and ended in the past. The action or event is viewed as a single, completed whole even though it may have taken place over a long period of time.

	TRABAJAR
yo	trabaj**é**
tú	trabaj**aste**
él, ella, usted	trabaj**ó**
nosotros, nosotras	trabaj**amos**
ellos, ellas, ustedes	trabaj**aron**

The preterit tense of regular **-ar** verbs is formed by adding the preterit endings to the infinitive stem. The **yo-** and **él/ella/usted-**forms have a written accent to indicate a stress on the final syllable. Note that the **nosotros-**form is the same in the preterit as in the present tense. Context usually makes clear which tense is intended.

A   Say that the following people listened to the news last night.

■III   Diego   *Anoche Diego escuchó las noticias.*

1. mis papás
2. yo
3. los Mendoza
4. tú

5. Mónica y yo
6. Laura
7. Uds.
8. nosotros

B   Ask a classmate whether he/she did the following things yesterday.

Game: Play *béisbol* to practice preterit forms. T gives subject and infinitive. S must supply correct preterit form. See Teacher's Guide for instructions.

■III   caminar hasta el colegio   —*¿Caminaste hasta el colegio ayer?*
—*Sí, caminé hasta el colegio.*
(No, no caminé hasta el colegio.)

1. trabajar mucho
2. cenar en un restaurante
3. hablar con tus profesores
4. ayudar a tus padres

5. llamar por teléfono
6. ganar el partido de tenis
7. comprar boletos para el cine
8. visitar a los tíos

Joven toreador en una corrida.

Definite articles with nouns in a general sense

La nieve es hermosa, ¿no?   *Snow* is beautiful, isn't it?
La fruta es buena.   *Fruit* is good.
Me gustan **los conciertos.**   I like *concerts*.

A definite article precedes a noun used in a general sense.

C Express to a classmate your opinion on the items below. Use one of the
following adjectives in your responses.

Point out that a singular
article is used with
nouns that normally
aren't counted (*nieve,
leche*). A plural article
is used with nouns that
can usually be counted
(*deportes*).

fácil	**bueno**	**interesante**	**maravilloso**
difícil	**malo**	**aburrido**	**horrible**

▪▥ películas mexicanas   —*¿Qué piensas de las películas mexicanas?*
                              —*Las películas mexicanas son buenas.*

1. comida española
2. carros italianos
3. deportes
4. cámaras alemanas
5. televisión

6. esquí
7. fútbol
8. música rock
9. verano
10. películas de terror

Preterit tense of verbs in -car, -gar, -zar

Toqué la guitarra anoche.	I *played* the guitar last night.
Llegué muy tarde.	I *arrived* very late.
Empecé a estudiar a las ocho.	I *began* to study at eight.

Verbs ending in **-car**, **-gar**, or **-zar** have a spelling change in the **yo-**form of the preterit tense. The letter **c** changes to **qu**, **g** changes to **gu**, and **z** changes to **c** to keep the original consonant sound of the infinitive. All other forms are regular.

Verbs like **tocar:** **buscar** *(to look for)*, **pescar** *(to fish)*, **practicar** *(to practice)*, **sacar** *(to take out)*

Verbs like **llegar:** **jugar** *(to play)*, **pagar** *(to pay)*

Verb like **empezar:** **organizar** *(to organize)*

D Specify what you did yesterday by answering the questions in the affirmative or negative.

■ll ¿Tocaste el piano anoche? Sí, *toqué el piano.*
(*No, no toqué el piano.*)

1. ¿Jugaste al vólibol?
2. ¿Pagaste la cuenta?
3. ¿Llegaste tarde al colegio?
4. ¿Pescaste en el lago?

5. ¿Buscaste un regalo para papá?
6. ¿Empezaste a pintar tu alcoba?
7. ¿Practicaste el violín?
8. ¿Sacaste muchas fotos?

Preterit tense of -ar stem-changing verbs

Game: Play *Ta Te Ti* to practice preterit verb forms. See Teacher's Guide for instructions.

Merendamos en el campo ayer.	*We picnicked* in the country yesterday.
¿Encontraste mi reloj?	*Did you find* my watch?

Most **-ar** verbs whose stems change from **e > ie** or **o > ue** in the present tense do not have a stem change in the preterit. Their preterit forms follow the pattern of regular **-ar** verbs.

Verbs like **merendar:** **empezar** *(to begin)*, **pensar** *(to think)*

Verbs like **encontrar:** **costar** *(to cost)*, **jugar** *(to play)*, **recordar** *(to remember)*, **sonar** *(to ring)*

E Say whether or not the following people planned to go fishing yesterday.

■ll Sara *Sara pensó ir a pescar ayer.*
(*No pensó ir a pescar ayer.*)

1. yo
2. Francisco
3. Uds.

4. Felipe e Ignacio
5. tú
6. Beatriz y yo

F Vicente had a bad day yesterday. Take his role and explain some of the day's mishaps.

Assignment: Have students record 5 things they did during the day. Use in next class as warm-up.

◾▥ no *recordar* el cumpleaños de papá   *No recordé el cumpleaños de papá.*

1. no *encontrar* mis libros para estudiar
2. *jugar* al ajedrez y *ganar* mi hermana
3. *llegar* tarde a casa y no *cenar*
4. *empezar* la película y *sonar* el teléfono
5. *comer* con Alicia y *costarme* $15

¡vamos a hablar!   Interview two classmates individually about their activities last weekend. Find out three things they did and then report each activity to the class.

¿Nadaste en el lago el sábado?   *Sí, nadé en el lago el sábado.*

[Ana] dice que nadó en el lago el sábado.

Preterit tense of **ir** and **ser**

	IR and SER
yo	fui
tú	fuiste
él, ella, usted	fue
nosotros, nosotras	fuimos
ellos, ellas, ustedes	fueron

Daniel **fue** al cine.   Daniel *went* to the movies.
Ayer **fue** miércoles.   Yesterday *was* Wednesday.

The verbs **ser** *(to be)* and **ir** *(to go)* have identical forms in the preterit. Context usually makes clear which verb is being used. Note that **ir** is normally followed by **a** or **de**.

G Claudio directed the school band at a concert last night and wants to know if the following people attended. Assure him that of course they went to the concert.

Add-an-element: S¹: *Fui al cine ayer.* S²: *Fui al cine y al banco ayer.* S: *Fui al cine, al banco y . . .*

◾▥   María   Claudio: *¿Fue María al concierto?*
                  Tú: *¡Claro que fue!*

1. tú   5. tú y Carmen
2. mi primo   6. tus padres
3. José Antonio   7. Ángela
4. Ramón y Gloria   8. la profesora de español

H   Fernando's trying to find out who was responsible for a class prank. Assure him that the following persons were not involved.

V: Have student playing Fernando react: ¿Seguro que no fue él? / Entonces, ¿quién fue? / ¡Caramba! ¿Quién fue?

■▮ Diego   Fernando: *¿Fue Diego?*
Tú: *No, no fue Diego.*

1. tú
2. Soledad y Javier
3. ustedes
4. Pilar

5. Jesús
6. Carmen y Ricardo
7. tú y Luis
8. Marta

Unos mariachis en Guadalajara.

Preterit of ver and dar

	VER	DAR
yo	vi	di
tú	viste	diste
él, ella, usted	vio	dio
nosotros, nosotras	vimos	dimos
ellos, ellas, ustedes	vieron	dieron

The verbs **ver** *(to see)* and **dar** *(to give)* have similar forms in the preterit.

I Margarita lost her dog Blanco. Report to her that the following people didn't see it this morning.

> ■ꕮ el Sr. Palacios *El Sr. Palacios no lo vio esta mañana.*

1. Claudia
2. yo
3. Jorge y Manuel
4. Cristina y yo
5. nuestros vecinos
6. mis papás
7. Gustavo
8. Pablo y Cecilia
9. tú

J Gabriel is organizing a sale to raise money for a class trip. Ask him what various people gave him for the sale.

> ■ꕮ Antonio (una bicicleta) Tú: *¿Qué te dio Antonio?*
> Gabriel: *Me dio una bicicleta.*

1. tus primos (unos libros)
2. Rosa (unos discos)
3. Isabel y Daniel (una lámpara)
4. Clara (el violín de su hermano)
5. Ana y José Manuel (unos carteles)
6. Luis (un radio viejo)
7. Teresa y Sara (unas pulseras viejas)

¡vamos a hablar! Exchange news with a classmate about somewhere that you went recently, what you saw, and what it was like.

> ¿Adónde fuiste el viernes? Fui al cine. Vi la película *Tigre.*
> ¿Qué tal es? Muy buena. Y tú, ¿adónde fuiste?

Audience approval or disapproval at a theater in a Spanish-speaking country is expressed in almost the same way as in the United States. To show approval, an audience may applaud, shout **¡Bravo!**, or give the performers a standing ovation. To request an encore, an audience may applaud rhythmically and shout **¡Otra! ¡Otra!** Disapproval may be expressed by silence at the end of a performance, or by whistling.

Al + infinitive

Al salir de la clase, Juan ve a su prima.	*On leaving* the classroom, Juan sees his cousin.
Al entrar en el teatro, compré un boleto.	*On entering* the theater, I bought a ticket.
Al llegar al lago, voy a nadar.	*On arriving* at the lake, I'm going to swim.

The construction **al** + infinitive is equivalent to English *on* or *upon (doing something)*. The action expressed may refer to the present, past, or future.

K Say whether or not the following things are generally true for you. Use *al* + infinitive in each statement.

V: Ask students to mention five things they are going to do after school, using the pattern: *Al salir de clase, voy a . . .*

■ ◁ ¿Lees el periódico cuando llegas a casa?

Sí, al llegar a casa, leo el periódico.
(No, al llegar a casa, no leo el periódico).

1. ¿Escuchas música cuando terminas tu trabajo?
2. ¿Sales del teatro cuando ves una película mala?
3. ¿Dices "¡Fantástico!" cuando recibes una invitación?
4. ¿Comprendes todo cuando oyes español?
5. ¿Juegas al béisbol cuando sales de la clase?
6. ¿Tienes miedo cuando ves un perro grande?

Los huicholes

Los huicholes son un grupo de indios de México que viven de una forma casi
primitiva, aislados° del resto de la civilización. La razón° de su aislamiento   isolated/reason
es principalmente geográfica. El pueblo huichol habita una región
montañosa de muy difícil acceso en la Sierra Madre al norte de Guadala-
5 jara. Su principal riqueza es la agricultura; viven del cultivo del maíz° y   corn
otros productos agrícolas°. Últimamente se les puede ver en los pueblos y   agricultural
ciudades cerca de sus montañas, adonde bajan a vender sus bordados° y   embroidery
artesanía°.   crafts

    La estructura social de los huicholes es muy simple. Es un pueblo que vive
10 agrupado en familias y que conserva las costumbres° de sus antepasados°.   customs/ancestors
La figura más importante es el curandero° o *mara'akame,* quien dirige° los   medicine man/leads
complejos° ritos religiosos de la comunidad. También dirige un peregri-   complex
naje° anual a una región sagrada° en busca del peyote, una planta con   pilgrimage/sacred
cualidades alucinógenas y medicinales. Este peregrinaje constituye una de
15 las bases de la religión de los huicholes. El uso del peyote se extiende a toda
clase de ritos religiosos, como pedir a los dioses una buena cosecha° de maíz,   harvest
conseguir° la cura de enfermedades o para obtener energía, valor° o fuerza°   to attain/courage/strength
para trabajar.

Las costumbres familiares están basadas en la igualdad°. Tanto el
20 hombre como la mujer participan en las decisiones, pero, según tradición, el
hombre sale a arar° la tierra y la mujer cuida° la casa. Cuando por alguna
razón la pareja se separa y uno de los esposos no regresa° al hogar° en dos o
tres semanas, la persona abandonada empieza a buscar una nueva
compañera o compañero. El noviazgo° de los jóvenes dura muy corto
25 tiempo. La gente joven suele mostrar° su afecto en público con besos° y
abrazos°. Si un chico quiere casarse° con una chica, él va a su casa con un
regalo, por ejemplo una ardilla°, un pescado, un cangrejo° o algo de valor
semejante°. Si la chica acepta, entonces ella le teje° una banda que representa una serpiente°. Esta banda expresa sus deseos por un buen resultado,
30 salud° y larga vida°. Los chicos, después de obtener el permiso de los
padres, se casan.

	equality
	to plough/takes care of
	return/home
	courtship
	usually show/kisses
	embraces/to get married
	squirrel/crab
	similar/weaves
	snake
	health/life

actividades

A. Give your opinion of some of the customs of the *huicholes*. Comment on
the following ideas.

1. el aislamiento de la civilización
2. ser curandero o *mara'akame*
3. el uso del peyote
4. la corta duración del noviazgo
5. lo que hace un chico si quiere casarse

B. ¿Te gustaría pasar un mes con los huicholes para ver de cerca sus
costumbres? ¿Crees que sería difícil adaptarte y aceptar su forma de
vivir?

En resumen

Preterit tense of **-ar** verbs (A, B, D–F)

	INVITAR
yo	invit**é**
tú	invit**aste**
él, ella, usted	invit**ó**
nosotros, nosotras	invit**amos**
vosotros, vosotras	invit**asteis**
ellos, ellas, ustedes	invit**aron**

1. The preterit tense is usually used to describe an action or event that began and ended in the past.
2. The **nosotros**-forms of **-ar** verbs are the same in the present tense as in the preterit. Context usually makes clear which meaning is intended: **Tomamos un refresco anoche.**
3. Verbs ending in **-car, -gar,** and **-zar** undergo a spelling change before **e** in the **yo**-form of the preterit: **c>qu, busqué; g>gu, pagué; z>c, empecé.**
4. Most verbs that change the stem vowel from **o>ie** or **o>ue** in the present tense do not have a stem change in the preterit: **Pensé visitarte mañana; ¿Jugaste al tenis ayer?**

Definite article with nouns in a general sense (C)

| ¿Te gusta **la música rock?** | Do you like *rock music?* |
| Me gustan **los deportes.** | I like *sports.* |

A noun used in a general sense is preceded by a definite article.

Preterit of some irregular verbs (G–J)

	IR/SER	VER	DAR
yo	fui	vi	di
tú	fuiste	viste	diste
él, ella, usted	fue	vio	dio
nosotros, nosotras	fuimos	vimos	dimos
vosotros, vosotras	fuisteis	visteis	disteis
ellos, ellas, ustedes	fueron	vieron	dieron

1. The verbs **ser** and **ir** have identical preterit forms.
2. The verbs **ver** and **dar** have similar preterit forms.

Al + infinitive (K)

Al terminar su trabajo, Elena fue al cine.

The construction **al** + infinitive is equivalent to English *on* or *upon (doing something)*.

A   Find out what various people did or what happened yesterday. Complete the following conversational exchanges with the appropriate preterit forms of the verbs in parentheses.

■III   ¿*(Encontrar)* tú la cámara de Beatriz?
—No. La *(buscar)*, pero no la *(encontrar)*.

¿*Encontraste tú la cámara de Beatriz?*
—No. *La busqué, pero no la encontré.*

1. ¿*(Pasear)* ustedes en bote?
   —No, *(montar)* a caballo.
2. ¿*(Comprar)* Uds. los boletos para el partido?
   —Sí, la taquillera nos *(dar)* unos boletos buenos.
3. ¿Cuánto *(pagar)* por esa lámpara?
   —Fue una ganga. Sólo *(costar)* $15.
4. ¿Con quién *(jugar)* al tenis? ¿con Roberto?
   —No, *(jugar)* con Irene.
5. ¿*(Celebrar)* Juan su cumpleaños?
   —Sí, sus amigos le *(dar)* una fiesta.

Cine en Cartagena, Colombia.

265

B Juan is having a party and some of the guests have already arrived. Give one or two lines of appropriate conversation to each person in the drawing below.

■⫿ Juan (en la puerta): *Hola, Carmen. ¡Bienvenida!*

C Elisa and Ramón are talking about Ramón's evening out last night. Complete their dialogue with the correct preterit forms of *ir, ser,* or *ver.*

Elisa: Oye, ¿_____ al cine anoche con Anita? Daniel dice que los _____ allí.

Ramón: Sí, Anita y yo _____ al cine, pero no _____ a Daniel.

Elisa: ¿_____ ustedes a comer también?

Ramón: Sí, primero _____ al Bodegón Español. La comida es siempre muy buena. Me gusta mucho ese restaurante.

Elisa: A mí también. Dime, ¿qué tal la película?

Ramón: ¡Uy! No me gustó. _____ algo horrible.

D State what each of the following people likes or dislikes, choosing from the items in column 3. Use the appropriate indirect-object pronoun and form of *gustar*.

1	2	3
1. a mí	gustar	deportes
2. a mi mamá		café
3. a ti		música rock
4. a mis hermanos		baile
5. a Pedro		hamburguesas
6. a nosotros		postres
7. a mi amiga Sara		fiestas

■III   *A mí me gustan los deportes.*

■III   *A mí no me gusta el café.*

E Combine the following pairs of sentences, using a phrase with *al* + infinitive.

■III   Llegué a casa. Tomé un   *Al llegar a casa, tomé un*
        refresco.   *refresco.*

1. Entré en mi cuarto. Empecé a estudiar.
2. Terminé mi trabajo. Escuché unos discos.
3. Fui a la biblioteca. Vi a una amiga.
4. Busqué mi libro de español. Encontré unas fotos viejas.
5. Pensé en las vacaciones. Recordé mi viaje a México.
6. Salí de la clase. Vi a Juan.

F Rafael is trying to make a date with Teresa. Read their conversation, then answer the questions based on it.

Rafael: Hola, Teresa. ¿Te gustaría ir al cine?
Teresa: No, gracias. Ya vi todas las películas interesantes.
Rafael: ¿Quieres ir al teatro?
Teresa: Sí, pero hoy no puedo ir. ¿Puedes ir mañana?
Rafael: Sí. ¿Te gustaría ver *Don Juan?* Puedo comprar los boletos hoy.
Teresa: Buena idea. Me gustaría mucho verlo. ¿Vas a invitar a Marcos y a Maricarmen también?
Rafael: No están aquí. Fueron a Veracruz la semana pasada.

1. ¿Van Rafael y Teresa al cine?
2. ¿Por qué no quiere ir al cine Teresa?
3. ¿Quiénes van al teatro?
4. ¿Quién compra los boletos?
5. ¿Por qué no invita Rafael a Marcos y a Maricarmen?

Vocabulario

SUSTANTIVOS

el acomodador, la acomodadora   usher
el asiento   seat
el baile   dance
el boleto   ticket
el concierto   concert
la culpa   fault
la fila   row
la orquesta   orchestra
el palco   box seat
la película (de terror)   film, movie (horror)
el pie   foot
la platea   orchestra seat
el programa   program
la taquilla   box office
el taquillero, la taquillera   ticket agent
el teatro   theater
el valor   cost
la vergüenza   shame; embarrassment

VERBOS

acompañar   to accompany
bailar   to dance
celebrar   to celebrate
discutir   to discuss
empezar (ie)   to begin
entrar   to enter
prometer   to promise
quedar   to remain, be left

OTRAS PALABRAS

anoche   last night
ayer   yesterday
malo, -a   bad
ocupado, -a   busy
pasado, -a   past
rápido   hurry, quickly
temprano   early

EXPRESIONES

así así   so-so
buen provecho   enjoy your food (meal)
¡cómo [lo siento]!   how [sorry I am]!
con permiso   excuse me, may I?
¡cuidado!   careful! watch out!
déme (Ud.)   give me
la música rock   rock music
[las seis] en punto   [six o'clock] sharp
me encanta [la música]   I like [music] a lot
pase (Ud.)   go ahead
perdone (Ud.)   pardon me, forgive me
¿te gustaría?   would you like?
tener la culpa   to be at fault

Fortaleza "El Morro" en San Juan.

capítulo 13
Con la familia

Puerto Rico, located in the northern Caribbean southeast of Miami, has close cultural, political, and economic relations with the United States which have significantly influenced the island's industrial and agricultural growth. With a raised standard of living and increased job opportunities, as well as a year-round warm climate and close family ties, many Puerto Ricans have chosen to remain on the island or to return from jobs in the United States.

269

La abuela cuenta sus memorias

Warm up: Encourage
students to relate their
own travel experiences,
using the preterit tense:
*Fui a Miami. Me gus-
taron mucho las playas.*

Hoy hace un año que visité a mis hijos en Nueva York y todavía recuerdo el frío tan terrible que hizo al llegar. ¡Diez grados bajo cero y yo sin abrigo! "Este clima — pensé — no se parece en nada al clima de mi querido Río Piedras."

Al ver a mis hijos y nietos en el aeropuerto, corrí hacia ellos y los besé con emoción. ¡Ay, bendito! ¡Qué alegría verlos de nuevo!

Los meses pasaron lentamente. Aunque visité muchos lugares de interés en la ciudad, asistí a muchas fiestas y reuniones con los amigos de mis hijos y aprendí un poco de inglés, no me adapté. "En Puerto Rico — pensé — tengo parientes, amigos y una forma de vivir agradable. ¿Por qué tratar de cambiarla?" Entonces, decidí volver y un día les dije a mis hijos:

"Es hora de irme."

Ellos no respondieron nada. Creo que me comprendieron. Sin embargo, les expliqué:

"Este país es para gente joven y yo estoy muy vieja para adaptarme."

comprensión

V: Have students retell
the *abuela*'s story in the
third person, after introducing preterit of *-er*
and *-ir* verbs.

1. ¿A qué fue la abuela a Nueva York?
2. ¿Cuándo fue?
3. ¿A quién vio en el aeropuerto al llegar?
4. ¿Cómo pasó el tiempo?
5. ¿Qué hizo en Nueva York?
6. ¿Qué decidió la abuela después de algunos meses? ¿por qué?

A. Welcome a friend you haven't seen in a year.

■Ⅲ ¡Hola, [Javier]! ¡Qué alegría verte!
¡Cuánto tiempo sin verte!
Tengo mucho que contarte°.

B. What is likely to be your reaction to a foreign country after spending three months there?

■Ⅲ ¿Qué tal te fue? Lo pasé° [muy bien].
¡Qué [rápidamente°] pasó el tiempo!
No me adapté.
Eché de menos° a [mis amigos].

C. Try to convince a friend to extend her/his visit to your home.

■Ⅲ Tengo que irme. ¿Por qué? Es pronto.
Tenemos mucho que hacer todavía.
Tu familia no va a echarte de menos.

Desacuerdos familiares

José y Elena están en casa con la abuela mientras trabajan sus padres. José está enojadísimo y pelea con su hermana. Está seguro que ella le rompió su radio. Como de costumbre, José llama a la abuela para resolver el problema.

JOSÉ	¡Abuela, abuela! ¡Pronto!
ABUELA	No, hijo. ¡Ven tú! ¿Qué pasa esta vez?
JOSÉ	Elena me rompió el radio y dice que no fue ella.
ABUELA	¡Ay, dios mío! Por favor, chicos, ustedes siempre están peleando.
ELENA	Te aseguro, abuela, que yo no hice nada. Pasé cerca y el radio se cayó de la mesa. Ya se lo expliqué a José.
ABUELA	¡Basta ya! No más pelea. ¡Elena, pídele disculpas a José!
ELENA	Pero, abuelita, yo . . .
ABUELA	¡Vamos, vamos, niña! ¡Pídeselas!
ELENA	José, lo siento . . . pero se cayó sólo.
JOSÉ	Bueno. Aunque sí fue tu culpa por correr.
ABUELA	¡Qué alivio! Ahora hay un poco de silencio sin ese radio a todo volumen.

V: Personalize *comprensión* by asking more questions: *¿Peleas con tu hermano/hermana? ¿Tienes una grabadora?*

1. ¿Por qué está enojado José?
2. ¿Por qué llama José a la abuela?
3. ¿Quién piensas tú que rompió el radio?
4. Según Elena, ¿qué pasó?
5. ¿Qué dice la abuela?
6. Al pedir disculpas, ¿piensa Elena que tiene la culpa?
7. ¿Por qué dice la abuela "ahora hay un poco de silencio"?

Optional: Have students act out *Desacuerdos familiares.*

V: Create a chain drill based on Act. A: S¹: *¡Idiota! ¡Rompiste mi raqueta!* S²: *No. No fui yo. Fue Carlos.* S³: *¿Yo? ¡No digas mentiras! No fui yo. Fue María.* S⁴: *¿Yo? Estás equivocado/a. No fui yo. Fue Alejandro.*

A. Last night Jorge found his tennis racket broken after you used it. He angrily blames you. Assure him that you didn't do it.

■ ¡Idiota°! ¡Rompiste mi raqueta°!

Te aseguro que no fui yo.
Estás equivocado°, lo juro°.
Yo no la rompí. Fue [Luis].
¿Yo? ¡Mentira°!

B. Elena accidentally dropped your radio on the floor and broke it. Reassure her by telling her not to worry.

■ ¡Ay! ¡Se me rompió tu radio!

No te preocupes.
No tiene importancia°.
No fue tu culpa.
No importa. No vale° mucho.

C. What would you say in the following situations?

Tu hermano rompió tu mejor disco.
Rompiste la grabadora de tu padre.
Un amigo piensa que rompiste su bicicleta.

No importa.
¡Idiota!
Fue [Paco]. Yo no fui.
Yo no hice nada.
¡Ay! ¡Mi disco!
Te juro que no sé quién fue.
¡Caramba! Estás equivocado/a.
No te preocupes.
No vale mucho.
Lo siento mucho.
¡Mentira!

_____ Estudio de palabras _____

Adverbios con -mente

rápido, -a	rápidamente	rapidly
fácil	fácilmente	easily
alegre	alegremente	happily

The Spanish suffix **-mente** is equivalent to the English suffix *-ly*. Many adverbs are formed by adding the suffix **-mente** to the feminine singular form of four-form adjectives, or to the singular form of two-form adjectives.

A   Form an adverb from each of the following adjectives, then use each one in an original sentence.

rápido	**alegre**
lento	**maravilloso**
fácil	**peligroso**

■‖   *Camino rápidamente al colegio por la mañana.*

■‖   *Mi hermano maneja peligrosamente.*

B   Tell a classmate something that you do slowly and something that you do rapidly.

■‖   *Como lentamente. ¿Y tú?*

■‖   *Hago mi trabajo rápidamente. ¿Y tú?*

Superlativos con **-ísimo**

La comida es **riquísima** aquí.
The food is *very delicious* here.

José está **enojadísimo.**
José is *extremely angry.*

Los ejercicios son **dificilísimos.**
The exercises are *very, very difficult.*

El helado me **gusta muchísimo.**
I *really* like ice cream *a lot.*

The superlative of many adjectives and adverbs is formed by adding **-ísimo** (**ísima, -ísimos, -ísimas**) to the word. A final vowel or an accent is dropped from the word before a superlative suffix is added. Adjectives ending in **-co** or **-ca** have a spelling change from **c** to **qu** before the superlative suffix: **rico > riquísimo.**

C Answer the following questions in the affirmative, using the superlative form of the adjectives or adverbs.

◼‖ ¿Fue interesante la clase?　　　*Sí, fue interesantísima.*

1. ¿Son simpáticos tus primos?
2. ¿Es grande tu casa nueva?
3. ¿Son caros los carros deportivos?
4. ¿Son hermosos los paisajes de Colombia?
5. ¿Tienes muchas fotos de tu viaje?
6. ¿Te gusta mucho pescar?
7. ¿Terminó tarde el concierto?

D Name two activities or things that you think are extremely good and two that you think are extremely bad.

◼‖ *Los deportes son buenísimos.*

◼‖ *La comida de la cafetería es malísima.*

El Yunque, a spectacular rain forest and bird sanctuary located near the eastern end of Puerto Rico, attracts thousands of visitors from all over the world. It harbors over 200 species of tropical birds, including a rare Puerto Rican parrot, and over 240 species of trees, as well as many kinds of tropical plants, including giant tree ferns and orchids. **El Yunque** generally has three or four brief but heavy downpours daily.

Pronunciación y ortografía

diphthongs

The letters **i** and **u** are often called weak vowels in Spanish. A diphthong is formed when an unaccented weak vowel combines with a strong vowel (**a, e, o**) or with another weak vowel. In a diphthong, the two vowel sounds are pronounced as a single syllable. The following words show examples of common weak + strong vowel combinations.

A Listen and repeat the following words after your teacher. Pronounce the weak + strong vowel combinations as a single syllable.

ia	ie	io	ua	ue
gracias	fiesta	radio	cuatro	nuevo
familia	siete	junio	cuánto	abuelo
estudiar	siempre	idiota	cuaderno	luego
demasiado	concierto	precio	cuando	bueno

B Read the following sentences aloud. Pay special attention to your pronunciation of the weak + strong vowel combinations.

Have students write Ex. B as a dictado.

1. Juan siempre come demasiado.
2. La fiesta empieza a las diez y media.
3. El concierto fue buenísimo.
4. Pienso llevar un radio a la escuela.
5. ¿Cuándo ve tu familia a los abuelos?

Más vale pájaro en mano que ciento volando.

Proverb: A bird in the hand is worth two in the bush (a hundred flying).

Preterit tense of **decir**

DECIR	
yo	dije
tú	dijiste
él, ella, usted	dijo
nosotros, nosotras	dijimos
ellos, ellas, ustedes	dijeron

Remind students that the preterit forms of *decir* and *hacer* (p. 277) have no written accents.

The verb **decir** *(to say, tell)* is irregular in the preterit tense. The stem vowel of **decir** changes to **i**, and **c** is replaced by **j** in the stem.

A Opinions vary as to whether it's going to rain today. Report who said it is, and who said it isn't.

▪▥ Anita (sí)   *Anita dijo que sí.*

1. David y Nicolás (no)
2. mi hermana (sí)
3. tú (sí)
4. nosotros (no)
5. yo (sí)
6. el Sr. Hernández (no)
7. Beatriz y yo (sí)
8. Uds. (sí)

Authority in Spanish-speaking families is often shared among various family members. Grandparents who live in the home care for children and may help them with homework, teach them tasks or crafts, and console them when problems arise. Brothers and sisters also watch after one another, and the oldest may be responsible for the younger children, acting almost with the authority of an extra parent.

Preterit tense of **hacer**

	HACER
yo	hice
tú	hiciste
él, ella, usted	hizo
nosotros, nosotras	hicimos
ellos, ellas, ustedes	hicieron

The verb **hacer** *(to do, make)* is irregular in the preterit tense. The stem vowel changes to **i.** The **c** changes to **z** in the **él/ella/usted**-form: **hizo.**

B   Claudia is trying to find out who wrote all over her Spanish notebook. Assure her that the people she asks about didn't do it.

> ▪▥   Clara   Claudia: *¿Lo hizo Clara?*
> Tú: *Te aseguro que ella no lo hizo.*

1. Cristina y Pilar
2. tú
3. Manuel y Alfredo
4. Sara

5. tú y Pedro
6. tus primas
7. Antonio
8. Uds.

Preterit tense of **-er** and **-ir** verbs

Review preterit forms of *-ar* verbs before introducing *-er* and *-ir* preterit forms. Stem-changing verbs *e* to *i* are presented in Chapter 14.

	CORRER	RECIBIR
yo	corrí	recibí
tú	corriste	recibiste
él, ella, usted	corrió	recibió
nosotros, nosotras	corrimos	recibimos
ellos, ellas, ustedes	corrieron	recibieron

The preterit tense of regular **-er** and **-ir** verbs is formed by adding the preterit endings to the infinitive stem. The preterit endings of **-er** and **-ir** verbs are identical. Note that the **yo-** and **él/ella/usted**-forms are stressed on the final syllable. The **nosotros-**form of **-ir** verbs is the same in the preterit and in the present tense.

> **Perdimos** el partido ayer.   *We lost* the game yesterday.
> Tomás **volvió** tardísimo anoche.   Tomás *returned* very late last night.

Most **-er** verbs whose stems change from **e > ie** or **o > ue** in the present tense, do not have a stem change in the preterit.

C   Say how many kilometers the following people ran last week to prepare for a 10-kilometer race. Use any number from 10 to 50.

> ◼▥   Miguel   *Miguel corrió [treinta] kilómetros.*

1. el señor Méndez
2. tú
3. Luisa
4. mis padres
5. yo
6. nosotros
7. los Caballero
8. tu profesora

D   Raquel and Carlos frequently disagree. Take the role of Carlos and correct Raquel's statements according to the cues.

> ◼▥   Ana subió a la montaña. (yo)   *Ana no. Yo subí a la montaña.*

1. Los Díaz vendieron su casa. (la Sra. Ramírez)
2. Juan aprendió a tocar el clarinete. (Fernando y yo)
3. Raúl y Ana recibieron un paquete. (Salvador y Patricia)
4. La Sra. Salinas escribió una novela. (el Sr. Salinas)
5. Sara bebió todos los refrescos. (tú)
6. Santiago volvió de Puerto Rico ayer. (Vicente y Clara)
7. Teresa perdió sus lentes. (Felipe)

E   Irene was absent from school yesterday and wants to know whether or not certain things happened. Answer her questions, supplying the correct preterit form of the *-ar, -er,* and *-ir* verbs.

Game: Play *Ta Te Ti* to practice *-er* and *-ir* preterit forms. See Teacher's Guide for instructions.

Assignment: Have students write eight sentences telling what they did yesterday.

Game: For additional practice of *-er* and *-ir* preterit forms, play *béisbol*. See Teacher's Guide.

> ◼▥   Tomás / ganar la carrera   Irene: *¿Ganó Tomás la carrera?*
>   Tú: *Sí, ganó la carrera.*
>   *(No, no ganó la carrera.)*

1. tus primas / insistir en ver *Noche de terror*
2. Elena / aprender a jugar al ajedrez
3. el profesor / anunciar el día del examen
4. Marta y Jesús / tocar bien en el concierto
5. tú / decidir qué hacer para tu cumpleaños
6. ustedes / discutir cuándo ir a bailar
7. Miguel / comprender el problema de álgebra
8. la Sra. Rojas / reparar la grabadora
9. tú / comer con Víctor

¡vamos a hablar!

Report to a classmate what various friends told you earlier in the day.

| ¿Qué te dijo María? | María me dijo que perdió el partido de tenis. |
| ¿Qué te dijeron Tomás y Bernardo? | Tomás y Bernardo me dijeron que merendaron en el campo ayer. |

Nada, nadie, and nunca

No tengo **nada** para tí.   I do *not* have *anything* for you.
No hay **nadie** en la puerta   There is *no one* at the door.
Nunca llegas tarde.   You *never* arrive late.

The negative words **nada, nadie,** and **nunca** can be used before or after a verb. When they are used after the verb, **no** must precede the verb.

F   You don't feel like doing anything today. Respond to various friends' suggestions, using *nada* or *nadie*.

> ▪‖   hablar con Manuel   Amigo/a: *¿Quieres hablar con Manuel?*
>   Tú: *¡No! No quiero hablar con nadie.*

1. mirar televisión
2. jugar al béisbol
3. tomar algo
4. ver a Marta
5. escribir a Carlos
6. comer un sandwich

G   Convince a friend that you never do the following things.

> ▪‖   ¿Peleas con tus hermanos?   *¿Yo? Nunca peleo con mis hermanos.*

1. Siempre vas a la piscina, ¿no?
2. ¿Sales al campo los fines de semana?
3. ¿Recibes cartas de tus amigos?
4. Siempre tienes exámenes los viernes, ¿verdad?
5. ¿Comes hamburguesas para la cena?

Alguno and ninguno

Javier me prestó **algunos** libros.   Javier lent me *some* books.
No encuentro **ningún** mapa aquí.   I can't find *any* map here.
No hay **ninguna** chica en la clase.   There's *not one* girl in the class.

Alguno, -a agrees in number and gender with the noun it precedes. **Alguno** and **ninguno** shorten to **algún** and **ningún** before a masculine singular noun. **Ninguno, -a** is almost always used in the singular.

H   Susana is always borrowing things from you. Refuse to lend her anything. Use *ninguno, -a* in the singular only.

> ▪‖   lápices   Susana: *Oye, ¿puedes prestarme algunos lápices?*
>   Tú: *Hoy no te puedo prestar ningún lápiz.*

1. cassette
2. bolígrafos
3. novela
4. pulsera
5. cuaderno
6. dólares

Double-object pronouns with **me, te, nos**

List direct- and indirect-object pronouns on board. Refer to list while introducing double-object pronouns.

¿**Me** compras un helado? Will you buy *me* an ice cream?
— Claro. **Te lo** compro ahora. — Of course. I'll buy *it for you* now.

When two object pronouns occur in the same sentence, the indirect-object pronoun usually precedes the direct-object pronoun. Object pronouns precede a conjugated verb.

FIRST POSITION	SECOND POSITION
me	
te	lo, la, los, las
nos	

The chart above shows the positions of indirect-object pronouns in relation to direct-object pronouns. Note that a pronoun beginning in **l** is always in second position.

Bús**came** el periódico. **Búscamelo.**
Quiero dar**te** esta foto. Quiero dár**tela.**

Object pronouns follow and are attached to commands. They often follow and are attached to infinitives. A written accent is added to the verb to maintain its original stress.

I Felipe notices that you have some new things. Tell him that your parents bought them for you.

▪ⅲ Este cartel es nuevo, ¿no? *Sí, me lo compraron mis padres.*

1. Esos zapatos son nuevos, ¿no?
2. ¡Veo que tienes un perro nuevo!
3. ¿Son nuevos tus lentes?
4. Esa lámpara es nueva, ¿verdad?
5. Esas novelas son nuevas, ¿no?
6. ¡Veo que tienes una guitarra nueva!

J You're eating out with your family, and your sister is impatient because the service is very slow. Assure her that you'll all be served soon.

▪ⅲ la ensalada Tu hermana: *¿Cuándo van a servirnos la ensalada?*
   Tú: *No te preocupes. Van a servírnosla pronto.*

1. el pan
2. los sandwiches
3. la sopa
4. las patatas
5. el postre
6. las manzanas

¡vamos a hablar!   You're trying to be especially nice to your brother after an argument. Offer to give him something of yours.

¿Te doy las monedas?   Sí, dámelas.

¿Te doy el cassette?   Sí, dámelo.

Double-object pronouns with **le** and **les**

¿Le	das un lápiz	a Carlos?
¿Le	das una cámara	a María?
¿Les	das unos collares	a ellas?
¿Les	das unas fotos	a ellos?

Sí,	**se lo**	doy a Carlos.
Sí,	**se la**	doy a María.
Sí,	**se los**	doy a ellas.
Sí,	**se las**	doy a ellos.

The indirect-object pronouns **le** and **les** change to **se** before **lo, la, los,** or **las.** An **a**-phrase, such as **a Carlos** or **a ellas,** is used to clarify or emphasize the person referred to by the indirect-object pronoun.

K   Tell a friend whether or not certain people gave Alejandro the following gifts for his graduation last week.

V: Place photos or actual objects in a box. Student selects item and says: S¹: *Tengo una calculadora. José me la dio.*

▪▥   ¿Le dio Pilar el disco?   *Sí, se lo dio Pilar.*
(No sé si se lo dio).

1. ¿Le dieron sus padres el carro?
2. ¿Le dio su hermano la trompeta?
3. ¿Le dieron sus abuelos el dinero?
4. ¿Le dieron sus tíos el reloj?
5. ¿Le dio Dolores la grabadora?
6. ¿Le dio Enrique los cassettes?
7. ¿Le diste tú las monedas?

L   You had a garage sale. Explain to a friend to whom you sold various possessions.

▪▥   los discos / a Pedro   Amigo/a: *¿A quién le vendiste los discos?*
Tú: *Se los vendí a Pedro.*

1. las monedas argentinas / a los Hernández
2. el juego de ajedrez / a Carmen
3. la calculadora / a Marta y a Julio
4. los carteles / a Fernando
5. el estante / a mis primas
6. la mesita / a una vecina
7. las novelas / a Felipe

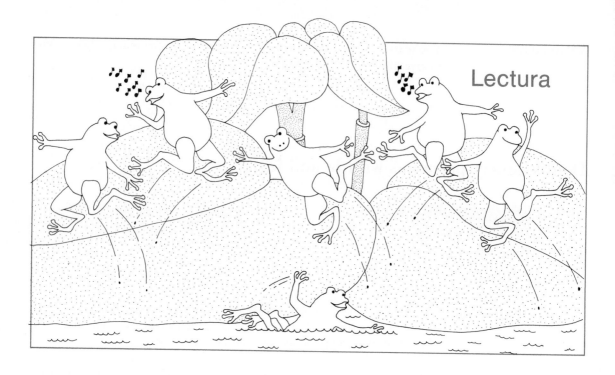

Lectura

La leyenda del coquí

OptionalOptional: Read or play a tape of the *Lectura*. Pause after each paragraph to ask comprehension questions.

Puerto Rico tiene una mascota nacional que es el coquí. Es una pequeña ranita° que rara vez se deja ver°. Vive una vida muy tranquila, casi siempre escondida° entre las plantas acuáticas y el follaje° húmedo de las matas° grandes.

5 Todos los días al caer de la tarde° empieza su canto° ensordecedor°:
¡Coquí! ¡Coquí! ¡Coquí!

De allí sacó su nombre. Aunque hay muchas ranas similares en las islas del Caribe, esta rana es exclusivamente puertorriqueña. Se diferencia de otras ranas de la región por tener los dedos separados en vez de unidos por
10 una membrana.

Hace algunos años°, según un cuento° popular, un presidente de la República Dominicana, después de residir algún tiempo en Puerto Rico, tuvo que regresar a su país. Como disfrutaba° tanto del canto del coquí, decidió llevarse una ranita para su tierra.

15 Días después le escribió una carta a uno de sus amigos en Puerto Rico diciendo, "El coquí que traje° está muy bien. Salta° y nada alegremente todo el tiempo, pero nunca volvió a cantar°."

very small frog/**se ... ver:** allows itself to be seen hidden/foliage/shrubs

al ... tarde: at sunset/song/ deafening

hace ... años: some years ago/story

he enjoyed

I brought/it jumps
nunca ... cantar: it never sang again

282   spanish today, one

A. Answer the following questions, based on your own experience.

1. ¿Tiene tu estado, colegio o equipo de fútbol una mascota? ¿cuál es?
2. ¿Qué símbolos (plantas o animales) tiene tu país? ¿tu estado?

B. Describe briefly an animal particular to your state or any animal that you think is unusual. Mention its habits and where it lives.

En resumen

Preterit of **decir** and **hacer** (A, B)

	DECIR	HACER
yo	dije	hice
tú	dijiste	hiciste
él, ella, usted	dijo	hizo
nosotros, nosotras	dijimos	hicimos
vosotros, vosotras	dijisteis	hicisteis
ellos, ellas, ustedes	dijeron	hicieron

The verbs **decir** and **hacer** are irregular in the preterit tense.

Preterit tense of **-er** and **-ir** verbs (C–E)

	VENDER	SUBIR
yo	vendí	subí
tú	vendiste	subiste
él, ella, usted	vendió	subió
nosotros, nosotras	vendimos	subimos
vosotros, vosotras	vendisteis	subisteis
ellos, ellas, ustedes	vendieron	subieron

1. The preterit endings of **-er** and **-ir** verbs are identical.
2. The **nosotros**-form of **-ir** verbs is the same in the preterit and present tenses.
3. Most **-er** verbs with a stem-change **e > ie** or **o > ue** in the present tense do not have a stem change in the preterit: **¿Perdiste tu reloj?**; **Volvimos de la playa ayer.**

Nada, nadie, and nunca (F, G)

The negative words **nada** *(nothing)*, **nadie** *(no one)* and **nunca** *(never)* can be used before or after a verb. When they are used after the verb, **no** must precede the verb: **Nunca peleo** or **No peleo nunca.**

Alguno and ninguno (H)

Alguno,-a *(some, any)* and **ninguno,-a** *(no, any, not one)* shorten to **algún** and **ningún** before a masculine singular noun: **No hay ningún papel aquí.**

Double-object pronouns (I–L)

FIRST POSITION	SECOND POSITION
me	
te	
nos	lo, la, los, las
le (se)	
les (se)	

1. When two object pronouns occur in the same sentence, the indirect-object pronoun usually precedes the direct-object pronoun: **Te di las fotos ayer; Te las di ayer.**
2. **Le** and **les** change to **se** before **lo, la, los,** or **las: Se lo di a Raquel.**
3. Object pronouns precede a conjugated verb, but follow and are attached to a command. They often follow and are attached to infinitives. Note the addition of a written accent: **Quiero dárselas a María.**

A Form eight logical sentences telling what the following people said or made or did. Use the preterit tense of *decir* or *hacer* and an appropriate phrase from column 3. You may add additional words if you like.

1	2	3
1. Jorge	decir	que no le gusta nadar
2. mi mamá	hacer	trampa en el juego
3. yo		un viaje a Puerto Rico
4. Daniel y Rosa		que no vas a pelear más
5. Elena		un postre buenísimo
6. tú		que no puede ir
7. Uds.		que no rompió la cámara
8. Paco y yo		todo su trabajo
		que fue de Ana la culpa

▪⦀ *Jorge dijo que no puede ir a la carrera.*

B Manuel just returned from a trip to Puerto Rico to visit relatives. Take his role and describe some of his impressions and activities. Use the superlative form of the adjective or adverbs given.

▪⦀ El viaje fue muy interesante. *El viaje fue interesantísimo.*

1. Mis parientes son muy simpáticos.
2. Visité el Yunque, un parque tropical muy hermoso.
3. La comida puertorriqueña es muy rica.
4. Saqué unas fotos muy buenas.
5. San Juan me pareció muy grande.
6. Las playas me gustaron mucho.
7. El clima es muy bueno allí.

Encourage students to retell Ex. B in the future. They should use the *ir + a* construction: *El viaje va a ser interesantísimo.*

C Say how you performed various activities by supplying an appropriate adverb ending in *-mente*. Use the following adjectives to form the adverbs.

lento	**alegre**	**rápido**
fácil	**inteligente**	**perezoso**

▪⦀ Acepté la invitación . . . *Acepté la invitación alegremente.*

1. Volví a casa . . .
2. Resolví el problema . . .
3. Paseé en bote . . .
4. Comprendí el ejercicio . . .
5. Escribí tres cartas . . .
6. Fui al colegio . . .

D Tell what happened or what the following people did recently by completing the conversational exchanges. Choose an appropriate verb from the list below and use the preterit tense.

perder	correr	comer	volver
recibir	llegar	prometer	encontrar

1. ¿ _____ Rosa alrededor del lago?
   —Sí. Ella y yo _____ cinco kilómetros.
2. ¿ _____ tus padres una carta de tu hermano?
   —Sí, y _____ hacernos una visita pronto.
3. ¿Dónde _____ Beatriz su cámara nueva?
   —En el parque, pero luego la _____.
4. ¿Cuándo _____ Julio y Bernardo de Puerto Rico?
   —El domingo pasado. _____ tardísimo a casa.
5. ¿ _____ tú en casa?
   —No, _____ en una cafetería.

E You're bored, but refuse to do anything your friends suggest. Reply negatively to the following suggestions. Use *nada, nadie, nunca,* or *ninguno,* as appropriate.

▪ⅰ Puedes leer algún libro. *No quiero leer ningún libro.*

1. Puedes jugar con Felipe.
2. ¿Quieres comer un sandwich?
3. ¿Por qué no escuchas algunos discos?
4. ¿Quieres ir al cine esta noche?
5. Puedes mirar algunas fotos.
6. ¿Quieres ir al parque esta tarde?
7. ¿Por qué no pintas algo?
8. ¿Quieres ver a Diana?

F What are you likely to say in the following situations? Use some of the phrases given below.

no tiene importancia	¡mentira!	otro día, quizás
¡cómo lo siento!	¡caramba!	estás equivocado/a
no fui yo	¡te [lo] pago!	fue tu culpa

▪ⅰ Un amigo pierde tu bolígrafo. *No tiene importancia.*

1. Rompes el collar de perlas de tu madre.
2. Tu hermano no te compra un boleto para el cine.
3. Una amiga cree que rompiste su cámara.
4. Rompes el tocadiscos de un amigo.
5. Invitas a una amiga al cine y no acepta.
6. Un amigo pierde tu raqueta de tenis.
7. Peleas con tu hermana y no quieres pedirle disculpas.

G   Alejandra had to take care of her brothers and sisters last Saturday. Read her description of how things went, then answer the questions that follow.

El sábado pasado, mamá y papá fueron a visitar a la tía Irene que está muy enferma. La mañana pasó rápidamente porque llevé a mi hermana Carmen y a mis hermanos Ricardo y Juanito al parque a jugar.

Luego comimos en una cafetería y entonces empezaron los problemas. A Juanito no le gustó la comida y peleó con Carmen porque ella lo llamó "tonto."

La tarde fue horrible. Ricardo jugó con un amigo y también pelearon. Por la noche cuando hice la cena, salió malísima. No comimos casi nada. Terminé enojadísima y con dolor de cabeza. ¡Nunca más quiero estar sola con los tres!

1.   ¿Por qué fueron los padres a ver a la tía?
2.   ¿Qué hicieron los chicos por la mañana?
3.   ¿Por qué pelearon Juanito y Carmen en la cafetería?
4.   ¿Con quién peleó Ricardo?
5.   ¿Por qué terminó con dolor de cabeza Alejandra?

H   Write a paragraph of at least ten sentences describing the Ochoa's family outing shown below. Include information such as where they went, what time they arrived, what the weather was like, what they did, and what time they returned home.

Vocabulario

SUSTANTIVOS

el abrigo   coat
el aeropuerto   airport
la alegría   happiness, pleasure
el alivio   relief
la emoción   emotion
la gente   people
el grado   degree (temperature)
el idiota, la idiota   idiot, fool
el interés   interest
la memoria   memory
la mentira   lie
la nieta   granddaughter, grandchild
el nieto   grandson, grandchild
la pelea   quarrel, fight
la raqueta (de tenis)   (tennis) racket
la reunión   social gathering; meeting
el silencio   silence
la vez   time

VERBOS

adaptarse   to adapt oneself
asegurar   to assure
asistir   to attend
besar   to kiss
cambiar   to change
contar (ue)   to tell
creer   to believe, think
explicar   to explain
jurar   to swear, promise (oath)
pasar   to pass, travel; to happen
pelear   to quarrel, fight
resolver (ue)   to resolve, solve
responder   to reply, answer
romper   to break
tratar (de)   to try (to)
valer   to be worth

OTRAS PALABRAS

agradable   pleasant, enjoyable
alguno, -a   some, any
aunque   although
bajo   below
como   like
de nuevo   again
enojado, -a   angry
equivocado, -a   mistaken
joven   young
lentamente   slowly
lento, -a   slow
nada   nothing
nadie   no one
ninguno, -a   no, not one
nunca   never
querido, -a   dear
rápidamente   quickly, rapidly
rápido, -a   fast, rapid
sin embargo   nevertheless
solo, -a   alone
terrible   terrible

EXPRESIONES

a todo volumen   at full volume
¡ay bendito!   my goodness! oh my!
¡basta ya!   that's enough now!
como de costumbre   as usual
echar de menos   to miss
están peleando   you/they are quarreling
hace [un año] que   it's been [one year] since
no tiene importancia   it's not important
pasarlo [bien]   to have [a good] time
pedir disculpas   to apologize
¡pronto!   quick!
se cayó   it fell
¡vamos!   come now!

Play Password to review vocabulary. See Teacher's Guide for instructions.

Murallas de la Catedral en el barrio gótico, Barcelona.

capítulo 14
En la ciudad

Barcelona, the capital of **Cataluña,** is a cosmopolitan port city on the Mediterranean and an important industrial and cultural center. The old sector of Barcelona, encompassing the port, **Las Ramblas,** and many of the city's theaters, museums, and monuments, forms the heart of activity in the city. Catalonians are proud of the **patria chica** (homeland), the **catalán** language, their customs, and the autonomy that has permitted them to direct many of their own affairs in recent years.

De compras

David, un estudiante norteamericano, va de compras por las tiendas de Barcelona. Lo acompañan sus amigos Pilar y Manolo. Entran en una tienda para mirar ropa y artículos de cuero.

DAVID	¡Cómo me gustan las chaquetas de cuero!
PILAR	Aquí hay unas estupendas.
MANOLO	¡Mira esta chaqueta, David! ¿Por qué no te la pruebas?
DAVID	¡Ay! ¡Me queda muy estrecha!
MANOLO	Tienes razón. Además, las mangas te quedan cortas. ¡Qué gracioso!
PILAR	Pruébate esta chaqueta marrón. ¿Te gusta el color?
DAVID	Sí. Es muy elegante. ¿Cuánto cuesta?
PILAR	12.000 pesetas. Está en rebaja.
MANOLO	Te queda muy bien, David.
PILAR	Estás guapísimo.
DAVID	Entonces, me la llevo.

comprensión

Complete the following statements, based on the dialogue.

Personalize: ¿Te gusta ir de compras? ¿Tienes una chaqueta de piel? ¿Te pruebas las cosas antes de comprarlas? ¿Compras tu ropa cuando está en rebaja?

1. David va de compras . . .
2. Los chicos entran en una tienda . . .
3. David se prueba . . .
4. La primera chaqueta . . .
5. La chaqueta que David compra . . .
6. Pilar y Manolo piensan . . .

extensión

A. You've just bought yourself a new sweater. Find out what a classmate thinks of it.

■‖‖ ¿Te gusta mi suéter° nuevo?

Sí. Estás guapísimo/a.
El color te queda [muy bien].
Sí. ¿Dónde lo compraste?
Te queda [grande], ¿no?

B. You're trying on a jacket in a clothing store, and the clerk asks you how you like it. How would you respond?

■⫶ ¿Le gusta, [señor/señorita]?   Sí, la llevo.
Sí, pero es muy cara.
Me queda un poco [ancha°].
No, no me gusta el color.

C. A friend compliments you on a jacket you've just bought. Respond appropriately.

■⫶ ¡Qué elegante es tu chaqueta!   ¡Eres muy amable°!
No, ¡qué va!°
Tu chaqueta es mucho más bonita.
Está a tus órdenes.°

Responding to compliments: In Spanish, *gracias* is usually accompanied by expressions such as *eres muy amable* or *está a tus órdenes. Gracias,* alone, may infer conceit.

Carta a una amiga

David escribe a una amiga de Madrid para contarle cómo le va en Barcelona.

Barcelona, 15 de abril

Querida Isabel:

Tienes razón. ¡Barcelona es fabulosa! Aunque todavía no conozco bien la ciudad, me divierto aquí mucho. Me encantan las Ramblas y el barrio gótico, y la gente me parece muy amable.

La familia con quien vivo aquí es muy buena y dos de los chicos asisten a mi escuela. Generalmente me levanto a las siete, igual que en casa y me desayuno con café y tostadas. Todavía no me acostumbro a comer a las dos, pues a esa hora ya me muero de hambre. Afortunadamente la comida catalana es riquísima, y la señora la prepara muy bien.

El único problema es el ruido de la calle que no me deja dormir. La otra noche me despertó un ruido horrible. Me levanté, pero no vi nada en la calle. Cuando busqué por la casa, sólo vi unos libros en el suelo. "Fue el gato" — pensé. ¡Qué susto me dio!

¿Cuándo vienes a Barcelona? El mes próximo hay dos días de fiesta y podemos organizar algo. Recuerdos a tu familia y escribe pronto.

Un abrazo,

David

David

Game: Play *College Bowl* to check comprehension of *carta.* Use *comprensión* questions and others. (See Teacher's Guide.)

1. ¿A quién escribe David?
2. ¿Cómo es Barcelona? ¿Qué le gusta a David de la ciudad?
3. ¿Qué hace David en Barcelona?
4. ¿Con quién vive David?
5. ¿Por qué no se acostumbra a las horas de comer?
6. ¿Por qué no duerme bien?
7. ¿Qué le despertó una noche?

extensión

A. Find out what a friend's day was like.

■ııı   ¿Cómo te fue hoy?   Bien. Nada especial°.
                                     ¡Excelente! Me divertí muchísimo.
                                     Así así.
                                     Mal. Me desperté [enfermo/a].

B. How are you likely to react if you're awakened in the middle of the night by a loud noise?

■ııı   ¡Cataplum!°   Grito° "¿Qué pasa?"
                                       Llamo a la policía.
                                     No hago nada. Me duermo° otra vez.
                                     Me escondo° debajo de la cama.

C. Evaluate your adaptability to new foods.

■ııı   ¿Te gusta probar nueva   Sí, me gusta probar de todo.
              comida?   Algunas veces.
                                     Si no es muy rara°.
                                     No, prefiero la comida que conozco.

Las Ramblas is an avenue that stretches between the harbor and the old city in downtown Barcelona, but it more closely resembles a park. The street is bordered by shops, cafés, hotels, theaters, and offices. Trees shade the broad central walk, alive with pedestrians and vendors selling birds, flowers, books, and magazines from kiosks. Residents of Barcelona as well as visitors to the city enjoy walking up and down **las Ramblas,** or sitting at outdoor cafés or on benches to watch the passersby.

Estudio de palabras

Una tienda de ropa

Introduce clothing with flashcards, magazine clippings, or actual items. See supplementary words in Appendix C.

1	el pantalón	5	el abrigo	9	el vestido	12	los blue jeans
2	la chaqueta	6	la camisa	10	el traje de baño	13	el cinturón
3	el traje	7	la blusa	11	la camiseta	14	los zapatos
4	el suéter	8	la falda				

A   Say what you generally wear to the following places.

■||| al cine   *Llevo [blusa y falda] al cine.*

Mention variants of clothing vocabulary, such as *pantalón vaquero* or *bluyines* for blue jeans.

1. a la playa
2. a la oficina
3. al partido de fútbol
4. al baile
5. al colegio
6. al teatro

B   Compliment a classmate on an item of clothing. He/she should respond appropriately.

Game: For practice of clothing vocabulary, play *Simón dice.* (See Teacher's Guide.)

■||| Me gusta tu pantalón.   *Eres muy amable.*

■||| ¡Qué abrigo más bonito!   *Está a tus órdenes.*

capítulo 14   **293**

Photo: Mexican students in uniform.

People in Spanish-speaking cities often dress quite formally. Men generally wear suits and ties, and women wear dresses or skirts as everyday attire for work as well as for casual wear. Young people frequently dress in jeans and blouses or shirts. Many schools require students to wear uniforms until they complete secondary school, and therefore, young people spend most of their clothing money on their out-of-school clothes.

Los colores

Use color flashcards or small national flags to introduce colors.

Optional: Mention color variants, such as *marrón, café, castaño, pardo*.

amarillo, -a	yellow	**negro, -a**	black
anaranjado, -a	orange	**gris**	gray
rojo, -a	red	**marrón**	brown
rosado, -a	pink	**azul**	blue
blanco, -a	white	**verde**	green

An adjective of color agrees in number and gender with the noun it modifies. When used as a noun, the name of a color is masculine in gender: **Me gusta el (color) rojo.**

A   Identify the color of different items of clothing you're wearing.

▪▥   ¿De qué color es tu camisa?   *Es amarilla.*

B   Take a poll in your class to determine what each person's favorite color is. Then determine which color is the class favorite.

▪▥   ¿Qué color te gusta más?   *El verde.*

Pronunciación y ortografía

diphthongs

The words in the exercises below show examples of strong + weak vowel combinations. Note that the semi-vowel **y** usually replaces **i** in strong + weak combinations when the sound of **i** comes last in a word: **hay.**

A   Listen and repeat the following words after your teacher. Pronounce the strong + weak vowel combinations as a single syllable.

ai, ay	au	ei, ey	oi, oy
baile	**au**to	s**ei**s	**oi**go
aire	c**au**sa	v**ei**nte	**hoy**
hay	rest**au**rante	r**ey**	**doy**

B   Read the following sentences aloud. Pay special attention to your pronunciation of the strong + weak vowel combinations.

1. Hay un restaurante en la calle 20.
2. Hoy voy a un baile.
3. Me gusta pintar paisajes al aire libre.

C   Many Spanish numbers contain diphthongs. Read aloud each of the following arithmetic problems and give the correct answer.

1. Seis y veinte son . . .
2. Siete menos cuatro son . . .
3. Diez y diez son . . .
4. Veintisiete menos nueve son . . .
5. Cincuenta menos cuarenta son . . .
6. Ciento y treinta son . . .

Los gatos quieren zapatos
y los ratones pantalones.

Proverb: Don't want what you can't have. (Lit: Cats want shoes, and mice want pants.)

Reflexive constructions

Luisa **la** lava.
Luisa washes *it.*

Luisa **se** lava.
Luisa washes *herself.*

El ruido **lo** despierta.
The noise wakes *him* up.

Ricardo **se** despierta.
Ricardo wakes up *(himself).*

A verb is reflexive in Spanish when the subject and pronoun object refer to the same person or thing. Reflexive verbs are more common in Spanish than in English and are often equivalent to non-reflexive verbs in English; for example, **despertarse** *(to wake up).* In vocabularies and dictionaries, the pronoun **se** is attached to the infinitive to indicate a reflexive verb.

	LAVARSE	DESPERTARSE
yo	**me** lavo	**me** despierto
tú	**te** lavas	**te** despiertas
él, ella, usted	**se** lava	**se** despierta
nosotros, nosotras	**nos** lavamos	**nos** despertamos
ellos, ellas, ustedes	**se** lavan	**se** despiertan

Reflexive verbs follow the same conjugation patterns as non-reflexive verbs. Reflexive pronouns agree with the subject of the verb. The reflexive pronouns **me, te, se,** and **nos,** like other object pronouns, precede a conjugated verb. They follow and are attached to commands, and they are often attached to infinitives. Note that the reflexive pronouns **me, te,** and **nos** are identical to direct-object and indirect-object pronouns.

The list below shows some verbs that are commonly used reflexively in Spanish.

Have students describe, in order, their morning routine: *Me levanto a las 6:30. Después me lavo, me visto, me peino*, etc.

acostarse (ue)	to go to bed
acostumbrarse	to accustom oneself
bañarse	to take a bath; to go swimming
desayunarse	to have breakfast
despedirse (i)	to say good-by
despertarse (ie)	to wake up
divertirse (ie)	to have a good time, enjoy oneself
dormirse (ue)	to fall asleep
lavarse	to wash oneself
levantarse	to get up
peinarse	to comb one's hair
ponerse (la ropa)	to put on (clothing)
probarse (ue)	to try on
quitarse (la ropa)	to take off (clothing)
sentarse (ie)	to sit down
vestirse (i)	to get dressed

A Complain to a friend that your younger brother Rafael imitates everything you do.

> ▣▥ me levanto *Cuando me levanto, Rafael también se levanta.*

1. me peino
2. me lavo
3. me quito los zapatos

4. me siento
5. me acuesto
6. me visto

B Say whether or not the following people are having a good time at a school party.

> ▣▥ Ramón *Ramón se divierte mucho.*
> *(Ramón no se divierte.)*

V: Have students describe situations in which they have a good time. *Me divierto cuando salgo con los amigos.* Or, ask: *¿Te diviertes en clase? ¿en las fiestas?*

1. tú
2. Manolo y Ana
3. nosotros

4. yo
5. ustedes
6. Clara

C You're studying in Barcelona for the summer. Explain to a Spanish friend what time you and your roommate generally do the following things.

> ▣▥ despertarse *Amigo/a: ¿A qué hora se despiertan Uds.?*
> *Tú: Generalmente nos despertamos a las siete.*

1. levantarse
2. sentarse a comer
3. desayunarse
4. lavarse

5. peinarse
6. acostarse
7. vestirse
8. bañarse

D Answer the questions below to confirm that various people do the things described.

■III   Daniel se levanta temprano. ¿Y tú?   *Yo también me levanto temprano.*

1. Mi hermana se duerme en clase. ¿Y Uds.?
2. Elena se viste de azul. ¿Y tú?
3. Nos acostamos tarde. ¿Y Marta?
4. Manuel se desayuna rápidamente. ¿Y David?
5. Todos se divierten en la playa. ¿Y Beatriz?
6. Uds. se preocupan cuando hay examen. ¿Y Carlos?

E Tell what time you and your friends did the following things yesterday.

For practice of colors, clothing and reflexives, ask questions such as: ¿Quién se vistió hoy con zapatos azules? ¿A qué hora te levantas todos los días? ¿Quién se sienta al lado de ti? ¿Quién se peinó muy bien hoy?

■III   Carmen / levantarse a las siete   *Carmen se levantó a las siete.*

1. yo / despertarse a las ocho
2. Elena / desayunarse a las nueve
3. nosotros / sentarse a leer a las tres
4. Alfonso / bañarse a las seis
5. yo / peinarse a las seis y cuarto
6. tú / lavarse a las diez
7. Uds. / acostarse a las diez y media

¡vamos a hablar!   Share information with a classmate about your daily routine. Use the reflexive verbs listed on page 297.

Generalmente me levanto a las seis y media. ¿Y tú?

Definite articles with clothing

Me quito **el** suéter.	I'm taking off *my* sweater.
Sara se pone **la** falda.	Sara is putting on *her* skirt.
Nos quitamos **el** abrigo.	We're taking off *our* coats.

In reflexive constructions, the definite article is generally used with articles of clothing. Note that when a plural subject is used, an article of clothing is in the singular if logically only one article belongs to each individual.

F Say that the following articles of clothing look well on their owner.

Personalize: Have students compliment each other on clothing and reply. S¹: *Te queda bien el suéter.* S²: *Eres muy amable.*

■III   a papá / traje   *A papá le queda bien el traje.*

1. a ti / zapatos
2. a mi hermana / vestido
3. a Julio / abrigo
4. a mamá / suéter
5. a mi tío / pantalón
6. a usted / chaqueta

Present tense of poner

	PONER
yo	**pongo**
tú	pones
él, ella, usted	pone
nosotros, nosotras	ponemos
ellos, ellas, ustedes	ponen

Poner *(to put, place)* is irregular in the **yo**-form in the present tense: **pongo.**

¿**Pones** la blusa nueva en la silla? — *Are you putting your new blouse on the chair?*

¿**Te pones** la blusa nueva? — *Are you putting on your new blouse?*

When **poner** is used in a reflexive construction with clothing, its meaning is equivalent to *to put on (oneself).*

G   Ask a classmate what he/she will wear for the occasions described below.

◼▥   para la fiesta   —*¿Qué te pones para la fiesta?*
                             — *Me pongo pantalón y suéter.*

1. para jugar al vólibol
2. para ir a clase
3. cuando vas a la piscina
4. cuando hace frío
5. para ir de compras
6. para estudiar

H   Describe the activities of the following people. Use a form of *poner* or *ponerse,* as appropriate.

◼▥   David / el abrigo nuevo   *David se pone el abrigo nuevo.*

◼▥   tú / los papeles en la mesa   *Tú pones los papeles en la mesa.*

1. Alberto / los libros en el estante
2. Marta / los zapatos
3. yo / el periódico en la silla
4. mamá / la comida en la mesa
5. papá y yo / el suéter
6. mis hermanos / el traje de baño
7. tú / el cinturón encima de la cama
8. nosotras / la lámpara en la mesita
9. Clara / la falda nueva

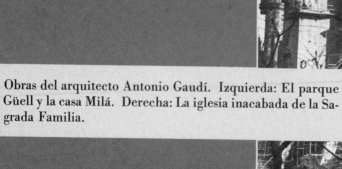

Obras del arquitecto Antonio Gaudí. Izquierda: El parque Güell y la casa Milá. Derecha: La iglesia inacabada de la Sagrada Familia.

Preterit of stem-changing -ir verbs

	DORMIR
yo	dormí
tú	dormiste
él, ella, usted	**durmió**
nosotros, nosotras	dormimos
ellos, ellas, ustedes	**durmieron**

Stem-changing **-ir** verbs that have a stem-vowel change **o > ue** in the present tense also have a stem change in the preterit tense. In the preterit, the stem vowel **o** changes to **u** in the **él/ella/usted-**form and in the **ellos/ellas/ustedes-**form.

I   Some of your classmates didn't sleep well last night and are sleepy today. Report who slept well and who didn't.

- ▪‖   Fernando tiene sueño.   *Sí, durmió mal anoche.*

- ▪‖   Tú no tienes sueño.   *No, dormí bien anoche.*

1. Pilar y yo no tenemos sueño.
2. Yo no tengo sueño.
3. Antonio tiene sueño.

4. Ana y Víctor no tienen sueño.
5. Dolores tiene sueño.
6. Tú tienes sueño.

	PEDIR
yo	pedí
tú	pediste
él, ella, usted	**pidió**
nosotros, nosotras	pedimos
ellos, ellas, ustedes	**pidieron**

Stem-changing **-ir** verbs that have a stem change **e > i** or **e > ie** in the present tense also have a stem change in the preterit tense. In the preterit, the stem vowel **e** changes to **i** in the **él/ella/usted-**form and the **ellos/ellas/ustedes-**form.

Stem-changing verbs like **pedir** are listed below:

despedir(se)	to say good-by
divertir(se)	to have a good time, enjoy oneself
preferir	to prefer
repetir	to repeat
servir	to serve
sugerir	to suggest
vestir(se)	to dress (oneself)

J   Fernando's class had a Spanish food festival last week. Take Fernando's role and tell what dish each person served.

Have second student give an appropriate re-action: ¡Qué [rico]! / No me gustó/gustaron.

■III   Susana / la sopa de ajo   *Susana sirvió la sopa de ajo.*

1. Elena y Víctor / los calamares
2. Javier / los refrescos
3. yo / la ensalada
4. los profesores / la paella
5. Ángela / el gazpacho
6. Teresa y yo / el queso
7. Manuel y Guillermo / el flan
8. Jaime / la tortilla

K   Raquel is leaving for a summer study program in Spain. Find out from a classmate whether or not the following friends said good-by to her.

■III   Ramón   *—¿ Se despidió Ramón de Raquel?*
— Sí, se despidió de ella.
(No, no se despidió de ella.)

1. tú   4. tú y Patricia
2. Diana   5. Ignacio
3. Salvador y Andrés   6. Mónica y Rosa

L   Enrique overslept yesterday and did the opposite of what he normally does every day. Report what he did.

■III   Se levanta temprano.   *Ayer se levantó tarde.*

■III   Se desayuna en casa.   *Ayer no se desayunó en casa.*

1. Se baña por la mañana.
2. Se peina con cuidado.
3. Se viste lentamente.
4. Se despide de su familia.
5. Se sienta para comer.
6. Se acuesta temprano.
7. Se duerme fácilmente.
8. Se lava antes de quitarse la ropa.

¡vamos a hablar!   Compare with a classmate some of the activities you did yesterday. Refer to the verbs listed on page 297.

Ayer me acosté tarde. ¿Y tú?   Yo también me acosté tarde.
Ayer me desayuné con la   Yo no me desayuné.
  familia. ¿Y tú?

La Tuna

After reading and discussion of *Lectura,* have class summarize with books closed.

La Tuna es un grupo de estudiantes universitarios que se dedica a cantar° · sing
las canciones° tradicionales y populares de España. Estas canciones se van · songs
transmitiendo de generación a generación de estudiantes y cada vez ad-
quieren° un nuevo sabor° de juventud y espíritu de alegría. · they acquire / flavor

5   Aunque el objeto principal de sus participantes es cantar y divertirse,
también es un medio° de ganar dinero para sus libros y otros gastos° uni- · means / expenses
versitarios.

  La Tuna sale por las calles de la ciudad con guitarras, laúdes°, pande- · lutes
retas°, bandurrias° y un acordeón. Sale a la hora en que la gente general- · tambourines / guitar-like instruments
10 mente va a pasear o a cenar en los restaurantes. Los jóvenes, con los
acordes° de sus instrumentos y sus alegres voces°, atraen la atención del · chords / voices
público de quien reciben contribuciones de dinero. La Tuna va también a
las casas de las amigas donde, desde la calle, les da una serenata. Tradi-
cionalmente, las amigas les regalan a los jóvenes las cintas° que llevan en sus · ribbons
15 capas.

  En la canción *La Aurora*°, la Tuna pide a una joven que tiene ese nombre · Dawn
que salga° a escuchar su canción. · that she come out

La Aurora

Use tape to present song, or record, if available.

Optional: Introduce other *Tuna* songs for class to listen to or sing. If students are musical, they might wish to organize a *Tuna* to perform at school functions.

Cuando la aurora tiende su manto°
Y el firmamento° viste de azul,
No hay un lucero que brille tanto°
Como esos ojos° que tienes tú.

robe
sky
lucero ... tanto: morning star that shines as bright
eyes

Bella Aurora, si es que duermes,
No evapores la ilusión.
Despierta, si estás dormida, morena sí,
Al eco de mi canción.

Bella niña, sal° al balcón
Que te estoy esperando° aquí,
Para darte la serenata
Sólo, sólo, para ti.

come out
I am waiting

actividad

Report in Spanish to the class on a band or singing group that you like. Give information such as what kind of music the group plays or sings, where it performs, and what instruments it uses.

En resumen

Reflexive constructions (A–E)

	LEVANTARSE Present tense	Preterit tense
yo	me levanto	me levanté
tú	te levantas	te levantaste
él, ella, usted	se levanta	se levantó
nosotros, nosotras	nos levantamos	nos levantamos
vosotros, vosotras	os levantáis	os levantasteis
ellos, ellas, ustedes	se levantan	se levantaron

1. A Spanish verb is reflexive when the subject and pronoun object refer to the same person or thing.
2. Reflexive verbs follow the same conjugation patterns as non-reflexive verbs.
3. The reflexive pronouns precede a conjugated verb. They follow and are attached to commands, and are often attached to infinitives: **Me levanto tarde los sábados; Levántate; Tengo que levantarme temprano.**

Definite articles with clothing (F)

Juan se pone **el** traje para la fiesta.
Cristina y Felipe se quitan **la** chaqueta.

The definite article is generally used with articles of clothing in reflexive constructions.

Present tense of **poner** (G, H)

	PONER
yo	**pongo**
tú	pones
él, ella, usted	pone
nosotros, nosotras	ponemos
vosotros, vosotras	ponéis
ellos, ellas, ustedes	ponen

When **poner** *(to put, place)* is used in a reflexive construction with clothing, its meaning is equivalent to *to put on (oneself):* **Me pongo la camisa.**

Preterit of stem-changing **-ir** verbs (I–L)

	DORMIR (o > u)	VESTIRSE (e > i)
yo	dormí	me vesti
tú	dormiste	te vestiste
él, ella, usted	**durmió**	**se vistió**
nosotros, nosotras	dormimos	nos vestimos
vosotros, vosotras	dormisteis	os vestisteis
ellos, ellas, ustedes	**durmieron**	**se vistieron**

1. The **-ir** verbs that have a stem change **o** > **ue** in the present tense have a change **o** > **u** in the **él/ella/usted-** and **ellos/ellas/ustedes-**forms in the preterit.
2. Stem-changing **-ir** verbs that have a stem change **e** > **i** or **e** > **ie** in the present tense have a stem change **e** > **i** in the **él/ella/usted-** and **ellos/ellas/ustedes-**forms in the preterit.

Repaso

A   Create six original sentences in which you describe the color of your clothing or different school supplies.

> ▰   *Llevo una camisa azul.*

> ▰   *Mi libro de español . . .*

B   Decide in which order Paloma is likely to do the following pairs of activities.

> ▰   dormirse / acostarse   *Primero Paloma se acuesta y después se duerme.*

1. bañarse / vestirse
2. peinarse / levantarse de la cama
3. quitarse la ropa / acostarse
4. sentarse a la mesa / desayunarse
5. ponerse el abrigo / ponerse el vestido
6. divertirse con los amigos / despedirse de la familia

C   Describe what the different members of the Torres family are wearing and what they are doing or about to do, based on the illustration below.

D   Interview a classmate and prepare a paragraph to report her/his activities.

1. ¿A qué hora te levantas generalmente?
2. ¿Cuándo te acuestas muy tarde, te levantas tarde también?
3. ¿Te desayunas antes o después de vestirte?
4. ¿Qué te pones para ir a la escuela?
5. ¿Cómo te despides de tu familia cuando sales?
6. ¿A qué hora te sientas a la mesa para cenar?
7. ¿A qué hora te acuestas?
8. ¿Te acuestas tarde o temprano los fines de semana?

◼ⁱⁱ   *Generalmente [Javier] se levanta . . .*

E   Julio and his friends went to the beach last Sunday. Complete his description with the appropriate preterit forms of the verbs given, and then answer the questions below.

Ayer yo *(levantarse)* temprano y *(desayunarse)* rápidamente con café y tostadas. *(Despedirse)* de la familia y después *(ir)* con los amigos a la playa. Allí nosotros *(divertirse)* mucho. *(Bañarse)* y *(comer)* en la playa y luego *(jugar)* al fútbol. Por la tarde *(pasear)* por el pueblo y *(tomar)* unos refrescos al aire libre. ¡Qué día más fabuloso y qué lástima tener que volver!

1. ¿Qué hizo Julio al levantarse?
2. ¿Adónde fue con los amigos?
3. ¿Qué hicieron ellos en la playa?
4. ¿Vieron el pueblo?
5. Según Julio, ¿cómo fue el día?

F   You and your friend Carmen go to a clothing store. Prepare a dialogue in Spanish to express the following.

1. Carmen asks what you're looking for.
2. Tell her that you need a new coat.
3. The clerk says that they have many coats. He/she shows you a blue coat and asks if you like it.
4. You say that it's very elegant and ask how much it costs.
5. The clerk answers, "Seventy-five dollars."
6. Say that you'll take it.

◼ⁱⁱ   Carmen: *¿Qué . . . ?*   Tú: *Necesito . . .*

G   Give a brief account of five or six things that happened or that you did during the past week.

◼ⁱⁱ   *Gané a mi padre al ajedrez.*

◼ⁱⁱ   *Fui a un baile y lo pasé muy bien.*

◼ⁱⁱ   *Mis padres me dijeron que van a comprar un coche nuevo.*

Vocabulario

SUSTANTIVOS

el abrazo   embrace, hug
la comida   food
el color   color
el cuero   leather
la fiesta   holiday
el gato   cat
la manga   sleeve
la ropa   clothing
el ruido   noise
el suelo   floor
el susto   scare, fright
la tienda   shop, store
la tostada   toast

LA ROPA

los blue jeans   blue jeans
la blusa   blouse
la camisa   shirt
la camiseta   T-shirt
el cinturón   belt
la chaqueta   jacket
la falda   skirt
el pantalón   pants, slacks
el suéter   sweater
el traje   suit
el traje de baño   bathing suit
el vestido   dress

LOS COLORES

amarillo, -a   yellow
anaranjado, -a   orange
azul   blue
gris   gray
marrón   brown
negro, -a   black
rojo, -a   red
rosado, -a   pink
verde   green

VERBOS

acostarse (ue)   to go to bed
acostumbrarse   to get used to
bañarse   to take a bath; to go swimming
dejar   to let, leave
desayunarse   to have breakfast
despedirse (i-i)   to say good-by
despertar (ie)   to wake
despertarse (ie)   to wake up
divertirse (ie-i)   to have a good time
dormir (ue-u)   to sleep
dormirse (ue-u)   to fall asleep
esconderse   to hide (oneself)
gritar   to shout
lavar   to wash
lavarse   to wash oneself
levantarse   to get up, stand up
llevar   to wear
peinarse   to comb one's hair
poner   to put, place
ponerse (la ropa)   to put on (clothing)
probar (ue)   to try, test
probarse (ue)   to try on
quitarse (la ropa)   to take off (clothing)
sentarse (ie)   to sit down
vestirse (i-i)   to get dressed

OTRAS PALABRAS

afortunadamente   fortunately
amable   kind
ancho, -a   wide
corto, -a   short
elegante   elegant
especial   special
estrecho, -a   narrow; tight
estupendo, -a   stupendous, wonderful
fabuloso, -a   fabulous
generalmente   generally
gracioso, -a   funny, amusing
guapo, -a   good-looking, handsome, beautiful
igual   similar, same
norteamericano, -a   North American
próximo, -a   next
raro, -a   strange, odd
único, -a   only

EXPRESIONES

¡cataplum!   bang!
está a tus órdenes   you're welcome to it
[me] queda/quedan   it fits [me], it is/they fit me, they are
¡qué va!   go on! nonsense!
recuerdos a [David]   regards to [David]

Ciclismo, deporte de gran popularidad en Colombia.

capítulo 15
Tráfico y ciclismo

Medellín, Colombia's second largest city, is one of the country's principal industrial centers. Its cotton, silk, and woolen textiles are shipped all over the world. Located in the mountains northwest of Bogotá, with a climate of eternal spring, Medellín has grown in population and rapidly expanded into a busy, modern city.

Locate *Colombia,*
Bogotá, and *Medellín*
on map of South
America.

Al final de la Vuelta

Desde Bogotá hoy nos transmiten la llegada a la meta de los participantes en la Vuelta
ciclística a Colombia, el acontecimiento deportivo más importante del año. Habla desde
Radio Medellín: Beto Sánchez.

LOCUTOR 1   Muy buenas tardes, señoras y señores. Les habla desde la meta en el
autódromo de Bogotá Beto Sánchez. Estoy transmitiéndoles la llegada de
los primeros corredores de la Vuelta a Colombia. Nuestros compañeros
de televisión están filmando los últimos kilómetros de la carrera. La
expectativa es enorme. Los aficionados siguen llegando a la meta para
darle la bienvenida al ganador.

LOCUTOR 2   Atención, Beto Sánchez, siento interrumpirte, pero ya se acerca el primer
grupo a la meta.

LOCUTOR 1   Señoras y señores, en la curva final está apareciendo el posible ganador. Su
cara muestra agotamiento . . . sus piernas trabajan como una máquina . . .
Ya llega a la meta, levanta las manos en señal de victoria y . . . ¡Señoras y
señores! Algo increíble ha ocurrido . . . nuestro ganador, Martín Baha-
montes, ha atropellado a la joven que le esperaba con un ramo de flores en
la línea de llegada.

comprensión

1. ¿Cuál es el acontecimiento deportivo más importante del año en Colombia?
2. ¿Desde dónde está hablando el locutor de radio?
3. ¿Qué pasa en el autódromo?
4. ¿Quién está apareciendo en la vuelta final?
5. ¿Cómo está el ganador al llegar a la curva final?
6. ¿Qué ocurre en la meta?

Assignment: Have stu-
dents write five true-
false statements as
comprehension check.

extensión

A. Imagine that you're at the finish line of a bicycle race and hear that the
winner has run over a young bystander. How do you react?

   ■ıı   ¡El ganador atropelló a un/a joven!   ¡No me digas!
    ¿Cómo ocurrió?
    ¡Ay, no quiero mirar!
    ¡Es increíble!

B. Your baseball team plays a good game against another school, but
loses. Do you accept the loss graciously or not?

   ■ıı   ¡Perdimos 6 a 7!   ¡Qué lástima!
    ¡Hicieron trampa!
    ¡Caramba! ¿Qué vamos a hacer?
    Tenemos que felicitarlos/las°.

The **Vuelta a Colombia** is an international bicycle race held annually in April or May. The grueling route, of over 1500 kilometers, changes each year. It usually begins on the northern coast and runs over mountainous terrain and through major cities where roads are completely blocked to traffic to accommodate the cyclists and spectators. The race lasts for fifteen days, with one day of rest, and generally ends in Bogotá with a final lap around the city's car racing track. The winner usually receives a trophy, car, house, and money, and also gains considerable prestige in the world of sports.

Cochise Rodríguez, a folk hero of the 60's and 70's, was a five-time winner of the Vuelta and twice world champion. Rafael Niño was a six-time winner in the 70's and world champion in 1980.

Un accidente

Accident insurance is not obligatory in Colombia, and many drivers have none; hence importance of establishing blame in accidents.

Son las seis de la tarde en Medellín y parece que toda la ciudad trata de volver a casa al salir del trabajo. En una calle central hubo un accidente que está causando enormes dificultades en la circulación.

PEATÓN	¡Señor agente! Hubo un accidente. Chocaron un camión y un carro.
POLICÍA	¿Hay heridos?
PEATÓN	Sí, pero nada grave. Parece que uno de los choferes se rompió el brazo.
POLICÍA	¡A ver, señores! ¿Qué pasó aquí?
CHOFER 1°	¡Este hombre pasó el semáforo en rojo!
CHOFER 2°	¡Usted se equivoca! Yo crucé la calle antes de cambiar la luz.
CHOFER 1°	¡Falso! Yo se lo explico, señor agente.
CHOFER 2°	¡Usted tuvo la culpa, pues no paró con la luz amarilla!
CHOFER 1°	¿No ve que me golpeó la parte de atrás del camión?
POLICÍA	Un momento, señores. ¡Basta ya! Voy a tomar todas las medidas necesarias, pues este asunto sólo lo resuelve un juez.

comprensión

Retell the accident from the point of view of a pedestrian at the scene. Give as many details as you can recall from the dialogue.

In many Spanish-speaking countries *chófer* has a written accent mark. In Colombia it does not.

Hubo un . . .
No fue . . .
Un policía . . .
El primer chofer . . .
El segundo chofer . . .

A. What are you likely to do if you witness an accident?

■▥ ¿Qué haces si ves un accidente?　Llamo [una ambulancia°].
　　　　　　　　　　　　　　　　　Ayudo a los heridos.
　　　　　　　　　　　　　　　　　Sirvo de testigo°.
　　　　　　　　　　　　　　　　　Nada.

B. You're visiting a friend in the hospital. Find out how he/she is getting along.

■▥ Dime, ¿cómo te sientes°?　¡Horrible! Me duele° todo el
　　　　　　　　　　　　　　　　cuerpo°.
　　　　　　　　　　　　　　　Me siento mejor.
　　　　　　　　　　　　　　　Bien, pero la comida del hospital°
　　　　　　　　　　　　　　　　es malísima.
　　　　　　　　　　　　　　　Aburrido/a.

C. A police officer stops you for speeding. What are you most likely to say?

■▥ ¿Por qué va tan rápido?　Por favor, tengo mucha prisa.
　　　　　　　　　　　　　　　¿Cuál es la velocidad máxima°?
　　　　　　　　　　　　　　　Sólo voy a 20 kilómetros por
　　　　　　　　　　　　　　　　hora.
　　　　　　　　　　　　　　　Lo siento, no me di cuenta°.

In most Spanish-speaking countries, the cost of buying and operating a car is much higher than in the United States. Compact cars are most common, not only because of the high price of gasoline in many countries, but also because they are easier to maneuver and park in cities with crowded, narrow streets. As more and more people have been able to purchase a car, cities have become plagued with traffic jams, despite the availability of numerous forms of public transportation. Since most families who own a car can afford only one, teenagers must depend on sharing the family car.

Photo: Caracas, Venezuela.

Estudio de palabras

Medios de transporte

Introduce, using flashcards or photos.

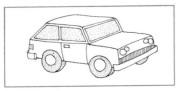

el carro, el coche

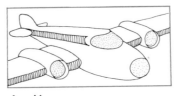

el avión

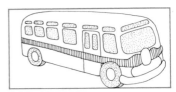

el autobús

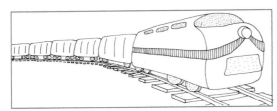

el tren

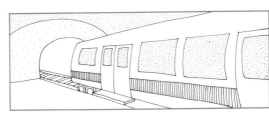

el metro

el barco

la bicicleta

la moto(cicleta)

A Imagine that you're going to make the trips described below. Say what form of transportation you will use to reach your destination.

■ɪɪ Vas de Bogotá a San Francisco. *Voy en avión.*

1. Tienes que ir a la biblioteca que está a doce cuadras.
2. Quieres viajar de Chicago a Los Ángeles.
3. Estás en el parque Chapultepec y quieres ir al Zócalo.
4. Tienes tres meses para ir de Barcelona a Buenos Aires.
5. Estás en Miami y tienes que estar en Nueva York en tres horas.
6. Quieres visitar parques nacionales en California, Utah y Arizona.

Point out regional vo-
cabulary differences for
bus: In Mexico, *el
camión;* in Puerto Rico
and Cuba, *la guagua.*

B State why you like or dislike each form of transportation shown above. Use some of the following words or phrases.

Game: Acrostic, using
transporte as key word.
Students supply *medios
de transporte.*

caro	**rápido**	**peligroso**	**un buen ejercicio**
barato	**lento**	**tener miedo**	**(no) poder mirar el paisaje**

■ɪɪ *No me gusta viajar en avión porque es muy caro.*

El cuerpo humano

Introduce, using student as model, biology department skeleton, or Halloween prop.

See Supplementary word sets for additional parts of the body.

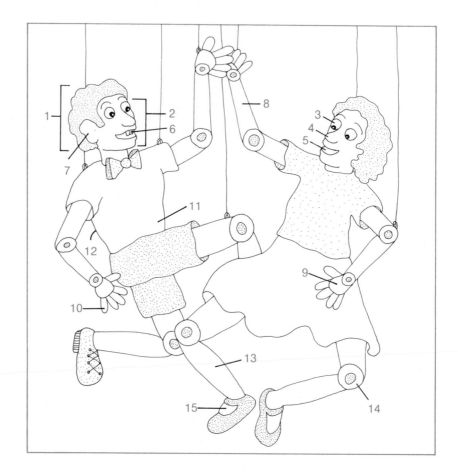

1   la cabeza
2   la cara
3   el ojo
4   la nariz
5   la boca
6   el diente
7   el oído, la oreja
8   el brazo
9   la mano
10   el dedo
11   el estómago
12   la espalda
13   la pierna
14   la rodilla
15   el pie

C   Name the part or parts of the body suggested by each of the following sentences.

   ■⫶   Corrí 5 kilómetros alrededor del lago.   *las piernas*

1. No puedo ver sin mis lentes.
2. ¿Quieres comer algo?
3. ¡Qué pequeños me quedan estos zapatos!
4. Las mangas de esta camisa me quedan cortas.
5. ¡Baja el volumen de ese radio!
6. No puedo escribir más.
7. ¡A . . . chú! Estoy muy resfriado.
8. Subí una montaña a pie.
9. Llevé diez paquetes grandes al correo.

Game: Play *Simón dice* for vocabulary practice.

Have students react: S¹: *las piernas.* S²: *Pobre-cito/a! / ¡Qué lástima! / ¿Te duelen mucho?*

D   Your class went on a 6-kilometer hike over rough terrain yesterday. Complain about your aches to a friend.

> ▪▥▯   Me duelen los pies. Y tú,   *Me duele mucho la espalda.*
> ¿qué tal?

Pronunciación y ortografía

diphthongs

When the two weak vowels **i** and **u** are combined in a diphthong, they are pronounced as a single syllable.

A   Repeat the following words after your teacher. Pay special attention to your pronunciation of the weak + weak vowel combinations.

Remind students that y usually replaces i in strong + weak vowel combinations when [i] is last in word: hay, muy, rey, hoy.

iu	ui, uy	
ciudad	ruido	fui
viuda	cuidado	muy

B   Read the following sentences aloud to practice various vowel combinations.

Optional: Review simple vowel sounds and diphthongs.

1. Sólo lo resuelve un juez.
2. Diana y yo fuimos en autobús.
3. Me duele todo el cuerpo.
4. El viaje de Buenos Aires a Miami es de dieciséis horas.
5. Quiero ir de San Diego a Nueva York.
6. La ciudad de San Juan está en Puerto Rico.

Un hombre de bien vale por cien.

Proverb: One man is worth a hundred and a hundred is not worth one. (Lit: A good man is worth a hundred others.)

vowel combinations with accent marks

A written accent on the strong vowel of a diphthong indicates a stressed syllable, as in **dieciséis** or **miércoles.** In vowel combinations that have a written accent on the weak vowel, the two vowels are pronounced as separate syllables, as in **día** or **policía.**

C Pronounce the following words aloud. Be sure to pronounce the diphthongs as a single syllable.

One-syllable diphthongs		Two syllables	
miércoles	televisión	día	gustaría
dieciséis	béisbol	oído	país
camión	¿cuándo?	policía	Raúl

D Read the following sentences aloud. Be careful to pronounce vowel combinations containing an accented weak vowel as two syllables.

1. Prefiero ir en avión.
2. ¿Con quién habla el policía?
3. Me gustaría visitar muchos países.
4. Raúl juega al béisbol los miércoles.

Gramática

Present progressive tense

Marta **está hablando** con Anita.
Estoy comiendo un sandwich.
¿Estás escribiendo una carta?

Marta *is talking* with Anita.
I'm eating a sandwich.
Are you writing a letter?

The present progressive tense is used to emphasize that an action is *in progress* at the moment of speaking.

INFINITIVE	STEM	PRESENT PARTICIPLE
hablar	habl-	hablando
beber	beb-	bebiendo
vivir	viv-	viviendo

The present progressive tense consists of a present-tense form of **estar** + present participle. The present participle of most verbs is formed by adding **-ando** to the infinitive stem of **-ar** verbs and **-iendo** to the infinitive stem of **-er** and **-ir** verbs.

Review *estar*, and practice various persons with participles given.

Have students mime an action for others to describe: *José está leyendo.*

Papá **está leyendo** el periódico.
Estoy vistiendo a mi hermanito.
Elena **está durmiendo.**

Dad *is reading* the newspaper.
I am dressing my little brother.
Elena *is sleeping.*

The present participle of **-er** and **-ir** verbs whose stem ends in a vowel is formed with **-yendo: leyendo.**

Stem-changing **-ir** verbs that have a vowel change **e > i** or **o > u** in the preterit show the same change in the present participle: **vistiendo, durmiendo.**

A Say what various people at the scene of an accident are in the process of doing.

▪▥ Un policía habla con los choferes.

Un policía está hablando con los choferes.

1. Los choferes discuten.
2. Un chofer dice que no tiene la culpa.
3. Un enfermero sale de la ambulancia.
4. Algunos peatones miran.
5. Un testigo explica lo que vio.
6. Una señora corre hacia el policía.
7. Un policía escribe en un cuaderno.
8. Un chofer pide disculpas al otro.

Medellín, contraste de lo antiguo y lo moderno.

B   Your sister Alicia wants you to take her to buy tickets for a concert, but she asks you at the wrong moment. Answer her impatiently, explaining what you're in the middle of doing.

> ▪▥   lavar el carro   Alicia: *¿Me llevas ahora?*
> Tú: *¿No ves que estoy lavando el carro?*

1. estudiar
2. comer
3. reparar la bicicleta

4. escribir una carta
5. leer el periódico
6. escuchar las noticias

C   Ramón is complaining because everyone is too busy for a soccer game. Take his role and report what his friends are in the process of doing.

> ▪▥   Carmen toca el clarinete.   *Carmen está tocando el clarinete.*

1. Tomás come en la cafetería.
2. Irene y Luis discuten qué hacer.
3. Tú haces los ejercicios de álgebra.
4. Pedro busca a su primo.
5. Miguel oye un concierto.
6. Manuel y Clara juegan al ajedrez.
7. Dolores espera a un amigo.
8. Ustedes celebran la victoria de Ramón.

Bring in pictures of people participating in activities suggested by the verbs below and ask your classmates to describe what is happening.

correr	leer	jugar [al béisbol]
bailar	comer	tocar [el piano]

¿Qué está haciendo este chico?   Está . . .

Definite article with parts of the body

¿Te duele **la cabeza?**   Does *your head* ache?
Víctor se rompió **el pie.**   Víctor broke *his foot.*
Nos lavamos **la cara.**   We're washing *our faces.*

A definite article is generally used with parts of the body in Spanish. Note that when a plural subject is used, a part of the body is in the singular if logically the sentence refers to one part per person.

D   Explain to your drama teacher various classmates' excuses for not attending rehearsal after school today.

    ■ⅲ   a Raúl / estómago   *A Raúl le duele el estómago.*

1. a Julio / pierna
2. a Diana y a Rosa / espalda
3. a mí / ojos
4. a Susana / brazo

5. a Isabel / rodilla
6. a nosotros / cabeza
7. a Diego y a Javier / pies
8. a Miguel / oídos

Object pronouns with present participles

Me la estoy lavando.   Estoy lavándo**mela.**
¿**Lo** estás leyendo?   ¿Estás leyéndo**lo?**
Se lo está escribiendo Ana.   Está escribiéndo**selo** Ana.

Object pronouns either precede the conjugated verb or follow and are attached to the present participle. Note that when one or two pronouns are attached to a present participle, a written accent is needed to maintain the original stress of the participle.

E   You and your sister are late for school. Your mother tries to hurry you. Tell her that you're in the process of doing the things she asks about.

    ■ⅲ   ¿Se levantaron ya?   *Estamos levantándonos ahora.*
                                   (Nos estamos levantando ahora.)

1. ¿Se bañaron ya?
2. ¿Se vistieron ya?
3. ¿Se peinaron ya?

4. ¿Se desayunaron ya?
5. ¿Se despidieron de papá ya?
6. ¿Se lavaron las manos ya?

F A number of your friends are impatiently asking for the belongings they left with you and Jorge. Assure each one that Jorge is looking for the items.

◼||| ¿Dónde está mi reloj? *Te lo está buscando Jorge.*
(Está buscándotelo Jorge.)

1. ¡Necesito mi radio!
2. ¡No encuentro mis libros!
3. ¿Dónde están mis zapatos?
4. ¿Tienes mi raqueta?
5. ¡Necesito mis lentes!
6. ¿Dónde está mi trompeta?
7. ¡Quiero mis discos!
8. ¡Quiero mi cuaderno!
9. ¿Tienes mis fotos?

Los pasajeros esperan la salida en un pueblo de Colombia.

Preterit tense of **tener, poder, poner**

	TENER	PODER	PONER
yo	tuve	pude	puse
tú	tuviste	pudiste	pusiste
él, ella, usted	tuvo	pudo	puso
nosotros, nosotras	tuvimos	pudimos	pusimos
ellos, ellas, ustedes	tuvieron	pudieron	pusieron

The verbs **tener** *(to have)*, **poder** *(to be able)*, and **poner(se)** *(to put; to put on)* are irregular in the preterit tense. Note that each verb has the same irregular endings.

G   Inform a friend that none of the following persons was to blame for breaking her/his record player.

◼‖‖   Ángela   *Ángela no tuvo la culpa.*

1. Miguel Ángel
2. Vicente y tú
3. Cristina y yo
4. Beatriz y Pedro
5. yo
6. María
7. Santiago y Felipe
8. Isabel y Roberto

H   Find out from a classmate whether or not various friends and family members were able to do the following things.

◼‖‖   Juan / ir a la carrera   Tú: *¿Pudo Juan ir a la carrera?*
                               Amigo/a: *Sí, pudo ir a la carrera.*
                               (No, no pudo ir a la carrera.)

1. Pilar / comprar los boletos
2. tú / encontrar el suéter
3. Silvia / vender su bicicleta
4. tus padres / oír el concierto
5. ustedes / resolver la pelea
6. tus hermanos / ver al ganador en la meta
7. Jaime / reparar su grabadora
8. tú / aprender a jugar al ajedrez

¡vamos a hablar!   Respond appropriately to the unfortunate news a friend tells you.

¡Estoy enojadísima! No pude ver la carrera.

¡Qué lástima! Fue una carrera magnífica.

¿Sabes que Ana se rompió un brazo?

No me digas. ¿Cómo ocurrió?

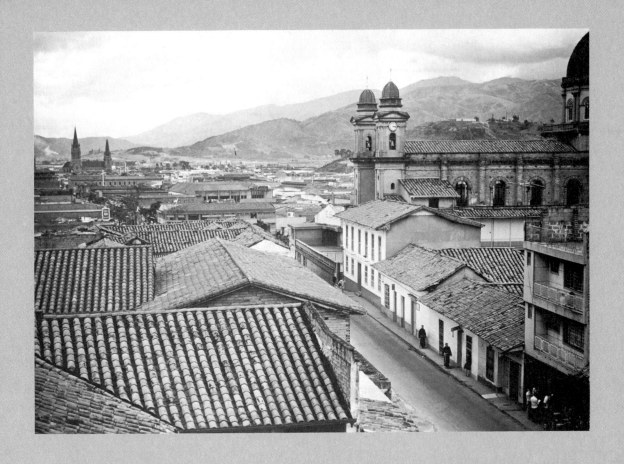

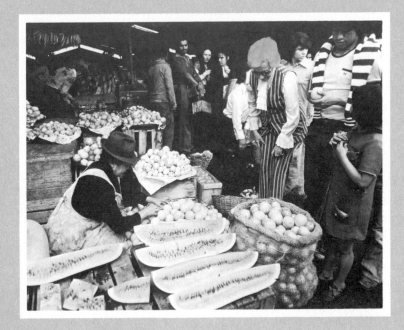

En los pueblos y ciudades de Colombia: Señora con frutas tropicales en Cartagena, a caballo en los llanos, Medellín y de compras en un mercado.

Lectura

Simón Bolívar, el Libertador

Simón José Antonio de la Trinidad Bolívar y Palacios es uno de los héroes más importantes de Suramérica por ser el Libertador de cinco naciones del continente. Nació° en Caracas, Venezuela, en 1783. Sus padres murieron cuando era° niño y se educó° con sus tíos. Su tutor, Simón Rodríguez, le
5 infundió° el ideal de la libertad. Al llegar a hombre, el sueño° de Bolívar fue expulsar a España del continente suramericano. Luchó en sangrientas batallas° por la independencia de Venezuela, Colombia, Perú, Ecuador y Bolivia con el anhelo° de formar la Gran Colombia.

Hubo varios atentados° contra la vida de Bolívar, a consecuencia de
10 rivalidades políticas. A continuación se cuenta uno de los atentados que se hizo contra el Libertador durante su presidencia en la Gran Colombia.

La conspiración del 25 de septiembre de 1828

Los enemigos° de Bolívar, con el consejo° y auxilio° del General Francisco de Paula Santander, vicepresidente de la nación, concibieron° el horrible
15 proyecto de asesinar° al Libertador. Después de dos atentados que fallaron°, los conspiradores se reunieron° en la noche del 25 de septiembre y resolvieron dar el golpe° esa misma noche. El Comandante Pedro Carujo, al frente de veinticinco soldados, se dirigió° al palacio presidencial donde dormía° Bolívar.

he was born

he was / he was educated

instilled / dream

luchó . . . batallas he fought in bloody battles
longing
attempts

enemies / advice / aid

conceived

assassinate

failed / met

dar . . . golpe to strike

went

was sleeping

20　El Libertador había pasado° el día enfermo de uno de muchos resfriados que padecía°, síntoma de la tuberculosis que lo tenía minado°, y por esa razón se retiró temprano. Doña Manuela Sáenz se presentó en la habitación para atender a Bolívar en su indisposición. Bolívar le habló de planes para una nueva revolución y luego, como de costumbre, puso su espada° y pis-
25　tolas a la cabecera°, se acostó y se durmió profundamente.

　　Bolívar dormía al cuidado de doña Manuela cuando ésta sintió° un tropel° de hombres que caminaba en el interior del palacio. Oyó además un ruido extraño° como el chocar de armas. Despertó al Libertador quien inmediatamente tomó su espada y una pistola y trató de abrir la puerta.
30　Doña Manuela lo contuvo° y con dificultad lo convenció de que escapara° por la ventana. Ella, mientras tanto, fue a enfrentarse con° los conspiradores que ya descerrajaban° la puerta. Cuando doña Manuela se les presentó, los desconocidos° le preguntaron con imperio°:

　　— ¿Dónde está Bolívar?
35　— En la sala de Consejo°, — les contestó doña Manuela con disimulo° y con la tranquilidad de las mujeres de valor.

　　Gritando "¡Muera el tirano!"°, los conspiradores se dispersaron por las salas de palacio con la esperanza° de encontrar al Libertador, hasta que vieron abierto el balcón por donde huyó° Bolívar.

	had spent
	he suffered from/sapped (of strength)
	sword
	head (of bed)
	heard
	mob
	strange
	restrained/lo . . . escapara convinced him to escape
	to face
	were forcing open
	strangers/command
	council/feigning ignorance
	¡muera . . . tirano! death to the tyrant!
	hope
	escaped

actividades

The Wars of Independence took place 1810–1822. Following the Sept. 25 attempt on Bolívar's life, he was acclaimed by the people, the cavalry was called in to restore order, and death sentences for Carujo and Santander were commuted to exile.

Game as comprehension check on *lectura:* Place in three envelopes questions of varying degrees of difficulty, assigning points to each. Student chooses category of question; if response is correct, team receives points.

A. With several classmates, create a brief dialogue and act out one of the following scenes of the attempt on Bolívar's life.

1. Bolívar and doña Manuela talk about Bolívar's health before he goes to sleep.
2. Doña Manuela hears strange noises in the palace and wakes Bolívar up.
3. Bolívar is ready to face the conspirators, but doña Manuela convinces him to escape.
4. The conspirators ask for Bolívar, and doña Manuela sends them on a search through the palace.

B. Research and prepare a brief description of a famous Hispanic leader, writer, sports figure, or artist.

Present progressive tense (A–C, E, F)

-ar		jugando	Estoy jugando al fútbol.
-er	estar +	comiendo	Está comiendo sandwiches.
-ir		saliendo	Estamos saliendo de la clase.

1. The present progressive tense describes an action *in progress*. It consists of a present-tense form of **estar** + present participle.
2. The present participle of most verbs is formed by adding **-ando** to the infinitive stem of **-ar** verbs and **-iendo** to the infinitive stem of **-er** and **-ir** verbs.
3. The present participle of **-er** and **-ir** verbs whose stem ends in a vowel is formed with **-yendo: ¿Estás leyendo el periódico?**
4. Stem-changing **-ir** verbs that have a change **e > i** or **o > u** in the preterit show the same change in the present participle: **pidiendo, durmiendo.**
5. With the present progressive, object pronouns precede the conjugated verb or follow and are attached to the present participle: **Te lo estoy explicando; Estoy explicándotelo.**

Definite article with parts of the body (D)

A definite article is generally used with parts of the body: **Me duele el oído; Se lava las manos.**

Preterit of **tener, poder, poner** (G, H)

	TENER	PODER	PONER
yo	tuve	pude	puse
tú	tuviste	pudiste	pusiste
él, ella, usted	tuvo	pudo	puso
nosotros, nosotras	tuvimos	pudimos	pusimos
vosotros, vosotras	tuvisteis	pudisteis	pusisteis
ellos, ellas, ustedes	tuvieron	pudieron	pusieron

Repaso

A

Pick out three words that best fit into one category from each set of words below.

1. accidente, cena, herido, ambulancia
2. semáforo, calle, camión, camisa
3. camión, testigo, juez, culpa
4. meta, ganador, pierna, trofeo
5. rodilla, fiebre, mano, nariz
6. avión, moto, barco, reloj
7. traje, cuerpo, falda, camisa

Assignment: Have students prepare five original lists for practice with partner.

B

You're having a cookout. Describe what various guests are in the process of doing, using the present progressive tense.

■▥ Carlos lleva unos refrescos al jardín.　*Carlos está llevando unos refrescos al jardín.*

Game for practice of present progressive: Place in hat slips of paper containing infinitives. Student chooses slip and pantomimes action. Others guess: *está esquiando, está tocando el piano, está bailando.*

1. Martín pide más hamburguesas.
2. Alicia toca la guitarra.
3. Antonio y Sara bailan.
4. Mónica come todo el postre.
5. Daniel, Vicente y Susana nadan en la piscina.
6. Tomás pone la comida en la mesa.
7. Claudia saca fotos.
8. Los otros juegan al vólibol.
9. Yo hago unas hamburguesas.

C

Your father went on a trip and calls to find out what everyone is doing. Answer his questions, using two object pronouns in your responses.

■▥ ¿Estás escribiendo una carta a tu amiga?　*Sí, se la estoy escribiendo.*

■▥ ¿Compró Juan los boletos para ustedes?　*Sí, nos los compró.*

1. ¿Les está haciendo mamá la cena?
2. ¿Te pusiste el traje de baño nuevo?
3. ¿Le dio Clara el tocadiscos a Pilar?
4. ¿Le vendió Juan su calculadora a Javier?
5. ¿Les prestaron los Jiménez una guitarra a ustedes?
6. ¿Se están probando los chicos los blue jeans nuevos?
7. ¿Se está lavando las manos Bernardo?
8. ¿Le pidió Clara disculpas a Vicente?
9. ¿Les dio mamá dinero para el cine?

D Cristina González is covering a street festival for a local newspaper. Take her role and describe what is happening, based on the illustration below. Include a statement describing what the people are celebrating.

E Give at least two logical forms of transportation that you can use between the places listed below.

▰▥ de tu casa a la casa de una amiga   *Puedo ir en bicicleta o en autobús.*

1. de San Francisco a Hawaii
2. del colegio al hospital
3. de Miami a Puerto Rico
4. de Nueva York a España
5. de tu ciudad a la playa
6. de tu casa al dentista

F   Tell who hurts where, after an especially strenuous gym class.

■III   Alicia / cabeza   *A Alicia le duele la cabeza.*

1. José / piernas
2. Marta / brazo
3. David y Ramón / rodilla
4. Elena / espalda
5. Teresa y Sara / pies
6. Miguel / dedos

G   Form eight complete sentences by combining logical elements from each column. Use the preterit tense of the verbs given.

1	2	3
1. Elena	tener	el suéter
2. mis primos	poder	la lámpara en la mesa
3. nosotros	poner	ver la carrera ciclística
4. Alfredo	ponerse	la culpa
5. tú		un anuncio en el periódico
6. los García		ver esa película ayer
7. Luisa		un accidente ayer
8. yo		un vestido nuevo para la fiesta
		un día maravilloso

■III   *Elena puso la lámpara en la mesa.*

H   Supply a logical reaction to each of the sentences below. Choose from the responses listed on the right.

1. ¡Usted tuvo la culpa!
2. ¡Me duele el brazo!
3. ¡Hubo un accidente!
4. No me queda bien la chaqueta.
5. El corredor atropelló al locutor de radio.
6. ¡Me rompiste la grabadora!
7. ¿Por qué pasó usted el semáforo en rojo?

Pruébate otra.
¿Fue grave?
¡Yo no fui!
¡Qué horror!
¡Cómo lo siento!
No me di cuenta.
Lo/a felicito.
¡Te equivocas!

I   You're looking out your window and see a man hit a car as he tries to park. Imagine the scene and describe it briefly to a family member. Include dialogue in your description if you wish.

golpear el carro   **servir de testigo**
llamar a un policía   **los choferes discuten**
tener la culpa   **hubo un accidente**

■III   *¡Diego! Hubo un accidente en la calle. Un señor . . .*

Vocabulario

SUSTANTIVOS

el accidente   accident
el aficionado   fan
el agente, la agente   police officer
el agotamiento   exhaustion
la ambulancia   ambulance
el asunto   matter
el avión   airplane
el barco   ship
la bienvenida   welcome
el camión   truck
el corredor   racer
el cuerpo   body
el chofer   driver
la expectativa   expectation
la flor   flower
el herido, la herida   injured person
el hombre   man
el hospital   hospital
el juez   judge
el kilómetro   kilometer
el locutor   radio announcer
la luz   light
la llegada   arrival; **la línea de llegada**   finish line
la máquina   machine
la medida   step, measure
la meta   finish line
la motocicleta (moto)   motorcycle
el peatón   pedestrian
el ramo   bouquet
el semáforo   traffic light
la señal   sign
el testigo   witness
el tren   train
la velocidad máxima   speed limit
la victoria   victory
la vuelta   turn; circuit

VERBOS

acercarse   to approach, draw near
aparecer   to appear
atropellar   to run over, trample; **ha atropellado**   he/she has run over
cruzar   to cross
chocar   to crash, collide
doler (ue)   to hurt, ache
equivocarse   to be mistaken
esperar   to wait (for); **esperaba**   he/she was waiting
felicitar   to congratulate
filmar   to film
golpear   to hit, strike
interrumpir   to interrupt
levantar   to raise
mostrar (ue)   to show
ocurrir   to occur; **ha ocurrido**   it has occurred
parar   to stop
romperse   to break
seguir (i-i)   to continue
sentir (ie-i)   to be sorry
sentirse (ie-i)   to feel

OTRAS PALABRAS

atrás   behind, at the back
ciclístico, -a   related to bicycles
enorme   enormous
final   final
grave   serious
increíble   incredible
necesario, -a   necessary
posible   possible

EXPRESIONES

darse cuenta   to realize
hubo   there was, there were

EL CUERPO

la boca   mouth
el brazo   arm
la cara   face
el dedo   finger
el diente   tooth
la espalda   back
el oído, la oreja   ear
el ojo   eye
la mano   hand
la nariz   nose
la pierna   leg
la rodilla   knee

Zunil, Guatemala, en un valle de volcanes.

capítulo 16
Fin de curso

Guatemala is a small, populous Central American country with numerous lakes, volcanoes, and beautiful mountain scenery. Despite repeated damage by volcanic eruptions and earthquakes, the country has been steadily growing and rebuilding. Because of the threat of earthquakes, most buildings in Guatemala City, the capital, are only one story high.

Temblor de tierra

Locate Guatemala, Guatemala City, and Lake Atitlán on map of Central America.

Alicia Díaz, una joven que vive en la Ciudad de Guatemala, cuenta de un temblor que hubo en la ciudad.

Hace unos días mi madre y yo fuimos de compras al centro con planes de quedarnos allí a cenar antes de volver a casa. Hicimos compras por varias horas cuando de pronto hubo un fuerte temblor de tierra y se apagaron las luces. ¡Qué susto tan terrible nos llevamos!

— Debemos salir inmediatamente — me dijo mamá.

— ¡Se fue la luz! ¿Quién tiene una linterna? — gritó alguien.

— ¡Cuidado con los ladrones! — gritó otro.

En pocos minutos nos encontramos en una gran confusión. La gente empezó a correr buscando la salida y algunos niños empezaron a llorar. Finalmente pudimos salir a buscar un lugar más seguro hasta poder volver a casa. Ya en casa oímos por radio que no hubo heridos. ¡Qué suerte tuvimos! Afortunadamente no fue un terremoto, sino sólo un fuerte temblor.

comprensión

Check comprehension with questions: *¿Quién es Alicia Díaz? ¿Dónde vive? ¿Cuándo fue de compras? ¿Con quién?* etc.

Personalize: *¿Vas de compras a la ciudad? ¿Te quedas a comer en el centro cuando vas de compras? ¿Qué es un apagón? ¿Hay frecuentes apagones en tu pueblo?*

Assignment: Have students prepare a short Spanish news item similar to Act. B, with questions for use in next class session.

A. Retell in your own words what happened to Alicia and her mother on the day of the tremor. The following words or phrases may help you.

ir de compras	el susto	un terremoto
gritar	¡cuidado!	la confusión
temblor de tierra	apagarse las luces	la gente

■III   Hace unos días Alicia y su madre fueron . . .

B. Read the following newspaper account of the tremor, and then answer the questions below.

La ciudad a oscuras°   in darkness

Guatemala, 21 de nov. En las horas de la tarde de ayer se registró un fuerte temblor de tierra, el cual ocasionó° un apagón° total en la ciudad que duró° varias horas. Los ladrones aprovecharon° la confusión general robando° almacenes y atracando° a algunos transeúntes°. La policía prontamente logró° controlar la situación y restaurar de nuevo el orden en la ciudad.

caused
blackout/lasted
took advantage/looting
holding up
passersby
managed to

1. ¿Qué causó el apagón?   3. ¿Qué pasó en la confusión?
2. ¿Cuánto tiempo duró?   4. ¿Qué hizo la policía?

extensión

A. Imagine that you're at school during a thunderstorm, and all the lights go out. How would you react?

■ꟷ   ¡Es un apagón° general!   ¡Ay, qué susto!
                                    ¿Quién tiene una linterna?
                                    Sí. Hay una tormenta°.
                                    No importa. No es nada.

B. How do you reassure a friend who is afraid of a thunderstorm?

■ꟷ   ¡Tengo miedo! ¡Qué   No te preocupes.
      tormenta!   ¡Cálmate!°
                                   ¡Tonto/a! No es nada
                                     serio°.
                                   Pronto va a pasar.

C. You're at a movie theater, and someone shouts "Fire!" Would you react calmly or not?

■ꟷ   ¡Hay fuego°!   Hay que llamar a los bomberos°.
                        ¡Socorro!°
                        ¡Tranquilos!° ¡Sin correr!
                        ¡No puedo abrir° la puerta!

V: Have students supply alternate catastrophes (accidente, temblor) to which others may respond or react.

Photo: Volcano on Lake Atitlán.

Earthquakes and volcanic eruptions are common occurrences in Guatemala, El Salvador, Costa Rica, and other areas close to the Pacific Ocean. Shifting continental plates are believed to be the cause of frequent tremors. The Circle of Fire, a string of volcanoes extending from Mexico southward through Central America, has been the site of a great deal of activity in recent years. Guatemala alone has three active volcanoes: **Pacaya, Fuego,** and **Santiaguito.**

¡Llegan las vacaciones!

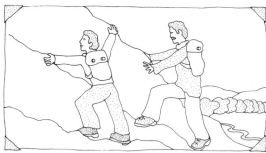

El año escolar en Guatemala ya va a terminar. Alicia y Moisés, dos compañeros de colegio, miran algunas fotos de las vacaciones del año pasado. También hablan de sus planes para las próximas vacaciones.

ALICIA
¡Mira estas fotos de nuestro viaje a la Argentina! ¡Cómo nos divertimos el año pasado . . . ! Aunque las pistas de Bariloche son dificilísimas.

MOISÉS
Supongo que tú sabes esquiar muy bien. Oye, ¿qué pasa en esta foto? ¿No es Eduardo?

ALICIA
Sí. Por tratar de hacerse el gracioso, se cayó y se rompió una pierna.

MOISÉS
¿Fue grave?

ALICIA
No, pero tuvimos que llevarlo al hospital. Por poco nos arruina el paseo. ¿Dónde pasaste tú las vacaciones?

MOISÉS
Nosotros fuimos al lago Atitlán. Mira, aquí estamos en la playa. Fue un mes maravilloso.

ALICIA
¡Parece un lugar muy hermoso!

MOISÉS
Lo pasamos muy bien. Nadamos, pescamos e hicimos varias caminatas. Pensamos volver de nuevo este año.

ALICIA
¡Estupendo! Nosotros vamos a quedarnos aquí. Pienso tomar unos cursos en las vacaciones.

MOISÉS
Pues no es mala idea.

1. ¿Dónde pasó Alicia las vacaciones del año pasado? ¿Qué hizo?
2. ¿Qué le pasó a Eduardo?
3. ¿Qué hizo Moisés durante las vacaciones?
4. ¿Qué va a hacer Moisés en las próximas vacaciones? ¿y Alicia?

extensión

Based on photos or drawings, have students retell personal experiences during vacations. Specific guidelines for assignment may be necessary.

A. You and your cousin Luisa are on a skiing trip and she has just fallen. It looks like she has a broken leg. What would you say?

◼ ¡Ay, me rompí la pierna!   ¡Caramba! ¡Qué mala suerte tienes!
¿Dónde hay un médico°?
¡Pobrecita! ¿Te duele mucho?
Sólo a ti te ocurren estas cosas.

B. You and a friend are about to set out on a camping trip. Your friend arrives with a lot of extra gear. How do you react?

◼ ¡Ya estoy listo/a!   ¿De camping° con todo eso°?
¿Qué llevas allí?
No te voy a ayudar a llevar nada.
¡Uy! ¡Tenemos que llevar todo en la espalda!
Tienes que dejar algo.

Photo: Skiers in Pyrenees, Spain.

C. Pepe's vacation last year was a complete disaster. Take his role and explain to a classmate why. Use some of the following words or phrases.

una tormenta   perderse   un accidente
romperse [un brazo] atropellar   doler [el estómago]

◼ ¿Cómo pasaste las vacaciones?   ¡Terrible! Fui a . . .

335

Estudio de palabras

Fenómenos naturales

el terremoto

el tornado

el huracán

la tormenta

la inundación

la nevada

A   You're a radio announcer. Report the following news items, indicating in each case when the event took place.

> ◼▐▌   terremoto en Guatemala   *Hoy a las cinco de la mañana hubo un terremoto en Guatemala.*

Personalize: ¿Hubo terremoto en California el año pasado? ¿Hubo inundación en Nueva York en septiembre? ¿Hubo una tormenta grave en el mar Caribe recientemente?

1. nevada en Washington
2. tornado en Wichita
3. huracán en Santo Domingo
4. inundación en México
5. tormenta grave en Puerto Rico
6. terremoto en Costa Rica
7. huracán en Florida

B   Describe the conditions that are usually present during each of the phenomenons illustrated above.

> ◼▐▌   *Cuando hay una nevada, . . .*

Pronunciación y ortografía

syllabication

1. Every Spanish syllable has one vowel or diphthong. Most Spanish syllables end in a vowel sound. A stressed weak vowel (**í** or **ú**) forms a separate syllable.

pa • la • bra   cau • sa   dí • a
mu • se • o   tie • ne   Ra • úl

2. A single consonant (including **ch, ll,** and **rr**) and most two-consonant groups ending in **-r** or **-l** form part of the following syllable.

pe • ro   mu • cho   o • tro
oi • go   ca • ba • llo   ha • blar
cui • da • do   pe • rro   a • tro • pe • llar

3. Other two-consonant groups are usually separated.

us • ted   don • de   tam • bién   ac • ci • den • te

4. In three-consonant groups, the first consonant generally forms part of the preceding syllable. Note that when **s** is between two consonants, it forms part of the preceding syllable: **cons • tan • te.**

siem • pre   es • cri • bir   se • cues • tro   en • con • trar

El sol brilla para todos.

Proverb: The sun shines upon all alike.

A   Pronounce the following words, then divide them into syllables.

Use Ex. A as *dictado*, with several students working at blackboard. Hold class competition dividing words into syllables.

cumpleaños	estudio	calculadora
país	doscientos	televisión
guitarra	bailar	policía
clase	idioma	prefieres
posible	adiós	puedo

B   Select five words from chapter vocabularies. Exchange words with a classmate, and divide them into syllables. Then check each other's work.

Lake Atitlán in Guatemala, nestled among green mountains, highlands, and volcanoes, is noted for the beauty of the constantly changing color of its water. Three different Indian tribes, each with its own language and customs, live in the numerous villages located along its shores. The lake attracts visitors from Guatemala and other countries to enjoy the mountain scenery, swimming, boating, and local markets.

Preterit with spelling changes

	LEER	CAERSE
yo	leí	me caí
tú	leíste	te caíste
él, ella, usted	**leyó**	**se cayó**
nosotros, nosotras	leímos	nos caímos
ellos, ellas, ustedes	**leyeron**	**se cayeron**

Optional: Have students conjugate all forms of *creer* and *oír.*

The verbs **leer** *(to read)* and **caerse** *(to fall down)* have a spelling change in the preterit tense. The unaccented **i** changes to **y** in the **él/ella/usted-** and **ellos/ellas/ustedes-**forms.

Other verbs like **leer** and **caer(se)** are **creer** *(to believe)* and **oír** *(to hear).*

A   Your English teacher wants to know how many books each student read last month. Inform her/him.

◼ⅠⅠ   Jorge / 2   *Jorge leyó dos libros.*

1. Mario / 4
2. nosotros / 5
3. yo / 1
4. tú / 7
5. Paquita y Raúl / 6
6. usted e Inés / 3

B   You and your friends heard an astounding bit of news about Tomás last night. State who believed it and who didn't.

◼ⅠⅠ   yo   *Lo oí y lo creí.*
   (Lo oí, pero no lo creí.)

1. Pepe
2. Marta y yo
3. Paco y Pablo
4. Isabel
5. tú
6. ustedes

C   Vicente wants to know if various friends plan to play soccer today. Explain to him why they can't.

V: Have students point to parts of their own body as cue for others to indicate where they hurt.

◼ⅠⅠ   A Alfonso le duele el pie.   Vicente: *¿Piensa Alfonso jugar al fútbol hoy?*
   Tú: *No, porque ayer se cayó y le duele el pie.*

1. A David y a Luis les duelen los brazos.
2. A Teresa le duele la mano.
3. A Pilar le duele la pierna.
4. A Miguel le duele la espalda.
5. A mí me duelen los dedos.
6. A nosotros nos duelen las rodillas.

¡vamos a hablar! Exchange news with a classmate about a number of recent events.

— ¿Oíste que hubo examen
en la clase de español ayer?
— Me lo dijo Ángela.

— ¡No me digas! ¿Cómo lo
sabes?

Infinitive after prepositions

Antes de ir al centro, llamé a Carlos.

Después de comprar una chaqueta,
salí del almacén.

Fui al colegio **sin desayunarme.**

Before going downtown, I called
Carlos.

After buying a jacket, I left the
department store.

I went to school *without having
breakfast.*

In Spanish, the infinitive is used after many prepositions, such as **antes de,
después de, sin, para, por,** and **en vez de.**

D   Combine each pair of sentences, using an appropriate preposition from the
list below. Use each preposition at least once.

al	por	antes de
sin	para	después de

Remind students of pronoun placement in D4 and 7.

▪Ⅲ   Fui al centro. Compré un
regalo.

*Fui al centro para comprar un
regalo.*

1. Leí el periódico. Miré televisión.
2. Me caí en la escalera. Salí de la clase.
3. Fui al colegio. Fui a la biblioteca.
4. Llamé a Ricardo. Le pedí ayuda.
5. Me rompí un dedo. No tuve cuidado.
6. Jugué al fútbol. Escuché las noticias.
7. Salí de casa. No me puse el suéter.

E   Find out whether or not a friend wants to change plans. Suggest an alternate activity.

Assignment: Have students prepare five original plans, based on Ex. E. Use in next class session as warm-up.

▪Ⅲ   ir al cine
o jugar al tenis

Tú: *¿Quieres ir al cine en vez de
jugar al tenis?*

Amigo/a: *Sí, de acuerdo.*
(No, prefiero jugar al tenis.)

1. quedar en casa o ir a la cafetería
2. mirar televisión o escuchar discos
3. jugar al fútbol o visitar a Lourdes
4. ir a bailar o tocar la guitarra
5. montar a caballo o pescar

Zona comercial en la Ciudad de Guatemala.

Si-clauses in the present tense

Si hoy hace sol, voy al centro.	*If it's sunny today,* I'm going downtown.
Si tú vas a la fiesta, yo voy también.	*If you go to the party,* I'll go, too.
Si llueve, no voy a salir.	*If it rains,* I won't go out.

The present tense is used in **si**-clauses that describe a fact or condition likely to exist or to happen. The present tense or **ir a** + infinitive may be used in the main clause.

F   Respond in the affirmative or negative, according to your mood.

■ꟼ   Si hace calor, ¿vas a la piscina conmigo?

Sí. Si hace calor, voy a la piscina contigo.
(No. Si hace calor, me quedo en casa.)

1. Si viene Alejandro a la fiesta, ¿vienes tú?
2. Si tienes tiempo, ¿me ayudas con el trabajo de español?
3. Si vas de camping, ¿vas a escribirme?
4. Si llueve esta tarde, ¿vas a salir?
5. Si llega Elena pronto, ¿vamos al parque?

Preterit tense of estar

	ESTAR
yo	estuve
tú	estuviste
él, ella, usted	estuvo
nosotros, nosotras	estuvimos
ellos, ellas, ustedes	estuvieron

The verb **estar** *(to be)* is irregular in the preterit tense. Note that **estar** has the same preterit endings as **tener.**

G   Help your class adviser by reporting who was sick and for how long after a class picnic.

◼ⅲ   María   *María estuvo enferma [tres] días.*

1. Javier
2. nosotros
3. Raquel y Felipe
4. yo
5. Carlos
6. tú

H   Tell a friend where the following people were during yesterday's storm.

◼ⅲ   Dolores / casa   Amigo/a: *¿Dónde estuvo Dolores durante la tormenta de ayer?*
    Tú: *Estuvo en casa.*

1. tú / la piscina
2. Marcos / la biblioteca
3. Ana e Ignacio / el restaurante
4. Pablo / el hospital
5. ustedes / el parque
6. tus padres / la oficina
7. Teresa / casa de Alfredo
8. tú y Fernando / la cafetería

¡vamos a hablar!   Ask a classmate about last year's vacation and what plans he/she has for the coming summer.

tomar unos cursos	**lo pasé [mal]**
aprender a [nadar]	**me divertí mucho**
ir a [la playa]	**me encanta(n) . . .**

¿Dónde estuviste el año pasado?   Estuve aquí, pero me divertí mucho.
¿Qué piensas hacer este verano?   Ir a las montañas.

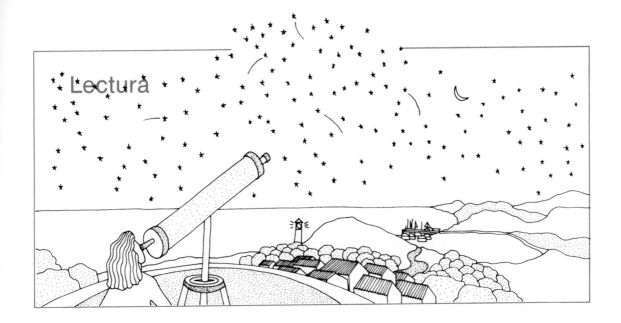

El horóscopo de la semana

Hablan las estrellas
Por la Profesora Qui-ki

Personalize: ¿Quién tiene este signo? ¿Cuándo es tu cumpleaños? ¿Debes ser aventuroso/a esta semana? ¿Qué puede pasar?

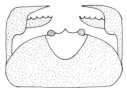

Aries: 21 de marzo al 19 de abril
¡Cuídate!° – especialmente el martes. Puedes caerte y romperte un brazo. Resiste el deseo de aventura°.

take care!

adventure

Tauro: 20 de abril al 20 de mayo
Buen tiempo para el amor°. Vas a estar más seguro/segura de tus sentimientos°.

love

feelings

Geminis: 21 de mayo al 20 de junio
Vas a tener mucho éxito° en tus estudios. Tiempo oportuno para tomar decisiones serias.

tener . . . éxito: to be very successful

Cancer: 21 de junio al 22 de julio
Debes estar alegre y confiado/confiada°. Hay grandes posibilidades para un viaje al extranjero.

confident

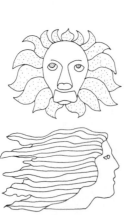

Leo: 23 de julio al 22 de agosto
Tus amigos están siempre en primer lugar. Tu magnetismo y espíritu emprendedor° te van a traer° muchas amistades°.

enterprising
bring/friendships

Virgo: 23 de agosto al 22 de septiembre
¡No te duermas! Organiza tu vida para darle un rumbo° más interesante. Haz° amistades con la gente de Escorpión.

direction/make

Libra: 23 de septiembre al 22 de octubre
Mira al futuro con optimismo. Ten paciencia° con tu familia y trata de mejorar° tus relaciones con los amigos.

be patient
improve

Escorpión: 23 de octubre al 21 de noviembre
Período importante. Debes llegar a una decisión pronto. Haz lo posible por cambiar de ambiente°. Puedes recibir noticias de un empleo o de alguien que te interesa muchísimo.

surroundings

Sagitario: 22 de noviembre al 21 de diciembre
Todo es armonía en tu familia, pero en el aspecto del dinero vas a tener algunas sorpresas desagradables°. Cuida tu salud. Acuéstate y levántate temprano.

unpleasant

Capricornio: 22 de diciembre al 19 de enero
Vas a conocer a una persona muy interesante y vas a querer saber todo acerca° de ella. Toma algunas precauciones pues va a influenciar tu vida en forma definitiva.

about

Acuario: 20 de enero al 18 de febrero
Esta semana vas a recibir muchos regalos importantes. Analiza a tus amigos para saber en cuáles puedes confiar°.

trust

Piscis: 19 de febrero al 20 de marzo
No debes esperar tontamente que la suerte te resuelva° los problemas. Aprende a mirarlos de frente y a resolverlos tú solo/sola. Días buenos desde el jueves hasta el domingo.

might solve

actividades

A. 1. ¿Crees en los horóscopos?
   2. ¿Cuál es tu signo?
   3. ¿Qué piensas de la predicción para tu signo?
   4. ¿Qué signo es el más afortunado?
   5. ¿Te gustaría tener otro signo?
   6. ¿Crees que la Profesora Qui-ki es optimista o no? ¿por qué?

B. Prepare an original horoscope for a friend. Your friend should tell you whether or not the horoscope suits her/his personality and character.

Ruinas mayas de Tikal en Guatemala.

Preterit with spelling changes (A–C)

	CREER
yo	creí
tú	creíste
él, ella, usted	**creyó**
nosotros, nosotras	creímos
vosotros, vosotras	creísteis
ellos, ellas, ustedes	**creyeron**

Verbs whose stems end in a vowel have a spelling change **i** to **y** in the **él/ella/usted-** and **ellos/ellas/ustedes-**forms in the preterit tense.

Infinitive after prepositions (D, E)

In Spanish, the infinitive is used after many prepositions: **Antes de salir, José cenó; Salí de casa sin ponerme el abrigo.**

Si-clauses in the present tense (F)

The present tense is used in **si**-clauses to state a fact or condition that is likely to exist or to happen: **Si hay una nevada, mañana vamos a esquiar.**

Preterit tense of **estar** (G, H)

	ESTAR
yo	**estuve**
tú	**estuviste**
él, ella, usted	**estuvo**
nosotros, nosotras	**estuvimos**
vosotros, vosotras	**estuvisteis**
ellos, ellas, ustedes	**estuvieron**

A Form a sentence about each person or pair of persons by combining logical elements from each column. Use the preterit tense and use each verb at least once.

1	2	3
1. Martín	caerse	mucho ruido anoche
2. yo	creer	que hubo una inundación en San Juan
3. ustedes	leer	de un árbol
4. Beatriz	oír	que Marta se rompió el brazo
5. mi mamá		que se acerca un huracán
6. Laura y Diego		en la piscina
7. tú		dos novelas la semana pasada
8. el Sr. Álvarez		que Sara lo hizo
9. Francisco y yo		una noticia increíble

■⫼ *Martín se cayó de un árbol.*

B Supply an appropriate ending to the following phrases.

■⫼ Me levanté temprano para . . .   *Me levanté temprano para ir a la playa.*

1. Escuché las noticias antes de . . .
2. Vi a Patricia al . . .
3. Fui al museo después de . . .
4. Me caí por . . .
5. Salí de casa rápidamente sin . . .
6. Me gusta hacer caminatas para . . .

A las orillas del lago en Santiago Atitlán.

C You witnessed a bank robbery. Describe the thief to a police artist. Include the following information.

1. what the thief's face is like
2. the color of her/his eyes
3. whether the thief is tall or short and blond(e) or brunet(te)
4. what clothing the thief wore and the color of each item

D Prepare an eight- to ten-line description of Antonio's vacation last year, based on the illustrations below.

E State what you or various friends are going to do, depending on the following conditions.

▪||| Si hace buen tiempo, Marcos . . .   *Si hace buen tiempo, Marcos va a jugar al tenis.*

1. Si termino mi trabajo, . . .
2. Si Elena va a Guatemala, . . .
3. Si Santiago y yo vamos de camping . . .
4. Si ganas la carrera, . . .
5. Si llueve esta tarde, Gloria . . .
6. Si voy al lago, . . .

F Tell about your experience in an earthquake last week. Use the preterit tense of the indicated verbs.

La semana pasada yo *(ir)* a una cafetería para comer. De pronto *(empezar)* un temblor bastante fuerte. *(Apagarse)* las luces. *(Oír)* mucho ruido y alguien *(gritar)* "¡Socorro!" Yo *(tratar)* de salir de la cafetería, pero no *(encontrar)* la puerta. *(Chocar)* con algo, *(caerse)* y *(romperse)* la mano. ¡Cómo me *(doler)!* Finalmente, *(llegar)* un señor con una linterna y me *(ayudar)* a salir. ¡Qué susto!

G What would you say to help or warn someone in these situations?

> ▪ǀǀǀ Tu hermanita tiene su bicicleta en la calle y no ve que viene un autobús.
>
> *¡Cuidado, Anita!*
> *Viene un bus.*

1. Estás en la oficina del médico con tu hermano menor. Él tiene mucho miedo y empieza a llorar.
2. Oyes en la radio que un tornado viene hacia la ciudad. Ves que tus vecinos trabajan en el jardín.
3. Vas a un concierto de música rock. Muchas personas quieren comprar boletos al mismo tiempo. Ves que va a caerse un chico.
4. Estás en el coche de un amigo. Un perro está cruzando la calle y piensas que tu amigo va a atropellarlo.
5. Estás volviendo a casa cuando de pronto ves fuego detrás de una casa. Hay gente en la casa.

Vocabulario

SUSTANTIVOS

el apagón blackout
el bombero fireman
la caminata hike
el centro center; downtown
el curso course (school)
el fuego fire
el huracán hurricane
la inundación flood
el ladrón thief, robber
la linterna flashlight; lantern
el médico, la médico doctor
la nevada snowstorm
el paseo walk; trip
la pista ski slope
el plan plan
la salida exit
el temblor tremor; **el temblor de tierra** earthquake
el terremoto earthquake
la tormenta storm
el tornado tornado

VERBOS

abrir to open
apagarse to go out
arruinar to ruin, spoil
caerse to fall down
encontrarse (ue) to be; to find oneself
llorar to cry
quedarse to remain, stay
suponer to suppose

OTRAS PALABRAS

alguien someone
eso that
fuerte strong
inmediatamente immediately
serio, -a serious
tranquilo, -a calm

EXPRESIONES

¡calmate! calm down!
hacer compras to shop
ir de camping to go camping
llevarse un susto to be frightened
por poco (+ present tense) almost, nearly
¡socorro! help!

A **Con los amigos.** Prepare a skit with three or four classmates about an outing to the movies, a play, a concert, or a race. Decide what to do and where to go. Arrange to meet, buy tickets, and make reservations. Act out what happens and what you say when you arrive. When the event is over, discuss what you think of it. Include an argument or mishap to make your skit lively.

B **Una entrevista.** Gather information about a Spanish-speaking person of international importance. The person may be living or dead and well known in sports, the arts, politics, the military, or any field that interests you. Learn as much as you can about that person. The class will then interview you to learn biographical details of the person you have chosen and what he/she has done to gain international fame.

C **Un periódico escolar.** Prepare a Spanish-language version of a school newspaper. Assign reporters to write varied news features, such as a Spanish Club party or event, a holiday celebration, school social events or trips, sports competitions, or a special class project. Include editorials, a horoscope, a review of a movie, play or concert, or a restaurant critic's column on the food in the school cafeteria. Compile the stories to simulate an authentic newspaper by pasting the articles in columns on a large sheet of paper or cardboard. Use illustrations when possible.

D **Los desacuerdos.** With two or three classmates, prepare and act out a disagreement. The cause of the argument might be related to a biking, skiing, car, or hiking accident or to the loss or destruction of a personal possession. One person should take the role of the victim, another the accuser, and one or two people should act as arbitrators.

E **Un concierto.** Find out what instruments various classmates can play. Then ask friends, your teacher, or a Spanish-speaking person you know to lend you sheet music for Hispanic songs. Form a singing group, choose one or two songs, and practice them. Give a concert at a Spanish-Club meeting or class party.

F **La moda.** Put on a fashion show in your classroom. Several classmates should volunteer to be models while others act as commentators, describing the outfits in Spanish. Commentaries may include a description of the color and fit of the outfit, and occasions when it may be worn. To make the show lively, models should try to put together unusual or humorous costumes. Select a panel of judges and students to serve as reporters for a column in your school newspaper. Award a prize for the best, funniest, or most original outfit.

G **Vendo a buen precio.** Choose a product that you would like to sell and prepare a television announcement to advertise the product. Your product can be clothes, sporting goods, furniture, books, or records. Find a way to make your product attractive and to convince prospective buyers to purchase it. Use posters or props and present your product to the class.

H **El mundo hispano.** Prepare a poster on a Spanish-speaking country. Gather information about two or three aspects of the country, such as its people, resources, geography, climate, government, or any aspects that particularly interest you. Then prepare your poster, using a map, illustrations, photographs from magazines, and brief descriptions about the country. Present your poster to the class.

I **Álbum.** By now, your album probably reflects many of the year's activities and the progress you've made in Spanish. Add to your album reports, scripts for skits, and articles that you've prepared for Spanish class. Also include any items previously suggested for the scrapbook or that you have collected from Spanish-speaking countries.

J **Las vacaciones.** Look at the color photographs on pages 241–248. Do any of the pictures show activities that you plan to participate in during the summer? Is there a scene that reminds you of a place where you will be? Is there a photograph of a place you would like to visit? Talk about your plans for the summer vacation, using one or more of the photographs as an illustration or background of what you plan to do or would like to do.

Reference
section

Appendix A
Spanish first names

The following list includes many common Spanish names. The popularity of some names varies from country to country.

girls

Adela	Leonor
Alejandra	Lucía
Alicia	Luisa
Amelia	Luz
Ana (Anita)	Manuela
Ana María	Margarita
Ángela	María
Bárbara	María del Carmen
Beatriz	(Maricarmen)
Carlota	María Isabel (Maribel,
Carmen	Marisa)
Cecilia	María Teresa (Maite)
Clara	Mariana
Claudia	Marta
Concepción (Concha,	Mercedes
Conchita)	Mónica
Consuelo	Nuria
Cristina	Paloma
Diana	Patricia
Dolores (Lola)	Paula
Elena	Pilar (Pili)
Elisa	Raquel
Emilia	Rosa
Esperanza	Rosario
Francisca (Paquita)	Sara
Gloria	Silvia
Graciela	Soledad
Inés	Susana
Irene	Teresa (Tere)
Isabel	Verónica
Juana	Victoria
Julia	Virginia
Laura	Yolanda

boys

Adolfo	Jesús
Alberto (Beto)	Joaquín
Alejandro	Jorge
Alfonso	José (Pepe)
Alfredo	José Antonio
Álvaro	José Luis
Andrés	José María
Ángel	Juan (Juanito)
Antonio (Tonio, Toño)	Juan Manuel
Arturo	Julián
Bernardo	Julio
Carlos	Luis
Claudio	Manuel (Manolo)
Cristóbal	Marcos
Daniel	Mario
David	Martín
Diego	Mateo
Eduardo	Miguel (Miguelito)
Emilio	Miguel Ángel
Enrique (Quique)	Nicolás
Ernesto	Pablo
Esteban	Pedro
Federico	Rafael (Rafa)
Felipe	Ramón
Fernando	Raúl
Francisco (Paco)	Ricardo
Gabriel	Roberto
Gonzalo	Salvador
Gregorio	Santiago
Guillermo	Sebastián
Ignacio (Nacho)	Tomás
Jaime	Vicente
Javier	Víctor

Appendix B

Core material equivalents *(Chapters 1–11)*

Below you will find English equivalents rather than literal translations of the dialogues and narratives in this book.

chapter 1   Who am I?

Who are you?

ANA	Hi! I'm Ana García. What's your name? (And you?)
PEDRO	Pedro López. Pleased to meet you, Ana.
ANA	Are you from around here?
PEDRO	No. I'm from Mexico.

What language do you speak?

TERESA	You speak English, don't you?
FELIPE	Yes, I'm bilingual. You are too, aren't you?
TERESA	Not really. I only speak a little English.

Who's that boy?

ISABEL	That's Juan Tovar, isn't it?
CARLOS	No. It's my friend Paco González. He's very nice.
ISABEL	Does he live here in Los Angeles?
CARLOS	No. He lives in Santa Barbara.

chapter 2   To school!

In biology class

Lucía, is the exam easy? (Rosa)
No. It's very hard. There are ten very long questions. (Lucía)
How awful! I don't know anything. (Rosa)
Don't worry. I'll help you study this afternoon. (Lucía)

Luis Lleras's schedule

Luis is a student at a school in Miami. He's studying six subjects. On Monday morning he has algebra with Mr. Rodríguez, Spanish with Miss Ibáñez, and biology with Mrs. Adams. At 11 he has lunch. In the afternoon he has history at 12, English at 1, and music at 2. His favorite class is history because the teacher is very good.

chapter 3   With friends

A birthday present

FELIPE	What do you have there, Pilar?
PILAR	A present for Rosa.
FELIPE	A present? Why?
PILAR	Because she's going to be fifteen tomorrow!
FELIPE	Don't tell me! What shall I buy her?
PILAR	A novel, or a record maybe . . . They're easy to find.
FELIPE	Hey, good idea. See you later.

| **How old are you?** | I'm looking for a young person between the ages of 16 and 18 to work in an office. Please call 515-2627. |

	CARMEN	Isabel, you're only fifteen, aren't you?
	ISABEL	Yes, but I'm almost sixteen.
	CARMEN	I don't believe you! When's your birthday?
	ISABEL	November 20th.
	CARMEN	How lucky! Then you can call about the job.

Will you lend me your calculator?	CARLOS	Say, Jaime! Will you lend me your calculator?
	JAIME	I can't. It's the teacher's.
	CARLOS	Please! I have an exam tomorrow.
	JAIME	Darn it! So do I.
	CARLOS	Can I study with you, then?
	JAIME	Good idea.

chapter 4 At home

Someone's calling (on the phone)	ENRIQUE	Hello!
	MR. PÉREZ	This is Mr. Pérez. Who's speaking? Enrique?
	ENRIQUE	Yes. Good afternoon, Mr. Pérez. How are you?
	MR. PÉREZ	Fine, thank you. Is your father home?
	ENRIQUE	No. He's in Puerto Rico. He'll be back Sunday.
	MR. PÉREZ	Very well. I'll call (back) Sunday, then.
	ENRIQUE	Good-by, Mr. Pérez.

Family pictures

Here's my family. In this picture you see Dad, Mom, and my Uncle Ignacio.
Look at this picture! It's my dog Sultán.
Here are my brother and sister with some friends. Manuel is my older brother and Cristina is my younger sister.
I look very happy here, don't I? That's my new bicycle.

Be quiet!	MOTHER	Good morning (children). How's everything?
	ROBERTO	I'm really sick, Mom. I have a cold. A . . . choo!
	ELENA	Oh, poor thing! I'm sorry! What about your algebra exam?
	ROBERTO	Be quiet, silly!
	MOTHER	Do you have an exam, Roberto? Off to school, then!

chapter 5 Work and pastimes

What do you want to be?

I live in Chicago, but I travel a lot because I'm a pilot. When I travel I like to visit new cities. In my spare time I watch television or listen to music.

I want to be a mechanic and fix cars. To learn, I work on weekends in my uncle's garage.

I want to be a painter. I'm an independent and creative person. I like to paint landscapes and to work outdoors.

I'm an interpreter because I speak three languages very well. My father is from Germany and my mother is from Spain. I like to help people from other countries.

Job application

Job application

Name: Jorge Castillo Santos
Address: 618 Michigan Avenue, Chicago
Telephone: 965-7428   Date of birth: 5/20/68
Father's name: Andrés Castillo   Occupation: Policeman
Mother's name: Elena Santos de Castillo Occupation: Nurse
School: Benito Juárez   Grade: 10
Job you are applying for: Assistant
Experience: None
Interests and pastimes: collecting coins, running, photography (taking photos)
References:
Name: Mr. Rubén Chávez   Telephone: 363-1542
Name: Mrs. Irene García   Telephone: 684-2322

chapter 6   Where are you going?

What confusion!   *Alfredo is a messenger and he wants to take the subway to deliver a package to the post office.*

POLICEMAN	Say, Mr., (You there!) where are you going?
ALFREDO	I'm going to the subway.
POLICEMAN	This entrance is closed.
ALFREDO	Oh, no! I'm going to arrive late. What can I do?
POLICEMAN	Don't worry. You have to go to the corner and then turn right. There's another entrance there. That's all.
ALFREDO	Thank you. Good-by.
POLICEMAN	You're welcome. Any time. (At your service.)

Mexico City's subway   *Verónica Chávez and her cousin Beatriz are visiting Mexico City for the first time. They want to take the subway, but they don't know where it is. Verónica asks at the information desk in the hotel.*

VERÓNICA	Pardon me, Sir. Where can I get the subway?
EMPLOYEE	Where are you going, Miss? There are three lines.
VERÓNICA	I'm going to the Zócalo.
EMPLOYEE	We're on the Paseo de la Reforma. In order to go to the Zócalo, you have to take line number 1. You should get off at Pino Suárez Station and take line number 2.
VERÓNICA	Oh, no! Is it difficult?
EMPLOYEE	No, Miss. With this map there's no problem.
VERÓNICA	Thank you very much. See you later.

chapter 7   Free time

The great race

Great Worldwide Circuit!

Admission prices

Sunday, Nov. 15, 1:30 P.M.

Pit pass $200 (pesos)
Reserved seats $200
General admission $30
Parking $10

Municipal automobile racetrack of Buenos Aires
Corner of Roca and General Paz Avenues

The world champion, Juan Manuel Alfaro, from Argentina, is organizing a large automobile race in the city of Buenos Aires. Everyone is reading with a lot of interest the news about the great race. Participants are coming from many countries and are driving Italian, French, and German cars. The winner of this competition is going to receive the World Cup. This trophy represents a lot of money and fame for the winner.

Spring in October?

In October, it is spring in Buenos Aires. It is a wonderful month to play tennis. Álvaro Ponti invites his friend Silvia Kaiser to play a game.

ÁLVARO   Hi, Silvia. Do you want to play tennis Saturday morning?
SILVIA   Thanks, Álvaro, but I can't.
ÁLVARO   Why? What are you doing?
SILVIA   I'm going to practice the guitar with Luisa.
ÁLVARO   If you prefer, we can play in the afternoon.
SILVIA   Great! I accept your invitation, then. What time?
ÁLVARO   Three?
SILVIA   Yes. O.K. Bye, Álvaro!

During the game

SILVIA   40 to 15 in your favor? You're cheating!
ÁLVARO   I'm not cheating. I just know how to play better than you.
SILVIA   Better than me? You're crazy! You're lucky today. That's all.
ÁLVARO   And you don't know how to lose. Well, would you like to go for a cold drink?

chapter 8   On vacation

An excursion to Monserrate

Leonor and Margarita are visiting their cousin Ernesto. They're from the Atlantic Coast and this is their first trip to Bogotá. Ernesto suggests going up Monserrate by funicular railway. They arrive at the top of the mountain at noon.

LEONOR   What a beautiful view! The air's so clean!
MARGARITA   Yes, but it sure is cold up here! There's a big difference from the temperature on the coast.
ERNESTO   For Bogotá, today's weather is nice. Why don't we climb down the mountain on foot? It's excellent exercise.

MARGARITA	Great idea! I'm very cold.
LEONOR	Isn't it dangerous? I'm afraid of a holdup.
ERNESTO	How silly you are! Come with us. During the day there's no danger.
LEONOR	Well . . . all right. If you insist.
	After walking all afternoon, the girls realize they are lost.
LEONOR	Ernesto! We're lost!
ERNESTO	Lost? I know the way very well.
MARGARITA	Are you sure?
ERNESTO	Well, now I'm not so sure.
LEONOR	How scary! And it's almost nighttime!
ERNESTO	Don't worry. I know how to get back. Look! Over there we can already see the first houses of the city.

"Warm country"

Melgar Hotel

Five reasons to spend your vacation at the Melgar Hotel!
An ideal climate? We have it!
Reasonable rates? You'll find them here!
Private pool? We have it!
Comfortable rooms? We have them!
Discotheque and restaurant? We have them here!

Please write to the hotel office for reservations.
Melgar, Tolima   Phones: 55 20 55   52 21 00

chapter 9   Let's eat!

Where are we going for dinner?

Luz María and Ricardo, two university students from Madrid, spend all Saturday at the library. It is 9:30 at night.

LUZ MARÍA	I've just finished my work. I'm dying of hunger.
RICARDO	Me too. Besides, I'm tired.
LUZ MARÍA	Let's go to the cafeteria to see what there is to eat.
RICARDO	Steaks, Spanish omelettes, sandwiches . . . You know, nothing new.
LUZ MARÍA	Why don't we go to a restaurant?
RICARDO	Good idea! But I don't have enough money.
LUZ MARÍA	It doesn't matter. I have enough. You can pay me later.
RICARDO	OK. Let's go to the Bodegón Español. They serve delicious meals there, and it's not very expensive.
LUZ MARÍA	Fantastic! Let's go then.

In the restaurant

Luz María and Ricardo arrive at the Bodegón Español. After deciding what they want, they order dinner.

WAITER	Good evening. What would you like for dinner?
LUZ MARÍA	For me, a salad and the hake.
RICARDO	And for me, gazpacho and the sirloin with mushrooms.
WAITER	Very well. What do you wish to drink?
LUZ MARÍA	White wine, please.
RICARDO	For me, too, and water, please. I'm very thirsty.

Bodegón Español
Menu

Appetizers
Fruit juice
Serrano ham (cured)
Mixed salad

Soups
Consommé
Garlic soup with egg
Gazpacho (cold vegetable soup)

Fish and shellfish
Clams sailor style
Grilled prawns
Hake in white sauce
Squid in their own ink
Trout, Navarre style

Meat
Roast suckling pig
Baked lamb
½ Roast chicken
Porkchops
Veal steak
Sirloin with mushrooms

Desserts
Ice cream
Flan (caramel custard)
Cheese
Fruit in season

Hours: Luncheon from 1:00 to 4:00. Dinner from 8:00 to 12:00.

chapter 10   Petroleum and prosperity

Everyone to Miami!

The Jiménezes, a fairly wealthy family from Caracas, are getting ready to go to Miami to visit their relatives, the Mendozas. They are going to spend a month there and want to take some presents.

Before going shopping, Doña Sofía checks the newspaper to see what's being advertised. She finds a jewelry store ad for pearls from the Island of Margarita and other gold jewelry. She decides to give her sister a pearl necklace.

Don Guillermo prefers to go to a large department store, since he wants to look for a chess set for his brother-in-law. His daughter Lola wants to look for a record for her cousin Julio and a bracelet for her cousin Ana.

<table>
<tr><td>At a department
store</td><td>Today the Jiménezes are shopping in Sabanagrande, a centrally located district in Caracas. Doña
Sofía goes to the jewelry store while Lola and Don Guillermo go to a department store. Lola is
looking for the record section on the first floor.</td></tr>
</table>

LOLA	What is the latest record by the *Melódicos?*
CLERK	Pardon me, Miss. What are you saying? I can't hear you.
LOLA	Can you lower the volume?
CLERK	Of course.
LOLA	I'm asking you what the latest record by the *Melódicos* is.
CLERK	There are several, Miss. You may look at the ones we have. Today they are two for the price of one.

Lola selects two records and takes them to the cashier.

CLERK	Will that be it? (Is that all?) That comes to 40 bolivars.
LOLA	Here you are. Thank you.

chapter 11   A house on the lake

A timely invitation

Pedro and Inés Castillo, two teen-agers from San Salvador, don't know what to do for the weekend. Suddenly, the phone rings. Pedro answers.

PEDRO	Hello?
MAN'S VOICE	Who's this? Pedro?
PEDRO	Yes. Uncle Arturo? What a surprise!
UNCLE ARTURO	Is your mother home?
PEDRO	No, she isn't. I'm sorry.
UNCLE ARTURO	Then tell her I want to invite you to see the new house near the lake.
PEDRO	Oh! How wonderful!
UNCLE ARTURO	Tell your mother to call me if you can come this weekend.
PEDRO	Yes. I sure will. See you soon.

By the lake

The Castillo family arrive at the house Uncle Arturo has by the shore of Lake Ilopango. It's a big house and is surrounded by many trees.

UNCLE ARTURO	Welcome (to my home)!
MRS. CASTILLO	It's a very beautiful place, Arturo. The children are going to be very happy.
UNCLE ARTURO	Yes, they can swim here, go out in a boat, or go fishing.
INÉS	Do you have a boat, Uncle Arturo?
UNCLE ARTURO	I don't, but I know some neighbors who have one. Let's see if we can go out with them tomorrow.
INÉS	Fantastic!

Looking for a house

Patricia and Julio Rodríguez, two young people from San Salvador, are reading the classified ads in the newspaper. Their parents want to buy a house near Lake Ilopango. Patricia finds the following ad.

On the lake, spacious, living room, dining room, 3 bedrooms, 2 baths, courtyard, garden (yard), parking. Telephone 23-9264.

Appendix C
Supplementary word sets

Some of the English words in the following lists have other Spanish equivalents, since terms may vary from country to country.

chapter 2

CLASSROOM OBJECTS

el altavoz   intercom, loudspeaker
el armario   closet; cupboard
el bloc, block   writing pad
el borrador   eraser (blackboard)
la carpeta   folder
la cartelera   bulletin board
la cartera, el portafolio   briefcase; bookbag
la engrapadora   stapler
el escritorio   desk
el estante   book shelf
la goma de borrar   eraser
el sacapuntas   pencil sharpener
la pluma   fountain pen
la presilla   paper clip
el pupitre   school desk
la regla   ruler
la tiza   chalk

chapter 3

SCHOOL SUBJECTS

el alemán   German
el arte   art
la economía   economics
la educación física   physical education
la física   physics
la geografía   geography
la literatura   literature
las matemáticas   mathematics
la mecanografía   typing
la psicología   psychology
la química   chemistry
la sociología   sociology
la taquigrafía   shorthand
la trigonometría   trigonometry

chapter 4

MEMBERS OF THE FAMILY

la bisabuela   great grandmother
el bisabuelo   great grandfather
la cuñada   sister-in-law
el cuñado   brother-in-law
la hermanastra   stepsister
el hermanastro   stepbrother
la madrastra   stepmother
la nieta   granddaughter
el nieto   grandson
la nuera   daughter-in-law
el padrastro   stepfather
la sobrina   niece
el sobrino   nephew
la suegra   mother-in-law
el suegro   father-in-law
el yerno   son-in-law

chapter 5

PROFESSIONS AND OCCUPATIONS

el actor   actor
la actriz   actress
el administrador, la administradora   administrator
el agricultor, el granjero   farmer
el/la analista de sistemas   systems analyst
el arquitecto, la arquitecta   architect
el carpintero   carpenter
el/la comerciante   tradesperson, merchant
el/la contable, contador   accountant
el/la detective   detective
el/la dibujante técnico   draftsperson
el escritor, la escritora   writer
el fotógrafo, la fotógrafa   photographer
el/la gerente   manager

el/la médico (la médica)   physician
el/la periodista   journalist
  el plomero, el fontanero   plumber
  el programador, la programadora   computer
      programmer
  el secretario, la secretaria   secretary
  el vendedor, la vendedora   salesperson

chapter 6

BUILDINGS AND PLACES

  el aeropuerto   airport
  el auditorio   auditorium
  la biblioteca   library
  el campo de golf   golf course
  la cancha de tenis   tennis court
  la estación de policía, la comisaría   police
      station
  el estadio   stadium
  el gimnasio   gymnasium
  el hospital   hospital
  la lavandería   laundromat, laundry
  la librería   bookstore
  el mercado   marketplace
  la papelería   stationery shop
  la piscina   swimming pool
  el supermercado   supermarket
  el teatro   theater

chapter 7

SPORTS

  el alpinismo   mountain climbing
  el buceo   scuba diving
  el ciclismo   cycling
  la equitación   horseback riding
  la esgrima   fencing
  el esquí acuático   water skiing
  el footing, correr   jogging
  la gimnasia   gymnastics
  el golf   golf
  el patín de ruedas   roller skating
  el patinaje sobre hielo   ice skating
  la pesca   fishing
    pista y campo   track and field
  la vela   sailing

MUSICAL INSTRUMENTS

  la bandurria   instrument similar to guitar
  la batería   percussion section
  la flauta   flute
  la gaita   bagpipes
  el arpa (f.)   harp
  el órgano   organ
  la pandereta   tambourine
  el saxófono (saxofón)   saxophone
  el trombón   trombone
  la trompeta   trumpet
  la viola   viola
  el violón   bass viol
  el violoncelo   cello

chapter 9

FOODS

  el aceite   oil
  el ajo   garlic
  el arroz   rice
  el batido   milkshake
  el caldo   broth
  el camarón, la gamba   shrimp
  la cebolla   onion
  el chile   chili (pepper)
  el chocolate   chocolate
  la chuleta   chop
  la fresa   strawberry
  el guisante   pea
  el jugo, el zumo   juice
  la limonada   lemonade
  la manzana   apple
  la mantequilla   butter
  la naranjada   orangeade
  la pasta   pasta (spaghetti, macaroni, etc.)
  el pastel   cake, pastry
  la piña   pineapple
  el queso   cheese
  el rosbif   roast beef
  la sal   salt
  la salsa   sauce
  la uva   grape

TABLE SETTING

la cuchara   spoon
la cucharita   teaspoon
el cuchillo   knife
el mantel   tablecloth
el platillo   saucer
el plato   plate
la servilleta   napkin
la taza   cup
el tenedor   fork
el vaso   glass

chapter 11

PARTS OF A HOUSE

la buhardilla   attic
la despensa   pantry, kitchen storage
el sótano   basement

FURNITURE AND APPLIANCES

el abrelatas   can opener
el armario   closet
la alacena   cupboard
la batidora   mixer
la cafetera   coffee pot
la cazuela, la olla   pot
la cómoda   chest of drawers
la cortina   curtain, drape
el cuadro   painting, picture
la chimenea   fireplace
la estufa   stove
el fregadero, la pileta   sink
el horno   oven
la lavadora   washing machine
el lavaplatos   dishwasher
la licuadora   blender
la nevera, el refrigerador   refrigerator
la sartén   frying pan
el sofá   sofa
la tostadora   toaster

chapter 14

CLOTHING

la bata   bathrobe
el bolso (la bolsa)   handbag, purse
las botas   boots
la bufanda   scarf (neck, woolen)
el camisón   nightgown
la cartera   billfold; brief case
los calcetines   socks
la gorra, el gorro   cap
los guantes   gloves
el impermeable   raincoat
los lentes de contacto, las lentillas   contact lenses
las medias   socks; stockings
el/la piyama, pijama   pajamas
las sandalias   sandals
el sombrero   hat
las zapatillas   slippers
los zapatos de tenis   sneakers

chapter 15

PARTS OF THE BODY

la cadera   hip
la ceja   eyebrow
el codo   elbow
el cuello   neck
el dedo de la mano   finger
el dedo del pie   toe
la frente   forehead
el hombro   shoulder
el labio   lip
la lengua   tongue
la mejilla   cheek
la muñeca   wrist
el tobillo   ankle

ADJECTIVES OF NATIONALITY

argentino, -a Argentine
belicense from Belize
boliviano, -a Bolivian
colombiano, -a Colombian
costarricense Costa Rican
cubano, -a Cuban
chileno, -a Chilean
dominicano, -a Dominican
ecuatoriano, -a Ecuadoran
español, -a Spanish
estadounidense from the United States
guatemalteco, -a Guatemalan
hondureño, -a Honduran
mexicano, -a Mexican
nicaragüense Nicaraguan
panameño, -a Panamanian
paraguayo, -a Paraguayan
peruano, -a Peruvian
puertorriqueño, -a Puerto Rican
salvadoreño, -a Salvadoran
uruguayo, -a Uruguayan
venezolano, -a Venezuelan

NATURE

el árbol tree
el bosque woods
el campo country
la cascada waterfall
el cielo sky, heaven
la colina hill
la flor flower
la isla island
el lago lake
el llano, la llanura plains
el/la mar sea
la mata bush
la montaña mountain
la nube cloud
el océano ocean, sea
la planta plant
la playa beach
el prado field
el río river
la sierra hills, mountain range
la tierra earth
el valle valley

ANIMALS

el caballo horse
el conejo rabbit
el hámster hamster
el loro parrot
el pájaro bird
el perico parakeet
el perro dog
el pez fish
el burro burro
la cabra goat
el cerdo pig
el cisne swan
la gallina chicken
el gallo rooster
la oveja sheep
el pato duck
la rana frog
el ratón mouse
el toro bull
la vaca cow

WILD ANIMALS

la culebra, la serpiente snake
el elefante elephant
el gorila gorilla
el hipopótamo hippopotamus
la jirafa giraffe
el león lion
el mono monkey
el oso bear
el tigre tiger
el zorro fox

INSECTS

la abeja bee
la hormiga ant
la mariposa butterfly
la mosca fly
el mosquito mosquito

Appendix D
Grammatical summaries

Agreement of adjectives

	FOUR-FORM ADJECTIVES	TWO-FORM ADJECTIVES
Masc. sing.	chico contento	chico alegre
Fem. sing.	chica contenta	chica alegre
Masc. plural	chicos contentos	chicos alegres
Fem. plural	chicas contentas	chicas alegres

Possessive adjectives

SINGULAR	PLURAL	
mi	mis	my
tu	tus	your
nuestro, nuestra	nuestros, nuestras	our
vuestro, vuestra	vuestros, vuestras	your (plural, familiar)
su	sus	his, her, its, your, their

Demonstrative adjectives

	ESTE this, these	ESE that, those	AQUEL that, those
Masc. sing.	este	ese	aquel
Fem. sing.	esta	esa	aquella
Masc. plural	estos	esos	aquellos
Fem. plural	estas	esas	aquellas

Pronouns

SUBJECT	DIRECT-OBJECT	INDIRECT-OBJECT	REFLEXIVE	OBJ. OF PREP.
yo	me	me	me	mí (conmigo)
tú	te	te	te	ti (contigo)
él, ella, usted	lo, la	le (se)	se	él, ella, usted
nosotros, -as	nos	nos	nos	nosotros, -as
vosotros, -as	os	os	os	vosotros, -as
ellos, ellas, ustedes	los, las	les (se)	se	ellos, ellas, ustedes

Verbs

regular verbs in -ar, -er, -ir

		TOMAR	COMER	ABRIR
Present	yo	tomo	como	abro
	tú	tomas	comes	abres
	él, ella, Ud.	toma	come	abre
	nosotros, -as	tomamos	comemos	abrimos
	vosotros, -as	tomáis	coméis	abrís
	ellos, ellas, Uds.	toman	comen	abren
Preterit	yo	tomé	comí	abrí
	tú	tomaste	comiste	abriste
	él, ella, Ud.	tomó	comió	abrió
	nosotros, -as	tomamos	comimos	abrimos
	vosotros, -as	tomasteis	comisteis	abristeis
	ellos, ellas, Uds.	tomaron	comieron	abrieron
Tú-command		toma	come	abre
Pres. part.		tomando	comiendo	abriendo

stem-changing verbs

		-ar verbs: e > ie pensar	-ar verbs: o > ue contar
Present	yo	pienso	cuento
	tú	piensas	cuentas
	él, ella, Ud.	piensa	cuenta
	nosotros, -as	pensamos	contamos
	vosotros, -as	pensáis	contáis
	ellos, ellas, Uds.	piensan	cuentan
Preterit	yo (etc.)	pensé	conté
Tú-command		piensa	cuenta
Pres. part.		pensando	contando

			-er verbs: e > ie perder	-er verbs: o > ue volver
Present		yo	pierdo	vuelvo
		tú	pierdes	vuelves
		él, ella, Ud.	pierde	vuelve
		nosotros, -as	perdemos	volvemos
		vosotros, -as	perdéis	volvéis
		ellos, ellas, Uds.	pierden	vuelven
Preterit		yo (etc.)	perdí	volví
Tú-command Pres. part.			pierde perdiendo	vuelve volviendo

			-ir verbs: e > i pedir	-ir verbs: e > ie or i sentir	-ir verbs: o > ue or u dormir
Present		yo	pido	siento	duermo
		tú	pides	sientes	duermes
		él, ella, Ud.	pide	siente	duerme
		nosotros, -as	pedimos	sentimos	dormimos
		vosotros, -as	pedís	sentís	dormís
		ellos, ellas, Uds.	piden	sienten	duermen
Preterit		yo	pedí	sentí	dormí
		tú	pediste	sentiste	dormiste
		él, ella, Ud.	pidió	sintió	durmió
		nosotros, -as	pedimos	sentimos	dormimos
		vosotros, -as	pedisteis	sentisteis	dormisteis
		ellos, ellas, Uds.	pidieron	sintieron	durmieron
Tú-command Pres. part.			pide pidiendo	siente sintiendo	duerme durmiendo

verbs with spelling changes

			Verbs in -car: c > qu before e	Verbs in -gar: g > gu before e	Verbs in -zar: z > c before e
			buscar	llegar	empezar
Preterit		yo	busqué	llegué	empecé
		tú	buscaste	llegaste	empezaste
		él, ella, Ud.	buscó	llegó	empezó
		nosotros, -as	buscamos	llegamos	empezamos
		vosotros, -as	buscasteis	llegasteis	empezasteis
		ellos, ellas, Uds.	buscaron	llegaron	empezaron

		Verbs in -ger and -gir: g > j before a and o	Verbs in -guir: gu > g before a and o
		escoger	seguir
Present	yo	escojo	sigo
	tú	escoges	sigues
	él, ella, Ud.	escoge	sigue
	nosotros, -as	escogemos	seguimos
	vosotros, -as	escogéis	seguís
	ellos, ellas, Uds.	escogen	siguen

		Verbs in vowel + -cer: c > zc before a and o	Verbs in consonant + -cer: c > z before a and o
		conocer	convencer
Present	yo	conozco	convenzo
	tú	conoces	convences
	él, ella, Ud.	conoce	convence
	nosotros, -as	conocemos	convencemos
	vosotros, -as	conocéis	convencéis
	ellos, ellas, Uds.	conocen	convencen

		Verbs in -eer: unstressed i > y
		leer
Preterit	yo	leí
	tú	leíste
	él, ella, Ud.	leyó
	nosotros, -as	leímos
	vosotros, -as	leísteis
	ellos, ellas, Uds.	leyeron

reflexive verbs

		LEVANTARSE
Present	yo	me levanto
	tú	te levantas
	él, ella, Ud.	se levanta
	nosotros, -as	nos levantamos
	vosotros, -as	os levantáis
	ellos, ellas, Uds.	se levantan
Tú-command		levántate
Pres. part.		levantándose

		LEVANTARSE
Preterit	yo (etc.)	me levanté
		te levantaste
		se levantó
		nos levantamos
		os levantasteis
		se levantaron

irregular verbs

		DAR	DECIR	ESTAR	HACER
Present	yo	doy	digo	estoy	hago
	tú	das	dices	estás	haces
	él, ella, Ud.	da	dice	está	hace
	nosotros, -as	damos	decimos	estamos	hacemos
	vosotros, -as	dais	decís	estáis	hacéis
	ellos, ellas, Uds.	dan	dicen	están	hacen
Preterit	yo	dí	dije	estuve	hice
	tú	diste	dijiste	estuviste	hiciste
	él, ella, Ud.	dio	dijo	estuvo	hizo
	nosotros, -as	dimos	dijimos	estuvimos	hicimos
	vosotros, -as	disteis	dijisteis	estuvisteis	hicisteis
	ellos, ellas, Uds.	dieron	dijeron	estuvieron	hicieron
Tú-command		da	di	está	haz
Pres. part.		dando	diciendo	estando	haciendo

		IR	JUGAR	OÍR	PODER
Present	yo	voy	juego	oigo	puedo
	tú	vas	juegas	oyes	puedes
	él, ella, Ud.	va	juega	oye	puede
	nosotros, -as	vamos	jugamos	oímos	podemos
	vosotros, -as	vais	jugáis	oís	podéis
	ellos, ellas, Uds.	van	juegan	oyen	pueden
Preterit	yo	fui	jugué	oí	pude
	tú	fuiste	jugaste	oíste	pudiste
	él, ella, Ud.	fue	jugó	oyó	pudo
	nosotros, -as	fuimos	jugamos	oímos	pudimos
	vosotros, -as	fuisteis	jugasteis	oísteis	pudisteis
	ellos, ellas, Uds.	fueron	jugaron	oyeron	pudieron
Tú-command		ve	juega	oye	—
Pres. part.		yendo	jugando	oyendo	pudiendo

		PONER	QUERER	SABER	SALIR
Present	yo	pongo	quiero	sé	salgo
	tú	pones	quieres	sabes	sales
	él, ella, Ud.	pone	quiere	sabe	sale
	nosotros, -as	ponemos	queremos	sabemos	salimos
	vosotros, -as	ponéis	queréis	sabéis	salís
	ellos, ellas, Uds.	ponen	quieren	saben	salen
Preterit	yo	puse	quise	supe	salí
	tú	pusiste	quisiste	supiste	saliste
	él, ella, Ud.	puso	quiso	supo	salió
	nosotros, -as	pusimos	quisimos	supimos	salimos
	vosotros, -as	pusisteis	quisisteis	supisteis	salisteis
	ellos, ellas, Uds.	pusieron	quisieron	supieron	salieron
Tú-command		pon	quiere	sabe	sal
Pres. part.		poniendo	queriendo	sabiendo	saliendo

		SER	TENER	VENIR	VER
Present	yo	soy	tengo	vengo	veo
	tú	eres	tienes	vienes	ves
	él, ella, Ud.	es	tiene	viene	ve
	nosotros, -as	somos	tenemos	venimos	vemos
	vosotros, -as	sois	tenéis	venís	veis
	ellos, ellas, Uds.	son	tienen	vienen	ven
Preterit	yo	fui	tuve	vine	vi
	tú	fuiste	tuviste	viniste	viste
	él, ella, Ud.	fue	tuvo	vino	vio
	nosotros, -as	fuimos	tuvimos	vinimos	vimos
	vosotros, -as	fuisteis	tuvisteis	vinisteis	visteis
	ellos, ellas, Uds.	fueron	tuvieron	vinieron	vieron
Tú-command		sé	ten	ven	ve
Pres. part.		siendo	teniendo	viniendo	viendo

Spanish-English vocabulary

The Spanish-English vocabulary contains the basic words and expressions listed in the chapter vocabularies, plus words that occur elsewhere, such as in headings and captions, excluding many cognates. The symbol ~ represents the key word for an entry. Chapter numbers following the definitions are given for words that are listed in the end-of-chapter vocabularies.

a   at, to, *2;* **al**   at the, to the, *6*
el abogado, la abogada
   lawyer, *5*
el abrazo   embrace, hug, *14*
el abrigo   coat, *13*
abril   April, *3*
abrir   to open, *16*
la abuela   grandmother, *4*
el abuelo   grandfather, *4;* **los**
   ~s   grandparents, *4*
aburrido, -a   boring, *2;* bored
acabar: ~ de *(+ inf.)*   to
   have just, *9*
el accidente   accident, *15*
el acento   accent
aceptar   to accept, *7*
acerca (de)   about
acercarse   to approach, draw
   near, *15*
acomodado, -a   well-to-do, *10*
el acomodador, la acomoda-
   dora   usher, *12*
acompañar   to accompany, *12*
el acontecimiento   happening
acostarse (ue)   to go to bed, *14*
acostumbrarse   to accustom
   oneself (to), get used to, *14*
la actividad   activity
de acuerdo   okay, all right, *5*
adaptarse   to adapt oneself, *13*
además   besides, *9*
adiós   good-by, *1*
¿adónde?   where to?, *6*
el aeropuerto   airport, *13*
el aficionado, la aficionada
   fan, *15*
afortunadamente   fortunately, *14*
el agente, la agente   police officer, *15;* agent

agosto   August, *3*
el agotamiento   exhaustion, *15*
agradable   pleasant, enjoyable, *13*
el agua *(f.)*   water, *9*
ahí   there, *3*
ahora   now, *3*
el aire   air; **al ~ libre**   outdoors, *5*
el ajedrez   chess, *10*
el ajo   garlic
la alcoba   bedroom, *11*
alegre   cheerful, happy, *1*
la alegría   happiness, pleasure, *13*
alemán, alemana   German, *7*
Alemania   Germany, *5*
la alfombra   carpet, rug, *11*
el álgebra *(f.)*   algebra, *2*
algo   something, *9*
alguien   someone, *16*
alguno, -a   some, any, *13*
el alivio   relief, *13*
el almacén   shop, store, department store, *10*
la almeja   clam
el almuerzo   lunch, *2;* **tomar**
   el ~   to have lunch, *2*
¡aló!   hello *(telephone),* *4*
alrededor   around, *11*
alto, -a   tall, high, *1*
la alubia   bean
allí   there, *6*
amable   kind, *14*
amarillo, -a   yellow, *14*
la ambulancia   ambulance, *15*
el amigo, la amiga   friend, *1;*
   ~ por correspondencia
   pen pal, *6*
el amor   love

amplio, -a   ample, spacious, *11*
anaranjado, -a   orange, *14*
ancho, -a   wide, *14*
andar   to go; to walk
anoche   last night, *12*
antes   before, *10*
antiguo, -a   old
antipático, -a   unpleasant, *1*
anunciar   to announce, *7*
el anuncio   advertisement
el año   year, *3;* **¿cuántos ~**
   tienes?   how old are you?, *3;*
   cumplir . . . ~s   to be, turn
   . . . years old, *3;* **tener . . .**
   ~s   to be . . . years old, *3*
apagarse   to go out (light,
   fire), *16*
el apagón   blackout, *16*
aparecer   to appear, *15*
aprender   to learn, *5*
aprovechar   to take advantage
   of
aquel, aquella   that (over
   there), *11*
aquí   here, *1*
el árbol   tree, *11*
argentino, -a   Argentinian, *7*
la armonía   harmony
arriba   above, up, *8*
arruinar   to ruin, spoil, *16*
la artesanía   handicrafts
el artículo   article
asado, -a   roasted
asegurar   to assure, *13*
así así   so-so, *12*
el asiento   seat, *12*
asistir   to attend, *13*
asomarse   to look or lean out
la astilla   chip, splinter

el asunto matter, *15*

atender to take care of, attend

la atracción attraction; **las ~es** amusements

el atraco holdup, *8*

atraer to attract

atrás behind, at the back, *15*

atropellar to run over, run into, trample, *15*

aunque although, *13*

la aurora dawn

el auto automobile

el autobús bus, *15*

el autódromo automobile race track

la avenida avenue

aventurarse to venture; to take a risk

el avión airplane, *15*

el aviso advertisement, *10*

¡ay! *expresses pain, alarm, surprise, 4;* **¡~ bendito!** my goodness! oh my!, *13*

ayer yesterday, *12*

el/la ayudante assistant, *5*

ayudar (a) to help, *5*

azul blue, *14*

bailar to dance, *12*

el baile dance, *12*

bajar to descend, *6;* to lower, turn down, *10*

bajo below, *13*

bajo, -a short, low, *1*

el balón ball

el banco bank, *6*

bañarse to take a bath; to go swimming, *14*

el baño bath

barato, -a cheap, *9*

el barco ship, *15*

el barrio district, *10*

el básquetbol basketball, *7*

basta: ¡~ ya! that's enough, *13*

bastante quite; enough, *7*

beber to drink, *9*

la bebida drink, *8*

el béisbol baseball, *7*

bello, -a beautiful

besar to kiss, *13*

la biblioteca library, *9*

la bicicleta bicycle, *3*

bien well, *4;* **bastante ~** quite well, *7*

la bienvenida welcome, *15*

bienvenido, -a welcome, *11*

bilingüe bilingual, *1*

la biología biology, *2*

el bistec beefsteak, *9*

blanco, -a white, *9*

los blue jeans blue jeans, *14*

la blusa blouse, *14*

la boca mouth, *15*

el bodegón tavern; restaurant

el boleto ticket, *12*

el bolígrafo ball-point pen, *2*

el bombero fireman, *16*

bonito, -a pretty, *4*

el bote rowboat, *11*

la botella bottle

el brazo arm, *15*

brillar to shine

bueno all right; well, *7*

bueno, -a good, *2;* **buen provecho** enjoy your food (meal), *12;* **¡qué bueno!** how nice! great!, *3*

el bus (autobús) bus, *6*

la busca search

buscar to look for, *3;* to get

el caballo horse, *8;* **montar a ~** to ride horseback, *8*

la cabeza head, *4;* **tener dolor de ~** to have a headache, *4*

el cacao cocoa

cada each, every

caerse to fall down, *16*

el café coffee, *9;* café

la cafetería cafeteria, *9*

la caja cash register, *10*

el calamar squid, *9;* **los ~es en su tinta** squid in their ink

la calculadora calculator, *3*

el caldo broth

caliente hot, warm, *8*

calmarse: ¡cálmate! calm down!, *16*

el calor heat, warmth; **hace ~** it's hot, warm, *8;* **tener ~** to be hot, *8*

la caloría calorie

callarse: ¡cállate! be quiet!, *4*

la calle street, *6*

la cama bed, *11*

la cámara camera, *8*

la camarera waitress

el camarero waiter, *9*

cambiar to change, *13*

caminar to walk, *8*

la caminata hike, *16*

el camino road, way, *8*

el camión truck, *15*

la camisa shirt, *14*

la camiseta T-shirt, *14*

el campeón champion, *7*

el camping: ir de ~ to go camping, *16*

el campo country, *8*

cansado, -a tired, *4*

cantar to sing

el capítulo chapter

la cara face, *15*

¡caramba! *expresses surprise, anger, annoyance, 3*

caraqueño, -a from Caracas, *10*

la carga load, burden

la carne meat, *9*

caro, -a expensive, *9*

la carrera race, *7*

el carro car, *5;* **~ deportivo** sports car, *6*

la carta letter, *5;* menu

el cartel poster, *7*

la casa house, home, *4;* **a ~** home; **en ~** at home, *4*

casi almost, *3*

el cassette cassette, *3*

el castillo castle

catalán, catalana Catalan, from Catalonia

¡cataplum! bang!, *14*

causar to cause

la cédula document (of identity)

celebrar to celebrate, *12*

la cena dinner, *9*

cenar to eat dinner, *9*

el centro center; downtown, *16*

cerca (de) near, *6*

el cerdo pork; pig

cerrado, -a closed, *6*

la cesta wastebasket, *2*; basket

el ciclismo cycling

ciclístico, -a related to bicycles, *15*

la cima summit, top, *8*

el cine cinema, movie theater, *6*

el cinturón belt, *14*

el circuito circuit

la circulación traffic

la ciudad city, *5*

el clarinete clarinet, *7*

claro of course, *3*

la clase class; classroom, *2*

la clave key

el clima climate, *8*

el cobre copper

la cocina kitchen, *11*

el coche car, *7*

el cochinillo suckling pig

coger to take

coleccionar to collect, *5*

el colegio school, *2*

el color color, *14*

el collar necklace, *10*

el comedor dining room, *11*

comer to eat, *9*

la comida meal, *9*; food, *14*

como like, *13*

¿cómo? how? what?, *1*; **¿~ es?** what is he/she like?, *1*

¡cómo . . . ! how . . . !; **¡~ lo siento!** I'm very sorry!

el compañero, la compañera classmate, *1*; partner, friend

la competencia competition, *7*

la compra: ir de ~s to go shopping, *10*; **hacer ~s** to shop, *16*

comprar to buy, *5*

comprender to understand, *6*

la comprensión comprehension

compuesto, -a compound

con with, *2*; **~ permiso** excuse me, may I?, *12*

el concierto concert, *12*

confortable comfortable, *8*

la confusión confusion, *6*

el conjunto group (music, dance, etc.)

conocer to know, be acquainted with, *11*; to meet

conocido, -a known

conservar to preserve

la conspiración conspiracy

constituir to constitute

contar (ue) to tell, *13*; to count

contento, -a happy, content, *4*

contestar to answer, *11*

la continuación continuation; **a ~** following

contrario, -a opposite

la copa cup, trophy

el cordero lamb

el corredor racer, *15*

el correo post office, *6*

correr to run, *5*

la correspondencia correspondence; **el amigo, la amiga por ~** pen pal

la corrida bullfight

la cortesía courtesy

corto, -a short, *14*

la cosa thing

la costa coast, *8*

costar (ue) to cost, *10*

la costumbre custom; **como de ~** as usual, *13*

creador, -a creative, *5*

creer to believe, *13*; **creo que sí** I believe so, *8*

cruzar to cross, *15*

el cuaderno notebook, *2*

la cuadra block; **a [tres] ~s** [three] blocks away, *6*

¿cuál? what? which?, *2*

la cualidad characteristic

cuando when

¿cuándo? when?, *2*

¿cuánto, -a? how much?; **¿cuántos? -as?** how many?, *2*

el cuarto quarter (hour), *7*; room; **~ de baño** bathroom, *11*

la cuenta bill, *9*; **darse ~ (de)** to realize, *15*

el cuero leather, *14*

el cuerpo body, *15*

el cuidado: ¡~! careful!, *12*; **tener ~** to be careful

la culpa fault, *12*; **tener la ~** to be at fault, *12*

el cultivo farming, cultivation

el cumpleaños birthday, *3*; **feliz ~** happy birthday, *3*

cumplir: ~ . . . años to be, turn . . . years old, *3*

la cuñada sister-in-law

el cuñado brother-in-law, *10*

el curso course (school), *16*

el chal shawl

el champiñón mushroom, *9*

chao good-by, *7*

la chaqueta jacket, *14*

charlar to talk, chat

la charreada rodeo (*Mexico*)

la chica girl, *1*

el chico boy, *1*

chocar to crash, collide, *15*

el chofer driver, *15*

el chorizo pork sausage

la chuleta chop (pork, veal)

la danza dance

dar to give, *10*; to show; **déme (Ud.)** give me (*formal*), *12*

de from, of, *1*; **de nuevo** again, *13*; **del** from the, of the, *3*

debajo de under, *10*

deber to be obligated to, ought, *11*

decidir to decide, *9*

decir to say, *10*; **dile** tell her/him, *11*; **¡no me digas!** you don't say! don't tell me!, *3*

dedicarse (a) to devote oneself (to)

el dedo finger, *15*

dejar to let; to leave, *14*

delante de in front of, *10*

delicioso, -a delicious, *9*

demasiado, -a too much, *4*

el/la dentista dentist, *5*

el/la dependiente clerk, *10*

el deporte sport, *7*

deportivo, -a related to sports

la derecha right; **a la ~
(de)** to the right (of), *6*

el desacuerdo disagreement

desayunar(se) to have breakfast, *14*

describir to describe

desde since, from, *10*

desear to desire, wish, *9*

el desfile parade, march

despacio slowly, *6*

despedirse (i-i) to say good-
by, *14*

despertar (ie) to wake, *14*

despertarse (ie) to wake up, *14*

después (de) after, *8*

detrás (de) behind, *6*

el día day, *2;* **buenos
~s** good morning, *1*

diciembre December, *3*

el diente tooth, *15*

diferenciarse (de) to be different (from)

difícil difficult, *2*

la dificultad difficulty

el dinero money, *5*

¡dios mío! oh my goodness!
oh my!, *6*

la dirección address, *5*

el director conductor (music);
director

el disco record, *3*

la discoteca discotheque, *8*

la disculpa: pedir ~s to
apologize, *13*

discutir to discuss, *12;* to argue

divertirse (ie-i) to have a
good time, enjoy oneself, *14*

doblar to turn; to fold

doler (ue) to hurt, ache, *15*

el dolor pain

el domingo Sunday, *2*

don *Spanish title (for man) used
with first name*

¿dónde? where?, *3*

doña *Spanish title (for woman)
used with first name*

dormir (ue-u) to sleep, *14*

dormirse (ue-u) to fall asleep, *14*

durante during, *7*

durar to last

económico, -a economical, *8*

echar: ~ de menos to miss, *13*

el ejercicio exercise, *8;* **hacer
~** to exercise, *8*

él he, *2;* him *(obj. prep.),* *9;*
ellos they, *4;* them *(obj. prep.),*
9

elegante elegant, *14*

ella she, *2;* her *(obj. prep.),* *9;*
ellas they, *4;* them *(obj.
prep.),* *9*

la emoción emotion, *13*

emocionante exciting; moving

empezar (ie) to begin, *12*

**el empleado, la emplea-
da** employee

el empleo job, *3*

en in, *1;* **~ punto** sharp
(with time), *12*

encantado, -a I'm pleased to
meet you, *1*

encantar: me encanta I like a
lot, *12*

encima de above, over, *10*

encontrar (ue) to find, *8*

encontrarse (ue) to be; to
find oneself, *16*

enero January, *3*

**el enfermero, la enfer-
mera** nurse, *5*

enfermo, -a sick, *4*

enfrente de in front of, *6*

enojado, -a angry, *13*

enorme enormous, *15*

la ensalada salad, *9*

entonces then, *3*

la entrada entrance, *6;* admission, ticket, *7*

entrar to enter, *12*

entre between, among, *3*

el entremés appetizer

el entretenimiento entertainment

entusiasmado, -a enthusiastic

enviar to send, *8*

la época epoch, era

el equipo equipment; team

equivocado, -a mistaken, *13*

equivocarse to be mistaken,
15

la escalera staircase, stairs, *11*

escoger to choose, *10*

escolar related to school

esconderse to hide oneself, *14*

escribir to write, *5*

el escritorio desk, *11*

escuchar to listen to, *5*

la escuela school, *5*

la escultura sculpture

ese, esa that, *1*

eso that, *16*

la espalda back, *15*

España Spain, *5*

el español Spanish (language), *1*

español, -a Spanish

especial special, *14*

el espectador, la espectadora
spectator

esperar to wait (for), *15*

el espíritu spirit

el esquí skiing, *7;* ski

esquiar to ski, *7*

la esquina corner (street), *6*

la estación station, *6;* season, *7*

el estacionamiento parking, *11*

el estadio stadium

el estado state

los Estados Unidos (EE.UU.)
the United States, *1*

el estante bookcase, *11*

estar to be, *4*

este, esta this, *2;* **estos, estas** these, *3*

el estilo style

estimado, -a dear

el estómago stomach, *4;* **tener dolor de ~** to have a stomachache, *4*

estrecho, -a narrow; tight, *14*

el/la estudiante student, *2*

estudiar to study, *2*

el estudio study

estudioso, -a studious, *1*

estupendo, -a stupendous, wonderful, *14*

el examen exam, *2*

excelente excellent, *8*

la excursión excursion, *8*

el éxito success

la expectativa expectation, *15*

la experiencia experience, *5*

explicar to explain, *13*

expulsar to expel

el extranjero: en el ~ abroad

extranjero, -a foreign

fabuloso, -a fabulous, *14*

fácil easy, *2*

la falda skirt, *14*

¡falso! -a! false!

faltar: me falta I need, *7*

la fama fame, *7*

la familia family, *4*

familiar family-related

fantástico, -a fantastic, *3*

el favor favor; **a tu ~** in your favor, *7;* **por ~** please, *3*

favorito, -a favorite, *2*

febrero February, *3*

la fecha date, *5;* **~ de nacimiento** birth date

felicitar to congratulate, *15*

feo, -a ugly, *4*

la fiebre fever, *4*

fiero, -a ferocious, savage

la fiesta party, festivity, *3;* holiday, *14*

la fila row, *12*

el filete steak, *9*

filmar to film, *15*

el fin end

el final end, *15*

final final, last, *15*

finalmente finally

la finca farm, ranch, *8*

fino, -a fine, *10*

el flan caramel custard

la flor flower, *15*

folklórico, -a folk

el fondo background; **al ~** at the back

la forma form, way, *13;* **de esta ~** in this way

la fortaleza fort

la foto(grafía) photo, picture; **sacar ~s** to take pictures, *5*

el francés French (language), *1*

francés, francesa French, *7*

fresco, -a cool, fresh; **hace ~** it's cool, *8*

el frío cold; **hace ~** it's cold, *8;* **tener ~** to be cold, *8*

la fruta fruit, *9*

el fuego fire, *16*

fuerte strong, *16*

el funicular cable railway, *8*

el fútbol soccer, *7;* **~ americano** football, *7*

la gallina hen, chicken

el ganador, la ganadora winner, *7*

ganar to earn, *5*

la ganga bargain, *10*

el garaje garage, *5*

el gato cat, *14*

el gazpacho *a cold vegetable soup*

generalmente generally, *14*

la gente people, *13*

el gol goal

golpear to hit, strike, *15*

la grabadora tape recorder, *2*

gracias thank you; **muchas ~** thank you very much, *3*

gracioso, -a funny, amusing, *14*

el grado grade, *5;* degree (temperature), *13*

la gramática grammar

gran great, *7*

grande large, great, *10;* big

grave serious, *15*

gris gray, *14*

gritar to shout, *14*

el grito shout

el grupo group

guapo, -a good-looking, handsome, beautiful, *14*

guatemalteco, -a Guatemalan

la guitarra guitar, *7*

gustar: ~le (a uno) to like, *10;* **me gusta** I like, *5;* **te gusta** you like, *7;* **me/te gustan** I/you like, *8;* **¿te gustaría?** would you like?, *12*

el gusto pleasure; **mucho ~** I'm pleased to meet you, *1;* **con mucho ~** with pleasure; I'll be glad to

la habitación room, *8*

habitar to live

hablar to speak, *5*

hacer to do or make, *11;* **~ compras** to shop, *16;* **~ trampa** to cheat (game), *7;* **hace [dos años] que** [two years] ago, *13;* **hace [buen] tiempo** the weather's [nice], *8;* **hace calor** it's warm, *8;* **hace fresco** it's cool, *8;* **hace frío** it's cold, *8;* **hace sol** it's sunny, *8;* **hace viento** it's windy, *8;* **¿qué tiempo hace?** what's the weather like?, *8*

hacerse to be; to pretend to be; to become

hacia toward, *10*

hallar to find

el hambre *(f.)* hunger; **me muero de ~** I'm dying of hunger, *9;* **tener ~** to be hungry, *9*

la hamburguesa hamburger, *9*

hasta until, *4;* **~ luego** see you later, *1;* **~ mañana** see you tomorrow, *1*

hay there is, there are, *2;* ∼ **que** it's necessary to, you must, *6*

el helado ice cream, *9*

el herido, la herida injured person, *15*

la hermana sister, *4*

el hermano brother, *4*

hermoso, -a beautiful, handsome

el héroe hero

la hija daughter, *4*

el hijo son, *4;* **los** ∼**s** children, *4*

la historia history, *2*

hola hello, hi, *1*

el hombre man, *15*

la hora hour, time; **¿a qué** ∼**?** at what time?, *6;* **¿qué** ∼**es?** what time is it?, *6*

el horario schedule, *2*

el horno oven; **al** ∼ baked

el horóscopo horoscope

horrible horrible, *9*

el horror horror; **¡qué** ∼**!** how terrible!, *2*

el hospital hospital, *15*

el hotel hotel, *6*

hoy today, *2*

hubo there was, there were, *15*

el huevo egg, *9*

húmedo, -a humid, moist

el huracán hurricane, *16*

la idea idea; **buena** ∼ good idea, *3*

el idioma language, *1*

el/la idiota idiot, *13*

la iglesia church, *6*

igual similar, same, *14*

la importancia importance; **no tiene** ∼ it's not important, *13*

importar: no importa it doesn't matter, *4*

inacabado, -a unfinished

increíble incredible, *15*

independiente independent, *5*

la información information, *6*

el ingeniero, la ingeniera engineer, *5*

el inglés English (language), *1*

iniciar to initiate, begin

inmediatamente immediately, *16*

insistir to insist, *8*

el instrumento instrument, *7*

inteligente intelligent *1*

el interés interest, *13*

interesante interesting, *2*

el interior inside, interior

el/la intérprete interpreter, *5*

interrumpir to interrupt, *15*

la inundación flood, *16*

el invierno winter, *7*

la invitación invitation, *7*

invitar to invite, *7*

ir to go, *7*

irse to go, leave, *13*

la isla island, *10*

italiano, -a Italian, *7*

la izquierda left; **a la** ∼ **(de)** to the left (of), *6*

el jai alai *Basque ball game*

el jamón ham, *9;* **el** ∼ **serrano** cured ham, *9*

el jardín garden, *11*

el/la joven young person, *3*

joven young, *13*

la joya jewel, *10*

la joyería jewelry store, *10*

el juego game, *7*

el jueves Thursday, *2*

el juez judge, *15*

jugar (ue) (a) to play (a sport or game), *7*

el jugo juice, *9*

julio July, *3*

junio June, *3*

jurar to swear, promise (oath), *13*

la juventud youth

el kilo kilogram

el kilómetro kilometer, *15*

la her, you, it, *8;* **las** them, you, *8*

el lado side; **al** ∼ **de** beside, next to, *6*

ladrar to bark

el ladrón thief, robber, *16*

el lago lake, *11*

la lámpara lamp, *11*

el langostino prawn, crayfish

el lápiz pencil, *2*

largo, -a long, *2*

el lavadero laundry area, *11*

lavar to wash, *14*

lavarse to wash oneself, *14*

le (to) him, her, it, you, *8;* **les** (to) them, you, *10*

la lectura reading

la leche milk, *9*

la lechuga lettuce, *9*

leer to read, *5*

lejos de far from, *6*

lentamente slowly, *13*

los lentes eyeglasses, *3*

lento, -a slow, *13*

el león lion

levantar to raise, *15*

levantarse to get up, stand up, *14*

la leyenda legend

libre free

el libro book, *2*

la línea route; line, *6*

la linterna flashlight; lantern, *16*

listo, -a ready, *8*

lo him, it, you, *8;* **los** them, you, *8*

el loco, la loca crazy person

loco, -a crazy, *7*

el locutor radio announcer, *15*

lograr to achieve

los que the ones that, *10*

luego later; **hasta** ∼ see you later, *1*

el lugar place, *11*

la luna moon

el lunes Monday, *2*

la luz light, *15*

llamar to call, *3;* ~ **por teléfono** to telephone

llamarse to be called, named; **¿cómo te llamas?** what's your name?, *1;* **me llamo** my name is, *1*

el llano plain

la llegada arrival; **la línea de** ~ finish line, *15*

llegar to arrive, come, *6*

lleno, -a full

llevar to bring, carry, *6;* to wear, *14*

llevarse: ~ **un susto** to be frightened, *16*

llorar to cry, *16*

llover (ue) to rain; **llueve** it's raining, *8*

la madre mother, *4*

el maestro, la maestra teacher

magnífico, -a magnificent, excellent, great, *7*

mal badly, *4;* **no está** ~ it's not bad, *4*

malo, -a bad, *12*

la mamá mother

mandar to send

manejar to drive, *7*

la manga sleeve, *14*

la mano hand, *15*

la manzana apple, *9*

la mañana morning; **de la** ~ A.M., *7;* **por la** ~ in the morning, *2*

mañana tomorrow, *2;* **hasta** ~ see you tomorrow, *1*

el mapa map, *6*

la máquina machine, *15*

el/la mar sea

maravilloso, -a marvelous, *7*

el marisco shellfish, *9*

marrón brown, *14*

el martes Tuesday, *2*

marzo March, *3*

más more, *6;* ~ **o menos** more or less, *7;* ~ **... que** more ... than, *11*

la materia subject, *2*

mayo May, *3*

mayor older, oldest, *4;* greater, larger

la mayúscula capital letter

me (to) me, *8, 10;* myself, *14*

el/la mecánico mechanic, *5*

la media: [las dos] y ~ half past [two], *6*

(la) medianoche midnight, *6*

el médico, la médica doctor, *16*

la medida step, measure, *15*

el medio means, method; ~ **de transporte** means of transportation

(el) mediodía noon, *6;* midday

medir (i-i) to measure, *5*

mejor better, *4*

la memoria memory, *13;* **de** ~ by heart, *8*

menor younger, youngest, *4*

menos less, minus, *7;* ~ **... que** less ... than, *11*

el mensajero, la mensajera messenger, *6*

la mentira lie, *13*

el mercado market

merendar (ie) to picnic, *8*

la merluza hake (fish), *9*

el mes month, *3*

la mesa table, *2*

la mesita small table; ~ **de noche** night table, *11*

la meta finish line, *15*

el metro subway, *6*

México Mexico, *1*

la mezquita mosque

mi my, *1;* **mis** my, *3*

mí me *(obj. prep.)*, *9;* **conmigo** with me, *9*

el miedo fear; **tener** ~ to be afraid, *8*

mientras while, during, *10*

el miércoles Wednesday, *2*

la minúscula small letter

mirar to look at, watch, *5;* **¡mira!** look!, *4*

mismo, -a same

la moda style, fashion

el momento moment; **un** ~ just a minute, *4*

la moneda coin, *5*

la montaña mountain, *8*

montañoso, -a mountainous

montar: ~ **a caballo** to ride horseback, *8*

el montón heap, pile

moreno, -a dark, brunet(te), *1*

morir to die

la mosca fly

mostrar (ue) to show, *15*

la moto(cicleta) motorcycle, *15*

mucho, -a much, a lot, *1;* ~ **gusto** I'm pleased to meet you, *1;* **muchos, -as** many, *2*

el mueble piece of furniture, *11*

la mueblería furniture store

la multa traffic ticket, fine

mundial worldwide, *7*

el mundo world

la muralla city wall; rampart

el museo museum, *6*

la música music, *2*

el músico, la música musician

muy very, *1*

el nacimiento birth

nada nothing, *13;* **de** ~ you're welcome, *6*

nadar to swim, *7*

nadie no one, *13*

la naranja orange, *9*

la nariz nose, *15*

la natación swimming, *7*

necesario, -a necessary, *15*

necesitar to need, *11*

negro, -a black, *14*

el nene, la nena baby

la nevada snowstorm, *16*

nevar (ie) to snow; **nieva** it's snowing, *8*

ni ... ni neither ... nor, *11*

la nieta granddaughter, grandchild, *13*

el nieto grandson, grandchild, *13*

la nieve snow

ninguno, -a no, not one, *13*

el niño, la niña child, *10*

no no, not, *1;* ¿~? isn't that right?, *1*

la noche night; **de la** ~ at night; P.M., *7*

el nombre name, *5*

norteamericano, -a North American, *14*

nos (to) us, *8, 10;* ourselves, *14*

nosotros, nosotras we, *4;* us *(obj. prep.), 9*

notar to note, notice

las noticias news, *7*

la novela novel, *3*

noviembre November, *3*

la nube cloud

nublado, -a cloudy; **está** ~ it's cloudy, *8*

nuestro, -a our, *4*

nuevo, -a new, *4;* **de** ~ again, *13*

el número number, *2*

nunca never, *13*

o or, *3*

el objeto object

la obra work (of art)

el obrero, la obrera worker, *5*

obtener to obtain

octubre October, *3*

la ocupación occupation, *5*

ocupado, -a busy, *12*

ocurrir to occur, happen, *15*

odiar to hate, *7*

la oficina office, *3*

el oído ear, *15*

oír to hear, *10;* **oiga (Ud.)** listen *(formal), 6;* **¡oye!** hey! listen!, *3*

el ojo eye, *15*

oportuno, -a timely

la orden command, order; **está a [tus] órdenes** you're welcome to it, *14*

la oreja ear, *15*

organizar to organize, *7*

la orilla bank (river, lake), *11*

el oro gold, *10*

la orquesta orchestra, *12*

la ortografía spelling

os (to) you *(pl.);* yourselves

oscuro, -a dark; **a oscuras** in the dark

el otoño autumn, *7*

otro, -a other, *5;* **otra vez** again

el padre father, *4;* **los padres** parents, *4*

la paella *Valencian rice dish with seafood*

pagar to pay (for), *9*

la página page

el país country (nation), *5*

el paisaje landscape, *5*

el pájaro bird

la palabra word

el palacio palace

el palco box seat, *12*

el palo stick

el pan bread, *9*

el pantalón or **los pantalones** pants, slacks, *14*

la papa potato, *9*

el papá father, *4;* **los papás** parents, *4*

el papel paper, *2*

el paquete package, *6*

para for; in order to, *3;* ~ **servirle** at your service

parar to stop, *15*

parecer to appear, seem, *10*

parecerse to resemble, be like

la pareja couple

el pariente relative, *10*

el parque park, *6*

la parte part, ¿**de** ~ **de quién?** who's calling?, *11*

el partido game, match, *7*

pasado, -a past, *12*

el pasajero, la pasajera passenger

pasar to spend (time), *8;* to pass, travel; to happen, *13;* ~**lo [bien]** to have a [good] time, *13;* **pase (Ud.)** go ahead *(formal), 13*

el pasatiempo pastime, *5*

pasear to go for a walk (drive, ride), *11*

el paseo walk, trip, *16*

el pasillo hallway, *11*

la patata potato, *9*

el patio courtyard, *11*

el peatón pedestrian, *15*

pedir (i-i) to ask for; to order, *9*

peinarse to comb one's hair, *14*

la pelea quarrel, fight, *13*

pelear to quarrel, fight, *13*

la película movie, *12;* ~ **de terror** horror movie, *12*

el peligro danger, *8*

peligroso, -a dangerous, *8*

el pelo hair; **¡me tomas el** ~! you're pulling my leg! you're joking!, *3*

pensar (ie) to think; to intend, *8;* to plan

pequeño, -a little, small, *7*

perder (ie) to lose, *7*

perdido, -a lost, *8*

perdonar to forgive; **perdón** excuse me, pardon me, *6;* **perdone (Ud.)** pardon me, forgive me *(formal), 12*

el peregrinaje pilgrimage

perezoso, -a lazy, *1*

el periódico newspaper, *10*

la perla pearl, *10*

el permiso permission

pero but, *3*

el perro dog, *4*

la persona person, *4*

pesar to weigh, *5*

el pescado fish, *9*

el pescador fisherman

pescar to fish, *11*

la peseta *monetary unit in Spain*

el peso weight; *monetary unit in many Latin American countries*

el petróleo crude oil

petrolífero, -a related to oil

el piano piano, *7*

el pie foot, *12;* **a** ~ on foot, *8*

la pierna leg, *15*

el/la piloto pilot, *5*

el pimiento pepper (red, green)

pintar to paint, 5

el pintor, la pintora painter, 5

la piscina swimming pool, 8

el piso floor, story, 10

la pista ski slope, 16

la pizarra chalkboard, 2

el plan plan, 16

la platea orchestra seat, 12

la playa beach, 8

la plaza square, plaza, 6

la población population

¡pobrecito, -a! poor thing!, 4

la pobreza poverty

poco: por ~ (+ present tense) almost, nearly, 16; un ~ (de) a little, 1

poco, -a little, few, some

poder (ue) to be able, can, 8

el/la poeta poet

el/la policía police officer, 5

la policía police force

el pollo chicken, 9

poner to put, 14

ponerse to put on, 14

por for; in exchange for, 10; around, through; ~ favor please, 3; ~ supuesto of course, 10

porque because, 2

¿por qué? why?, 2

la posibilidad possibility

posible possible, 15

el postre dessert, 9; de ~ for dessert, 9

la práctica practice, 7

practicar to practice, 7

práctico, -a practical, 10

el precio price, 7

preferir (ie-i) to prefer, 8

la pregunta question, 2

preguntar to ask, 6

preocuparse to worry; no te preocupes don't worry, 2; no se preocupe (Ud.) don't worry (formal), 6

preparar to prepare, 9

prepararse to get ready, 10

prestar to lend; to borrow, 3

la primavera spring, 7

primero, -a first, 3

el primo, la prima cousin, 4

la prisa hurry; tener ~ to be in a hurry, 8

privado, -a private

probar (ue) to try, test, 14

probarse (ue) to try on, 14

el problema problem; ¡qué ~! what a problem!, 2

el profesor, la profesora teacher, 2

el programa program, 12

prometer to promise, 12

pronto soon; ¡~! quick! hurry up!, 13; de ~ suddenly, 11; hasta ~ see you soon, 3

próximo, -a next, 14

el proyecto project

el pueblo town; people

la puerta door, 11

puertorriqueño, -a Puerto Rican

pues well, 1; then, 4

la pulsera bracelet, 10

el punto point; en ~ sharp, right on time, 12

puro, -a pure, clean, fresh

que that, which; who

¿qué? what?, 1; ¿~ tal? how are you?, 4

¡qué! how!, what!; ¡~ lástima! what a shame!, 4; ¡~ va! go on! nonsense!, 14

quedar to remain, be left, 12; [me] queda(n) it/they fit(s) [me], it is/they are, 14

quedarse to remain, stay, 16

querer (ie) to want, 5

querido, -a dear, 13

el queso cheese

¿quién? who?, 1; ¿de ~? whose?, 3

la quinceañera fifteen-year-old girl

quitarse to take off (clothing), 14

quizás perhaps, 3

el rábano radish

el/la radio radio, 8

el ramo bouquet, 15

rápidamente quickly, rapidly, 13

¡rápido! quickly! hurry!, 12

rápido, -a fast, rapid, 13

la raqueta (de tenis) (tennis) racket, 13

raro, -a strange, odd, 14

la raza race

la razón reason; no tener ~ to be wrong, 8; tener ~ to be right, 8

la rebaja discount, 10; en ~ on sale

recibir to receive, 7

recordar (ue) to remember, 8

el recuerdo: recuerdos a [tu familia] regards to [your family], 14

el refresco refreshment, soft drink, 7

regalar to give as a present

el regalo gift, present, 3

regular so-so, 4

el reloj wrist watch, 3

reparar to repair, fix, 5

el repaso review

repetir (i-i) to repeat, 6

el reportero, la reportera reporter

representar to represent

el resfriado cold, chill

resfriado, -a: estar ~ to have a cold, 4

resolver (ue) to solve, 13

responder to reply, answer, 13

el restaurante restaurant, 8

restaurar to restore

el resto the rest, remainder

el resumen summary

la reunión social gathering, meeting, 13

el rey king

rico, -a delicious, 9; rich

la rivalidad rivalry

robar to steal, loot

rock rock (music), 12

la rodilla knee, 15

rojo, -a   red, *14*
romper   to break, *13*
romperse   to break (a bone), *15*
la ropa   clothing, *14*
rosado, -a   pink, *14*
rubio, -a   blond(e), *1*
el ruido   noise, *14*

el sábado   Saturday, *2*
saber   to know, *7*
sabroso, -a   tasty
sacar   to remove; ~ **fo-tos**   to take pictures, *5*
el saco   sack
la sala   living room, *11*
la salida   exit, *16*
salir   to leave, *11*
la salsa   sauce, dressing
el sandwich   sandwich, *9*
el santo, la santa   saint
la sardana   *folk dance of Cata-lonia*
se   himself, herself, itself, yourself, yourselves, them-selves, *14*
la sed   thirst; **tener ~**   to be thirsty, *9*
seguir (i-i)   to continue, *15*
según   according to, *7*
seguro, -a   sure, *8*
el semáforo   traffic light, *15*
la semana   week, *2;* **el fin de ~**   weekend, *5*
sentarse (ie)   to sit down, *14*
sentir (ie-i)   to be sorry, *15;* **¡cómo lo siento!**   how sorry I am!, *12;* **lo siento**   I'm sorry, *1*
sentirse (ie-i)   to feel, *15*
la señal   sign, *15*
el señor *(abbr.* **Sr.)**   Mr., Sir, *1;* man
la señora *(abbr.* **Sra.)**   Mrs., Madam, *1;* woman
la señorita *(abbr.* **Srta.)**   Miss, *1;* young woman
separado, -a   separated
separar   to separate
septiembre   September, *3*

ser   to be, *1, 3, 5*
el ser humano   human being
la serenata   serenade
serio, -a   serious, *16*
servir (i-i)   to serve, *9*
si   if, *7*
sí   yes, *1*
siempre   always, *4*
siguiente   following, succes-sive, *11*
el silencio   silence, *13*
la silla   chair, *2*
el sillón   armchair, *11*
simpático, -a   nice, pleasant, *1*
sin   without, *10;* ~ **embar-go**   nevertheless, *13*
sinfónico, -a   symphonic
sino   but
el síntoma   symptom
sobre   about, concerning, *7*
¡socorro!   help, *16*
el sol   sun; **hace ~**   it's sunny, *8*
solamente   only
el soldado   soldier
solicitar   to ask for; to apply for
la solicitud   application
solo, -a   alone, *13*
sólo   only, *1*
el solomillo   sirloin, *9*
solucionar   to solve
sonar (ue)   to ring, *11*
la sopa   soup, *9*
la sorpresa   surprise; **¡qué ~!**   what a surprise!, *2*
su   his, her, its, your, their, *2;* **sus**   his, her, your, their, *3*
la subida   rise
subir   to ascend, climb, *8*
el suelo   floor, *14*
el sueño   sleep; dream; **tener ~**   to be sleepy
la suerte   luck; **tener ~**   to be lucky, *7*
el suéter   sweater, *14*
suficiente   sufficient, enough, *9*
sugerir (ie-i)   to suggest, *8*
suponer   to suppose; to as-sume, *16*

el sustantivo   noun
el susto   fright, scare, *14;* **lle-varse un ~**   to be fright-ened, *16*

tal   such
también   also, *1;* **yo ~**   me too, *3*
el tambor   drum, *7*
tan   so, *8;* ~ **... como**   as ... as, *11*
la taquilla   box office, *12*
el taquillero, la taquillera   ticket agent, *12*
la tarde   afternoon, *2;* **buenas ~s**   good afternoon, *1;* **de la ~**   P.M.; **por la ~**   in the afternoon, *2*
tarde   late, *6*
la tarjeta postal   post card
te   (to) you, *8, 10;* yourself, *14*
el teatro   theater, *12*
el teleférico   cable car
el teléfono   telephone, *3*
la televisión   television, *5*
el temblor   tremor, *16;* ~ **de tierra**   earthquake, *16*
la temperatura   temperature, *8*
temprano   early, *12*
tener   to have, *2;* **¿qué tienes?**   what's the matter?, *4;* **no ~ razón**   to be wrong, *8;* ~ **años**   to be ... years old, *3;* ~ **calor**   to be hot, *8;* ~ **cuidado**   to be careful; ~ **la culpa**   to be at fault, *12;* ~ **dolor de cabeza**   to have a headache, *4;* ~ **dolor de estómago**   to have a stomachache, *4;* ~ **fiebre**   to have a fever, *4;* ~ **hambre**   to be hungry, *9;* ~ **lugar**   to take place; ~ **miedo**   to be afraid, *8;* ~ **prisa**   to be in a hurry, *8;* ~ **que** *(+ inf.)*   to have to, *6;* ~ **razón**   to be right, *8;* ~ **sed**   to be thirsty, *9;* ~ **sueño**   to be sleepy, *8*

el tenis   tennis, *7*
terminar   to finish, *9*
la ternera   veal
la terraza   terrace, *11*
el terremoto   earthquake, *16*
terrible   terrible, awful, *13*
el testigo   witness, *15*
el testimonio   evidence; proof
ti   you *(obj. prep.)*, *9;* **contigo**   with you, *3*
la tía   aunt, *4*
el tiempo   weather; time; **a
~**   in/on time; **del ~**   in
season, *9;* **hace [buen] ~**
the weather's [nice], *8;* **¿qué
~ hace?**   what's the
weather like?, *8;* **~ libre**
spare (free) time, *5*
la tienda   shop, *14;* tent
la tierra   land, soil, *8;* homeland
el tío   uncle, *4*
la toalla   towel
el tocadiscos   record player, *10*
el tocador   dresser, *11*
tocar   to play (instrument), *7*
todavía   still; yet, *5*
todo   all; **eso es ~**   that's
all, *6;* **~ el mundo**   everybody, *7;* **~s**   everybody
tomar   to take, *6;* to eat or
drink, *9;* **~ el almuerzo**   to
have lunch, *2*
el tomate   tomato, *9*
¡tonto, -a!   silly, foolish (person)!, *4*
el toreador   toreador, bull-
fighter
la tormenta   storm, *16*
el tornado   tornado, *16*
la tortilla   omelette, *9*
la tostada   toast, *14*
trabajar   to work, *3*
el trabajo   work, *5*
traer   to bring
el tráfico   traffic
el traje   suit, *14;* **~ de baño**
bathing suit, *14*

la trampa   trap; trick; **hacer
~**   to cheat, *7*
la tranquilidad   calm
tranquilo, -a   calm, quiet, *16*
transmitir   to broadcast; to
transmit
el transporte   transportation
tratar   to try, *13*
el tren   train, *15*
el trofeo   trophy, *7*
la trompeta   trumpet, *7*
la trucha   trout
tu   your, *1;* **tus**   your, *3*
tú   you, *1*
la tuna   *university musical group
in Spain*

últimamente   lately
último, -a   last, *10*
un, una   a/an, *3;* **unos, unas**
some, *4*
único, -a   only, *14*
unido, -a   united
usar   to use
el uso   use, usage
usted, ustedes   you, *4;* you
(obj. prep.), *9*

las vacaciones   vacation, *8*
valer   to be worth, *13*
el valor   cost, *12;* courage
el valle   valley
¡vamos!   come now!, *13;* come
on!; let's go!
varios, -as   various, several, *10*
vasco, -a   Basque
el vaso   glass, *9*
el vecino, la vecina   neighbor
la velocidad: ~ máxima
speed limit, *15*
vender   to sell, *10*
venir   to come, *8;* **ven(tú)**
come, *8*
la ventana   window, *11*
ver   to see, *8;* **a ~**   let's see,
let's hope

el verano   summer, *7*
la verdad   truth; **¿~?**   isn't
it so? right?, *1*
verde   green, *14*
la verdura   vegetable, *9*
la vergüenza   shame, embarrassment, *12*
el vestido   dress; clothing, *14*
vestirse (i-i)   to get dressed, *14*
la vez   time, *13;* **a veces**
sometimes, *8;* **en ~ de**   instead of, in place of, *10;*
otra ~   again, *7;* **rara ~**
seldom; **una ~**   once, *6*
viajar   to travel, *5*
el viaje   trip, *8*
la victoria   victory, *15*
la vida   life
viejo, -a   old, *10*
el viento   wind; **hace ~**   it's
windy, *8*
el viernes   Friday, *2*
el vino   wine, *9*
el violín   violin, *7*
visitar   to visit, *5*
la vista   view, *8*
la viuda   widow
vivir   to live, *1*
volar (ue)   to fly
el volcán   volcano
el vólibol   volleyball, *7*
el volumen   volume, *10;* **a
todo ~**   at full volume, *13*
volver (ue)   to return, *8*
vosotros, vosotras   you *(pl.)*
la voz   voice
la vuelta   turn; circuit, *15*
vuestro, -a   your *(pl.)*

y   and, *1*
ya   already, *6*
yo   I, *1;* **~ no**   not me, *1*

el zapato   shoe, *10*
la zona   area
el zumo   juice

English-Spanish vocabulary

a/an   un, una
able: to be ~   poder (ue)
afraid: to be ~   tener miedo
after   después de; **~wards**
despúes
afternoon   la tarde; **good ~**
buenas tardes; **in the ~**
por la tarde
again   otra vez; de nuevo
airplane   el avión
all   todo, -a
all right   de acuerdo
already   ya
also   también
always   siempre
angry   enojado, -a
answer   la respuesta; **to ~**
contestar
appear   parecer; aparecer
arrive   llegar
ask   preguntar
assignment   la tarea
athlete   el/la atleta
aunt   la tía
autumn   el otoño

bad   malo, -a
band   la banda *(music)*
bank   el banco
bargain   la ganga; **to ~**   re-
gatear
be   ser; estar
beach   la playa
beautiful   hermoso, -a
because   porque
become   llegar a ser; hacerse
bed   la cama; **to go to ~**
acostarse (ue)
bedroom   el cuarto; la alcoba
before   antes de
begin   empezar (ie); comenzar
(ie)
believe   creer
big   grande

bill   el billete *(money);* la
cuenta *(price)*
birthday   el cumpleaños;
happy ~   feliz cumpleaños
black   negro, -a
blind   ciego, -a
blue   azul
bore   aburrir; **to be ~d**
estar aburrido, -a; **to be boring**   ser aburrido, -a
bother   molestar
boy   el muchacho; el chico
breakfast   el desayuno; **to eat
~**   desayunar(se)
bridge   el puente
bring   traer
brother   el hermano
brown   marrón; castaño, -a;
pardo, -a; café
building   el edificio
business   el comercio; el nego-
cio
busy   ocupado, -a
but   pero
buy   comprar

cake   el pastel; la tarta
call   llamar; llamar por
teléfono *(on the phone)*
can   poder (ue)
car   el coche; el carro; el auto
careful: to be ~   tener cuidado
carry   llevar
cat   el gato
check   la cuenta *(bill)*
checkers   las damas
chess   el ajedrez
child   el niño, la niña
choose   escoger
church   la iglesia
city   la ciudad
class   la clase
clerk   el/la dependiente
clock   el reloj

close   cerrar (ie)
clothing   la ropa
cloud   la nube; **to be ~y**
estar nublado
coat   el abrigo
coin   la moneda
cold   frío; **to be (feel) ~**
tener frío; **to be ~**   hacer frío
(weather); **to have a ~**
estar resfriado, -a
come   venir
corner   la esquina *(street);* el
rincón *(interior)*
cost   costar (ue)
country   el país *(nation);*
~side   el campo; el paisaje
course: of ~   claro; por supuesto
cousin   el primo, la prima
crazy   loco, -a
cry   llorar
cup   la taza
customer   el/la cliente

dance   el baile; **to ~**   bailar
date   la fecha *(calendar);* la
cita *(appointment)*
daughter   la hija
day   el día
deaf   sordo, -a
die   morir (ue-u)
dining room   el comedor
dinner   la comida; la cena
discovery   el descubrimiento
do   hacer
dog   el perro
door   la puerta
downtown   el centro
dream   el sueño; **to ~**   soñar
(ue)
drink   la bebida; **soft ~**   el
refresco; **to ~**   beber;
tomar
drive   manejar; conducir

each cada
early temprano
earn ganar
easy fácil
eat comer; tomar
egg el huevo
embassy la embajada
employee el empleado, la empleada
end el fin; **to ~** terminar; acabar
enjoy divertirse (ie-i) *(oneself)*
enough bastante
enter entrar
everybody todo el mundo; todos
everything todo
expensive caro, -a

face la cara
factory la fábrica
fail salir mal *(subject, exam)*
fall caer; caerse
fan el aficionado, la aficionada *(enthusiast)*
farming la agricultura; el cultivo
father el padre; el papá
feel sentir (ie-i); sentirse (ie-i)
few pocos, -as
fight la pelea; **to ~** pelear; luchar
find encontrar (ue)
finish terminar; acabar
fish el pez *(live)*; el pescado *(food)*; **to ~** pescar
floor el piso *(story)*; el suelo *(room)*
flower la flor
food la comida; el alimento
foot el pie; **on ~** a pie
forget olvidar
friend el amigo, la amiga
frog la rana
fun: to be ~ ser divertido, -a; **to have ~** divertirse (ie-i); pasarlo bien

game el partido *(sports, contest)*; el juego
garden el jardín
get obtener; conseguir (i-i); **to ~ up** levantarse
gift el regalo
girl la muchacha; la chica
give dar
glass el vaso
go ir; **to ~ down** bajar; **to ~ shopping** ir de compras; **to ~ up** subir
good bueno, -a
good-looking guapo, -a
grade la nota *(mark)*; **to get [good] ~s** sacar [buenas] notas
grandfather el abuelo
grandmother la abuela
gray gris
green verde
ground la tierra; el suelo
guest el huésped, la huéspeda; el invitado, la invitada
guitar la guitarra
gymnasium el gimnasio

hair el pelo
hand la mano
happen ocurrir; pasar
happy alegre; contento, -a
hard difícil
have tener
head la cabeza
hear oír
heart el corazón
help la ayuda; **~!** ¡socorro! **to ~** ayudar
here aquí; acá
holiday el día festivo; la fiesta
home la casa; **at ~** en casa
hope esperar
host el anfitrión
hostess la anfitriona
hot caliente; **to be (feel) ~** tener calor; **to be ~** hacer calor *(weather)*

house la casa
how ¿cómo?; **~ many?** ¿cuántos, -as?; **~ much?** ¿cuánto, -a?; **~ are you?** ¿qué tal?; **~ old are you?** ¿cuántos años tienes?
hungry: to be ~ tener hambre
hurry: to be in a ~ tener prisa
husband el esposo; el marido

ice el hielo
ice cream el helado
if si
imagine: ~! ¡fíjate!; ¡imagínate!
in en
inexpensive barato, -a
instead of en vez de
instrument el instrumento
invite invitar

jacket la chaqueta
jeans los blue jeans
job el trabajo; el empleo
joke el chiste
juice el jugo; el zumo
jump saltar
jungle la selva

keep guardar
key la llave
king el rey
kiss el beso; **to ~** besar
kitchen la cocina
know conocer *(someone)*; saber *(a fact or how)*

land la tierra
language el idioma; la lengua
last último, -a
late tarde
laugh reír (i-i)
learn aprender

leave salir; dejar
left: to the ~ a la izquierda
leg la pierna
legend la leyenda
lend prestar
less menos
letter la carta *(mail);* la letra *(alphabet)*
library la biblioteca
life la vida
lift levantar
like gustarle; **I** ~ me gusta(n)
listen (to) escuchar
little pequeño, -a; **a** ~ **bit** un poco (de)
live vivir
living room la sala
long largo, -a
look (at) mirar; **to** ~ **for** buscar; **to** ~ **like** parecerse a
lose perder (ie)
lot, lots mucho, -a; muchos, -as
love amar; querer (ie)
luck la suerte; **to be** ~**y** tener suerte
lunch el almuerzo; **to eat** ~ almorzar (ue); tomar el almuerzo

magazine la revista
make hacer
man el hombre; el señor
maybe tal vez; quizás
meal la comida
mean querer (ie) decir
meet encontrarse (ue); conocer *(preterit)*
midnight (la) medianoche
milk la leche
mistake el error; la falta; **to be mistaken** estar equivocado, -a; no tener razón; **to make a** ~ equivocarse
money el dinero
month el mes
moon la luna

morning la mañana; **in the** ~ por la mañana
mother la madre; la mamá
mouth la boca
movie la película; **movies** el cine
must deber; tener que

name el nombre; **to be named** llamarse
near cerca (de)
necklace el collar
need necesitar
neighbor el vecino, la vecina
neighborhood el barrio; la vecindad
never nunca
new nuevo, -a
news las noticias
newspaper el periódico; el diario
night la noche; **good** ~ buenas noches; **last** ~ anoche
noon (el) mediodía
notebook el cuaderno
nothing nada
now ahora
nurse el enfermero, la enfermera

obey obedecer
oil el petróleo; el aceite
okay de acuerdo
old viejo, -a
older mayor
open abrir
orange la naranja *(fruit);* anaranjado, -a *(color)*
ought deber *(+ inf.)*
outdoors al aire libre
owe deber

paint pintar
pants el pantalón
parents los padres

party la fiesta
pass aprobar (ue) *(exam, subject);* pasar
pay pagar
pen la pluma; **ballpoint** ~ el bolígrafo
pencil el lápiz
people la gente; el pueblo
pink rosado, -a
place el lugar; el sitio; **to** ~ poner
plan pensar (ie) *(+ inf.);* planear
plate el plato
to play jugar a (ue) *game, sport);* tocar *(instrument)*
please por favor
pool la piscina
poor pobre; ~ **thing!** ¡pobrecito, -a!
post card la tarjeta postal
pretty bonito, -a
price el precio
promise prometer
purse la bolsa
put poner; **to** ~ **on** ponerse

queen la reina
question la pregunta
quiet: to be ~ callarse; estar callado, -a
quite bastante

rain la lluvia; **to** ~ llover (ue)
read leer
reading la lectura
record el disco; ~ **player** el tocadiscos
record grabar
red rojo, -a
relative el pariente
remain quedar; quedarse
remember recordar (ue)
return volver (ue)
rich rico, -a

right: to the ~   a la derecha;
  to be ~   tener razón
road   el camino; la calle
room   el cuarto; la habitación
run   correr

sad   triste
save   ahorrar
say   decir
scholarship   la beca
see   ver
sell   vender
send   mandar; enviar
shoe   el zapato
shout   el grito; to ~   gritar
show   mostrar (ue); enseñar
sick   enfermo, -a
sing   cantar
singer   el/la cantante
singing: ~ group   el coro; el
  conjunto
sister   la hermana
sit down   sentarse (ie)
sleep   dormir (ue-u); to go to
  ~   dormirse (ue-u)
sleepy: to be ~   tener sueño
snow   la nieve; to ~   nevar (ie)
some   unos, -as; algunos, -as
something   algo
son   el hijo
song   la canción
soon   pronto
speak   hablar
sport   el deporte
spring   la primavera
stay   quedarse
still   todavía
stomach   el estómago
stop   parar; dejar de (+ inf.)
store   la tienda; el almacén
story   el cuento; la historia; el
  piso (floor)
strong   fuerte
study   estudiar

summer   el verano
sun   el sol; it's sunny   hace
  sol
swim   nadar

take   tomar; to ~ pictures
  sacar fotos
tall   alto, -a
teach   enseñar; dar clase (de)
team   el equipo
tear   la lágrima
tell   decir (someone something);
  contar (ue) (story)
thank you   gracias
there   allí; allá; ~ is/are
  hay
thief   el ladrón, la ladrona
thing   la cosa
think   pensar (ie)
thirsty: to be ~   tener sed
throat   la garganta
tie   la corbata; to ~   atar
tired   cansado, -a
today   hoy
tomorrow   mañana
tonight   esta noche
town   el pueblo; la aldea
travel   viajar
tray   la bandeja
tree   el árbol
true   verdad; cierto, -a
try   tratar de; probar; to ~
  on   probarse

ugly   feo, -a
uncle   el tío
understand   entender (ie);
  comprender
until   hasta

very   muy
visit   visitar

wait   esperar; to ~ for
  esperar a
waiter   el camarero
waitress   la camarera
walk   caminar; pasear
want   querer (ie); desear
wash   lavar; to ~ oneself
  lavarse
watch   el reloj
water   el agua (f.)
weak   débil
wear   llevar
weather   el tiempo; the ~'s
  [nice]   hace [buen] tiempo;
  what's the ~ like?   ¿qué
  tiempo hace?
week   la semana; ~end   el
  fin de semana
welcome   bienvenido, -a;
  you're ~   de nada
what?   ¿qué?; what is (are) . . .
  like?   ¿cómo es (son) . . . ?
when?   ¿cuándo?
where?   ¿dónde?
white   blanco, -a
who?   ¿quién?
whose?   ¿de quién?
why?   ¿por qué?
wife   la esposa; la mujer
win   ganar
winter   el invierno
woman   la mujer; la señora
word   la palabra
work   trabajar
write   escribir
wrong: to be ~   no tener
  razón

yard   el jardín
year   el año
yellow   amarillo, -a
yesterday   ayer
young   joven; ~ person
  el/la joven

Index

Art Credits